SCHIZOPHRENIA RESEARCH TRENDS

SCHIZOPHRENIA RESEARCH TRENDS

KONSTANCE V. ALMANN
EDITOR

Nova Biomedical Books
New York

For permission to use material from this book please contact us:
Telephone 631-231-7269; Fax 631-231-8175
Web Site: http://www.novapublishers.com

LIBRARY OF CONGRESS CATALOGING-IN-PUBLICATION DATA

Schizophrenia research trends / Konstance V. Almann (editor).
p.; cm.
Includes bibliographical references and index.
ISBN-13: 978-1-60021-746-3 (hardcover)
ISBN-10: 1-60021-746-X (hardcover)
1. Schizophrenia. I. Almann, Konstance V.
[DNLM: 1. Schizophrenia. 2. Cognition. WM 203 S337986 2007]
RC514.S33638 2007
616.89'80072--dc22

2007016464

Published by Nova Science Publishers, Inc. ✢ New York

CONTENTS

PREFACE

Schizophrenia is a chronic, severe, and disabling psychosis, which is an impairment of thinking in which the interpretation of reality is abnormal. Psychosis is a symptom of a disordered brain. Approximately 1 percent of the population worldwide develops schizophrenia during their lifetime. Although schizophrenia affects men and women with equal frequency, the disorder often appears earlier in men, usually in the late teens or early twenties, than in women, who are generally affected in the twenties to early thirties. People with schizophrenia often suffer symptoms such as hearing internal voices not heard by others, or believing that other people are reading their minds, controlling their thoughts, or plotting to harm them. The current evidence concerning the causes of schizophrenia is a mosaic. It is quite clear that multiple factors are involved. These include changes in the chemistry of the brain, changes in the structure of the brain, and genetic factors. Viral infections and head injuries may also play a role.

New molecular tools and modern statistical analyses are allow focusing in on particular genes that might make people more susceptible to schizophrenia by affecting, for example, brain development or neurotransmitter systems governing brain functioning. State-of-the-art imaging techniques are being used to study the living brain. They have recently revealed specific, subtle abnormalities in the structure and function of the brains of patients with schizophrenia. In other imaging studies, early biochemical changes that may precede the onset of disease symptoms have been noted, prompting examination of the neural circuits that are most likely to be involved in producing those symptoms. This book presents new and important research in the field.

Chapter I – Background: Body image aberration in schizophrenia was earlier conceived as delusional and hallucinatory symptoms. However, perceptions of schizophrenia have changed dramatically, especially with the concept of negative symptoms in the 1980s and in the 1990s, to include the neurocognitive aspects of schizophrenia. Deviations in schizophrenics' body image from the standard underlying various behaviors or allegations concerning the body should be now refocused. In this chapter, using the Body Image Questionnaire (BIQ), comprised of three hypothetical components, anatomical, functional and psychological, attempts were made to resolve some primary questions. They were (1) whether or not there is any related clinical characteristics to schizophrenic body image abberation, (2) whether there are aberrant components of body image specific to schizophrenia, (3) whether or not there is unique link between depression and body image in schizophrenia.

Methods: In study 1, correlations between body image assessed by the BIQ and clinical characteristics as positive and negative symptoms assessed by SAPS and SANS, insight assessed by SAI, and daily dose of conventional antipsychotic drugs were examined. In study 2, three components of body image, that is, anatomical, functional and psychological, were compared between schizophrenic and non-schizophrenic groups. In study 3, the correlation between depression assessed by SDS and body image assessed by the BIQ was examined. In these studies, 93 chronic schizophrenics, 177 normal adults, and 43 patients with anxiety disorders according to DSM-IV criteria, were examined. In studies 4-5, the additional finding of Rorschach percepts concerning body image in schizophrenia was reported.

Results: Schizophrenics' body image aberration proved to be independent of symptoms and medication. It was also shown that the aberration proved to be limited to functional imageries, and that the anatomical component remained intact. As to depression, a specific link of body image, especially with functional imageries, with the depression characteristic to schizophrenia was found.

Conclusion: All these results showed that body image aberration in schizophrenics is not the result of symptoms or effects of conventional neuroleptic medications, but they are germane to schizophrenia, which is comprised of aberration mainly in functional body imageries. This body image deviation proved to be linked to some serious depressive signs and symptoms in schizophrenia. The subsidiary findings, that is, the Rorschach percepts as a mass of flesh quite often seen in schizophrenia, are congruent with the main findings that schizophrenic patients showed an anticipation of becoming unmovable.

Chapter II - This review is an attempt to present recent progress in the pathophysiology of schizophrenia. It is based on human research and lower animal models, with special emphasis on models, i.e. on theoretical constructs that sustain them. Theories and their outcomes will be briefly explained rather than deeply discussed. A selection of the literature in which the reader will find a more detailed analysis is provided whenever necessary rather than for justifying each aspect.

Chapter III - Glutamate is one of the most abundant neurotransmitters in the brain; it may be responsible for mediating synaptic neurotransmission at 40 percent or more of the brain's synapses. The glutamatergic signal is recognized by both metabotropic and ion channel receptors. The N-methyl-D-aspartic acid (NMDA) receptor is an example of a glutamate-gated ion channel receptor; the binding of glutamate to this receptor increases the likelihood that its channel will transiently assume an open-configuration, allowing the influx of calcium ions. Importantly, there are allosteric modulatory sites, including an obligatory co-agonist site that recognizes glycine, on the NMDA receptor complex that influence glutamate's ability to promote calcium ion conductance. Abnormalities of NMDA receptor-mediated neurotransmission are implicated in a variety of major neuropsychiatric disorders, especially schizophrenia. Specifically, NMDA receptor hypofunction (NRH) is implicated in the pathophysiology of schizophrenia because of the ability of phencyclidine (PCP) to precipitate a schizophreniform psychosis. PCP is a noncompetitive NMDA receptor antagonist that binds to a hydrophobic site within the channel; it is referred to as an open-channel blocker. Descriptively, the PCP-model of schizophrenia is the best pharmacological model of this disorder with symptoms manifest in all of the relevant domains of psychopathology, including positive (e.g., hallucinations), negative (e.g., affective flattening), cognitive (e.g., abnormalities of attention), mood (e.g., dysphoria) and motor symptoms (e.g., posturing).

Because of PCP's pharmacological action as a noncompetitive NMDA receptor antagonist and the PCP-model of schizophrenia, our laboratory has been engaged in characterizing and quantifying behaviors in mice, including genetically-inbred strains, elicited by MK-801 (dizocilpine), a high-affinity analogue of PCP that binds to the same hydrophobic channel domain. Presumably, blockade of the NMDA receptor by MK-801 is a pharmacological strategy for creating NRH in the intact animal. The authors characterized two behavioral outcome measures: the dose-dependent ability of MK-801 to raise the threshold voltage required for the precipitation of tonic hindlimb extension and elicit irregular episodes of intense jumping behavior (referred to as "popping") in mice. Moreover, 24 hours after mice are forced to swim for up to 10 minutes in cold water, the ability of MK-801 to antagonize electrically precipitated seizures is reduced. Thus, stress affects the endogenous tone of NMDA receptor-mediated neurotransmission. Genetically inbred strains of mice differ in their behavioral sensitivity to MK-801 on these two measures; interestingly, the BALB/c inbred mouse strain is more sensitive than other inbred strains and the NIH Swiss outbred mouse strain. Stress and genetic strain differences interact to affect behavioral sensitivity to MK-801. Importantly, these animal models serve to test the ability of glycinergic interventions to modulate NMDA receptor-mediated neurotransmission in the intact animal. Thus, they are used as screening procedures for NMDA receptor agonist interventional strategies that may be developed as medications for the treatment of schizophrenia. A series of glycinergic interventions have been tested in these models. Also, these paradigms are useful in demonstrating that drugs, whose direct actions are on other neurotransmitter systems, affect NMDA receptor-mediated neurotransmission in the intact animal. Preliminary clinical trials of a few NMDA receptor agonist interventions have been conducted in patients with schizophrenia. In general, the medications are well-tolerated and the results suggest that the adjuvant therapeutic efficacy of specific glycinergic interventions may be influenced by state of illness and the specific antipsychotic medication chosen for maintenance pharmacotherapy (e.g., clozapine). The chapter will concentrate on the results of our laboratory and clinical investigations, whose primary aim was modulation of NMDA receptor-mediated neurotransmission in mice and man.

Chapter IV - This author explores major evolutionary ideas related to schizophrenia, covering four general topics. First, the essential groundwork that justifies the application of evolutionary principles to psychiatric disorders is established. Second, the authors examine evolutionary theories that frame schizophrenia in its classical orientation, as a disease or accident of normal brain evolution. Third, theories that attribute some evolutionary advantage to schizophrenia are reviewed. Last, a more detailed description of the authors' hypothesis is presented, suggesting that the origins of schizophrenia may involve shamanism and group selection.

Chapter V - One of the key features of schizophrenia is the inability to filter out irrelevant stimuli which consequently leads to stimulus overload. There are different paradigms which aim at investigating these deficient filter mechanisms; one of these is latent inhibition (LI). LI refers to the retardation of associative learning that normally occurs when the to-be-conditioned stimulus (CS) is previously preexposed without reinforcement. It is based on a form of selective attention and reflects the ability of normal individuals to ignore irrelevant external and internal stimuli. In schizophrenia, the LI effect is disrupted. This LI disruption is due to faster learning of the CS-US (unconditioned stimulus) association which results in better performance of preexposed schizophrenic subjects compared to healthy controls. Because of this, attenuated LI has become an important tool to model cognitive and attentional deficits in schizophrenia.

In recent studies a newly developed visual learned irrelevance (LIrr) paradigm has been applied. Learned irrelevance is yet another attentional paradigm related to latent inhibition. In contrast to LI, in a LIrr test procedure both the CS and the US are preexposed in an unrelated manner. LIrr has been shown to retard associative learning even more than LI.

In the following chapter the advantages of LI and LIrr, respectively, in schizophrenia research are discussed. Moreover, the differences between the currently applied LI paradigms will be presented as well as the LI modulations in healthy controls, first-episode and chronic schizophrenia patients.

Chapter VI - In recent decades, evidence has accumulated that cognitive impairments are a central feature of schizophrenic disorder. Many research findings have indicated that cognitive impairments limit the rate of improvement in various kinds of psychological interventions for schizophrenic patients. The lack of awareness of mental disorder is another important correlate of patients' response to treatment, compliance and prognosis. In this study the authors hypothesized that schizophrenic patients' ability to be aware of the illness is dependent on more basic ability to directly acquire verbal information, in particular information given throughout treatment interventions. Twenty-seven outpatients with long illness duration were rated on the Scale to Assess Unawareness of Mental Disorder (SUMD) and assessed on verbal learning and memory test. The authors obtained several significant correlations indicating the presence of the relationship between "learning potential" and insight about psychosis. Afterwards, some of the patients participated in 12 sessions of cognitive training and/or 12 sessions of psychoeducation. The effectiveness of these interventions on illness awareness was assessed and the influence of verbal learning abilities on insight change was explored and discussed.

In: Schizophrenia Research Trends
Editor: Konstance V. Almann, pp. 1-53
ISBN 13: 978-1-60021-746-3

Chapter I

BODY IMAGE DEVIATION IN CHRONIC SCHIZOPHRENIA: NEW RESEARCH

Reiko Koide* and Akira Tamaoka
Institute of Clinical Medicine, University of Tsukuba, Tsukuba-Shi, Ibaraki-Ken, Japan

ABSTRACT

Background

Body image aberration in schizophrenia was earlier conceived as delusional and hallucinatory symptoms. However, perceptions of schizophrenia have changed dramatically, especially with the concept of negative symptoms in the 1980s and in the 1990s, to include the neurocognitive aspects of schizophrenia. Deviations in schizophrenics' body image from the standard underlying various behaviors or allegations concerning the body should be now refocused. In this chapter, using the Body Image Questionnaire (BIQ), comprised of three hypothetical components, anatomical, functional and psychological, attempts were made to resolve some primary questions. They were (1) whether or not there is any related clinical characteristics to schizophrenic body image abberation, (2) whether there are aberrant components of body image specific to schizophrenia, (3) whether or not there is unique link between depression and body image in schizophrenia.

Methods

In study 1, correlations between body image assessed by the BIQ and clinical characteristics as positive and negative symptoms assessed by SAPS and SANS, insight assessed by SAI, and daily dose of conventional antipsychotic drugs were examined. In study 2, three components of body image, that is, anatomical, functional and

* Correspondence concerning this article should be addressed to: R. Koide. 1-6-2-905-305, Takezono, Tsukuba-Shi, Ibaraki-Ken, Japan. E-mail: ttn5aks258@mx6.ttcn.ne.jp

psychological, were compared between schizophrenic and non-schizophrenic groups. In study 3, the correlation between depression assessed by SDS and body image assessed by the BIQ was examined. In these studies, 93 chronic schizophrenics, 177 normal adults, and 43 patients with anxiety disorders according to DSM-IV criteria, were examined. In studies 4-5, the additional finding of Rorschach percepts concerning body image in schizophrenia was reported.

Results

Schizophrenics' body image aberration proved to be independent of symptoms and medication. It was also shown that the aberration proved to be limited to functional imageries, and that the anatomical component remained intact. As to depression, a specific link of body image, especially with functional imageries, with the depression characteristic to schizophrenia was found.

Conclusion

All these results showed that body image aberration in schizophrenics is not the result of symptoms or effects of conventional neuroleptic medications, but they are germane to schizophrenia, which is comprised of aberration mainly in functional body imageries. This body image deviation proved to be linked to some serious depressive signs and symptoms in schizophrenia. The subsidiary findings, that is, the Rorschach percepts as a mass of flesh quite often seen in schizophrenia, are congruent with the main findings that schizophrenic patients showed an anticipation of becoming unmovable.

Keywords: body image, schizophrenia, symptom, insight, depression, perception

PART I. INTRODUCTION

Schizophrenics' Body Image Aberration: An Overview

Since the time of Kraepelin (1919) and Bleuler (1911/1950), schizophrenics' deviant perceptions, feelings, and beliefs concerning their bodies have been described. In this section, the symptoms relevant to body image aberration that have been discussed for over the past half century, as well as psychological measures that were developed to understand these aberrations, are reviewed, to lead to the current status and future prospects for the study of the body image aberration in schizophrenia.

(1) Symptoms Relevant to Body Image Aberration

Disturbances of body experience in schizophrenic patients occur frequently. They have been observed as somatic delusions (McGlichrist & Cutting, 1995), coenaesthesis (Huber, 1957/1971; Rohricht & Priebe, 1997, Schmoll & Koch, 1989; Schmoll, 1994), disturbances of pain perception (Dworkin & Caligor, 1988; Rosenthal et al., 1990; Dworkin, 1994; Guieu et al., 1994; Lautenbacher & Krieg, 1994), out-of-body experiences (Blackmore, 1986;

Twemlow et al., 1982), dysmorphophobia (Connolly & Gipson, 1978; Hay, 1983; Birtchnell, 1988; Snaith, 1992; Philips & McEloroy, 1993; deLeon et al., 1989; Phillips et al., 1994), and self-injury or self mutilation (Feldman, 1988; Burgess, 1991; Martin & Gattaz, 1991; Sonneburn & Vanstraelen, 1992; Weiser et al., 1993; Kennedy & Feldmann, 1994). In addition, the effects of body-oriented psychotherapy have been suggested (Darby, 1968; Berman, 1972).

According to Roehricht and Priebe (1997) in a report by Huber and Zerbin-Rueden (1979), although symptoms relevant to body distortion were seen in more than 74% of cases of schizophrenia, little attention has been paid to the evaluation of such symptoms. These symptoms are not included as a prominent component in psychometric approaches to measuring symptoms, such as the Brief Psychiatric Rating Scale, BPRS, (Overall & Gorham, 1962) or the Positive and Negative Symptoms Scale, PANSS (Kay et al., 1987). It is, however, not fair to regard that the issue as being rather neglected. Specifically, bizarre somatopsychic phenomena, e.g., feelings that the body is "being radiated," "being controlled by others," and "being cut up" have been reported in schizophrenia. Some of these abnormal body perceptions have been designated as "Schneiderian first rank symptoms" (Schneider, 1959/1976). Dysmorphophobia was relabeled as “one of the Somatoform Disorders” in 1980. “Body Dysmorphic Disorder,” and its counterpart, “Delusional Disorder, Somatic Subtype” in 1987, were included in the *Diagnostic and Statistical Manual of Mental Disorders* (American Psychiatric Association, 1987), which produced considerable concern over delusions regarding appearance of the body (deLeon et al., 1989; Phillips et al., 1994). First, studies of these symptoms relevant to disturbances in body experiences in schizophrenia are reviewed to give an overview of how the problems have been described and treated.

Before Antipsychotics

Even in the era before antipsychotic agents, body image was rather attractive to those who studied the psychopathology of schizophrenia. Since Wernicke foreshadowed the idea of body image in his concept of "somatopsyche," this whole psychological field has been recognized as important in the understanding of psychotic patients, especially in relation to hallucinatory and delusional disturbances (Schilder, 1935; Angyal, 1936; Gerstmann, 1942; Bychowsky,1943).

The initial study of body image was a description of phantom limb. It was succeeded by neurological research from the 1910s to the 1950s (Head, 1911/1926; Pick, 1922; Schilder, 1935), and body image was conceived as the equivalent of "body schema" or "postural schema." This became the traditional definition of the concept. It was introduced to the field of psychiatry by Schilder (1935), and attempts were made to find similar distortions in psychiatric patients (Schilder, 1935; Angyal, 1936).

Bodily Hallucination and Somatic Delusion

Lukianowicz (1967) and McGlichrist and Cutting (1995) classified somatic delusions of psychotic cases including schizophrenia, showing that bodily delusions and hallucinations occur mostly inseparably. Bodily hallucination and somatic delusion have been treated as coenaesthesis in non-English speaking psychiatry, especially in Germany, where it was often reported to herald the onset of schizophrenia (Huber 1957,1971; Rohricht & Priebe, 1997; Schmoll & Koch, 1989; Schmoll, 1994).

Disturbances of Pain Perception

A disorder of proprioception in schizophrenic patients was earlier described by Rado (1959) as a basic element in schizophrenia. He speculated that extensive proprioceptive deficits could lead to distorted awareness of body image and eventually to the thought disorder characteristic of schizophrenia. Rosenbaum et al. (1965) and Ritzler and Rosenbaum (1974) conducted a series of experiments based on his theory with schizophrenic and non-schizophrenic subjects using weight discrimination as a measure of proprioception. They found that schizophrenics performed almost as well as normals do when asked to discriminate heavy weights, but did not discriminate light weights nearly as well as normals. Since light weights do not provide as much proprioceptive feedback as do heavy weights, these results were interpreted as demonstrating a proprioceptive deficit in the schizophrenics. These results, however, were not replicated by other authors (Ritzler, 1977; Leventhal et al., 1982), who showed that a proprioceptive deficit is not unique to schizophrenia.

Since the time of Kraepelin and Bleuler, “pain insensitivity” or “reduced sensitivity to pain” in schizophrenia has been documented. Kraepelin (1919) observed that patients with schizophrenia are often “less sensitive to bodily discomfort; they endure uncomfortable positions, pricks of a needle, injuries…burn themselves with their cigar, hurt themselves.” Bleuler (1911/1950) noted that even in well-oriented patients one may often observe the presence of a complete analgesia which includes the deeper parts of the body as well as the skin. The patients “pluck out an eye, sit down on a hot stove and receive severe burns”.

Although some authors reported that schizophrenic patients suffer headache (Varsamis & Adamson, 1976; Watson et al., 1981; Philips and Hunter, 1982; Torrey, 1989), the prevalence of pain complaints in schizophrenia appears to be lower than in other psychiatric disorders (Merskey, 1965; Spear, 1967; Delapaine et al., 1978; Watson et al., 1981). There are many descriptions of pain insensitivity in schizophrenia by surgeons and internists (Arieti, 1945; Marchand, 1959; West and Hecker, 1952; Vanderkampt, 1970; Apter, 1981, Fishbain 1982; Bickerstaff et al., 1988, Katz et al., 1990; Rosenthal et al., 1990). Dworkin (1994) reviewed the literature on this issue and argued that the insensitivity, although currently neglected, has important implications for physical health, self-mutilation, homelessness, premorbid development, and affective flattening in schizophrenic patients. Lautenbacher and Krieg (1994) also reviewed the literature and pointed out that pain insensitivity is important in elucidating pathophysiological mechanisms because pain perception is controlled by neurochemical and neurohormonal functions known to be affected by psychiatric disease processes. Guieu et al. (1994), however, assessed the pain thresholds of ten schizophrenic patients and ten controls by measuring the leg flexion nociceptive reflex threshold, and concluded that in most cases the increase in pain threshold is the result of attitude and not alterations in brain function.

Out-of-Body Experiences

A number of studies have pointed out the confusion in the existing psychiatric literature concerning the status of consciousness in which there is an altered perception of the mind/body relationship. They defined out-of-body experience (OBE) as an altered state of consciousness in which one's mind or awareness is experienced as separated from one's physical body. They argued that the increasing numbers of patients who are involved in such phenomena, traditionally classified as psychopathological, should not be treated in the way that a symptom is usually treated (e.g., interpretation or medication) but should be viewed by a physician with "benign neglect" (Twemlow, et al., 1982).

Gabbard et al. developed a questionnaire, Profile of Out-of-Body Experiences, POBE, that included 51 items based on reports of near-death experiences, mystical-religious literature, and philosophical-occult-psychotic literature describing OBE experiences. They tried to clarify this group of phenomena by differentiating OBE from depersonalization, autoscopic phenomena, and schizophrenic body distortions (such as boundary loss). They selected seven points to differentiate OBE from the disturbances in corporal perception found in schizophrenia. That is, the bodily distortions in schizophrenic patients are characterized by loss of reality testing, chronic difficulty with delineation of body boundaries, varied bodily distortions, being uncertain of the location of the body, profound regression in personality, blurred identity, and being experienced as "going crazy," whereas those experiencing OBE show intact reality testing, have episodic and short-lived experiences, basically unvaried distortion, are certain of their location, show no evidence of regression, have an intact identity, and are not experienced as "going crazy."

Blackmore (1986) administered POBE to schizophrenic patients, along with two other questionnaires to assess perception and symptoms, and showed that there is no evidence to consider the typical OBE as pathological or as symptomatic of schizophrenia.

Dysmorphophobia

Extreme concern with aspects of personal appearance was called dysmorphophobia by Morselli in 1886 (Birtchnell, 1988; Phillips, 1991), who defined it as "a subjective feeling of ugliness or physical defect that the patient feels is noticeable to others, although his appearance is within normal limits." Despite its relative neglect in American psychiatry, it is now termed "Somatoform Disorder" in DSM III (1980), "Body Dysmorphic Disorder (BDD)" in DSM III-R with its counterpart, "Delusional Disorder, Somatic Subtype (DDSS)" (1987). It is a distressing and impairing disorder that may lead to occupational and social dysfunction as well as unnecessary and costly cosmetic surgery and dermatologic treatment (Phillips, 1991), and an increase in this disorder has been reported (Phillips et al., 1993; Hollander et al., 1993). It is still described with the term BDD under the heading of Somatoform Disorder in DSM-IV (1994).

In the 19th century, the term "dysmorphophobia" described those patients who present with "a fear of being misshapen" when in fact objectively they have no cause for complaint. However, numerous reports of dysmorphophobia in psychiatric morbidity, including schizophrenia, have been reported (Connolly and Gipson, 1978; Edgerton et al., 1960; Jacobsen et al., 1960; Hay, 1970). In the 1980s, there were continuing debates as to its status as a symptom or discrete psychiatric illness; that is, it is not a phobia because there is no fear of physical abnormality per se—the ugliness of others is tolerated. It was remarked that dysmorphophobia is non-specific as a symptom and can occur in a variety of different psychiatric syndromes, from a sensitive personality development to an attenuated schizophrenic illness (Hay, 1970/1983).

In the 1940s to the 1960s, psychodynamic theories attempted to recognize that a complaint about appearance might be understood in terms of psychological defense mechanisms (Meyer et al., 1960; Jacobsen et al., 1960; Linn and Goldman, 1949; Hill and Silver, 1950). Body parts took on a psychological significance and symbolic function, and a complaint might reflect an underlying conflict. However, reports of excellent results from surgery on the minimally deformed led to criticism to these theories, suggesting neurotic, and even psychotic, patients can benefit from cosmetic surgery (Edgerton et al., 1960; Hay, 1973).

Although the original definition of dysmorphophobia states that the appearance is within normal limits, diagnostic criteria proposed for dysmorphophobia allow for a slight physical anomaly to be present, but with the patient's concern judged disproportionately great (Andreasen and Bardach, 1977). Birtchnell (1988) regarded it as important to maintain a distinction between those patients with minimal deformity (the normal but less than attractive) who might considerably benefit from surgery and those with primary dysmorphophobia distinguished by the vagueness of the complaint, e.g., "the skin under my eyes joins my nose in a funny way," where surgery is contraindicated, rather than, for example, "the tip of my nose is rather bulbous."

The disorder once termed dysmorphophobia was renamed body dysmorphic disorder (BDD) in DSM III-R. As Snaith (1992) reviewed, DSM III-R considered the disorder under two headings: (1) delusional disorder, somatic type, and (2) body dysmorphic disorder. The distinctions between these two categories rests on whether the bodily concern has the characteristics of a true delusion, but a clear distinction cannot always be made. DSM III-R differentiated BDD, a nonpsychotic somatoform disorder in which insight is present, from its delusional counterpart, a psychotic disorder in which insight is absent. The delusional variant of BDD was reported as a more severe form of the disorder (Phillips et al., 1994).

Self-Injury or Self Mutilation

Self-injurious behaviour of various sorts occurs in an appreciable number of individuals with schizophrenia, as well as in those with other disorders (Burgess, 1991). Self-mutilation has been defined as "painful , destructive and injurious acts upon the body without the apparent intent to commit suicide" (Pattison and Kahan, 1983). Reports of self-mutilation in patients with schizophrenia include descriptions of unilateral and bilateral eye enucleation (Feldman, 1988; Kennedy and Feldmann, 1994), self-laceration (Shore et al., 1978; Sweeny and Zamecnik, 1981), and self-amputation of various parts of the body, including the hand (Schweitzer, 1990), breast (Coons et al., 1986), ear (Silva, et al., 1989; Weiser et al., 1993), penis and testicles (Schweitzer, 1990; Martin and Gattaz, 1991), and in what is arguably the most extreme case reported to date, virtually the entire face (Scheftel et al., 1986).

Burgess (1991) studied the relationship of depression and cognitive impairment to self-injury in psychiatric patients including schizophrenics, showing that self-injury was correlated with neurocognitive deficits in borderline and schizophrenic groups.

Body-Oriented Psychotherapy

An early theoretical assumption, currently recognized as invalid, was that the core disturbance in schizophrenia is a breakdown of ego boundaries leading to a dedifferentiation of the self from the non-self (Federn, 1952; Freeman et al., 1958). According to this theory, what is sensed as thought (a process occurring within the mental and physical boundary) is no longer distinguished from what is sensed as lying outside the ego boundary (Berman, 1972). Psychoanalytic theorists have stressed the important role the individual's body plays in bringing about the formation of the ego (e.g., Federn, 1952; Fenichel, 1954; Ferenczi, 1926; Freud, 1962), and the maintenance of the distinction between ego and non-ego was a controversial issue for psychotherapeutic treatment of schizophrenia.

Des Lauriers (1962) theorized that the recovery process in schizophrenia could be conceptualized as a progressive definition and demarcation of the schizophrenic's ego boundaries through a systematically increased awareness of body limits and bodily self. In order to accomplish this, the psychotherapist attempted to stimulate in the schizophrenic patient awareness of, and interest in, the bodily self as the separating boundary from that which is not himself (Darby, 1968; Des Lauriers, 1962). Studies conducted with an inkblot boundary index developed by Fisher and Cleveland (1958), the Barrier and Penetration scores, lend some support to the above conception of schizophrenia and the recovery process, in that schizophrenics were differentiated from neurotics and normals on the basis of their lower Barrier and higher Penetration scores (Fisher and Cleveland, 1958; Reitman and Cleveland, 1964; Holtzman et al., 1961) and that as a schizophrenic improved clinically, his Penetration scores decreased (Cleveland, 1960a). Fisher and Cleveland (1968) suggested that special treatment efforts, aimed at re-identifying and redefining bodily limits, should improve these patients. Because a question arises as to whether directly focusing the schizophrenic patient's awareness and attention on his own body can effect a redefinition of boundaries, attempts were made to demonstrate that focusing on somatic stimuli leads to subsequent changes in inkblot boundary indexes, implying, at least, that it can (Fisher and Renik, 1966; Renik and Fisher, 1968). Attempts were also made to expect alteration of body image change in these indexes by inducing somatic awareness in groups of hospitalized schizophrenics (Darby, 1968). Quinlan and Harrow (1974) examined the boundary in a sample of acute schizophrenics by the use of four types of Rorschach indexes including Barrier and Penetration scores. Their results support the hypothesis that schizophrenics give certain types of responses considered indicative of boundary disturbance, such as contamination responses, although Barrier and Penetration indexes are more benign signs of boundary diffusion.

(2) Psychological Measurement of Body Image Aberration

The above observations have led to an assumption that body image aberration or deviation exists in schizophrenia, and that it is related to the core of schizophrenia. Attempts were made, using the Rorschach test (Quinlan & Harrow 1974; Fisher & Cleveland, 1958/1968; Fisher, 1963), Drawing test (Kokonis, 1972) and inquiries (Fisher & Seidner, 1963; Chapman et al., 1978; Coleman et al., 1996; Koide, 1985; Oosthuizen et al., 1998), to point to characteristic deviations of body image in schizophrenic patients. These are the Body Distortion Questionnaire, BDQ, (Rohricht & Priebe, 1996), the Perceptual Aberration Scale, PAS, (Coleman et al., 1996; Chapman et al., 1978), Dysmorphic Concern Questionnaire,

DCQ (Oosthuizen et al., 1998), and the present Body Image Questionnaire, BIQ (Koide, 1985). However, none of these measures are regarded as well-established (Rohricht & Prieb, 1997).

Projective Method

Early attempts to measeure body image aberrations were made through indirect means, that is, projective techniques. Figure-drawing techniques (Goodenough, 1928; Machover, 1949), have been used often by researchers (Cancro, 1971; Jasker and Reed, 1963; Sugarman and Cancro, 1964); however, most of the differences between schizophrenic and normal subjects appear to reflect nothing more than general inadequacy of drawing skill by schizophrenics (Swensen, 1957/1968). Barrier and penetration percepts on the Rorschach Test were inferred from body image (Fisher and Cleveland, 1958/1968). Barrier percepts are ones that emphasize peripheral-boundary-defining qualities of the percepts (e.g., flower pot or knife in armor). Penetration percepts involve penetration of outer surfaces of things (e.g., squashed bug or x-ray picture). Lowered barrier scores and heightened penetration scores have been reported in schizophrenia (Fisher and Cleveland, 1958/1968; Reitman and Cleveland, 1964; Holtzman et al., 1961/64). A lack of difference has also been reported (Jasker and Reed, 1963). While support for schizophrenic deviancy on the barrier and penetration scores is strong, acceptance of such evidence as support for schizophrenic body-image aberration requires belief in the projective hypothesis (Chapman et al., 1978).

Experimental Measurement

More direct attempts were made to measure body image aberration in the laboratory setting. Traub et al. (1967) performed an experiment in which the subjects adjust a body-distorting mirror until they believe that it reflects them accurately, with the result that schizophrenic patients erred more than the normal control subjects. Controversial results were presented in studies in which the patients were asked to judge the size of their own body. Cleveland (1960) and Cleveland et al. (1962) reported that schizophrenics overestimate the size of their various body parts (hand, foot, stomach, heart) more than control subjects do, although Weckowicz and Sommer (1960) found that schizophrenics underestimate sizes of their hands and feet. Dillon (1962) and Fisher (1966) found no difference between schizophrenic and normal subjects.

Questionnaire Measurement

The first questionnaire that attempted to measure body image aberration in schizophrenia is the Body Experience Questionnaire, BEQ, which is a true-false questionnaire developed by Fisher and Seidner (1963) and Fisher (1964). Their findings showed greater body image aberration in schizophrenics than in non-schizophrenic subjects, but their BEQ focused to a large extent on hypochondriacal concerns and feelings of body inadequacy rather than the more extreme psychosis-like deviancy of perception of the body that is usually attributed to schizophrenia.

Chapman et al. (1978) developed another questionnaire to measure schizophrenic body image aberration, the Perceptual Aberration Scale, PAS, which is composed of 28 items and a four-point rating sale. Items were intended to tap five kinds of deviant experiences that are uncommon in normal people. The experiences dealt with (a) unclear boundaries of the body, (b) feeling of unreality of, or estrangement from, parts of the body, (c) a sense of deterioration of the body, (d) perceptions of change in size, relative proportions, or spatial relationships of body parts, and (e) changes in the appearance of the body. The scale was standardized on normal control groups. Male schizophrenics reported more body image aberration than normal control subjects, but only a portion of the schizophrenics were deviant. In addition, schizophrenic body image aberrations were negatively correlated with time since first hospitalization and had no correlation with the Physical Anhedonia Scale (Chapman et al., 1976) for schizophrenia, suggesting that the two scales, PAS and Physical Anhedonia Scale, may identify alternative manifestations of proneness toward the same schizophrenia, that is, schizophrenia and schizophrenia-proneness. Coleman et al. (1996) administered PAS to a sample of 2000 students to detect a group of schizotypy in a study conducted to examine the empirical links between schizophrenia and schizotypic psychopathology. Through comparisons of thought disorder assessed by the Thought Disorder Index, TDI (Coleman et al., 1993), between high and low PAS groups, the authors supported the hypothesis that psychometrically identified schizotypic individuals tapped by PAS display thought disorder similar to that of schizophrenia.

Oosthuizen et al. (1998) developed a four-point questionnaire, the Dysmorphic Concern Questionnaire, DCQ, to assess dysmorphic concerns, and tried to establish a correlation with clinical variables. The DCQ was loosely based on the General Health Questionnaire, GHQ. A series of seven statements was devised, based on the dysmorphic concern literature, to capture the essence of the problem (e.g., concern about physical appearance, considering oneself misshapen) and past attempts to deal with the problem (e.g., consulting a plastic surgeon, covering up supposed defects). The DCQ was administered to 63 patients including 33 schizophrenics. The results showed dysmorphic concern is often a reflection of cognitive set rather than a diagnosis itself.

The Body Image Questionnaire, BIQ, is a seven-step self-rating questionnaire with 59 body referring items, especially devised to measure schizophrenic body image deviation (Koide, 1985). The BIQ was developed on the basis of the clinical observations made through contact with chronic schizophrenic patients by clinicians and the attempts to grasp their deviations through assessing rather persistent attitudes or feelings toward the patients' own bodies, which are measurable on a graded continuum with those of normals. Thus, what is assessed by the BIQ is not a psychosis-like body distortion experience itself but an underlying readiness for observable aberrant behaviors including distorted body experiences. The patients' deviated concern about their body is revealed by observations. A middle-aged female schizophrenic patient tried to eat her glasses to exemplify the strength of her teeth (image of strong teeth). A young male patient continued to reject walking outside the hospital in the treatment programs because he felt tight like a stone when he tried to go out (image of tightness caused by relaxation). One young female patient talked about her wish to commit suicide because, she said, she wanted to avoid situations in which she imagined herself unable to move her own body by herself (image of becoming immobile). The items of the BIQ were arranged to include three prospectively hypothetical components: namely, anatomical, functional and other psychological elements such as mood and primitive sensation.

Objective of the Study

A wide variety of studies has appeared on body image aberration in schizophrenia; however, the problem inherent in schizophrenic body image aberration remains elusive. Earlier, the body image problems in schizophrenia were regarded as something related to psychotic symptoms, particularly with delusion and hallucination. Our perceptions of the schizophrenia have changed dramatically, particularly over the past two decades. During 1980s, the predominant view of the phenomenology of schizophrenia broadened beyond a narrow focus on psychotic symptoms to include negative symptoms, proprioceptive deficits, and self-injury representing body image problems. In the 1990s, another fundamental change in our perception of the disorder occurred. With this change, we have expanded the phenomenology of schizophrenia even further, beyond symptoms altogether, to include a strong emphasis on neurocognitive aspects of schizophrenia (Green & Neuchterlein, 1999).

Schizophrenia has consequently been investigated using "neuropsychological" procedures in order to uncover evidence of discrete neurological damage or dysfunction that may account for the great impairments in judgment, attention, concentration, planning ability and anticipation. In the late 1970s, a new era of neuropsychological study of schizophrenia began with three different review articles in which the low performance on neuropsychological test in functional patients was compared to organic patients (Goldstein, 1978; Heaton et al., 1978; Malec, 1978), and with the initial publication of in vivo evidence of ventricular enlargement in schizophrenia, as revealed by computerized tomography (CT) (Johonstone et al., 1976; Weinberger et al., 1979).

Focus has been on clarifying the relationships between neurocognitive deficits and psychotic symptoms (Cornblatt et al., 1985; Green & Walker, 1985; Neuchterlein et al., 1986; Green et al., 1992) and negative symptoms (Neuchterlein et al., 1986; Censits et al., 1997; Buchanan et al., 1997), between neurocognitive deficits and functional outcome (Green, 1996), between neurocognitive deficits and insight (Silverstein & Zerwic, 1985; Young et al., 1993; Lysaker & Bell, 1994; Cuesta & Peralta, 1994) and social cognition (Schneider et al., 1995; Bryson et al., 1997). In a current overview, Green and Nuechterlein (1999) searched for meaningful psychopharmacological and cognitive/behavioral interventions for neurocognitive deficits in schiziophrenia. Conventional antipsychotic agents are generally effective for psychotic symptoms, but their effects on neurocognition are relatively weak (Cassens et al., 1990; Strauss, 1993). Novel antipsychotic medications are more encouraging (Hagger et al., 1993; Green et al., 1997; Jeste et al., 1998; Keefe et al., 1999; Kern et al., 1999; Meltzer & McGurk, 1999). Conventional antipsychotic medications involve much coadministration of anticholinergic medications (e.g., benoztropine mesylate) that are known to have a negative effect on neurocognition (Spohn & Strauss, 1989).

To consider body image aberration in the above context, which deficit of body image comes from symptoms and which from medication should be clarified first. The questions are (1) Is body image aberration a result of symptoms seen in attenuated schizophrenic illness? (2) Is body image aberration an effect of medications? (3) What is the schizophrenics' body image's inherently aberrational part? Is there any intact part? (4) Is it remediable by behavioral/cognitive or psychopharmacological intervention? A full investigation of these basic questions is now required. Each section in this chapter is the attempt to clarify these basic problems.

PART II. STUDIES USING BODY IMAGE QUESTIONNAIRE (BIQ)

Study 1. Body Image Aberration and Clinical Characteristics

Introduction

In the era of pre-antipsychotics, disturbance of body experiences in schizophrenia had been documented as pathological experiences, especially in relation to hallucinatory and delusional disturbances. Since the 1970s, several concepts about the course of schizophrenia and recovery from it have been developed in the search for new perspectives (Strauss 1989; Harding et al., 1992). Because there is a growing interest in the recovery phase of schizophrenia, their body image characteristics should be refocused as multi-phased deviation from the normal experiences. In this context, the body image should be redefined rather comprehensively as persistent attitudes and feelings toward one's own body, which would preserve deleterious as well as ameliorative effects in the illness-environment interaction of disorder and recovery. In addition, with the availability of neuroleptics since mid. 1950s, undesirable physical reactions caused by drugs may also contribute to negative body image.

The aim of the study in this section was to reexamine the body image distortion perceived by schizophrenics, using the Body Image Questionnaire, BIQ, (Koide,1982/1985). Special inquiries were made concerning the influence of the clinical variables such as positive and negative symptoms, insight and neuroleptic dosage on body image aberration. The questions addressed in this sections are (1) What are the components of body images? (2) Which phases of body image are aberrant in schizophrenia? (3) Which aberrant body images are related to symptoms? (4) Which aberrant body images are associated with favorable signs of remission? (5) Is body image aberration related to neuroleptic dosage?

Method

Assessment of Body Image Deviation

Body image was assessed using the BIQ, a seven-step self-rating scale (scored as 1 to 7) with three hypothetical components, anatomical, functional and psychological. (See Appendix 1.)

Assessment of Clinical Characteristics

Positive symptoms were assessed using the Scale for Assessment of Positive Symptoms, SAPS, (Andreasen, 1983). Negative symptoms were assessed using the Scale for Assessment of Negative Symptoms, SANS, (Andreasen, 1981). Insight was assessed through Schedule for Assessing Insight, SAI, which comprises three main component scores that include acceptance, recognition of illness, and relabeling of pathological experiences, and one supplemental component, i.e., the hypothetical contradiction, which measures amenability to delusional experiences (David, 1990).

Subjects

The study sample consisted of 93 chronic schizophrenics; 44 were men and 49 were women. The mean (SD) age of the patients was 48.5 (10.1) years. All of them were inpatients at chronic psychiatric wards of a mental hospital in Ibaraki Prefecture in Japan. They were diagnosed as schizophrenic, on the basis of medical records, according to DSM-IV criteria (Subtypes: 24 Paranoid types, 40 Disorganized types, 25 Residual types, 4 Undifferentiated types). The mean (SD) duration of hospitalization was 24.1 (10.6) years, and the mean (SD) age of onset was 24.0 (7.0) years old. Their mean (SD) dose of neuroleptics was 469.8 (397.5) mg/day of chlorpromazine equivalent dose. The mean SAPS scores of the subjects was 26.2. The mean of SANS scores was 67.8. The mean SAI score was 8.4. The normal control group was comprised of 177 normally functioning adults of whom 78 were men and 99 were women. The mean (SD) age was 44.9 (12.6) years old. The normal adults were attending university summer school classes in psychology, and were confirmed to be normal by the General Health Questionnaire, the GHQ (short form, Goldberg, 1972; Goldberg & Williams, 1988). All subjects were informed of the purpose of the study and actively participated with written informed consent. (See Table 1.)

Table 1. Demographic and clinical characteristics of subjects. (Studies 1 and 5.)

	Schizophrenic	Normal
	(N=93)	(N=177)
Demographic characteristics		
Mean Age	48.5	44.9
Gender (% male)	47.3	44.1
Clinical characteristics	Mean (Range)	
Age of Onset	24.0 (14-45)	
Years of Hospitalization	24.1 (3-47)	
Dose of CPZ (mg/day)	469.8 (30-2156)	
SAPS	26.2 (0-94)	
SANS	67.8 (9-152)	
SDS	42.5 (24-64)	
SAI (Insight)	8.4 (0-14)	

Data Analysis

Comparisons of Means of each BIQ Item Scores

The means of the scores of 59 BIQ items were compared between schizophrenic and normal control groups using t-test.

Factor Analysis of the Body Image Questionnaire

On the bases of tentative preliminary analysis, 32 out of the original 59 items that proved to be not relevant to the factor analysis were excluded. However, two exceptional functional items (items 37, 41) from the excluded non-contributing items that proved to be important for discrimination when each item score was compared were re-included. The items of the final version pertain to smallness (items 8, 40, 54, 55), fatness (items 15, 28, 56) and roundness (items 24, 52) for the anatomical body image component; difficulty in manipulating his/her own body into action (items 9, 13, 21), lack of strength (items 1, 3), unusual concern over digestive functions (items 38, 53) and exceptional criterion-oriented standards (items 37, 41) for the functional component; and dissatisfaction and ugliness (items 10, 12, 27, 32), lack of vitality (items 31, 59) and fragility (items 19, 26, 39) for the psychological component.

Table 2. Means of BIQ items differentiating diagnostic groups. (Study 1.)

	Schizophrenic	Normal
01. My body is weak.	3.913	3.175***
03. I often get sick.	3.774	2.943***
06. My body is underdeveloped.	3.612	3.176**
07. My body is clean. ®	3.065	2.604**
09. I move slowly	4.193	3.649**
13. I am good at athletics.®	4.301	3.556**
17. I often lose my balance.	3.591	3.153*
19. I am often injured.	4.010	3.508**
23. My mood is numb.	4.279	3.875*
25. I am clumsy with my hands.	4.064	3.593*
26. I seldom catch a cold. ®	4.173	3.519**
29. My voice is feeble.	4.011	3.491**
31. I am always cheerful. ®	3.752	3.255**
37. I can work well in dark rooms. ®	5.258	4.429***
39. My body is susceptible to infection.	3.892	3.278**
41. I cannot move my body freely.	3.239	2.858*
42. My heart is strong. ®	3.397	2.949*
43. I don't mind being touched by others. ®	4.591	4.000**
44. My body is not meager. ®.	3.709	3.339*
45. I seldom get excited.	4.043	3.653*
47. My teeth are weak.	4.826	4.079***
55. My arms are unusually long. ®	3.989	3.680*
59. I always feel energetic.®	3.957	3.491**

*P<0.05, **P<0.01, ***P<0.001

The combined (schizophrenic and normal) data of the three BIQ hypothetical components, viz., anatomical, functional and psychological, were separately factor-analyzed using varimax rotation as the principal method, and the means of the factor scores were compared between the schizophrenic and normal control groups using *t*-tests. The factors that proved to be significant in differentiating schizophrenic and normal groups were compared further between the schizophrenic subgroups using *t*-tests. The schizophrenic subgroups were compared according to high (above or equal to mean) and low (lower than mean) scores on subscales and total scores of SAPS, SANS and SAI. Sub-grouping was also done according to the clinical factors of years of hospitalization and age at onset of disease, as well as daily equivalent dose of chlorpromazine. The SPSS (version 10) was used for statistical analysis.

Results

Group Differences of the BIQ Item Scores

The 23 out of 59 BIQ items proved to be differentiating two diagnostic groups. They were being weak, being prone to sickness, being underdeveloped, being dirty, moving slowly, being poor at athletics, being prone to losing balance, being prone to injury, being numb, being clumsy with hands, being prone to catching colds, speaking with a feeble voice, being always gloomy, being unable to work in dark rooms, being susceptible to infection, being unable to move his/her body freely, having a weak heart, minding being touched by others, being meager, not being prone to becoming excited, having weak teeth, having unusually long arms and being listless. (See Table 2.)

Factor Analysis and Obtained Differential Factors

Factor Analyses

Factor analyses of the three BIQ components, anatomical, functional, and psychological, using varimax rotation as the principal method, identified three factors with eigenvalues greater than 1 for each component. All items except two (items 37 and 41) had substantial loading on each of the factors. Total variances explained were 47.15%, 52.16% and 44.96%, respectively. Each of the three anatomical factors was composed of items indicating the images of smallness, fatness and roundness, respectively. Each of the three functional factors was composed of items indicating the images of dullness in movement, powerlessness and unusually strong gastrointestinal function, respectively. Each of the three psychological factors was composed of items indicating the images of dissatisfaction, lifelessness and fragility, respectively. (See Table 3 & 4.)

Differentiating Factors

Based on the results of the *t*-test of means of obtained factor scores of schizophrenic and normal control groups, five proved to be factors that differentiated the two groups. These factors are F-1 (dullness in movement, t=3.099, df=159.101, p=0.002), F-2 (powerlessness, t=4.458, df=136.065, p=0.000), F-3 (unusually strong gastrointestinal function, t=2.332, df=263, p=0.020), P-2 (lifelessness, t=3.042,df=260, p=0.003) and P-3 (fragility, t=4.507, df=260, p=0.000). (See Table 4.)

Related Clinical Characteristics

Symptoms

The results of the *t*-test of differentiating factor scores between schizophrenic subgroups composed of SAPS and SANS scores are shown in Table 5. The high-score (>5.28) group on hallucinations (SAPS-1) showed a statistically significantly higher factor score on F-2 (powerlessness, t=2.567, df=89, p=0.012) and P-2 (lifelessness, t=2.426, df=89, p=0.017) than the low-score group. The high-score (>10.12) group on delusions (SAPS-2) showed a statistically significantly higher factor score on F-2 (powerlessness, t=2.100, df=89, p=0.039) and P-2 (lifelessness, t=3.814, df=89, p=0.000) than the low-score group. The high-score (>8.96) group on positive formal thought disorder (SAPS-4) showed a statistically significantly higher factor score on F-2 (powerlessness, t=2.819, df=89, p=0.006) than the low-score group. The high-score (>26.2) group on total SAPS showed a statistically significantly higher factor score on F-2 (powerlessness, t=2.358, df=89, p=0.021) and P-2 (lifelessness, t=2.175, df=89, p=0.032) than the low-score group.

Table 3. Factor structure of BIQ. (Study 1.)

Items of BIQ components	Factors and Factor Loadings			h^2
Anatomical	*A-1*	*A-2*	*A-3*	
55. My arms are short.	0.716			0.539
08. I am short.	0.65			0.463
54. My legs are short.	0.636			0.418
40. My hands are small.	0.457			0.239
28. I am fat.		0.796		0.673
15. My body is not skinny.		0.792		0.629
56. My neck is short.		0.437		0.348
24. My body is not rough.			0.731	0.536
52. My body is round.			0.413	0.401
Functional	*F-1*	*F-2*	*F-3*	
13. I am poor at athletics.	0.808			0.654
09. I move slowly	0.783			0.644
21. I walk slowly.	0.693			0.492
37. I cannot work well in dark rooms.				0.027
03. I often get sick.		0.881		0.804
01. My body is weak.		0.802		0.693
41. I cannot move my body freely.				0.250
38. My stomach is unusually strong.			0.812	0.666
53. My bowels are unusually strong.			0.673	0.462
Psychological	*P-1*	*P-2*	*P-3*	
32. My body is unattractive.	0.693			0.535
27. I am satisfied with my body.	0.684			0.487
12. My body is ugly.	0.671			0.476
10. My body is defective.	0.568			0.385
59. I always feel listless.		0.933		0.903
31. I am always gloomy.		0.506		0.290
26. I often catch colds.			0.586	0.352
39. My body is susceptible to infection.			0.554	0.339
19. I am often injured.			0.496	0.279

Note: Only items that loaded at >.400 are shown.

Table 4. Means of factor scores in schizophrenic and control groups. (Study 1.)

Anatomical Factors	Schizophrenic	Control
A-1. Smallness	0.092	-0.047
A-2. Fatness	0.114	-0.058
A-3. Roundness	0.057	0.029
Functional Factors		
F-1. Dullness in movement	0.246	-0.128**
F-2. Powerlessness	0.373	-0.195**
F-3. Unusually strong gastrointestinal function	0.168	-0.088*
Psychological Factors		
P-1. Dissatisfaction	0.003	-0.018
P-2. Lifelessness	0.239	-0.127**
P-3. Fragility	0.278	-0.147**

*p<0.05, **p<0.01.

The high-score (>12.2) group on avolition-apathy (SANS-3) showed a statistically significantly higher factor score on F-2 (powerlessness, t=3.852, df=89, p=0.000) than the low-score group. The high-score (>13.7) group on anhedonia-asociality (SANS-4) showed a statistically significantly higher factor score on F-2 (powerlessness, t=2.983, df=89, p=0.004) and P-2 (lifelessness, t=3.272, df=89, p=0.002) than the low-score group.

Insight

The results of the *t*-test of differentiating factor scores between schizophrenic subgroups composed of SAI scores are shown in Table 6. The high-score (>3.29) group on acceptance (SAI-1) showed a statistically significantly lower factor score on F-3 (unusually strong digestive function, t=-2.482, df=89, p=0.015) and higher factor score on P-3 (Fragility, t=2.135, df=89, p=0.036) than the low-score group. The high-score (>1.7) group on hypothetical contradiction (SAI-supplement) showed a statistically significantly lower factor score on F-3 (unusually strong gastrointestinal function, t=-2.348, df=89, p=0.021) than the low-score group.

Other Clinical Characteristics

There was no significant difference between subgroups of body image factor scores in years of hospitalization, age at onset of disease or the daily chlorpromazine-equivalent dose.

Discussion

The factor analysis identified five differentiating factors, which showed that there is body image aberration in schizophrenic patients: dullness in movement, powerlessness, unusually strong digestive function, lifelessness and fragility. These findings, along with those of other investigations (Roehricht & Priebe, 1996; Coleman et al., 1996; Chapman LJ, Chapman & Raulin, 1978), revealed that schizophrenics manifested perceptual and cognitive deficits in body image.

Table 5. Differential BIQ factor scores in high and low score groups of SAPS and SANS. (Study 1).

	Positive symptoms		Negative symptoms	
	SAPS		SANS	
Factors	High	LOW	High	LOW
	SAPS-1		SANS-1	
	Hallucinations		Affective flattening or blunting	
F-1	–	–	–	–
F-2	0.789	0.178*	–	–
F-3	–	–	–	–
P-2	0.608	0.058*	–	–
P-3	–	–	–	–
	SAPS-2		SANS-2	
	Delusions		Alogia	
F-1	–	–	–	–
F-2	0.708	0.208*	–	–
F-3	–	–	–	–
P-2	0.794	-0.033**	–	–
P-3	–	–	–	–
	SAPS-3		SANS-3	
	Bizarre Behaviour		Avolition Apathy	
F-1	–	–	–	–
F-2	–	–	0.805	-0.013**
F-3	–	–	–	–
P-2	–	–	–	–
P-3	–	–	–	–
	SAPS-4		SANS-4	
	Positive formal Thought Disorder		Anhedonia-associality	
F-1	–	–	–	–
F-2	0.723	0.098**	0.718	0.064**
F-3	–	–	–	–
P-2	–	–	0.599	-0.082**
P-3	–	–	–	–
	SAPS-5		SANS-5	
	Inappropriate affect		Attention	
F-1	–	–	–	–
F-2	–	–	–	–
F-3	–	–	–	–
P-2	–	–	–	–
P-3	–	–	–	–
	SAPS-Total		SANS-Total	
F-1	–	–	–	–
F-2	.729	0.180*	–	–
F-3	–	–	–	–
P-2	0.556	0.067*	–	–
P-3	–	–	–	–

High =High score group. Low=Low score group. *–p<0.05, **=p<0.01.

Table 6. Differential BIQ factor scores in high and low score groups of SAI. (Study 1.)

BIQ	SAI		SAI	
Factors	High	Low	High	Low
	SAI-1a.		SAI-1b.	
	Treatment compliance (passive)		Treatment compliance (unprompted)	
F-1	–	–	–	–
F-2	–	–	–	–
F-3	0.047	0.546*	–	–
P-2	–	–	–	–
P-3	0.368	-0.059*	–	–
	SAI-2a.		SAI-2b.	
	Awareness of illness		Awareness of illness	
	(mental, physical)		(mental, psychiatric)	
F-1	–	–	–	–
F-2	–	–	–	–
F-3	–	–	–	–
P-2	–	–	–	–
P-3	–	–	–	–
	SAI-2c.			
	Explanation of illness			
F-1	–	–		
F-2	–	–		
F-3	–	–		
P-2	–	–		
P-3	–	–		
	SAI-3a.		SAI-3b.	
	Relabelling		Explanation	
	of psychotic experience		of psychotic experience	
F-1	–	–	–	–
F-2	–	–	–	–
F-3	–	–	–	–
P-2	–	–	–	–
P-3	–	–	–	–
	SAI-total		SAI-supplemental	
			Hypothetical Contradiction	
F-1	–	–	–	–
F-2	–	–	–	–
F-3	–	–	-0.135	0.303*
P-2	–	–	–	–
P-3	–	–	–	–

*=p<0.05

Among the five differential body image factors, only two factors showed correlation with positive symptoms measured by SAPS: powerlessness and lifelessness, and the same factors correlated with negative symptoms. These results highlighted the close relationships between powerless and lifeless body images and severity in symptoms, both positive and negative, implying that the patients with severe symptoms would have powerless and lifeless body images.

Although the current view is that schizophrenics lack insight (Amador et al. 1994, 1991,; Cuesta & Peralta, 1994), the results of the present study showed that there is variation in degree of insight measured by SAI. The results also showed that acceptance of treatment, as one component of insight, as assessed by the SAI, proved to be related negatively with unusual gastrointestinal function and positively with the fragile body image, showing that patients who comply with treatment have fragile body images and have images of digestive organs that are not too strong. It might be well estimated that the fragile body image and the reduction of strength of images of digestive organs enhance the patients' feeling of needing help, which makes them compliant to treatment. Another insight component that showed a relationship with the deviated body image factor was the double-awareness phase, as assessed by the hypothetical contradiction, a supplemental item of the SAI. This was conceived as the degree of the patient's conviction about the delusion, as it appeared in the recovery from delusion (Sacks et al, 1974), and arising "from rapid oscillations between belief and disbelief." The score suggests "the amenability to test still firmly held beliefs against reality" (Sacks et al, 1974). The degree of double awareness was shown to be inversely related with the image of unusual strength of gastrointestinal function, showing that the patients with flexible amenability to delusional ideas have images of digestive organs that are not very strong.

The overall results proved two out of the five factors that differentiated the schizophrenic from the normal group to be related to positive and negative symptoms and two to insight. It is important that one major differentiating factor, dullness in movement, did not show any correlation with symptoms or insight. During the 1990s, observations focused on the fact that while patients' symptoms were improved markedly by antipsychotic agents, the patients still required assisted living arrangements and could not work in highly competitive situations (Goldberg et al, 1993). The fact that the main part of the body image deviancy assessed by BIQ did not relate to positive or negative symptoms is assumed to have some relation to these observations, and suggests the possibility that the main component of body image deviancy, which is independent from severity of symptoms, is closely related to some deficits that are germane to schizophrenia.

Conclusion

The factor analysis of BIQ showed some aberrant phases of schizophrenics' body image. They were: dullness in movement, powerlessness, unusually strong gastrointestinal function, lifelessness and fragility. Powerlessness and lifelessness proved to be related to positive and negative symptoms and unusually strong gastrointestinal functions and fragility, to insight.

Study 2. Schizophrenics' Body Images: What Are They?

Introduction

In Study 1, the attempts with factor analysis to find out the linkage of schizophrenics' aberrant body image with clinical characteristics proved to be exhaustive. However, the results of factor analysis showed that there are some differential body image factors, none of which seemed to relate to an anatomical component of body image of schizophrenia. It was further observed that most of the BIQ differential items were functional and psychological.

Distorted body experiences in schizophrenic patients, especially regarding their images of their body shape or proportions, have been reported since the 1960s. DeLeon et al (1989) denoted dysmorphophobia as a symptom which occurs in a number of different disorders, notably in schizophrenia. Dysmorphophobia as seen in somatoform disorders (1980), body dysmorphic disorder (1987) and delusional disorder, somatic subtype, were included in the Diagnostic and Statistical Manual of Mental Disorders, which produced considerable concern about delusion regarding the appearance of the body. (deLeon et al, 1989; Phillips et al, 1994). There has also been much discussion on distorted body experiences, which are legitimately categorized as psychological derivative imageries, including coenaesthesis (Huber, 1957; Rohricht & Priebe, 1996; Schmoll, 1994). Much concern has been placed on the blurred nature of body boundaries (Quinlan & Harrow, 1974; Fisher S, 1966), and the Rorschach test has been used to examine the vulnerable characteristics of body boundaries such as penetrability. In spite of all these attempts, clinical relevance of body image aberration remains unclear. It is still uncertain whether or not the body images are deviated in the area of visual imagery, or in feelings about their body such as being hard as stone or being fragile.

Thus, the question of which phase of body image links with symptoms and which to recovery? leads to the next question, "What are schizophrenics' body images, or what are their aberrations?" In this section, attempts were made to clarify this question simply by comparing three hypothetical components of BIQ, that is, anatomical, functional, and psychological, between schizophrenic and non-schizophrenic groups.

Method

Assessment of Body Image Deviation

Body images were assessed using the BIQ. The three BIQ component scores, *anatomical, functional,* and *psychological,* were obtained using scoring system with reverse items. (See, Appendix 1-1.) Items included in each component are shown in the Appendix. (See Appendix 1-3, 1-4 and 1-5.)

Subjects

The study sample consisted of 83 chronic schizophrenics; 44 were men and 39 were women. The mean (SD) age of the patients was 48.2 (10.0) years. All of them were inpatients in chronic psychiatric wards of a mental hospital in Ibaraki Prefecture in Japan. They were diagnosed as schizophrenia, according to DSM-IV criteria (Subtypes: 20 Paranoid types, 36 Disorganized types, 23 Residual types, 4 Undifferentiated types). The mean (SD) duration of hospitalization was 23.7 (10.5) years, and the mean (SD) age of onset was 24.2 (7.0) years old. Their mean (SD) dose of neuroleptics was 437.0 (396.9) mg/day of chrolpromazine equivalent dose. The group with anxiety disorders was comprised of 43 patients with anxiety disorders in DSM-IV, including 23 men and 20 women. They were outpatients of a private clinic in Ibaraki Prefecture in Japan. The mean (SD) age was 39.1 (14.1) years old. The normal control group of study 1 was used. All of the study participants were informed of the purpose of the study and actively participated with a written informed consent. (See Table 7.)

Table 7. Demographic and clinical characteristics of subjects. (Study 2.)

	Schizophrenia	Anxiety Disorders	Normals
	(N=83)	(N=43)	N=177
Demographic characteristics			
Mean Age	48.2	39.1	44.9
Gender (Male %)	53.0	53.4	44.0
Clinical characteristics of the schizophrenic patients			
	Mean (Range)		
Age of Onset	24.2 (14-45)		
Years of Hospitalization	23.7 (3-47)		
Dose of CPZ (mg/day)	437.0 (30-1256)		

Data Analysis

Means of the three BIQ component scores were compared among groups with schizophrenia, anxiety disorders and normals using ANOVA, followed by multiple comparisons using the Tukey method. The means of each item score of the differential component scores obtained were compared between the schizophrenic and non-schizophrenic groups using ANOVA.

Results

The results of ANOVA are shown in Table 8, and the results of succeeded multiple comparisons are shown in Table 12. Statistically significant group differences in means were found in the BIQ functional component score (F=12.478, df=2/284, p=0.000). Further multiple comparisons of differences of means showed a statistically significant difference between groups with schizophrenia and anxiety disorders (p =0.021), and between groups with schizophrenia and normal groups (p = 0.000). There was no statistically significant difference among the three diagnostic groups in the BIQ anatomical component score or in the BIQ psychological component score.

The mean scores of BIQ functional items, which composed the differential component, were further compared between schizophrenic and non-schizophrenic groups. Eight out of 17 items showed statistically significant differences, including being weak (F=7.262, df=2, p<.001), being liable to get sick (F=10.810, df=2, p<.000), moving slowly (F=6.065, df=2, p<.003), being poor at athletics (F=7.743, df=2, p<.001),, being liable to lose balance(F=5.092, df=2, p<.007), walking slowly(F=3.314, df=2, p<.038), being unable to work in dark rooms(F=10.415, df=2, p<.000), and having weak teeth (F=5.614, df=2, p<.004). The means of each functional item arc shown in Table 9.

Table 8. Group means of BIQ component Scores. (Study 2.)

	Schizophrenia (N=83)	Anxiety Disorders (N=43)	Normals (N=177)	F
Anatomical	80.6	70.71	79.1	1.818
Functional	78.4	73.07	71.4	12.478***
Psychological	78.4	84.77	72.5	2.800
Total	238.8	228.34	223.1	18.046***

*P<0.05, **P<0.01, ***P<0.001

Table 9. Means of BIQ-Functional items of three diagnostic groups. (Study 2.)

	SC	AD	NO	F
01. My body is weak.	3.853	3.558	3.175	7.264***
03. I often get sick.	3.734	3.558	2.945	10.810***
09. I move slowly.	4.253	3.857	3.649	6.065**
13. I am good at athletics.®	4.465	4.432	3.626	7.743**
17. I often lose my balance.	3.790	3.566	3.153	5.092**
21. I walk slowly.	4.409	3.690	4.101	3.314*
37. I can work well in dark rooms. ®	3.570	3.418	2.783	10.415***
47. My teeth are weak.	4.817	4.209	4.079	5.614**

®=reverse item.
*P<0.05, **P<0.01, ***P<0.001.

Discussion

Results of this study showed aberration restricted to functional imageries, revealing that there are both intact and deficient phases in schizophrenics' body images. Of three hypothesized components, that is, anatomical, functional, and psychological body images, only functional imageries proved to be deviant.

The results of the comparisons of means of the various functional items between groups showed that differences included three categories of ill-functional body imageries. First was vulnerability to illness, including images of being weak and of being liable to get sick. Second was difficulty in manipulating their bodies, including images of being unable to work in dark rooms, being poor at athletics, walking slowly and of moving slowly. The third category was unusual concern over gastrointestinal functions reflected in having weak teeth.

Conclusion

Via the analysis of three hypothetical components of BIQ, the schizophrenic body image deviation proved to be comprised of deviation in functional imageries.

Study 3. Depression and Body Image in Chronic Schizophrenia

Introduction

Although mood disorders are conventionally viewed as nosologically distinct from schizophrenia, depression in schizophrenia has been recognized from the time of Mayer-Gross (1920) and Bleuler (1911/1950). Comorbid depressive signs and symptoms (DSS) in schizophrenia were earlier described as postpsychotic depression (McGlaschan & Carpenter, 1976), resulting from realization of disability once psychosis has abated and insight is recovered. A second view is described as post-treatment depression in which neuroleptic medication causes depression in schizophrenia (Van Puttan & May, 1978;Galdi, 1983). The concept has been further elaborated by Van Putten and May (1978), who argued that depression in schizophrenia might be specifically associated with extrapyramidal side effects of neuroleptic medication. A third view relates depression to the schizophrenic process itself. According to this hypothesis, depression forms an integral part of the illness, predicting that depressive symptoms would be most prevalent during the acute phase of illness and subside with treatment (Knights & Hirsch, 1981; Hirsch, 1982).

Recently, DSS have become a target of treatment because novel antipsychotic agents introduce new avenues that may differentially affect schizophrenic signs and symptoms, including depression (Pickar, 1995; Tollefson et al., 1998), and its association with a higher risk of suicide and self-harm (Siris, 1991; Hu et al., 1991; Drake & Cotton, 1986; Caldwell & Gottesman, 1990; Cohen et al., 1990; Roy et al., 1983) has been highlighted. There are studies that reported depressive schizophrenics attempt at unusual self-mutilation (Feldman, 1988; Burgess, 1991; Martin & Gattaz, 1991; Weiser et al., 1993; Kennedy & Feldmann, 1994), which suggest a close relationship between DSS in schizophrenia to body image aberrations.

The report in this section looks at depression in schizophrenia by detecting its unique relationship to patients' body image using BIQ.

Method

Subjects

The subjects in study 1 were used. (See Table 1.)

Assessment of Depression

Depression was assessed by Zung's Self-rating Depression Scale (SDS, Zung, 1965). The SDS scores ranged from 24 to 64, and their mean (SD) was 40.0 (7.9). Based on the distribution, the (schizophrenic and normal) depressive groups were comprised of those who scored 48 or higher, which included 20.3% of all subjects, including schizophrenicc and normal populations. The non-depressive groups were comprised of those who scored 32 or lower, which included 18.9% of all subjects.

Data Analysis

The means of the factor scores obtained in study 1 were compared between the depressive (SDS scores >=48) and non-depressive (SDS scores =<32) groups in schizophrenic and normal control samples, respectively, using *t*-tests. In addition, 59 item scores of BIQ were compared between high and low score groups in these comparative sets using *t*-tests.

Results

Based on the results of the *t*-test of means of obtained factor scores of schizophrenic depressive and non-depressive groups, 5 of these proved to be factors that differentiated the two groups. These factors and their interpretations are factor A-3 (roundness, t=-2.420, df=37, *p*=0.021), factor F-2 (powerlessness, t=2.407, df=38, *p*=0.021), factor F-3(Unusually strong gastrointestinal function, t=-2.588, df=38, *p*=0.014), factor P-1 (Dissatisfuction, t=2.491, df=38, *p*=0.015) and factor P-2 (Lifelessness, t=2.556, df=38, *p*=0.015). Among these factors, significant differences were found among normal population in factor P-1 (t= 5.010, df=40, p=0.000), and factor P-2 (t=2.756, df=40, *p*=0.009), showing that schizophrenic and normal groups had common relationships of depression to body image along with these factors. The other three of the five factors did not differentiate depressive and non-depressive groups in normal samples. Also, there was no factor differentiating depressive and non-depressive group uniquely found in the normal samples. (See Table 10.)

Table 10. BIQ Factors differentiating depressive and non-depressive state. (Study 3.)

Factors	Schizophrenic		Control	
	D	Non-D	D	Non-D
A-1	_	_	_	_
A-2	_	_	_	_
A-3	-2.220	.449*	_	_
F-1	_	_	_	_
F-2	.794	-.030*	_	_
F-3	-.165	.620*	_	_
P-1	.262	-.513*	.764	-.331***
P-2	.751	-.198*	.411	-.356*
P-3	_	_	_	_

D=Depressive group, Non-D=Non-depressive group. *P<.0.05, **P<0.01, ***P<0.001.

There were BIQ items which differentiated depressive and non-depressive groups only in schizophrenic samples. These were; having small eyes, being not meager, being weak, being clumsy with hands, having unusually strong stomach, having strong heart, having strong bowels, being underdeveloped, feeling cold, being dissatisfied, not minding being touched by others, and being getting worse. Schizophrenic and normal control samples shared the most of the differentiating items in the psychological element. (See table 11.)

Table 11. BIQ items differentiating depressive and non-depressive state. (Study 3.)

	Schizophrenics		Normals	
BIQ items	D	Non-D	D	Non-D
Anatomical				
18. I have small eyes.	4.200	3.181*		
44. My body is not meager.®	4.266	3.000**		
Functional				
01. My body is weak.	4.600	3.454*		
03. I often get sick.	4.400	3.000*	3.461	2.655*
17. I often lose my balance.			4.461	2.714***
25. I am clumsy with my hands.	4.833	3.181**		
37. I can work well in dark rooms. ®	5.666	4.181**	3.692	4.655*
38. My stomach is not unusually strong. ®	3.600	5.181**		
42. My heart is strong. ®	3.933	2.272**		
53. My bowels are unusually strong.	3.766	5.000*		
Psychological				
06. My body is underdeveloped.	.3.866	2.636*		
07. My body is clean.®			3.153	2.413**
10. My body is defective.	4.400	3.363*	4.692	3.448**
11. My body feels cold.	4.233	5.363*		
12. My body is beautiful.®	4.333	3.272*	4.769	3.482***
22. I seldom feel tired.®			5.461	4.206**
23. My mood is numb.	3.833	5.090*	2.000	4.724***
27. I am satisfied with my body. ®	3.200	4.727*		
31. I am always cheerful. ®			3.923	2.931**
32. My body is unattractive.			5.153	3.931***
34. I always feel sick.	4.433	3.181*	4.615	3.413***
43. I don't mind being touched by others. ®	4.866	3.636*		
45. I seldom get excited			2.833	4.275**
46. My health is getting better. ®	5.000	3.900*		
49. I am seldom tense.	2.400	3.909**	2.076	3.241**
59. I always feel energetic.®	4.666	3.363**	4.307	3.137**

D=Depressive group, Non-D=Non-depressive group. *P<.0.05, **P<0.01, ***P<0.001.

Discussion

The depression assessed by SDS correlated to 5 factors of body image assessed by BIQ. The findings further demonstrated that 3 among these 5 factors correlated with depression in schizophrenic groups, interpreted as roundness, dullness in movement, and unusually strong gastrointestinal function, none of which differentiated depressive from non-depressive group in normal subjects. It would be reasonable to assume that there is some close link between depression and body image, which is unique and specific to schizophrenia.

Dissatisfied and lifeless body images were found to be related to depression in schizophrenic as well as in normal samples. Dissatisfaction and lifelessness would be a common body image factors they shared regardless of diagnosis. In the schizophrenic sample, three differentiating factors were further observed, one anatomical factor, and two functional factors. It was observed that the more the schizophrenic patients becomes depressed, the less round and the less powerful their imagined body becomes and that the more they depressed, the less powerful their gastrointestinal function becomes in their body images. The results of the comparisons of means of each BIQ item also demonstrated that the variety of functional body image items differentiated depressive from non-depressive patients in the schizophrenic sample. The concern on bodily function proved to be prominent in schizophrenic depressive patients.

These observations may suggest that these depression-related body images in schizophrenia have characteristics, which lead to the anticipation of the serious corporeal deterioration of becoming immovable. This close linkage between depression and undesirable functional body images in schizophrenic patients would be connected with the self-mutilation or higher risk of self-harm observed in schizophrenia.

PART III. STUDIES USING RORSCHACH TEST: SUBSIDIARY FINDINGS

Study 4. A Unique Rorschach Response Observed in Schizophrenic Patients

Introduction

Although recognized as closely linked with psychopathology, distortion of body image has seldom been studied in schizophrenia. The major cause of the neglect of this concept is methodological, i.e., the difficulty in developing assessment techniques. In this section, a new finding concerning body image of schizophrenia, as observed in their Rorschach responses, is reported.

In the attempts to detect body image aberration in the studies using the BIQ, we found that responses that evoke images of a mass of flesh are often seen in schizophrenic Rorschach responses. This was first noticed in the response of a schizophrenic patient (Case A of this study) as "This looks like a mass of flesh of some kind of animal, though I cannot specify which," to Card VI. This response followed to the failure to construct the response "a gorilla" in Card IV, in which she could not identify its legs, arms, or head. According to this Rorschach sequence, a process is assumed to exist in schizophrenic thought that the their bodies are becoming a mere mass of flesh, as if they were being vivisected though still alive, which forms a core of fear of schizophrenic patients. Difficulty in identifying legs, arms, and head of perceived animals or human beings also proved to be a process of perceiving "a mass of flesh."

Starting with these observations, an attempt was made to explore similar responses in schizophrenics' Rorschach responses, and it was found that these responses are quite common in schizophrenic patients. We call the characteristics revealed in these responses as body image "becoming a mass of flesh" and present the hypothesis that this might form a core characteristic of body image of schizophrenia.

Responses such as "mass of flesh", or "muscles in the shoulder of a man," are typical mass of flesh responses because the image of a mass of flesh is clearly verbalized in these responses. Responses such as "a rat without legs" or "a girl, but I cannot see her hands" are also mass-of-flesh responses, because these responses, though indirect, vaguely imagine a mass of flesh through the diminution of head, legs, and arms and emphasis on the trunk.

Four cases are presented. All of them were inpatients of a chronic care ward of a mental hospital in Ibaraki Prefecture and were diagnosed as schizophrenia according to DSM-IV. All patients were informed of the purpose of the study and actively participated with written informed consent. The socio-demographic and clinical characteristics, such as illness type, onset age, years of hospitalization, BPRS scores (Overall & Gorham, 1962), and daily dose of neuroleptics, are shown in Table 12.

Table 12. Demographic and clinical characteristics of subjects. (Study 4.)

	Case A	Case B	Case C	Case D
Age	62	46	33	28
Gender	Female	Female	Male	Female
Years of education	9	7	13	12
Years of employment	2	0	0	4
Illnessl types	Paranoid	Disorganized	Disorganized	Residual
Age at onset	19	16	19	22
Years of hospitalization	37	30	33	5
BPRS	51	49	64	25
Daily dose of neuroleptics (mg)	400	1525	175	350

Case Reports

Case A

Miss A was a 62-year-old woman. She was born to a farmer in Ibaraki Prefecture in Japan as the first of seven children. After she graduated from high school, she went to Tokyo and worked as a housekeeper, but one year later she became restless, sleepless, and went back home. At the age of 22, she was admitted to the hospital with prominent delusional experiences. She left the hospital once, but soon left home, wandered around, stole food from a store and was returned the hospital. Since then, she has been in the hospital for 37 years.

In a semi-structured interview, she said, "A fox is controlling me. He exchanges my body with that of a victim of a traffic accident, so that I feel great pain in my legs, head, and arms. The fox is one of the foxes I keep at home. He changes my body because he gets money through traffic accidents. I am a splendid and super woman. If I had not been ill, I would have made a country. I sculpted on the moon as well as the sun."

In the Rorschach Test, she gave one response per card and gave in seven responses among ten animals with unclear or absent legs, arms, or head, or irregular emphasis on the legs. "Two elephants, but the legs are too short for elephants"(Card II). "A bat, legs are just like those of a bat" (Card V). "An animal I have never seen before. It looks like a gorilla, but this has no head, no legs, and no arms" (Card IV, IX). "A shrimp, with big tails and many small legs"(Card IX).

Case B

Miss B was a 46-year-old woman. She was a third of four children in the family of a public official. She suffered from tuberculosis in the junior high school. One day she was made a fun of by her classmates and refused to go to school. At the age of sixteen, she began to speak in monologues and to spend almost all day in bed. She showed delusions and hallucinations, and entered into the hospital when she was seventeen years old.

In the interview, she said, "I have been suffering from hallucinations everyday for twenty or thirty years. I hear the voice of a middle-aged woman, and she always says bad things about me. It causes severe pain in my shoulder. But I still continue knitting. When I brush my teeth, I feel like I am dying. When I am in bed, and also I am walking, germs move and frighten me, and dogs and cats are lying on me. All animals are transparent so that I cannot see them but they certainly exist."

She presented feelings of "being pressed" in 3 responses among a total of 7. "A calf oppressed by a fixed butterfly" (Card II). "Human beings are pressed down with their hands on the floor" (Card III). "A crab which is compressed, narrow in width" (Card X). She also showed an image of becoming a mass in the response, "A rat, there are no legs" to Card VIII.

Case C

Mr. C was a 55-year-old man. He was born the fourth child of a wealthy family in Tokyo. His father owned a company, and he went to private school. When he was in university, in the first year, he went to a supermarket with the group of his friends to steal some small things. He was expelled from the university. Since then, he complained of anxiety at meeting people, and visited many clinics for medication and psychotherapy, but he gradually came to stay at home almost all day. When he was 22 years old, he entered the hospital with prominent delusions and hallucinations.

In the interview, the patient said, "I suffer from nightmares every night. It is a dream of hell and I feel I cannot survive any more with these ominous ideas. I cannot concentrate. I am slow in thinking. And I have become old-fashioned. Somebody is talking ill of me. I feel suspected as a criminal every time a crime is broadcast on the television. It is because I know the names of the criminals, so that this is my referential delusion."

He showed five human movement responses, none of which identified the agent. "Hitting each other with both hands" (Card I), "Washing" (Card III), "Dancing" (Card VI), "Being astonished (Card VII), and "Talking, with each other" (Card X). He also showed over-clarification of ages in his human percepts, as "old" (Card II), "middle-aged" (Cards III, X), and "young" (Card VII). These estimations of age without evidence suggest the possibility that there might be strong conflict in his subjective inability to experience time, from which he feels excluded.

Case D

Miss D is a 28-year-old woman. She was the second of two children of a family of an artisan in Ibaraki Prefecture. When she was 16 years old, she felt that her classmates are talking ill of her so she refused to go to school. She once consulted with a psychologist. After she graduated from high school, she went to Tokyo and worked for a large company there for five years. When her mother got sick, she came back home to see her mother. Soon after her mother died, she became sleepless, violent especially toward her father, suffered from hallucinations and entered the hospital at the age of 23. After her admission, the hallucinations disappeared, and she returned home to stay several times, although she was not successful in staying home every time because of her violent behaviour toward her father.

In the interview, she said, "I feel miserable because I am under the protection of my father who is so slovenly that he spends a lot of money on bicycle races. My father hit me. But it is because I poured water on him. I am worried that I cannot be independent, though I am old enough to be. To tell the truth, I want to be a child of my elder sister."

She presented the body image as a mass of flesh in the response, "A crab, with torso with a carapace and nippers" (Card III), in which the mass-of-flesh image was covered with the hard shield of a crab and the impression of the whole response was aggressive and defensive, ready for fight. She also showed withdrawal of the body from the outer world in the response, "A piece of clothing, too showy for me." She showed helpless feelings in the response, "A flower, with leaves hanging down and connected with the roots in this way" (Card IX). In this response, the psychological process is presented as a feeling of helplessness that was developed into an attempt to confirm that she was related to her support system.

Discussion

The body image becoming a mass of flesh was seen in four cases as a common characteristics of body image, regardless of their variety of illness type, of degree of severity of symptoms assessed by BPRS, life history and daily dose of neuroleptic medication. Clarification of how this mass-of-flesh image is expressed and is related to the patients' clinical pictures is necessary. Three questions need to be discussed with regard to these patients: (1) Is mass-of-flesh image really related to delusion?: (2) Is it related to hallucinatory behaviour? (3) Is it related to symptoms other than delusional and hallucinatory experiences?

Case A refers to the first question. In this case, body image as a mass of flesh was expressed in a typical form as "a mass of flesh of some animal with a bamboo stick." From this response, it is assumed that she has a catastrophic fear of her body being exposed to the outer world without protection, being penetrated. It is further guessed that this fear is elaborated into a delusional belief to clarify and explain its origin, by thinking that a naughty fox exchanged her body with that of a victim of a traffic accident, and that the fox is one of many foxes she kept at home.

Case B exemplifies to the second question. In this case, the body image of becoming a mass of flesh was expressed as "a rat without arms and legs" and also as "a crab which was compressed" and "a calf that was oppressed by a butterfly." These responses imply that body image as becoming a mass of flesh modified into more sensory form as "being pressed" and developed into a hallucination. She suffered from being oppressed at shoulder presumably caused by a middle-aged woman's voice. She also suffered from being oppressed by germs creeping on her and by transparent animals lying on her.

Case C refers to the third question. In this case, the agents in human Rorschach percepts are frequently not identified. Omission of the head is an indirect expression of body image as a mass of flesh. The lack of identification of the agents of the human percepts implies his avoidance of committing himself to the percepts. With this withdrawal, he tries to maintain distance by regarding the whole situation in which he lives as if it were a fiction, acted on a stage, and regarding himself as an audience. He described his own symptoms as "referential delusion" as if others observe him and felt himself "like a criminal who appears on television". His over-concern about age and many attempts to guess age without enough evidence would be derived phenomenon from this withdrawal from the real world, in which time passes, into a fictional narcissistic world, in which there is no lapse of time. He is worried about "becoming old-fashioned." This concern toward age seems consistent with the age-disorientation of schizophrenia (Crow & Johnstone, 1980; Crow & Stevens, 1978). It was reported that 25% of the schizophrenic patients mistake their own ages by more than 5 years.

In Case D, the mass-of-flesh percepts appeared in the perception, "A crab, with a torso with a carapace and nippers" (Card III). A mass of flesh was seen in the elimination of the legs with armor. This is consistent with her clinical picture, in which her violent acting-out is a prominent problem. As the risk of violence has come to be one of the current issues of schizophrenia (Taylor, 1995; Fottrell,1980; Humphreys et al., 1992) the present finding seems to relate to some illness-specific risk factor to evoke violence in schizophrenic patients. In this case, it is assumed that an "armored mass-of-flesh body image" would be a compromised product of an aggressive premorbid personality and schizophrenic illness.

The body image as becoming a mass of flesh is considered to have four connotations. First, it suggests an image of the body, which is still alive, though exposed to the outer world. Second, it suggests an image of the body that is helplessly threatened and unprotected. Third, it suggests an image of the body that is unmovable. Fourth, it suggests an image of the body that is weakened and helpless. These would constitute an image of potential catastrophe concerning the patients' own body.

The image of becoming a mass of flesh was recognized in two stages. Stage 1 is presented directly with reference to "a mass of muscles" or "mass of flesh," as seen as a typical response one. Stage 2 as presented indirectly as an animal or a human being without legs or arms, or without clarifying them, in which the mass of flesh is vaguely imagined through the diminution of head or legs. In observation of these four cases above, stage 1 presumably works with delusion, especially being closely linked with bizarre delusions and enhancing psychological factors for it. Stage 2 would exist as a rather general, though underlying, disposition in schizophrenic patients. In the case of stage 2, it was further shown that image of becoming a mass of flesh leads to some readiness for age-disorientation as one of the major thought disorders, as well as violent acting-out behaviours, so that one of the future topics to be discussed should be the effect of the image of becoming a mass of flesh on the formation of a variety of schizophrenic symptoms.

Conclusion

Rorschach responses that imply the body images of becoming a mass of flesh were shown in four chronic schizophrenic cases. The body images of becoming a mass of flesh were experienced in two forms: one is experienced by the percept of a mass of muscles. The other is by percepts of an animal or a human being with diminished legs, head, or arms. In studying four cases carefully, these responses were found regardless of the illness type, duration of illness, life history, and neuroleptic doses, but they related not only to delusional and hallucinatory symptoms but also to some other thought disorders such as age-disorientation as well as violence. Because this is just an initial phase of the study, further studies are required to determine whether this finding is a general intrinsic trend of schizophrenia or not.

Study 5. A Mass of Flesh: Schizophrenic Rorschach Percepts

Introduction

The Rorschach test is important in the diagnosis of schizophrenia. Since 1966, 1728 studies using the Rorschach test, among which 126 were concerned with the diagnosis of schizophrenia, have been indexed in Medline. Rorschach protocols have been documented in thought disorders, sometimes in terms of ego impairment, to provide information concerning diagnosis of schizophrenia. Rappaport et al. (1968) are historically credited with systematically identifying deviant aspects of the patient's verbal responses to the inkblot. Attempts have been made to develop specific criteria on the Rorschach designed to make a more accurate assessment of thought disorders, including the Delta Index (Watkins & Stauffacher, 1952), Thought Disorder Index (Johnston & Holzman, 1979), and Schizophrenia Index (Exner, 1974, 1978, 1986a, 1986b, 1991, 1993; Mason et al., 1985). Earlier, methods were developed to assess "primary process" manifestations (Holt, 1977; Meloy, 1984) or boundary disturbance manifestations (Quinlan and Harrow, 1974). During the 1970s to 1980s, methods to assess object relations were developed to differentiate borderline personality disorders from schizophrenia (Urist, 1977; Kwawer, 1980). In the 1990s, Wagner and Frye (Wagner & Frye, 1990) reported the diagnostic implication of the "fragmented" Rorschach W:D (Whole Responses vs. Detail Responses) ratio in schizophrenia, and Perry developed perseveration measures (Perry & Braff, 1998). One of the most widely used of these Rorschach criteria for the evaluation of schizophrenia is the Comprehensive System's Schizophrenia Indices, SCZI (Exner, 1974; Mason et al., 1985). The Comprehensive System began to pay more attention to the importance of systematically measuring unusual verbalizations and identifying reliable test signs that capture a range of aberrations in thought and language. The diagnostic indicators of disordered thinking in Exner's approach pointed to large differences between schizophrenia and control subjects, confirming an impairment of perceptual accuracy, reality testing and reduced emotional control (Di-Nuovo et al., 1988), and the Exner Rorschach was judged to be a valid test for schizophrenia (Vincent & Harman, 1991; Hilsenroth et al., 1998). Another index, the Ego Impairment Index, proved to differentiate among schizophrenics according to the severity of their ego impairment (Perry et al., 1992). Recently, investigators have placed much emphasis on Rorschach indications for thought disorders in regard to sensorimotor gating abnormalities or other information processing in the neurocognitive context (Perry & Braff, 1994; Perry et al., 1999).

In the previous section (study 4), a new finding was reported concerning Rorschach percepts of schizophrenia, that images of a mass of flesh were often seen in schizophrenic Rorschach responses. This was first noticed in the Rorschach response to Card VI of a middle-aged female (Case A) with chronic schizophrenia in the statement, "This looks like a mass of flesh of some kind of animal, although I cannot specify which animal." Before producing this response, the patient had failed to make the response of " a gorilla" to Card IV, in which she could not identify its arms, legs or head. According to these Rorschach sequences, it would be considered that if the patient has failed to see the legs and arms, a gorilla is perceived as a mass of flesh. A similar response was found in another middle-aged male with chronic schizophrenia, who responded to Card IX, "Part of a naked man, the swelling muscles of his shoulder." This patient also responded to Card VIII, "The carcass of an animal. Only bones here, for the flesh is gone." In this response, he imagined a mass of flesh and quickly eliminated it by thinking of it as having been taken away in his fantasy. The third patient, a middle-aged female with chronic schizophrenia, who gave another such response, by responding to Card VIII, saying "Two seals. They are seals, because their legs and arms are quite short. They look like muscles. Only the muscles of seals. With backbones here." In this response, she saw two aquatic animals that have intrinsically diminished (short) legs and arms, and this image soon became muscles with backbones.

Starting with these findings, the attempts were made further to find similar responses in their Rorschach percepts. It was found that the responses in which a mass of flesh or muscles are explicitly verbalized are not often seen in their Rorschach percepts, but that the responses with the same implications in modified and implicit forms, especially in the form of animals or human beings with diminution of head, legs or arms, were quite common in schizophrenic patients.

Although apparently different, these responses share the common characteristic of revealing the perception of a mass of flesh in the Rorschach pattern. The author called the above percept "a mass of flesh" (MF) and considered that the implications of the MFs should be studied further in the diagnosis of schizophrenia. In order to detect MFs reliably, inclusion and exclusion criteria for MFs were developed which describes the details to identify the MFs.

First, this study is an attempt to develop inclusion criteria for detecting these responses based on these observations. Second, to examine whether perception of MFs is characteristic in schizophrenia or not, the presence or absence of the MFs was examined in the Rorschach protocols of patients in the diagnostic groups of acute schizophrenia, anxiety disorders according to DSM-IV criteria, and healthy adults.

Method

Inclusion and Exclusion Criteria for the MF Percept

The idea that schizophrenics produce percepts of a mass of flesh evolved through our earlier observations in the evaluation of 7 chronic schizophrenia patients. Thereafter, particular attention was given to the responses of 69 consecutive chronic schizophrenic patients (76 in total) to confirm whether or not they produced any response which had a connotation of a mass of flesh or its implicit representation, mainly reflected in diminution of head, arms or legs, of any living thing. After it was confirmed that 75 out of 76 (98%) chronic schizophrenic patients produced some MFs, a list of criteria for MFs was made to detect them reliably.

MFs are, in their explicit and typical form, responses in which a mass of flesh or muscle is explicitly verbalized. The MFs, in their implicit forms, include responses in which diminution of arm, leg, and head is mentioned. In these responses, absence, unusual shortness or vagueness of arms, legs or head is verbalized. The things or living things with a mass-like shape, or perceived as folded or unfolded, are also included because these responses reflect the image of a mass of flesh or the process of becoming a mass of flesh or its denial. Exclusion criteria were made as a guide to exclude misleading responses. Inclusion and exclusion criteria are summarized in Appendix 2.

Test Administration and Scoring

All Rorschach tests were administered by the present authors. The presence or absence of any response that fit the criteria was examined in each case. The cases were divided into two groups, that is, one with MFs and one without.

Inter-Rater Reliability

Inter-rater agreement was determined by evaluating the MFs according to the protocols of 20 chronic schizophrenics. Independent ratings was made by two raters. Nineteen among 20 protocols were scored as showing MF (MF +) by two independent scorers, and 95% inter-rater agreement was obtained.

Subjects

The socio-demographic data of the subjects used for evaluation of the MFs are shown in Table 13. The chronic schizophrenic patients were those of Study 2, who agreed to participate to the study using the Rorschach test. There were 41 men and 35 women. The mean (SD) age of the patients was 49.4 (9.4) years. The mean (SD) chlorpromazine-equivalent dose was 474.8 (406.3) mg. Twenty-two acute schizophrenic patients, 10 male and 12 female, are inpatients of a hospital in a Tokyo suburb. The Rorschach test was administered within one month after their first admission. Their mean (SD) age was 21.8 (3.3) years. All of them were medicated, and the mean (SD) chlorpromazine-equivalent dose was 1082.3 (536.8) mg. All of them had been diagnosed with schizophrenia, according to DSM-IV criteria. Thirty patients with anxiety disorders according to DSM-IV, 16 male and 14 female, were outpatients of a private clinic in Tokyo. Their mean (SD) age was 35.9 (13.4) years. Twenty-eight healthy adults, 14 men and 14 women, were graduate students, hospital staff members, businessmen, office employees, and housewives. The mean (SD) age was 34.1 (12.8) years old. All normal adults were demonstrated to be healthy by administering General Health Questionnaire (Goldberg, 1972; Goldberg & Williams, 1988). Written informed consent was also obtained. (See Table 13.)

Table 13. Demographic characteristics of subjects. (Study 5.)

	Schizophrenia		Anxiety Disorders	Nprmals
	Chronic	Acute		
	(N=76)	(N=22)	(N=30)	(N=22)
Mean Age	49.4	21.8	35.9	34.1
Gender (% male)	53.9	45.5	53.3	50.0

Statistics

The number of subjects perceiving MFs and those not perceiving MF was calculated in each diagnostic group.

Results

Seventy-five out of 76 chronic schizophrenic patients (98%) saw MFs. All 22 acute schizophrenic patients saw MFs. Twenty-eight out of 30 patients with anxiety disorders did not perceive MF. None of the healthy adults saw the MF. It would be reasonable to regard the MFs as characteristic of schizophrenia. The number of subjects perceiving MFs (MF+) and those not perceiving MF (MF-) in schizophrenic and non-schizophrenic groups are shown in Table 14 ($x^2 = 11.308$, df=1, p=0.001).

Both of two patients with anxiety disorders who perceived MFs were young adolescent males and had brief psychotic episodes in their life histories. One patient with chronic schizophrenia who did not perceive MF was a middle-aged male patient who scored the least total response to the inkblots. (His total response was less than ten.)

Table 14. MFs in schizophrenic and non-schizophrenic groups. (Study 5.)

	Schizophrenic		Non-schizophrenic	
	Acute	Chronic	Anxiety Disorders	Normal
	(N=22)	(N=76)	(N=30)	(N=28)
MF+	22	75	2	0
MF-	0	1	28	28

Discussion

The primary contribution of this investigation is to find that Rorschach percepts of a mass of flesh are characteristic of schizophrenia. It was found that although there are some differences in their responses, the perception of a mass of flesh in Rorschach inkblot stimuli was broadly seen as living things with diminished arms, legs or head. By developing inclusion and exclusion criteria for MFs, detection of MFs would become easier and more reliable. To test whether the perception of MFs in inkblots is unique to schizophrenia or not, we examined the Rorschach Test data of 22 acute schizophrenia, 30 anxiety disorders and 28 healthy adults. Ninety-seven out of 98 schizophrenic patients saw MFs, although only two out of 30 patients with anxiety disorders saw MFs. Further, healthy adults did not see any MF. Thus, MFs proved to be characteristic of schizophrenia.

An index for detecting such responses is particularly important because it provides a tool for detecting schizophrenia in its early phase. Ninety-eight percent of chronic schizophrenics, as well as 100% of acute schizophrenic patients, perceived MFs. The perception of MFs might exist from the time of onset and therefore be able to detect a very early phase of schizophrenia, suggesting the diagnostic predictive value of MF perception. As a greater understanding of the nature of schizophrenia has refocused attention on the early course of psychosis in the from of early detection and intervention around the onset (McGlashan & Johannessen, 1996) the inclusion and exclusion criteria would have more value if MFs are found in the prodrome of schizophrenia.

The findings that schizophrenic patients produce MF percepts may lead to improvement of our understanding of thought disorder of schizophrenia. The use of the Rorschach test in the study of thought disorder is well established. However, using the Rorschach test for the purpose of eliciting perceptual deficits, manifested in global and affective percepts such as MFs, might provide a new opportunity to understand the cognitive dysfunction of schizophrenia patients.

Conclusion

The Rorschach test was given to schizophrenic and non-schizophrenic subjects to determine whether schizophrenic patients more frequently produced the "mass of flesh" percept than the non-schizophrenic groups did.

PART IV. DISCUSSION AND CONCLUSION

Discussion

The major findings of the studies on schizophrenics' body image aberration in this chapter are: (1) There is some aberration in schizophrenics' body image. (2) There are aberrant as well as intact phases in their body images. (3) Aberration was found in functional imageries, while anatomical imageries are intact. (4) Aberration is independent of symptoms and conventional neuroleptic medication.

The main questions raised in the introduction were whether aberration comes from symptoms or is an effect of neuroleptics, and whether it is remediable or not. What the components of body image are and which phase of body image is aberrant in schizophrenia was the first question we tried to answer by attempts at classification of body image items by factor analysis. Nine body image factors were obtained, and some factors proved to differentiate schizophrenics from normal controls. Although these factors were variously named, after rather exhaustive attempts, the only discrete common feature among factor-analytic studies was that functional imageries may contribute substantially to the factors that meaningfully differentiated groups or were related to depression. In addition, almost no significant correlation was found between aberrant body image factors and clinical characteristics such as symptoms, insight, or neuroleptic dosage. The results of Study 1 showed that when each component of symptoms and insight was cross-validated to the BIQ factors, there were some symptoms and some insight components related to body image factors; however, the overall results showed their relationship was quite weak. The only strong evidence gained through these studies was the fact that there are some differential body image factors, most of which seemed to relate to functional body imageries, but none of which seemed to relate to the anatomical component of body image of schizophrenia.

Thus the question of which phase of body image links with symptoms and which to recovery? leads to the next question, "What are the body images of schizophrenics and what is aberrant for them?" In Study 2, attempts were made to clarify this question simply by comparing three hypothetical components of body image, that is, anatomical, functional, and psychological, between schizophrenic and non-schizophrenic groups. The results showed clearly that anatomical, that is, the visual or the spatial, component is intact in schizophrenia and limited their aberration mainly to functional component.

The fact that schizophrenics have aberrant body images in function, i.e., they have unmovable body images, is controversial with regard to the possibility that it reflects perseverance in motor activity. Schizophrenic patients might have difficulty in the shifting the response set in motor activity in light of the feedback that a previous response was incorrect and consequently "persevere" in making the same response, creating difficulty in movement cognition. Perseveration is a cardinal feature of frontal lobe disease (Bilder & Goldberg, 1987). It is one of the presenting basic neurocognitive deficits, observed since the time of Bleuler (1911/1950), who wrote that schizophrenic patients "remain fixed to the same circle of ideas, the same words, the same sentence structure or at any rate, return to them again and again without any logical need."

The degree of perseverance of schizophrenic patients is similar to that of patients with known frontal pathology (Levin, 1984). Since Weinberger et al. (1986) reported a negative correlation between the percentage perseveration as measured by the Wisconsin Card Sorting Test, WCST, (Milner, 1963) and prefrontal blood flow, these associations have supported the hypothesis that schizophrenic patients have an impairment of the frontal or prefrontal cortex.

Because the clinical interpretation of test data can often point to multiple studies that converge on a set of frequent severe and selective deficits, patients with schizophrenia typically demonstrate abnormalities in attention, memory, and executive function that stand out against a background of diffuse impairment (Pantelis et al., 1996). However, some areas of function appear to be relatively more intact than others, i.e., some aspects of language (Gold et al., 1994; Saykin et al., 1991; Daniels et al., 1988; Barr et al., 1989; Frith, 1993) and some types of visual spatial processing (Kolb & Whishaw, 1983; Goldberg et al., 1990; Goldberg et al., 1993a). These neuropsychological profiles implicate specific brain regions, i.e., frontal-medial dysfunction (Kolb & Whishaw, 1983; Taylor and Abrams, 1984). The finding that the aberration referred to functional body imageries would imply body image deficits that have some relation to dorsolateral deficits, and the fact that the anatomical, that is, visual and spatial, imageries remain intact is consistent with the previous finding that some types of visual spatial processing is intact in the neuropsychological profile of schizophrenics.

In Study 3, body image aberration was considered through an attempt to detect specific body image characteristics related to depression in schizophrenia by comparing the BIQ factor scores between depressive and non-depressive groups comprised by Zung's Self-rating Depression Scale (SDS) in normal and schizophrenic groups respectively. The results showed some body image factors related uniquely to depression in schizophrenia, which, again, referred to functional body images. The result of this part of the study might cast light on future prospects of the study of body image aberration using a device such as the BIQ because of its link with DSS which has become a target for treatment of schizophrenia, with the novel antipsychotic medications. The studies performed for this chapter all revealed that neuroleptics did not relate to body image aberration; however, novel antipsychotic agents were not discussed or studied. This would be relevant to the final question as to whether or not the body image aberration is remediable.

Study 4 and Study 5 are reports of subsidiary findings of our main studies using the BIQ, in which schizophrenic patients produced Rorschach responses implying or referring to "mass of flesh." Study 4 is composed of the initial observations. In Study 5, the Rorschach test was given to schizophrenic and non-schizophrenic subjects to determine whether schizophrenic patients more frequently produced the "mass of flesh" percept than the non-schizophrenic groups did. These findings suggest that there might be a fear of immobility in schizophrenia that is congruent with our main findings.

Conclusion

Schizophrenic body image aberration was considered in the current context. The schizophrenic body image aberration was unrelated to symptoms, insight, or conventional neuroleptic medication, but proved to be germane to schizophrenia. The schizophrenic body image aberration also proved to be limited to functional imagery while anatomical imageries remained intact.

Acknowledgements

We would like to express our appreciation to Dr. Chin-Piao Chien, professor emeritus of UCLA, and Dr. Shoji Shin'ichi and Dr. Susumu Oda, professors emeriti of Tsukuba University. We also thank Dr. Toshihiko Maeda of tne Institute of Statistical Mathematics for the statistical consultation.

Part of the text was re-edited from *Psychiatry and Clinical Neurosciences*, Vol. 56, pp9-15, "Body image, symptoms and insight in chronic schizophrenia" by Koide et al (2002), with permission from Blackwell Publishing, and from *Comprehensive Psychiatry,* Vol.43, pp474-477, "A mass of flesh: Schizophrenic Rorschach Percepts" by Koide R., et al (2002), with permission from Elsevier.

References

Amador, X. F., Flaum, M,, Andreasen, N.C., Strauss, D. H., Yale, S. A., Clark, S. C. & Gorman, J. M. (1994). Awareness of illness in schizophrenia and schizoaffective and Mood disorders. *Archives of General Psychiatry, 51*, 826-836.

Amador, X. F., Strauss, D.H., Yale, S.A., & Gorman JM. (1991). Awareness of illness in schizophrenia. *Schizophrenia Bulletin, 17*,113-132.

American Psychiatric Association. (1980). *Diagnostic and statistical manual of mental disorders (3rd edition)*. Washington, DC: American Psychiatric Association.

American Psychiatric Association. (1987). *Diagnostic and statistical manual of mental disorders (3rd edition revised)*. Washington, DC: American Psychiatric Association.

American Psychiatric Association. (1994). *Diagnostic and statistical manual of mental disorders (4th edition)*. Washington, DC: American Psychiatric Association.

Andreasen, N. C. (1981). *Scale for the assessment of negative symptoms*. Iowa City, IA: The University of Iowa Press.

Andreasen, N. C. (1983). *Scale for the assessment of positive symptoms*. Iowa City, IA: The University of Iowa Press.

Andreasen, N. C., Arndt, S., Alliger, R., Miller, D., & Flaum, M. (1995). Symptoms of schizophrenia: methods, meanings, and mechanisms. *Archives of General Psychiatry, 52*, 341-351.

Andreasen, N, & Bardach, J. (1977). Dysmorphophobia:Symptom or disease? *American Journal of Psychiatry, 134*, 673-676.

Angyal, A. (1936). Experiences of body self in schizophrenia. *Archives of Neurology and Psychiatry, 35*, 1629-1634.

Apter, J.T. (1981). The "silent" acute abdomen in schizophrenia. *Journal of the Medical Society of New Jersey, 78*, 679-680.

Arieti, S. (1945). Primitive habits and perceptual alterations in the terminal stage of schizophrenia. *Archives of Neurology and Psychiatry, 53*, 378-384.

Barr, W. B., Bilder, R. M., Goldberg, E. H., Caplan, E., & Mukherjee, S. (1989). The neuropsychology of schizophrenic speech. *Journal of Communication Disorders, 22*, 327-349.

Berman, A. L. (1972). Videotape self-confrontation of schizophrenic ego and thought processes. *Journal of Consulting and Clinical Psychology, 39*, 78-85.

Bickerstaff, L. K., Harris, S. C, Leggett R S, & Cheah K. C. (1988). Pain insensitivity in schizophrenic patients: A surgical dilemma. *Archives of Surgery, 123*, 49-50.

Bilder, R. M., & Goldberg, R. E. (1987) Motor perseverations in schizoiphrenia. *Archives of Clinical Neuropsychology, 2*, 195-214.

Birtchnell, S. A. (1988). Dysmorphophobia - a centenary discussion. *British Journal of Psychiatry, 153 (suppl 2)*, 41-43.

Blackmore, S. (1986). Out-of-body experiences in schizophrenia. A questionnaire survey. *Journal of Nervous and Mental Disease, 174*, 615-619.

Bleuler, E. (1911) *Dementia Praecox, or the Group of Schizophrenias*. Translated by J Zinkin. New York: International Universities Press (1950).

Braff, D. L., Heaton, R., Kuck, J., Cullum, M., Moranville, J., Grant, I., & Zisook, S. (1991). The generalized pattern of neuropsychological deficits in outpatients with chronic schizophrenia with heterogeneous Wisconsin Card Sorting Test results. *Archives of General Psychiatry, 158*, 340-345.

Brebion, G., Smith, M. J., Amador, X., Malaspina, D., & Gorman, J.M. (1997). Clinical correlates of memory in schizophrenia: differential links between depression, positive and negative symptoms, and two types of memory impairment. *American Journal of Psychiatry, 154*, 1538-1543.

Bryson, G., Bell, M., Lysaker, P. (1997). Affect recognition in schizophrenia: A function of global impairment or a specific cognitive deficit. *Psychiatry Research, 71*, 105-113.

Buchanan, R. W., Strauss, M. E., Breier, A., Kirkpatrick, B., & Carpenter, W.T. (1997). Attentional impairements in deficit and nondeficit forms of schizophrenia. *American Journal of Psychiatry, 154*, 363-370.

Burgess, J. W. (1991). Relationship of depression and cognitive impairment to self-injury in borderline personality disorder, major depression, and schizophrenia. *Psychiatry Research, 38*, 77-87.

Bychowsky, G. (1943). Disorders of the body image in the clinical picture of psychoses. *Journal of Nerveous and Mental Disease, 97*, 310-334.

Caldwell, C. B., & Gottesman, I.I. (1990). Schizophrenics kill themselves too: a review of risk factors for suicide. *Schizophrenia Bulletin, 16*, 571-589.

Cancro, R. (1971). Sophistication of body concept in process-reactive schizophrenia. *Perceptual and Motor Skills, 32*, 567-570.

Cassens, G., Inglis, A. K., Appelbaum, P. S., & Gutheil, T. G. (1990). Neuroleptics: Effects on neuropsychological function in chronic schizophrenic patients. *Schizophrenia Bulletin, 16*, 477-499.

Censits, D. M., Ragland, J. D., Gur, R. C., & Gur, R. E. (1997). Neuropsychological evidence supporting a neurodevelopmental model of schizophrenia: A longitudinal study. *Schizophrenia Research, 24*, 289-298.

Chapman, L. J., Chapman, J.P., & Raulin, M. L. (1976). Scales for physical and social anhedonia. *Journal of Abnormal Psychology, 85*, 374-382.

Chapman, L. J., Chapman, J. P., & Raulin, M. L. (1978). Body-image aberration in schizophrenia. *Journal of Abnormal Psychology, 87*, 399-407.

Cleveland, S. E. (1960a). Body image changes associated with personality reorganization. *Journal of Consulting Psychology, 24*, 256-261.

Cleveland, S. E. (1960b). Judgements of body size in a schizophrenic and a control group. *Psychological Reports, 7*, 304.

Cleveland, S. E., Fisher, S., Reitman, E. E., & Rothaus, P. (1962). Perception of body size in schizophrenia. *Archives of General Psychiatry, 7*, 277-285.

Cohen, L. J., Test, M. A. & Brocon, R. L. (1990). Suicide and schizophrenia: data from a prospective community treatment study. *American Journal of Psychiatry, 147*, 602-607. Correction, 147, 1110.

Coleman, M. J., Carpenter, J. T., Waterneaux, C., Levy, D. L., Shenton, M. E., Perry, J., Medoff, D., Wong, H., Manoach, D., Meyer, P., O'Brien, C., Valentino, C., Robinson, D., Smith, M., Makowski, D. & Holzman, P. S. (1993) The Thought Disorder Index: A reliability study. *Psychological Assessment, 5*, 336-342.

Coleman, M. J., Levy, D. L., Lenzenweger, M. F. & Holzman, P. S. (1996) Thought disorder, perceptual aberrations, and schizotypy. *Journal of Abnormal Psychology, 105*, 469-473.

Connolly, F. & Gipson, M. (1978). Dysmorphophobia. A long term study. *British Journal of Psychiatry, 132*, 458-470.

Coons, P. M., Ascher-Svanum, H, & Bellis, K. (1986). Self-amputation of the female breast. *Psychosomatics, 27*, 667-668.

Cornblatt, B. A., Lenzenweger, M. F., Dworkin, R. H. & Erlenmeyer-Kimling, L. (1985). Positive and negative schizophrenic symptoms, attention, and information processing. *Schizophrenia Bulletin, 11*, 397-408.

Crider, A. (1997). Perseverations in schiziophrenia. *Schizophrenia Bulletin, 23*, 63-74.

Crow, T. J. & Johnstone, E. C. (1980). Dementia praecox and schizophrenia: was Bleuler wrong? *Journal of the Royal College of Physicians, 14*, 238-240.

Crow, T. J. & Stevens, M. (1978). Age disorientation in chronic schizophrenia: the nature of the cognitive deficit. *British Journal of Psychiatry, 133*, 137-142.

Cuesta, M. J. & Peralta, V. (1994). Lack of insight in schizophrenia. *Schizophrenia Bulletin, 20*, 359-366.

Cuesta, M. S., Peralta, V., Caro, F, & de Leon, J. (1995). Schizophrenia syndrome and Wisconsin Card Sorting Test dimensions. *Psychiatry Research, 58*, 45-51.

Daniels, E. K., Shenton, M. E., Holzman, P. S., Benowitz, L. I., Coleman, M. ,Levin, S. & Levine, D. (1988). Patterns of thought disorder associated with right cortical damage, schizophrenia, and mania. *American Journal of Psychiatry, 145*, 944-949.

Darby, J. A. (1968). Pychotheraputic treatment of schizophrenia: Theory and case study. *Psychotherapy: Theory, Research, and Practice, 5*, 234-239.

David, S. A. (1990). Insight and psychosis. *British Journal of Psychiatry, 156*, 798-808.

Delaplaine, R., Ifabumuyi, O. I., Merskey, H. & Zarfas, J. (1978). Significance of pain in psychiatirc hospital patients. *Pain, 4*, 361-366.

deLeon, J., Bott, A. & Simpson, G. H. (1989). Dysmorphophobia: body dysmorphic disorder or delusional disorder, somatic type? *Comprehensive Psychiatry, 30*, 457-472.

Des Lauriers, A. M. (1962). *The experience of reality in childhood schizophrenia.* New York: International Universities Press.

Dillon, D. J. (1962) Measurement of perceived body size. *Perceptual and Motor Skills,14*, 191-196.

Dingman, C. W. & McGlashan, T. H. (1986). Discriminating characteristics of suicides: Chestnut Lodge follow-up sample including patients with affective disorder, schizophrenia and schizoaffective disorder. *Acta Psychiatrica Scandinavica, 74*, 91-97.

Dingman, C. W. & McGlaschan, T. H. (1988). Characteristics of patients with serious suicidal inpatients who ultimately commit suicide. *Hospital and Community Psychiatry, 39*, 295-299.

Di-Nuovo, S., Laicardi, C. & Tobino, C. (1988). Rorschach indices for discriminating between two schizophrenic syndromes. *Perceptual and Motor Skills, 67*, 399-406.

Drake, R. E. & Cotton, P. G. (1986). Depression, hopelessness and suicide in chronic schizophrenia. *British Journal of Psychiatry, 148*, 554-559.

Dworkin, R. H. (1994). Pain insensitivity in schizophrenia: A neglected phenomenon and some implications. *Schizophrenia Bulletin, 20*, 235-248.

Dworkin, R. H. & Caligor, E. (1988). Psychiatric diagnosis and chronic pain: DSM III-R and beyond. *Journal of Pain and Symptom Management, 3*, 87-98.

Edgerton, M., Jacobsen, W. & Meyer, E. (1960) Surgical/ psychiatric study of patients seeking plastic (cosmetic) surgery: 98 consecutive patients with minimal deformity. *British Journal of Plastic Surgery, 13*, 136-145.

Exner, E. J. Jr. (1974). *The Rorschach: A Comprehensive System: Vol.1.* Basic Foundations. New York: Wiley.

Exner, E. J. Jr. (1978). *The Rorschach: A Comprehensive System: Vol.2.* Current Research and Advanced Interpretation. New York: Wiley.

Exner, E. J. Jr. (1986a). *The Rorschach: A Comprehensive System: Vol.1.* Basic Foundations. 2nd ed. New York: Wiley.

Exner, E. J. Jr. (1986b). Some Rorschach data comparing schizophrenics with borderline and schizotypal personality disorders. *Journal of Personality Assessment, 50*, 455-471.

Exner, E. J. Jr. (1991). *The Rorschach: A Comprehensive System: Vol.2*. Current Research and Advanced Interpretation. 2nd ed. New York: Wiley.

Exner EJ Jr. (1993). *The Rorschach: A Comprehensive System: Vol.1*. Basic Foundations (3rd edition). New York: Wiley.

Federn P. (1952). *Ego Psychology and the psychosis*. New York: Basic Books.

Feldman MD. 1988 The challenge of self-mutilation: a review. *Comprehensive Psychiatry, 29*, 252-269.

Ferenczi, S. (1926). The problem of acceptance of unpleasant ideas: Advances in knowledge of the sense of reality. *International Journal of Psychoanalysis, 7*, 312-323.

Fishbain, D. A. (1982) Pain insensitivity in psychosis. *Annals of Emergency Medicine, 11*, 630-632.

Fisher, S. (1963). A further appraisal of the body boundary concept. *Journal of Consulting Psychology, 27*, 62-74.

Fisher, S. (1964). Body image and psychopathology. *Archives of General Psychiatry, 10*, 519-529.

Fisher, S. (1966). Body image in neurotic and schizophrenic patients. *Archives of General Psychiatry, 15*, 90-101.

Fisher, S. & Cleveland, S. E. (1958). *Body image and personality*. Princeton, NJ; Van Nostrand.

Fisher, S. & Cleveland S. E. (1968). *Body image and personality 2nd edition)*. New York: Dover Publications.

Fisher, S. & Renik, O.D. (1966). Induction of body image boundary changes. *Journal of Projective Techniques and Personality Assessment, 30*, 429-434.

Fisher, S. & Seidner, R. (1963). Body experiences of schizophrenic, neurotic and normal women. *Journal of Nervous and Mental Disease, 137*, 252-257.

Fottrell, E. (1980). A study of violent behaviour among patients in psychiatric hospitals. *British Journal of Psychiatry, 136*, 216-221.

Freeman, T., Cameron, J. L. & McGhie, A. (1958). *Chronic Schizophrenia*. New York: International Universities Press.

Freeman, T. & Gathercole, L. E. (1966). Perseveration in chronic schizophrenia and organic dementia. *British Journal of Psychiatry, 112*, 27-32.

Freud, S. (1962). *The ego and the id*. New York: Norton.

Frith, C. (1993). *The Cognitive Neuropsychology of Schizophrenia*. Erlbaum, Hove.

Galdi, J. (1983). The causality of depression in schizophrenia. *British Journal of Psychiatry, 142*, 621-624.

George, L. & Neufeld, R. W. (1985). Cognition and symptomatology in schizophrenia. *Schizophrenia Bulletin, 11*, 264-285.

Gerstmann, J. (1942). Problem of imperception of disease and of impaired body territories with organic lesions. Relation to body schema and its disorders. *Archives of Neurology and Psychiatry, 48*, 890-913.

Gold, J. M., Hermann, B.P., Wyler, A., Randolph, C., Goldberg, T.E. & Weinberger, D. R. (1994). Schizophrenia and temporal lobe epilepsy: a neuropsychological study. *Archives of General Psychiatry, 51*, 265-272.

Goldberg, D. P. (1972). *The detection of psychiatric illness by questionnaire*. Maudsley Monograph 21. London: Oxford University Press.

Goldberg, D. & Williams, P. (1988). *A user's guide to the General Health Questionnaire*. Windsor, Berkshire: Neer-Nelson.

Goldberg, T. E., Gold, J. M., Greenberg, R., Griffin, S., Schulz, S. C., Picker, D., Kleinman, J. E., & Weinberger, D. R. (1993a). Contrasts between patients with affective disorder and patients with schizophrenia on a neuropsychological screening test battery. *American Journal of Psychiatry, 150*, 1355-1362.

Goldberg, T. E., Greenberg, R. & Griffin, S. (1993b). The impact of clozapine on cognition and psychiatric symptoms in patients with schizophrenia. *British Journal of Psychiatry, 162*, 43-48.

Goldberg, T.E., Ragland, D.R., Gold, J., Bigelow, L.B., Torrey, E.F. & Weinberger, D. R. (1990). Neuropsychological assessment of monozygotic twins discordant for schizophrenia. *Archives of General Psychiatry 47*, 1066-1072.

Goldstein, G. (1978). Cognitive and perceptual differences between schizophrenics and organics. *Schizophrenia Bulletin, 4*, 160-185.

Goodenough, F. L. (1928). Studies in the psychology of children's drawings. *Psychological Bulletin, 25*, 272-279.

Green, M. F. (1996). What are the functional consequences of neurocognitive deficit in schizophrenia? *American Journal of Psychiatry, 153*, 321-330.

Green, M. F., Marshall, B. D., Wirshing, W. C., Ames, D., Marder, S. R., McGurk, S., Kern, R. S. & Mintz, J. (1997). Does risperidone improve verbal working mempry in treatment–resistant schizophrenia? *American Journal of Psychiatry, 154*, 799-804.

Green, M. F. & Nuechterlein, K. H. (1999). Should schizophrenia be treated as a neurocognitive disorder? *Schizophrenia Bulletin, 25*, 309-318.

Green, M. F., Nuechterlein, K. H. & Geier, D.J. (1992). Sustained and selective attention in schizophrenia. *Progress in Experimental Personaity and Psychopathology Research, 15*, 290-313.

Green, M. F. & Walker, E. (1985). Neuropsychological performance and positive and negative symptoms in schizophrenia. *Journal of Abnormal Psychology, 94*, 460-469.

Guieu, R., Samuelian, J. C. & Coulouvrat, H. (1994). Objective evaluation of pain perception in patients with schizophrenia. *British Journal of Psychiatry, 164*, 253-255.

Hagger, C., Buckley, P., Kenny, J. T., Friedman, L., Ubogy, D. & Meltzer, H. Y. (1993). Improvement in cognitive functions and psychiatric symptoms in treatment –refractory schizopherenic patients receiving clozapine. *Bioliogical Psychiatry, 34*, 702-712.

Harding, C. M., Zubin, J. & Strauss, S. (1992). Chronicity in schizophrenia. *British Journal of Psychiatry, 161 (Suppl 18)*, 27-37.

Hay, G. (1970). Dysmorphophobia. *British Journal of Psychiatry, 116*, 399-406.

Hay, G. (1973). Changes in psychometric test results following cosmetic nasal operations. *British Journal of Psychiatry, 122*, 89-90.

Hay, G. (1983). Paranoia and dysmorphophobia. *British Journal of Psychiatry, 142*, 309-310.

Head, H. (1911). Sensory disturbunce from cerebral lesions. *Brain, 34*, 187-189.

Head, H. (1926). *Aphasia and Kindred Disorders of Speech*. London: Cambridge University Press.

Heaton, R. K., Baade, L. E. & Johnson, K. L. (1978). Neuropsychological test results associated with psychiatric disorders in adults. *Psychological Bulletin, 85*,141-162.

Hill, G. & Silver, G. (1950). Psychodynamics and esthetic motivations for plastic surgery. *Psychosomatic Medicine, 12*, 345-355.

Hilsenroth, M. J., Fowler, J. C. & Padawer, J. R. (1998). The Rorschach Schizophrenia Index (SCZI): an examination of reliability, validity, and diagnostic efficacy. *Journal of Personality Assessment, 70*, 514-534.

Himelhoch, S., Taylor, S. F., Goldman, R. S. & Tandon, R. (1996). Frontal lobes, antipsychotic medication, and schizophrenic symptoms. *Biological Psychiatry, 39*, 227-229.

Hirsch, S. R. (1982). Depression "revealed" in schizophrenia. *British Journal of Psychiatry, 140*, 421-424.

Hollander, E., Cohen, L. T. & Simeon, D. (1993). Body dysmorphic disorder. *Psychiatric Annals, 23*, 359-364.

Holt, R. (1977). A method for assessing primary process manifestations and their controls in Rorschach responses. In M. Rickers-Ovsiankina (Eds), *Rorschach Psychology (2nd edition, pp375-420)*. Huntington, NY: Krieger.

Holtzman, W. H., Gorham, D. R. & Moran, L. J. (1964). A factor-analytic study of schizophrenic thought processes. *Journal of Abnormal and Social Psychology, 69*, 355-364.

Holtzman, W. H., Thorpe, J. S., Swartz, J. D. & Herron, E.W. (1961*). Inkblot perception and personality: Holtzman inkblot technique*. Austin: University of Texas Press.

Hu, W. H., Sun, C. M., Lee, C. T., Peng, S. L., Lin, S. K. & Shen, W. W. (1991). A clinical study of schizophrenic suicides: 42 cases in Taiwan. *Schizophrenia Research, 5,* 43-50.

Huber, G. (1957). Die coenaesthetische Schizophrenie. *Fortschritte der Neurologie und Psychiatrie, 25*, 491-520.

Huber, G. (1971). Die coenaesthetische Schizophrenie als Praegnanztyp schizophrener Erkrankungen. *Acta Psychiatrica Scandinavica, 47*, 349-362.

Humphreys, M. S., Johnstone, E. C., MacMillan, J. F. & Taylor, P. J. (1992). Dangerous behaviour preceding first admission s for schizophrenia. *British Journal of Psychiatry, 161*, 501-505.

Jacobsen, W., Edgerton, M., Meyer, E., Canter, A. & Slaughter, R. (1960). Psychiatric evaluation of male patients seeking cosmetic surgery. *Plastic and Reconstructive Surgery, 16*, 356-372.

Jasker, R. O. & Reed, M. R. (1963). Assessment of body image organization of hospitalizd and non-hopspitalized subjects. *Journal of Projective Techniques, 27*, 185-190.

Jeste, D. V., Lohr, J. B., Eastman, J. H., Rockwell, E. & Caligiuri, M. P. (1998). Adverse neurobiological effects of long term use of neuroleptics: Human and animal studies. *Journal of Psychiatric Research, 32*, 201-214.

Johnston, M, & Holzman, P. (1979). *Assessing Schizophrenic Thinking*. San Francisco: Jossey-Bass.

Johnstone, E. C., Crow, T. J., Frith, C. D., Husband, J. & kreel, L. (1976). Cerebral ventricular size and cognitive impairment in chronic schizophrenia. *Lancet II,* 924-926.

Katz, E., Kluger, Y., Rabinovici, R., Stein, D. & Gimmon, Z. (1990). Acute surgical abdominal disease in chronic svhizohrenic patients: A unique clinical problem. *Israel Journal of Medical Sciences, 26,* 275-277.

Kay, S. R., Fiszbein, A. & Opler, L.A. (1987). The positive and negative syndrome scale (PANSS) for schizophrenia. *Schizophrenia Bulletin, 13,* 261-276.

Keefe, R. S. E., Silva, S. G., Perkins, D. O. & Lieberman, J. A. (1999). The effects of atypical antipsychotic drugs on neurocognitive impairmaent in schizophrenia: A review and meta-analysis. *Schizophrenia Bulletin, 25,* 201-222.

Kennedy, B. L. & Feldmann, T. B. (1994). Self-inflicted eye injuries: case presentation s and a literature review. *Hospital Community Psychiatry, 45,* 470-474.

Kern, R. S., Green, M. F., Marshall, B. D., Wirshing, W. C., McGurk, S. R., Marder, S. R. & Mintz, J. (1999). Risperidone vs haloperidol on secondary memory: Can newer antipsychotic medications aid learning? *Schizophrenia Bulletin, 25,* 223-233.

Knights, A. & Hirsch, S. R. (1981). "Revealed" depression and drug treatment for schizophrenia. *Archives of General Psychiatry, 38,* 806-811.

Koide, R. (1985). Body image differences between schizophrenic and normal female adults. International *Review of Applied Psychology, 34,* 335-347.

Kokonis, N. D. (1972). Body image disturbance in schizophrenia. A study of arms and feet. *Journal of Personality Assessment, 36,* 573-575.

Kolb, B. & Whishaw, .IQ. (1983). Performance of schizophrenic patients on tests sensitive to left or right frontal temporal, and parietal function in neurologic patients. *Journal of Nervous and Mental Disease, 171,* 435-443.

Kraepelin, E. (1919). *Dementia Praecox and Paraphrenia.* Edinburgh, Scotland: E. and S. Livingstone.

Kuechenhoff, J. (1984).Dysmorphophobie. *Nervenarzt, 55,* 122-126.

Kwawer, J. (1980). Primitive interpersonal modes, borderline phenomena and Rorschach content. In J. Kwawer, H. Lerner, P. Lerner & A. Sugarman (Eds). *Borderline Phenomena and Rorschach Test* (pp. 257-274). New York: International University Press.

Lautenbacher, S. & Krieg, J. C. (1994). Pain perception in psychiatric disorders: a review of the literature. *Journal of Psychiatry Research, 28,* 109-122.

Leventhal, D. B., Schuck, J. R., Clemons, J. T. & Cox, M. (1982). Proprioception in schizophrenia. *Journal of Nervous and Mental Disease, 170,* 21-26.

Levin, S. (1984). Frontal lobe dysfunction in schizophrenia II. Impairments of psychological and brain functions. *Journal of Psychiatric Research, 18,* 27-55.

Liddle, P. F. & Morris, D.L. (1991). Schizophrenic syndromes and frontal lobe performance. *British Journal of Psychiatry, 158,* 340-345.

Linn, L. & Goldman, I. (1949). Psyciatric observations concerning rhinoplasty. *Psychosomatic Medicine, 11,* 307-309.

Lukianowicz, N. (1967). Body image disturbances in psychiatric disorders. *British Journal of Psychiatry, 113,* 31-47.

Lysaker, P. & Bell, M. (1994). Insight and cognitive impairment in schizophrenia: Performance on repeated administrations of the Wisconsin Card Sorting Test. *Journal of Nervous and Mental Disease, 182*, 656-660.

Machover, K. (1949). *Personality projection in the drawing of the human figure. Springfield, Ill.*: Chales C Thomas.

Malec, J. (1978). Neuropsychological assessment of schizophrenia versus brain damage: a review. *Journal of Nervous and Mental Disease, 166*, 507-516.

Manschreck, T. C., Maher, B. A., Hoover, T. M. & Ames D. (1985). Repetition in schizophrenic speech. *Language and Speech, 28*, 327-349.

Marchand, W. E. (1959). Practice of surgery in a neuropsychiatric hospital. *Archives of General Psychiatry, 1*, 123-131.

Martin, R. L., Cloninger, C. R. & Guze, S. B. (1985). Frequency and differetial diagnosis of depressive syndromes in schizophrenia. *Journal of Clinical Psychiatry, 46*, 9-13.

Martin, T. & Gattaz, W. F. (1991). Psychiatric aspects of male genital self-mutilation. *Psychopathology, 24*, 170-178.

Mason, B., Cohen, J. & Exner, J. E. Jr. (1985). Schizophrenic, depressive, and nonpatient personality organizations described by Rorschach factor structures. *Journal of Personality Assessment, 49*, 295-305.

Mayer-Gross, W. (1920). Uber die Stellungsnahme auf abgelaufenen akuten psychose. *Zeitschrift fuer die Gesamte Neurologie Psychiatrie, 60*, 160-212.

McGlaschan, T. H. & Carpenter, W. T. Jr. (1976). An investigation of the post psychotic depressive syndrome. *American Journal of Psychiatry, 133*, 14-19.

McGlashan, T. H. & Johannessen, J. O. (1996). Early detection and intervention with schizophrenia: Rationale. *Schizophrenia Bulletin, 22*, 201-222.

McGlichrist, I. & Cutting, J. (1995). Somatic delusions in schizophrenia and the affective psychoses. *British Journal of Psychiatry, 167*, 350-361.

Meloy, J. (1984). Thought organization and primary process in the patients of schizophrenics. *British Journal of Medical Psychology, 57*, 279-281.

Meltzer, H. Y. & McGurk, S. R. (1999). The effects of clozapine, risperidone, and olanzapine on cognitive function in schizophrenia. *Schizophrenia Bulletin, 25*, 233-255.

Merriam, A. E., Kay, S., Opler, L. A., Kushner, S. F. & van Praag, H. M. (1990). Neurological signs and the positive-negative dimension in schizophrenia. *Biological Psychiatry, 28*, 181-192.

Merskey, H. (1965). The characteristics of persistent pain in psychological illness. *Journal of Psychosomatic Research, 9*, 291-298.

Meyer, E., Jacobsen, W., Edgerton, M. & Canter, A. (1960). Motivational patterns in patients seeking elective plastic surgery (women who seek rhinoplasty). *Psychosomatic Medicine, 22*, 193-199.

Milner, B. (1963). Effect of different brain lesions in card sorting. The role of the frontal lobes. *Archives of Neurology, 9*, 100-110.

Nuechterlein, K. H., Edell, W. S., Norris, M. & Dawson, M. E. (1986). Attentional vulnerability indicators, thought disorder, and negative symptoms. *Schizophrenia Bulletin, 12*, 408-426.

Oosthuizen, P., Lambert, T. & Castle, D. J. (1998). Dysmorphic concern: prevalence and associations with clinical variables. *Australia and New Zealand Journal of Psychiatry, 32*, 129-132.

Overall, J. E. & Gorham, D. R. (1962). Brief Psychiatric Rating Scale (BPRS). *Psychological Reports, 10*, 799-812.

Pantelis, C., Nelson, H. E. & Barnes, T. R. E. (1996). *Schizophrenia: A neuropsychological perspective*. Chichester, West Sussex: John Wiley & Sons.

Pattison, E. M. & Kahan, T. (1983). The deliberate self-harm syndrome. *American Journal of Psychiatry, 140*, 867-872.

Perry, W. & Braff, D. L. (1994). Information processing and thought disorder in schizophrenia. *American Journal of Psychiatry, 151*, 363-367.

Perry, W. & Braff, D. L. (1998). A multimethod approach to assessing perseveration in schizophrenia patients. *Schizophrenia Research, 33*, 69-77.

Perry, W., Geyer, M. A. & Braff, D. L. (1999). Sensorimotor gating and thought disturbance measured in close temporal proximity in schizophrenic patients. *Archives of General Psychiatry, 56*, 277-281.

Perry, W., Viglione, D. & Braff, D. L. (1992). The Ego Impairment Index and schizophrenia: a validation study. *Journal of Personality Assessment, 59*, 165-175.

Phillips, K. A. (1991). Body dysmorphic disorder: The distress of imagined ugliness. American *Journal of Psychiatry, 148*, 1138-1149.

Phillips, K. A. & McElroy, S. L. (1993). Insight, overvalued ideation, and delusional thinking in body dysmorphic disorder: Theoretical and treatment implications. *Journal of Nervous and Mental Disease, 181*, 699-702.

Phillips, K. A. & McElroy, S. L., Keck, P. E., Hudson, J. I. & Pope, H. G. Jr. (1994). A comparison of delusional and nondelusional body dysmorphic disorder in 100 cases. *Psychopharmacology Bulletin, 30*, 179-186.

Philips, C. & Hunter, M. (1982). Headache in a psychiatric population. *Journal of Nervous and Mental Disease, 170*, 34-40.

Pick, A. (1922). Stoerung der Orientierung am eigenen Koerper. *Psychologische Forschung, 1*, 303-315

Pickar, D. (1995). Prospects for pharmacotherapy of schizophrenia. *Lancet, 345(8949)*, 557-562.

Quinlan, D. M. & Harrow, M. (1974). Boundary disturbance in schizophrenia. *Journal of Abnormal Psychology, 83*, 533-541.

Rado, S. (1959). Dynamics and classification of disorder behavior. *American Journal of Psychiatry, 1*, 651-656.

Reitman, E. E. & Cleveland, S. E. (1964). Changes in body image following sensory deprivation in schizophrenic and control groups. *Journal of Abnormal and Social Psychology, 68*, 168-176.

Renik, O. D. & Fisher, S. (1968). Induction of body image boundary changes in male subjects. *Journal of Projective Techniques and Personality Assessment, 32*, 45-49.

Ritzler, B. & Rosenbaum, G. (1974). Proprioception in schizophrenics and normals: Effects of stimulus intensity and interstimulus interval. *Journal of Abnormal Psychology, 83*, 106-111.

Ritzler, B. (1977). Proprioception and schizophrenia: A replication study with nonschizophrenic patient controls. *Journal of Abnormal Psychology, 86*, 501-504.

Roehricht, F. & Priebe, S. (1996). Body image of patients with acute paranoid schizophrenia: A follow-up study. (Das Koerpererleben von Patienten mit einer akuten paranoiden Schizophrenie. Eine Verlaufsstudie.) *Nervenarzt, 67*, 602-607.

Roehricht, F. & Priebe, S. (1997). Disturbances of body experience in schizophrenic patients.(Stoerungen des Koerpererlebens bei schizophrenen Patienten.) *Fortschritte der Neurologie-Psychiatrie, 65*, 323-336.

Rosenbaum, G., Flenning, F. & Rosen, H. (1965). Effects of weight intensity on discrimination thresholds of normals and schizophrenics. *Journal of Abnormal Psychology, 70*, 446-450.

Rosenthal, S. H., Porter, K. A. & Coffey, B. (1990). Pain insensitivity in schizophrenia: Case report and review of the literature. *General Hospital Psychiatry, 12*, 319-322.

Roy, A., Thompson, R. & Kennedy, S. (1983). Depression in chronic schizophrenia. *British Journal of Psychiatry, 142*, 465-470.

Sacks, M. H., Carpenter, W. T. & Strauss, J. S. (1974). Recovery from delusions. *Archives of General Psychiatry, 30*, 117-120.

Saykin, J. A., Gur, R. C., Gur, R. E., Mozley, P. D., Mozley, L. H., Resnick, S. M, Kester, D. B. & Stafiniak, P. (1991). Neuropsychological function in schizophrenia: selective impairment in memory and learning. *Archives of General Psychiatry, 48*, 618-624.

Schafer, R. (1960). Bodies in Schizophrenic Rorschach Responses. *Journal of Projective Techniques, 24*, 267-281.

Schafer, R. (1986). *Projective Testing and Psychoanalysis. Selected Papers.* International Universities Press, INC.

Scheftel, S., Nathan, A. S., Razin, A. M. & Mezan, P. (1986). A case of radical facial self-mutilation: An unprecedented event and its impact. *Bulletin of the Menninger Clinic, 50*, 525-540.

Schilder, P. (1935). *The image and appearance of the human body.* London: Kegan Paul, Trench, Trubner & Co.

Schmoll, D. (1994). Coenaesthetische Schizophrenie. *Fortschritte der Neurologie Psychiatrie, 62*, 372-378.

Schmoll, D. & Koch, T. (1989). Leibgefuehlsstoerungen in der schizophrenen Psychose. Eine Kasuistik. *Nervenarzt, 60*, 619-627.

Schneider, F., Gur, R. C., Gur, R. E., Shtasel, D. L. (1995). Emotional processing in schizophrenia: Neurobehavioral probes in relation to psychopathology. *Schizophrenia Research, 17*, 67-75.

Schneider, K. (1959). *Klinische Psychopathologie, 12th ed.* Stuttgart: Georg Thieme Verlag, (5th eds. Translated by M. W. Hamilton. Clinical Psychopathology. New York: Grune and Stratton, 1976.)

Shore, D., Andreasen, D. J. & Cutler, N. R. (1978). Prediction of self-mutilation in hospitalized schizophrenics. *American Journal of Psychiatry 135*:1406-1407.

Schweitzer I. 1990 Genital self-amputation and the Klingsor Syndrome. *Australian and New Zealand Journal of Psychiatry, 24*, 566-569.

Silva, J. A., Leong, G. B. & Weinstock, R. (1989). A case of skin and ear self-mutilation. *Psychosomatics, 30*, 228-230.

Silverstein, M. L. & Zerwic, M. J. (1985). Clinical psychopathologic symptoms in neuropsychologically impaired and intact schizophrenics. *Journal of Consulting and Clinical Psychology, 53*, 267-268.

Siris, S. G. (1991). Diagnosis of secondary depression in schizophrenia: Implications for DSM-IV. *Schizophrenia Bulletin, 17*, 75-98.

Snaith, P. (1992). Body image disorders. *Psychotherapy and Psychosomatics, 58*, 119-124.

Sonneburn, C. K. & Vanstraelen, P. M. (1992). A retsospective study on self-inflicted burns. *General Hospital Psychiatry, 14*, 404-407.

Spear, F. G. (1967). Pain in psychiatric patients. *Journal of Psychosomatic Research, 11*,187-193.

SPSS. (1997). *SPSS Base 7.5 Application Guide*. Chicago, Illinois: SPSS.

Spohn, H. E. & Strauss, M. E. (1989). Relation of neuroleptic and anticholinergic medication to cognitive functions in schizophrenia. *Journal of Abnormal Psychology, 98*, 367-380.

Strauss, M. E. (1993). Relations of symptoms to cognitive deficits in schizophrenia. *Schizophrenia Bulletin, 19*, 215-231.

Strauss, S. (1989). Subjective experiences of schizophrenia: Toward a new dynamic psychiatry – II. *Schizophrenia Bulletin, 15*, 179-187.

Sugarman, A. A. & Cancro, R. (1964). Field dependence and sophistication of body concept in schizophrenics. *Journal of Nervous and Mental Disease, 138*, 119-123.

Sweeny, S. & Zamecnik, K. (1981). Predictors of self-mutilation in patients with schizophrenia. *American Journal of Psychiatry, 138*, 1086-1089.

Swensen, C. H. (1957). Empirical evaluations of human figure drawings. *Psychological Bulletin, 54*, 431-466.

Swensen, C. H. (1968). Empirical evaluations of human figure drawings: 1957-1966. *Psychological Bulletin, 70*, 20-44.

Taylor, M. A. & Abrams, R. (1984). Cognitive dysfunction in schizophrenia. *American Journal of Psychiatry, 141*, 196-201.

Taylor, P. J. (1995). Schizophrenia and the risk of violence. In S. R. Hirsh & D. R. Weinberger (Eds). *Schizophrenia*. Oxford: Blackwell Science Ltd.

Tollefson, G. D., Sanger, T. M., Lu, Y. & Thieme, M.E. (1998). Depressive signs and symptoms in schizophrenia: a prospective blinded trial of olanzapine and haloperidol. *Archives of General Psychiatry, 55*, 250-258.

Torrey, E. F. (1989). Headache in schizophrenia and seasonality of births. *Biological Psychiatry, 26*, 847-858.

Traub, A. C., Olson, R., Orbach, J. & Cardone, S. C. (1967). Psychophysical studies of body image: III. Initial studies of disturbance in a chronic schizophrenic group. *Archives of General Psychiatry, 17*, 664-670.

Twemlow, S. W., Gabbard, G.O. & Jones, F. C. (1982). The out-of-body experience: a phenomenological typology based on questionnaire responses. *American Journal of Psychiatry, 139*, 450-455.

Urist, J. (1977). The Rorschach test and the assessment of object relations. *Journal of Personality Assessment, 41*, 3-9.

Vanderkampt, H. (1970). Clinical anomalies in patients with schizophrenia. *Experimental Medicine and Surgery, 28*, 291-293.

Van Puttan, T. & May, P. R. A. (1978). 'Akinetic depression' in schizophrenia. *Archives of General Psychiatry, 35*, 1101-1107.

Varsamis, J., Adamson, J. D. (1976). Somatic symptoms in schizophrenia. *Canadian Psychiatric Association Journal, 21*, 1-6.

Vincent, K. R. & Harman, M. J. (1991). The Exner Rorschach: an analysis of its clinical validity. *Journal of Clinical Psychology, 47*, 596-599.

Wagner, E. E. & Frye, D. (1990). Diagnostic and intellectual implications of the fragmented Rorschach W:D ratio. *Perceptual and Motor Skills, 71*, 887-890.

Watkins, J. & Stauffacher, J. (1952). An index of pathological thinking in the Rorschach. *Journal of Projective Techniques, 16*, 276-286.

Watson, G. D., Chandarana, P. C. & Merskey, H. (1981). Relationships between pain and schizophrenia. *British Journal of Psychiatry, 138*, 33-36.

Weckowicz, T. E. & Sommer, R. (1960). Body image and self-concept in schizophrenia, an experimental study. *Journal of Mental Science, 106*, 17-39.

Weinberger, D. R., Berman, K. F. & Zec, R. F. (1986). Physiologic dysfunction of dorsolateral prefrontal cortex in schizophrenia: I. Regional cerebral blood flow evidence. *Archives of General Psychiatry, 4*, 114-124.

Weinberger, D. R., Torrey, E. F., Neophytides, A. N. & Wyatt, R.J. (1979). Lateral cerebral ventricular enlargement in chronic schizophrenia. *Archives of General Psychiatry, 36*, 735-739.

Weiser, M., Levy, A. & Neuman, M. (1993). Ear Stuffing: An unusual form of self-mutilation. *Journal of Nervous and Mental Disease, 181*, 587-588.

West, B. M. & Hecker, A.O. (1952). Peptic ulcer: Incidence and diagnosis in psychotic patients. *American Journal of Psychiatry, 109*, 35-37.

Young, D. A., Davila, R. & Scher, H. (1993). Unawareness of illness and neuropsychological performance in chronic schizophrenia. *Schizophrenia Research, 10*, 117-124.

Zung, W. W. K. (1965). A self-rating depression scale. *Archives of General Psychiatry, 12*, 63-70.

APPENDIX

Appendix 1. Manual for Scoring the Body Image Questionnaire

Appendix 1-1. Overview of the questionnaire and the scoring system

Reverse items The BIQ is composed of 59 items, including 28 reverse questions. Reverse items are Nos. 2, 4, 7, 12, 13, 14, 15, 22, 26, 27, 28, 30, 31, 33, 35, 36, 37, 38, 42, 43, 44, 46, 48, 50, 52, 55, 57 and 59.

Scoring system In *Regular items*, answers are scored as 7 when one "strongly agrees" with the statements, and scored as 1 when one "strongly disagrees" to the statements. In the *Reverse items*, answers are scored as 1 when one "strongly agrees" with the statements, and scored as 7 when one “strongly disagrees” with the statements. Answers as “neither agree nor disagree” are scored as 4.

BIQ component BIQ has three Components, Anatomical, Functional and Psychological. *Anatomical items* are Nos. 4, 8, 15, 16, 18, 20, 24, 28, 36, 40, 44, 48, 52, 54, 55, 56, 57 and 58. (See Apendix 1-3.) *Functional items* are: Nos. 1, 2, 3, 5, 9, 13, 17, 21, 25, 33, 37, 38, 41, 42, 47 and 53. (See Appendix 1-4.) *Psychological items* are Nos. 6, 7, 10, 11, 12, 14, 19, 22, 23, 26, 27, 29, 30, 31, 32, 34, 35, 39, 43, 45, 46, 49, 50, 51 and 59. (See Appendix 1-5.)

Appendix 1-2. Body Image Questionnaire (BIQ)

	Strongly disagree	Moderately disagree	Slightly agree	Neither agree nor disagree	Slightly agree	Moderately agree	Strongly agree
01. My body is weak.							
02. My eyesight is good. ®							
03. I often get sick.							
04. My complexion is pale. ®							
05. My body is limber.							
06. My body is underdeveloped.							
07. My body is clean.®							
08. I am short.							
09. I move slowly							
10. My body is defective.							
11. My body feels cold.							
12. My body is beautiful.®							
13. I am good at athletics.®							
14. I am becoming stronger. ®							
15. My body is skinny. ®							
16. My body is small.							
17. I often lose my balance.							
18. I have small eyes.							
19. I am often injured.							
20. I am poorly proportioned.							
21. I walk slowly.							
22. I seldom feel tired.®							
23. My mood is numb.							
24. My body is rough.							
25. I am clumsy with my hands.							
26. I seldom catch a cold.®							
27. I am satisfied with my body. ®							
28. I am thin.®							

Appendix 1-2. Body Image Questionnaire (BIQ) (Continued)

29. My voice is feeble.							
30. My skin is not easily poisoned. ®							
31. I am always cheerful. ®							
32. My body is unattractive.							
33. My posture is good. ®							
34. I always feel sick.							
35. I am not allergic to many things. ®							
36. My skin is smooth.®							
37. I can work well in dark rooms. ®							
38. My stomach is not unusually strong. ®							
39. My body is susceptible to infection.							
40. My hands are not unusually large.							
4I. I cannot move my body freely.							
42. My heart is strong. ®							
43. I don’t mind being touched by others. ®							
44. My body is not meager.®							
45. I seldom get excited.							
46. My health is getting better. ®							
47. My teeth are weak.							
48. My body is symmetrical.®							
49. I am seldom tense.							
50. I am not prone to bump into others. ®							
51. My body is not consistent with my sex.							
52. My body is rectangular. ®							
53. My bowels are unusually strong.							
54. My legs are unusually short.							
55. My arms are unusually long. ®							
56. My neck is unusually long.							
57. My head is large. ®							
58. My hair is unusually short.							
59. I always feel energetic.®							

®=reverse item.

Appendix 1-3. BIQ-Anatomical items.

04. My complexion is pale. ®
08. I am short.
15. My body is skinny. ®
16. My body is small.
18. I have small eyes.
20. I am poorly proportioned.
24. My body is rough.
28. I am thin. ®
36. My skin is smooth. ®
40. My hands are not unusually large.
44. My body is not meager. ®.
48. My body is symmetrical. ®.
52. My body is rectangular. ®
54. My legs are unusually short.
55. My arms are unusually long. ®
56. My neck is unusually long.
57. My head is large. ®
58. My hair is unusually short.

®=reverse item.

Appendix 1-4. BIQ-Functional items

01. My body is weak.
02. My eyesight is good. ®
03. I often get sick.
05. My body is limber.
09. I move slowly
13. I am good at athletics.®
17. I often lose my balance.
21. I walk slowly.
25. I am clumsy with my hands.
33. My posture is good. ®
37. I can work well in dark rooms. ®
38. My stomach is not unusually strong. ®
41. I cannot move my body freely.
42. My heart is strong. ®
47. My teeth are weak.
53. My bowels are unusually strong.

®=reverse item.

Appendix 1-5. BIQ Psychological items

06. My body is underdeveloped.
07. My body is clean. ®
10. My body is defective.
11. My body feels cold.
12. My body is beautiful. ®
14. I am becoming stronger. ®
19. I am often injured.
22. I seldom feel tired. ®
23. My mood is numb.
26. I seldom catch a cold. ®
27. I am satisfied with my body. ®
29. My voice is feeble.
30. My skin is not easily poisoned. ®
31. I am always cheerful. ®
32. My body is unattractive.
34. I always feel sick.
35. I am not allergic to many things. ®
39. My body is susceptible to infection.
43. I don't mind being touched by others. ®
45. I seldom get excited.
46. My health is getting better. ®
49. I am seldom tense.
50. I am not prone to bump into others. ®
51. My body is not consistent with my sex.
59. I always feel energetic.®

Appendix 2. Inclusion and exclusion criteria for perception of flesh masses

Inclusion
1. Explicit verbalization of a mass of flesh or muscles.
2. The remains of a mass of flesh.
3. Diminution of head, arm or leg.
4. Elongation of neck, arm or leg.
5. Plants or vehicles described as "without arms or legs.[1]"
6. A creature with the shape of a mass[2].
7. A single organ vaguely detected with no further explanation.
8. "Being cut and opened," "being folded," "being unfolded," or "being stuck together".
Exclusion
1. Underdeveloped animals or human beings, or animals that have intrinsically short arms or legs, without further explanation concerning diminution of arms or legs.
2. Omission of legs in the response to Card VII.

Note: 1. Examples are: "A tropical flower. I cannot find its arms or legs." "An airplane. It doesn't have any arms or legs." 2. Example is: "A prawn. It is in this globular shape, with his back hunching up in this way."

In: Schizophrenia Research Trends
Editor: Konstance V. Almann, pp. 55-93
ISBN 13: 978-1-60021-746-3

Chapter II

SCHIZOPHRENIA: A COGNITIVE SCIENCE VIEWPOINT

Guy Sandner

INTRODUCTION

This review is an attempt to present recent progress in the pathophysiology of schizophrenia. It is based on human research and lower animal models, with special emphasis on models, i.e. on theoretical constructs that sustain them. Theories and their outcomes will be briefly explained rather than deeply discussed. A selection of the literature in which the reader will find a more detailed analysis is provided whenever necessary rather than for justifying each aspect.

CLINICAL ASPECTS OF SCHIZOPHRENIA

Schizophrenia is a chronic disease with a high incidence (1%). A brief description of its symptoms is provided in **Box 1**. It comprises "*positive symptoms*" that reflect an excess or distortion of normal functions. Rigorous scaling methods were developed for research purposes, for example the SAPS (Scale of the Assessment of Positive Symptoms) [4]. It gathers 34 precise items noted by a trained observer along a 0 to 5 scale, which ends in a score. On the opposite, one may observe also *"negative symptoms"* in patients. Negative symptoms reflect a diminution or loss of normal function. For them also, a scaling method has been established comprising 25 items. It is called SANS (Scale of the Assessment of Negative Symptoms). Both positive and negative symptoms can be evaluated together using the 30 items PANSS scale (Positive and negative scale) [105].

Subsets of the Disease

Because of the diversity of its symptoms and the minimal criteria used to diagnose schizophrenia, one may wonder whether they constitute specific subsets of the disease. Statistical studies on populations of patients (cluster analyses) have identified four subsets at the onset of the disease [112]. One third of the patients show predominant negative symptoms. One tenth of them show predominant positive symptoms. One fifth of them show mainly signs of disorganization added to significant indexes of positive and negative symptoms. The remaining third have been qualified as "mixed" by some authors and were found to have all symptoms but at a low level. Whether these patients belong to a form of "mild schizophrenia" or have been tested during an interval between two active episodes is unclear. This is perhaps the reason why other authors accept only three subsets.

Cognitive Disabilities in Schizophrenia

Cognitive deficits have become accepted as robust and core characteristics of the disorder to such a degree that it has been recently suggested that the diagnostic criteria for schizophrenia should be reconsidered by including a new category of "schizotaxia" in the next edition of the DSM [86,120]. According to the present stage of the possibilities to characterize such deficits, it remains premature to do so in the close future. A delay is necessary to further develop their theoretical background. Important also, will be the clear identification of the cognitive skills that remain preserved by the disease. Another point that requires more research is the determination of the time course of each cognitive deficit along the disease. Cognitive deficits manifest before the occurrence of the first active phase and there appears to emerge now a consensus that some of them are constant along the evolution of the disease. The cognitive impairment observed in the adult has even been proposed to be a fossilized way of childish thinking, a failure of normal cognitive maturation. The cognitive aspects of schizophrenia have been considered to represent a kind of "endophenotype", more proximal to this disease's cause than to the symptoms. Their early manifestation has been used as an argument in favor of the idea that schizophrenia is a neurodevelopmental disease. Being present also in relatives of patients or in schizotypal personality people they have been called "traits" of the disease, and suspected to account for a state of vulnerability leading to the disease or not, depending on deleterious or protective environmental influences.

Diverse cognitive functions have been found altered in patients. They will be considered in turns, below. What they have in common is that they require an effortful psychological activity, a controlled management of attention or an appropriate management of complex memories.

1. Mixed disabilities are commonly observed using the standard Wechsler Adult Intelligence Scale (WAIS IQ). Altered executive functions gather a difficulty to manage the temporary storage of memories (working memory), a reduced access to inferential reasoning, and a decreased mental shifting capacity. Awareness, sustained attention and vigilance may be also affected. Classical global evaluations have found

memory deficits which clearly differ from those observed in dementia. At the higher level of Cognitive Sciences, we have to consider the alteration of the capacity to analyze "one's behavior at the third person", which refers to consciousness.

2. It is essential to consider apart, the cognitive functions required for social interactions because the social isolation that occurs in schizophrenia needs to be correctly understood. It renders extremely difficult to proceed to vocational reinsertion [136, 183]. To interact with others, we need to express our emotions and understand those of others (emotional interplay). We also need to express our intentions and understand those of others to cooperate with them (cooperative interplay). Specifically human, language may be used to convince someone else through argumentation, as we can change our mind after hearing an argumentation (intellectual interplay, closely related to the "theory of mind") [117].

Analysis of the Alterations of Cognitive Functions

Dysfunctional Awareness in Schizophrenia

The concept of awareness covers different properties of the brain, some of which may be specific to human beings. Emphasis has been put initially on operational properties of awareness. Using empirical measurement scales like the Scale to Assess Unawareness of Mental Disorder (SUMD), it has been shown that schizophrenia is the disease that elicits the strongest perturbation of awareness. Patients are suspected of having a decreased awareness of their environment, their thoughts or their disease. The latter is a result of a decrease of insight capacity [148]. This has been noticed since the first descriptions of schizophrenia were made. Patients were reported to remain unaware of their symptoms, of their state of illness, of the beneficial effect of treatment and of the social consequences of their disorder [163]. This reminds us of some neurological consequences of strokes or trauma where patients forget that the lost function has ever existed. But before concluding that patients with schizophrenia are really unaware of their abnormal mental state, it is essential to consider an alternate possibility, namely that they deny it because it is too painful to acknowledge it. This point has been addressed experimentally by correlating the schizophrenics' level of impairment of general executive functions with their level of unawareness [131]. Deny tendencies have been observed, but only in the less impaired cases.

"Poor insight" is a real cognitive impairment whose cause has been documented by theoretical studies. There is no reason to consider that insight differs from any other individual experience. It differs only by its content that gathers mainly the following four aspects: 1. *self-agency*: the consequences of our own actions may be represented in a different way than the actions of others; 2. *self-coherence*: the mental representation includes some constant somatic references; 3. *self-affectivity*: emotional status is part of the representation; 4. *self-history*: there is a sequential organization of represented events, serving as the leading rope of biography [107]. Alteration of anyone of these aspects, or worsening several of them, may elicit the impairment of insight. Such primary "self-experiences" have not been directly evaluated, but the following corresponding operational cognitive properties have been tested: 1. "action monitoring" - anticipation and verification of sensory outcomes of self-triggered actions; 2. "self-recognition" on a photograph or on a drawing; 3. "taking perspectives", which is closely related to the "theory of mind" [36]; 4. "telling one's autobiography". We shall notice in the next sections that several of these properties have been found altered in patients. Insight impairment is only one facet of unawareness. It seems difficult for patients to proceed to conscious recollection of events when they have to distinguish in their memories what they *clearly remember* from what they recognize with a raw *feeling of familiarity* [9,173].

Another interesting interrogation concerns the capacity of patients to remain aware of their intentions. The deficit of this form of awareness would represent a bridge towards an explanation of delusion, especially the so characteristic "delusion of control". Frith et al. [76] have proposed an interesting parable for explaining the difference between the insight perturbation of schizophrenic patients, and that one of patients having an "anarchic hand" symptom. Let us figure out that, during a seminar, the remote control of the slide projector becomes chaotic because of some radio-electric interference. Then, the speaker does his best to counter the resulting unwanted effect. This is how a patient behaves when his 'anarchic hand' moves independently of his will. Now, consider that added to the possibility to control the slide projector by a remote control device, there is also a technician who supervises the talk and anticipates the speaker's needs. The slides will then appear appropriately, but without the speaker pressing the button of the remote control. In this case, he will readily understand that someone else has control on the projector. This resembles the attitude of a schizophrenic patient who lost the feeling that he controls his actions (except that the speaker hopefully would not believe that an angel controls the projector). Patients with delusion of control have indeed a biased recognition of their own actions [71]. When the position of a patient's hand is shown to him with a video device with some spatial or temporal distortion during a targeted movement, the patient is less sensitive to the spatial or temporal biases than healthy control subjects. In other words, patients are less conscious of what they really control [6, 88]. This unawareness of the source of an event could even explain the auditory hallucinations. Imagined voices would no more be recognized as a product of the subject's brain. Taken together, all these could express the deterioration of the comparison process between the sensori-motor models of the environment managed by the brain, and the perceived reality [3]. Thalamic brain areas could play a crucial role in this process.

ALTERATION OF ATTENTION IN PATIENTS

Impairment of attention in schizophrenia has been evoked since the beginning of the 20th century. But it has been difficult to link what was then no more than a clinical intuition with any precise aspects of attention. The four classical aspects of attention that need to be considered are: *1) sustained attention, 2) switching attention (to a new target), 3) selective attention and 4) control of attention* [27].

1. *Sustained attention:* The most common test of attention used has been the Continuous Performance Test (CPT) with its impressive number of avatars. It is assumed to evaluate "sustained attention", i.e. the capacity of a subject to keep attentive along a repetitive task. It consists in pressing a lever upon detection of a specific letter, a number or a picture that has

to be identified among irrelevant items. Popular avatars are situations where the subject has to react to a specific succession of numbers, for example 3 followed by 7 (CPT 3-7), or a pair of identical numbers (CPT-IP), or to detect a degraded stimulus (DS-CPT) [31]. This diversity makes the interpretation of CPT hazardous. Most studies have pointed to an alteration of CPT performance in patients, especially for its more difficult avatars, like DS-CPT [32, 54, 124]. This deficit of attention has been correlated with unawareness [175], with negative and disorganized symptoms [83]. It is not amenable to neuroleptic treatment, which raises the possibility that it corresponds to a trait of the disease. This trait was also found in a subgroup of relatives totally blank of schizoid personality [53, 113]. Therefore, it was suggested to use it as a criterion for genetic studies [37]. It has been proposed as a standard test by the NIMH-MATRICS conference[1]. It was found to be associated with specific minor neurological signs, as assessed by using the "Cambridge Neurological Inventory", relative to "motor coordination" and "disinhibition" [29]. Such a finding reminds the hypothesis of Posner [14, 149] who assimilates attention to a covert movement by reference to the overt orienting response. This raises the question of the involvement of a common substrate in attention and the preparatory phase of movement. CPT has also been directly used to get insight into the neuroanatomical substrate of the perturbation of attention in patients. Precise morphological studies using MNR (voxel based morphometry) have showed that grey matter density of the left thalamic nucleus, left angular and supramarginal gyrus, and left inferior and postcentral gyri correlated with CPT performances only in patients [165]. Two aspects are particularly interesting in this list of differences, the involvement of the thalamus and the left-right asymmetry. Data have also been collected using functional imaging techniques [143]. Such studies have pointed to the involvement of the superior temporal cortex, superior parietal gyrus and the cerebellum. The involvement of the parietal cortex reminds us that patients with parietal cortex lesions lose their awareness of the opposite part of their body, together with minor motor control difficulties [45]. Therefore, the parietal cortex has been considered as an essential structure for the production of some critical aspects of attention. But psychological testing is not the only means to analyze sustained attention. Another means used, is to evaluate the capacity of a subject to detect the occurrence of a particular sensory event in a series of other events, without requiring an overt verbal response. It consists in recording the electro-encephalographic reaction evoked by a tone. The most characteristic response is called mismatch negativity (MMN). It is obtained by subtracting the waveform elicited by frequent standard tones, from slightly deviant non-target tones [140]. MMN amplitudes are lower in patients [87]. MMN responses are found to be reduced in frontal recordings and are related to negative symptoms [168]. MMN seems to correspond to an early pre-attentive detection mechanism whose perturbation in some patients would explain their difficulty to attend to new stimuli.

2. *Switching attention*: Attention can be governed by an automatic mechanism. But, we can also decide what aspect of our environment we have to consider. That is a top-down mechanism [80]. It can be moved voluntarily to enhance the contrast of incoming information like a spotlight does [149]. This point of view has some interesting outcomes: 1) by adhering to the view that attention is no more than a motor function, but a covert one (scrutiny), itself

[1] website => www.matrics.ucla.edu

linked to the ongoing intention of the subject, it is difficult to discriminate between orientation reactions and attention; 2) to switch attention, the brain has to inhibit the possibility to come back to the previous focus of attention, and at the same time, it has to facilitate the new one, these two opponent processes being difficult to discriminate experimentally; 3) In everyday life, the top-down voluntary control is challenged by bottom up calls from the reflex driven form of attention. One wonders how the priorities among both of them are managed; 4) The final executors of the switching process are the sensory filters, located in the brain stem, but other levels of the chain of sensory treatment, such as the thalamus, are also involved. In humans, the model for investigating such questions has been the visual system. We can privilege a part of our visual field without moving the eyes. This is tested either by a transient cue placed at the periphery of the visual field – attracting attention - or by a central cognitive cue, like an arrow, indicating where the focus of the attention has to be. This tests respectively the bottom-up and top-down management of attention. Patients have a decreased reactivity of their prefrontal cortex, the latter being the source of top-down orientation reactions accompanied by an inhibition of the reflexive orientation reactions at the level of the superior colliculus. If the attention management system is organized likewise, one should observe a decrease in the top-down control of attention together with facilitation of the reflexive form of attention. This has been consistently observed in schizophrenic patients [135, 170].

3. *Selective attention*: Stroop observed that it is difficult to name the color used to print the name of a color, when they differ. Errors occur and the responses are delayed. There is a semantic preference, as an opposite interference, i.e. the "reverse Stroop effect" remains extremely weak. Many studies have been conducted using the Stroop test in patients. Contradictory effects have been reported, and iterative attempts have been done to find out whether the discrepancies result from differences in subgroups of patients, or in the stage of the disease, or in its treatment [30, 47, 50]. No firm conclusion has come out of such studies. But, a recent review has provided interesting explanations of the discrepancies and has opened the gate for new researches in this field [92]. The main discrepancy arose when the Stroop test was transferred from printed cards to the computer screen. In the traditional card version, schizophrenic patients showed to be more sensitive to interference. It has been concluded that the Stroop test models the everyday life distractibility of the patients. But, this effect has not occurred in computerized versions of the test. The cards presented to the subject a list of many color names that he/she had to read in sequence. On the computer screen, they appeared one after the other. It was suggested that patients have enough attention capacity to avoid interference in the latter case, but they are distracted by the neighboring color names on the card version of the test. This observation has a strong heuristic value because it meets other observations showing the difficulty of patients to avoid target-context interferences.

Besides this approach, another one is based on acoustic stimuli. A dichotic listening test consists in presenting to the subject's ears syllables having the same vowel (ba,da,ga,pa,ta,ka) but a different one for each ear. The subject has to tell what he hears ("non-forced condition"), or what he can identify with his right or left ear ("forced-right" or "forced-left" conditions). It tests the capacity to privilege the source of a sound according to its location, which is typically a top-down control process in the auditory system. In healthy people there is a right ear advantage in the non-forced condition, enhanced in the forced-right condition, and suppressed in the forced-left one. Schizophrenic patients cannot reverse their right ear advantage [98]. During hallucinations there is a reversal of the spontaneous ear advantage [125]. Such observations indicate that the latter is a state marker of ongoing hallucinations, and that hallucinations interfere with natural auditory perceptions, challenging the capacity of the patients to attend to natural phonemes [133]. These observations were submitted to functional anatomical studies that showed that patients over-activated their right temporal lobe.

4. *Control of attention*: According to what has already been seen, it is essential to consider the source of the top-down control mechanism of attention, namely the cognitive processes that modify the focus and the level of attention. Correlation studies have shown that in patients, but not in control subjects, the capacity to gather scattered visual information to identify an object (Hooper visual organization task) as well as the ability to detect a detail in a visual scene (Judgment of fine orientation test) are impaired [118]. Such kind of global approaches have been followed by more specific interrogations about the involvement of attention in the understanding of visual scenes. Studies on the management of overt or covert exploration movements indicate that they are poor. They do not allow a normal representation of the environment [102]. When given the instruction to attend to something, the subsequent recognition performance is enhanced. But who knows if a patient understands and keeps such instruction along a test. Better are the experimental strategies in which automatic mental processes are used. Attention is enhanced and its target governed automatically by outlying events, i.e. unexpected or unfitted with their context. An illustration of this approach has been provided by evoked potential studies using delayed evoked potentials, namely the P300 or N400 (respectively a weak evoked positive potential occurring about 300 ms, and a negative one, 400 ms beyond the unexpected event). Complementary to these evoked potentials, the events were followed by bursts of high frequency, gamma wave brain activities. A brief explanation of these physiological measurements is given below.

P300: For the production of P300 potentials, oddball paradigms are used. Some 2000 Hz non-target sounds are presented within a series of sounds to be recognized (to be counted). They trigger the P300 response [95]. Its amplitude is proportional to the amount of attention resources devoted to the task. It was viewed as a measure of the central nervous system activity that occurs when representations are generated [103]. It was considered as an assessment of quick stimulus classification, unrelated to response selection. More than a hundred studies have been published about the effect of schizophrenia on P300 [19]. The P300 latency is delayed in patients and its amplitude reduced. It is believed to represent a trait of the disease as it has been found early along the course of the disease, remaining independent of the treatment and evolution of the disease. Unfortunately, it has also been observed in numerous other severe mental diseases (depression, Alzheimer disease, drug dependency).

N400: For the production of a N400 potential, the subject has to listen to a verbal comment and read words on a computer screen. For example he hears "the opposite of white" and reads "cat" that is obviously not congruent ("black" would have been congruent). The amplitude of the N400 response, dominating in the temporo-parietal cortical area, is inversely correlated with its predictability [144]. Overall, reduced N400 amplitudes were correlated with the severity of negative symptoms and cognitive impairment.

BURST OF GAMMA VAWE: Paradigms like those used to evoke P300 or N400 responses have also been used to elicit a transient gamma wave activity. The neural activity corresponding to the gamma range (around 40 Hz) are believed to correspond to the mental stage when the brain bounds the diverse aspects of a new stimulus [116]. The decreased evoked gamma wave activity in schizophrenia indicates a disturbance of integrative processing [114]. It is predominant in the right hemisphere.

ALTERATION OF THE MANAGEMENT OF ACTIONS IN PATIENTS

Accuracy of Fine Motor Patterns

The prototypical experimental approach of the control of movements consisted in observing the fast and precise movements of the eyes, easy to measure. It evidenced deficits in the production of *visual exploration, target pursuit movements, pro-saccades and anti-saccades*. In fact, their exploration had a practical aim [180] – finding an objective means to characterize a trait or a particular clinical state or stage of schizophrenia - and a theoretical ambition – understanding the reciprocal link between action and sensation [108]. All classes of eye movement disorders cited above have been proposed as phenotype markers of the disease [180], with a few contradictory reports. The existence of other minor motor perturbations before the occurrence of the first acute episode of the disease [159] strengthens this position and, subsequently, justifies theoretical speculations about the movement management disorders in schizophrenia. The following brief review of each class of eye movement deficit will place the emphasis on this theoretical aspect.

1. *Visual exploration*: Disturbed recognition of faces, and the emotions that they express, have been related to a particular visual scan path of patients looking at photographs of faces. According to the here over mentioned debate about being a phenotype marker or not, it has been clearly shown that relatives of patients have also shown such deficits [126] and treatments did not alter them in patients [99, 130]. This means that it is a trait marker, even if some of its detailed aspects have also been reported to change along the disease. A better understanding of the deficit has been obtained through constrained experiments, for example using schematic images of faces [143] or abstract geometrical drawings that the subject had to remember [177] (he/she was asked to draw them later on). These studies have shown patients ameliorating their performance when complementary instructions were provided (for example if someone asked them to find a small change in the drawing). Such instructions might have facilitated the production of plans of action or replaced their deficient willed intention. Another point of interest of such studies is the correlation between the decrease in exploratory activity with negative symptoms and a frontal cortex functional impairment. It means that the deficit expresses high level of visuo-motor coordination defect. But there is another interesting hypothesis to consider, proposed by Korn [108]. The part of a picture standing at the left of the fixation point (optic axis of the eye) feeds the right visual cortex and vice versa. This needs a complex organization of the visual neuronal paths with half of

the axons of the retinal ganglion cells crossing the midline in the optic chiasma. Let us suppose that the fixation point moves to another spot, for example with a rightward gaze. Along the course of this eye movement, what was previously at the right, treated by the left hemisphere, comes suddenly to feed the right one. This organization is all but simple, and there is no doubt that a powerful cortico-cortical inter-hemispheric dialogue is needed to keep the representation of the world coherent. Even more complicated, each eye has its own optical axis and motor command system and both eyes need to keep their motor control coordinated. Korn proposes simple methods to investigate such coordination features, like to fixate with both eyes a figure placed between the subject's face and a mirror. Patients have shown a bad repartition of the inflow of visual information to the two hemi-cortices, a lack of information exchange between the bilaterally treated images, and a poor motor coordination. What these deficits have in common is to express different consequences of a bad functional connectivity in the brain.

2. *Target pursuit movements*: In opposition to the previous type of eye movement, smooth pursuit of a target is an automatically driven action that results in keeping the image of a target in the centre of the fovea, when it moves at predictable speed and direction. The central question, yet not understood, is how this movement is controlled. From a neurobiological point of view, two parallel systems are in play, the colliculus-mibrain reflexes and top-down management by the visual cortex area, located at the border between the medial temporal lobe and the occipital cortex [97]. This raises, once more, the question of central integrative properties of the brain and top-down control of brain stem automatisms. The eye follows a target even if it is omitted for a short period of time, which indicates that the pursuit movement includes prediction. There is a slight difference between the position of the target and the optical axis of the eyes. It has been evaluated as the "gain of the eye tracking system", or as "position error" (distance between target and eye position). This pursuit gain was enhanced in patients. Added to this parameter, some small movements, called saccades, occur along the pursuit task. The two major ones are: the catch-up saccades, a kind of hesitation of the gaze, delayed in relation to the target, and the leading saccades, a movement of the eye looking ahead of the position of the target. Most anatomo-functional studies (using functional imaging in patients submitted to pursuit tasks) have shown that the bad management of the pursuit movement might be linked to a hypo-reactivity of the frontal cortex correlated with its decrease in grey matter content [10], and a hyperactivity in the hippocampus [179]. The hypo-frontality of patients does not deserve any more comments. The hippocampus has a number of classical functions that may have some interest. It was presented as a comparator between predicted features and reality [109]. Its over-activity may reveal an inadequate prediction. It is also crucially involved in the management of spatial references [189], therefore its activation may correspond to a compensatory attempt to fit for a bad representation of the position of the target or its background. The eye movement abnormality is an accepted trait of schizophrenia, independent of any treatment. Classical antipsychotic drugs may even worsen the eye pursuit capacity [67]. Some of its aspects were found to be so consistent that testing them was proposed as a predictive test for children at high risk to develop schizophrenia [162]. But a debate remains according to some detailed features of the pursuit movements within groups of patients and along the disease. Lee et al [115] brought convincing arguments in favor of a major correlation between disorganization

(general thought disorder) and the magnitude of the alteration of pursuit capacity. Looking closely at the leading saccades, their increase has been considered to express a deficit in the capacity to inhibit them, linking this deficit of inhibition with a number of other such deficits common to schizophrenia. A prospect of the consequences of an abnormal eye pursuit system could be grounded on ethological considerations. Pursuit is necessary to predict the movement of a prey or the movement of a predator. Catching a prey, i.e. food, as opposed to escape from a predator (imagine a snake approaching your body) is closely linked with reward and punishment. Inability to manage correctly such essential appraisal of emotional factors elicited by the actual world may progressively deteriorate severely the basic behavior with a dominant feeling of uncontrolled threat. This would well turn into paranoid delusion in humans.

3. *Pro-saccades and Anti-saccades:* We should consider these two types of eye movements separately as they differ on methodological and neurobiological grounds, as well as on their susceptibility to schizophrenia. But, they have often been considered together in theoretical and experimental studies. When a target suddenly appears, the reaction of subjects is to shift their gaze to it with a rapid eye movement called "pro-saccade". Subjects can decide to look away from it, or be instructed to look at its contra-lateral mirror image. The movement is then an "anti-saccade". The saccades are characterized by their ratio of occurrence, their latency, speed and accuracy. For the test, the subject has to look at a central fixation spot. The saccade-eliciting stimulus may appear at the left or right at various distances of this fixation point. The stimulus may appear with different delays after switching off the fixation point, or the latter may remain on. Considering patients, the anti-saccades seem more altered [84]. Between 2 and 25% of errors occurred in control subjects, and up to 71 % in patients [153, 155]. Their latency, but not their speed, was sensitive to the gap between the fixation spot and the target [22, 172]. Alteration of the gain, both for the pro-saccades and the anti-saccades, remained marginal [64]. A number of theoretical assumptions have been raised, what complements the speculations initiated in the previous section. Guidance of eye movements involves two neural systems, an automatic one that has to obey the second one, a top down volitional control. The automatic system organized at the level of the midbrain manages the pro-saccade. It seems to be preserved in patients. Submitted to top-down control mechanisms, it may be boosted or countered according to the circumstances. The presence of the target boosts it, but not in patients. This means that, even if the automatic mechanism is not altered, it may show some indirectly induced change. When a patient has to look to a spot shown before he was allowed to produce a saccade, i.e. a memorized spot, most parameters of the saccade are considerably altered [139]. In this case, automatic control is substituted by volitional management. It is believed to involve the frontal eye field, the prefrontal and dorsolateral frontal cortex, and an occulomotor system in the basal ganglia. Complementary to this top-down activation, potent top-down inhibitions also exist. They are needed for the production of anti-saccades. Anti-saccade generation is based on an internal representation of the task and its goal. It is altered by schizophrenia. In other words, the disease would elicit some kind of goal neglect [100]. Anti-saccade alterations are correlated with disturbances of the executive function (working memory, see below) mediated by the prefrontal cortex. Anti-saccade tasks are not only altered in the patients themselves, but in their relatives, so that these tasks could be proposed for genetic researches [119].

4. *Intention and action.* Patients showed longer reaction times in volitional tasks. This might express a general difficulty in the initiation of actions. A volitional action is sustained by an intention. Intention looks like a kind of counterpart of attention, but on the motor side of behavior. This has been the starting point of a theoretical approach in a recent study by Frecska et al. [72]. Using the classical study of attention where a pointer indicated to the subject where a target would be shown in the spatial location, they added another pointer indicating with which hand the subject had to respond, imposing an intended movement. Schizophrenic patients were unable to use the intended cue as effectively as control subjects did.

MEMORY DEFICITS IN PATIENTS

Theoretical Background

Memory refers to the fact that past experiences influence behaviors. Several categories of memories have been identified by neuropsychological studies in humans. Some of them are effortless, involving recording and recall processes with minimal awareness. Access to such memories generates a feeling of familiarity, and they are spared in schizophrenic patients. With enhanced awareness, we can reconstruct past experiences through an effortful mental "reliving". Patients show obvious impairment of this form of memory [173]. I shall consider below the different subdivisions of human memory [26] to delimit those that are impaired by the disease. A more thorough account on this subject can be seen on Chapter 7. Neuropsychology has developed an approach of memory based on the identification of series of pairs of opponent forms of memory. This approach is helpful because it is simple and easy to remember. The best known of such pair consists of short-term opposed to long-term memory. Baddeley [8] proposed a model explaining how the short-term memory works. It was called "working memory". It comprises at least three components, a central executive and two subsidiary storage loops, the "phonological loop" and the "visuo-spatial sketchpad", respectively storing a limited number of words and locations (Figure 7.4). The loops are fed by sensory information as well as by elements from the long-term memory, which opens the possibility for the working memory to be an interface between the ongoing experiences and the representation of the world. Long-term memory is also made of several components. Some forms of organic amnesia showed that skills were acquired implicitly, i.e. without any memory of the corresponding learning circumstances. There are several forms of such "implicit" memory. Associative memory is usually opposed to non-associative memory. Associative memory refers to what is obtained by "conditioning", namely the automatic link established between contingent events (associative conditioning) or actions and events (instrumental conditioning). Non-associative learning covers a broad spectrum of phenomena, among which are sensory priming and procedural memory. Easy identification of an object presented in a degraded picture when it had been already seen in a not degraded form, defines sensory priming. Producing a new complex motor activity (like riding a bicycle, for example), after having repeated it a number of times, characterizes procedural memory. Both priming and working memory are implicit memories. They are spared in heavy amnesic patients. These implicit forms of memory are opposed to declarative memory. Declarative memory is further divided in two opposite forms of memory [181], semantic and episodic memory (Figure 7.6). Semantic memory refers to our capacity to record, link to each other, and recover general knowledge. It is tested through questions about cultural knowledge shared by most people (for example "what is the capital of USA, of Brazil...?") or by specific learning tests where the subject has to remember items belonging to specific semantic categories (flowers, transportation means, names of persons...). This form of memory does not refer to the temporal dimension of the items to be remembered. When one is asked about what happened on a special occasion, we should be able to reconstruct the corresponding sequence of events with some effort ("try to remember the circumstances and food eaten on your last meal"), which is representative of "episodic memory". "Autobiographic memory" is a specific form of episodic memory consisting of the selection of very long-term memories concerning episodes of the subject's own life. This treelike categorization of human memories is beset with two difficulties. Firstly, some neuropsychologists have rejected it, claiming that this oversimplified presentation would be misleading in face of the actual complexity of memory processes in humans. Secondly, the corresponding classification departs too much from theories about lower animals' memory. But, opposed to such limitations, this presentation of human memory proved to be efficient, inclusive for the analysis of pathological cases. The tests developed to this end have been used to characterize which aspect of memory is impaired by schizophrenia.

1. *Working memory alterations in schizophrenic patients:* Mistakes and delayed responses have occurred in tests where the two loops had to interfere [23] and in tests in which the patient had to tell back a series of items in the reverse order than the one learned [33]. From a theoretical point of view, the deficit consisted of an alteration of the phonological loop [61] and/or its management by the central executive system. Alterations of the visuo-spatial sketchpad were also reported in patients and their relatives [160]. These deficits were attributed to a decreased activity of the prefrontal cortex and parietal cortex [7], more severe in patients with negative symptoms [25, 137].

2. *Preserved implicit forms of learning in schizophrenic patients:* Apart from a few observations, implicit memories, like conditioning, priming and procedural learning [85], are preserved in schizophrenic patients. This observation has been extended to the implicit learning of grammatical rules related to the acquisition of language, using "artificial grammar" tests [44]. Briefly, subjects were submitted to abstract sentences constructed according to rules not explained to them. Later on, they had to indicate their feeling of familiarity for new sentences constructed according to the same rules or not. For procedural learning, using iteratively a simple form of the "Tower of Toronto" task, an improvement occurred even in patients having much difficulty in finding the ideal solution of the task. A contradictory report came from the difficulty in learning mirror image movements, another classical testing method for procedural memory. Two points have to be considered for solving the contradiction. Firstly, the latter implicit memory test does not really impose the acquisition of a new movement but the reversal of an already existing one [110]. This was difficult for patients, as perseverance is a characteristic feature of the disease. Secondly, patients had difficulties in using visual information for managing their actions, which was precisely required at the beginning of the test.

3. *Deteriorated explicit memory in schizophrenic patients: difficulties in linking memories to each other and to the context of learning:* A meta-analysis published in 1999 [2], showed that explicit memory deficits in schizophrenia were the major cognitive deficits of this disease. It was even labeled as "schizophrenic amnesia". Free recall of long-term memories was more impaired than in other severe mental diseases (for example depression). Spontaneous encoding of information during learning sessions is weak in patients. This lower degree of encoding holds true for verbal as well as non-verbal material, for example faces [34]. This memory deficit has strong social consequences [65]. Understanding the memory disorders of schizophrenia rests on two key words, both corresponding to the learning stage: "source monitoring" and "temporal-spatial contextual indexation of events". Patients seem less aware of the causes of events (source) and of the co-occurrence of other minor events occurring during learning (context). This fact represents an impaired spontaneous strategy of organizing the information to be memorized. It has been suggested that patients cannot keep new information long enough in their working memory to build source or contextual links, before storing it into their long-term memory [184]. That could result from the decreased functional capacity of their prefrontal and temporal brain areas [42]. *Source memory deficits* have been reported in many studies. Many of them were focused on the necessity to discriminate who was involved in an event, the subject himself, a relative or an unknown person. A typical test consisted in asking a subject to prepare an answer to a question (verbalization). Then, the subject had, or not, to tell his/her answer to the experimenter. Later on, the memories of his/her answers (corresponding respectively to a mute or speaking one) were compared. The answers were labeled by the action in the corresponding memories. But, patients reported more often, having verbalized the answer than they actually did. Memorized events may also be labeled using features of the learning context, which is the essence of reality monitoring, or on the basis of an internally generated context, a process referred to as self-monitoring [93]. It is noteworthy that source monitoring deficit leads to a coherent explanation of delusion [46]. Delusion, and even hallucination, can result from an abnormal salience of internally generated stimuli, or from the disruption of a comparison process leading to abnormal readiness to accept mental events as real [20]. The crucial point is the degree of confidence that the subject can keep about his/her memories. It is also closely related to his/her awareness of the source of memories. This has been investigated in patients using a confidence scale of remembering (guess/know/remember) that corresponds to their degree of awareness. Patients were unable to link the separate components of events into a cohesive whole, leading to a quantitative and qualitative impairment of high level awareness [43]. Such a finding was not limited to the source-target relationship but extended to the incapacity for linking any specific memory with other events, for example "when", "where", and "in which circumstances" something happened. This aspect has also been documented in patients [157]. For example, patients do not remember sentences that have a coherent syntax, better than random words [134]. To summarize all this, it appears that patients do not link spontaneously their memories to each other. This explains their dramatic failures in autobiographic memories. Analysis of the content of their autobiographic memory has been done to find out at what period of their life their autobiographic memories started to become abnormally fuzzy [62,156]. Clear positive results were obtained, and they corresponded to the period when the initial clinical signs had occurred, though some disturbances were detected

as soon as their early adolescence. This could be interpreted as a progressive deterioration of memorization, starting before the visible onset of the disease.

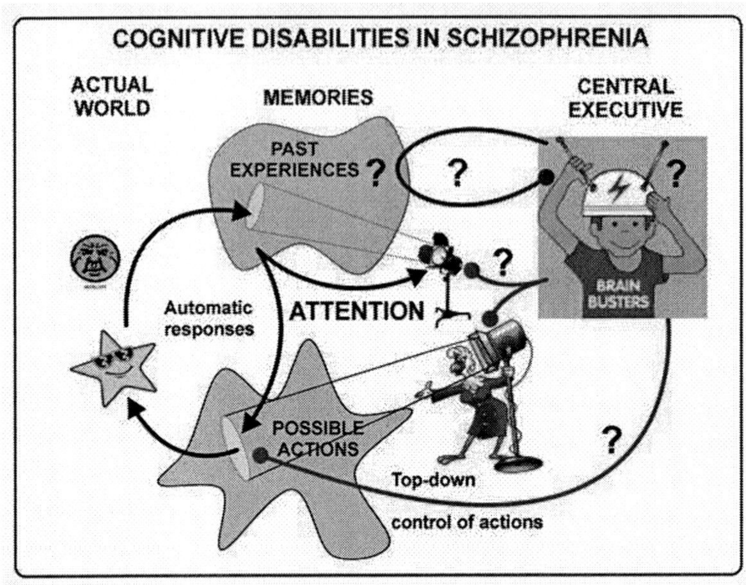

Figure 4.1. Cognitive disabilities in schizophrenia: This drawing shows that representations of sensory experiences as well as of possible actions (memories) are inserted between the actual world (on the left) and the central executive system (on the right). The automatic process that triggers actions or guides the attention and intention spotlights in response to changes in the environment - according to standard past experiences (red arrows) - remains unaffected by schizophrenia. However, the top-down management of such stimulus-response process is altered because of: 1. abnormal memory organization, 2. poor central executive (cortical) functioning or 3. modified top-down commands.

Consequences of the Impairment of Attention, Awareness and Memory on Social Interaction

A new subfield has arisen recently in Cognitive Sciences, namely Social Cognition. It may provide specific explanations for the poor relationship of patients with other people, initially interpreted as a mere consequence of the perturbation of their personal cognitive possibilities. Now it is admitted that the individual cognitive disorder of patients only accounts for a part of their social difficulties [190], and this implicates that communicating with others is a specific brain function. Its study rests on specific theoretical development and new, original methods have been developed in this field. Rather than drawing a list of theories and methods, I will consider them in turns, using a concrete illustrative model, focused on the difficulty in remaining or returning to a vocational activity [183]. Furthermore, this model allows delimiting what results come from personal disabilities, or from what expresses a social communication disorder.

Prototypal tasks: Let us imagine that a patient gets a job where he has to prepare packages of little mechanical parts for a supermarket, a realistic and simple task for a healthy person. Let us suppose that the task consists in preparing, sealing and labeling small bags, each one containing five cheese-headed metal screws, washers and butterfly nuts, before packing them into parcels to be delivered. I will consider below each of several sources of difficulties for this patient (which may turn into stigmatization, if underestimated [147], what is especially harmful as it occurs in a social environment.

Predictable consequences of the alteration of personal cognitive functions: This should help to make obvious the practical consequences of the alteration of cognitive functions mentioned in the previous sections. 1) The model task requires *sustained attention* (usually impaired). 2) The description of the patient's task comprises purposely some technical words. Workers need to master specific *semantic memories*. Semantic memories related to vocational activity are usually acquired in the late adolescence, i.e. after onset of the disease. 3) *Episodic memory* alterations may also hinder the working ability. Patients at work have to remember some sequences of their activity, from one to the next day. 4) A preserved procedural memory could be a substitute for that. 5) When something has to change in the activity, *patients may persevere* with some aspects of their prior activity (according to their degree of "frontality"). 6) *Working memory* deficit is another source of difficulty. It is common that workers listen to a radio set during their job. One would suspect that such acoustic information would interfere with the visuo-spatial sketchpad, intensely used in the given example of working task. 7) A last personal cognitive function not detailed previously, as less required in the job itself than in general organization of life and interaction with fellow workers, must be considered. Patients may find it very difficult to organize their activity because the *construction of sub-goals* (getting the components of the set of screws together) and their organization to reach a general aim (place the screws into the bag) is a serious challenge for them [28]. If we consider now other forms of tasks, more intellectual ones, patients may have difficulties because of their hindered *syllogistic* [171] and *analogical* [81] reasoning. The incidence of these impairments on social life can be evaluated by specific methods, as for example the « Social Cognitive Problem-Solving » test (SCPS) [192]. The global effect of individual cognitive disorders can also be evaluated by situational tasks in the real world (or using virtual computerized constructions). Two standardized testing situations have been validated: the "Grocery test" [89,154], the patient having to purchase a number of goods while being observed by a psychologist – and the "Kitchen test" [52, 169] – the patient being required to follow a recipe to prepare lunch.

Three aspects of these personal cognitive hindrances have to be underlined: 1) clinical observations are useless to predict them, 2) the treatment usually does not ameliorate them, and 3) they vary from one to another patient. From this, it can be concluded that they should be evaluated in each outpatient.

Hindrance of social cognitive functions: The tests aimed at finding out specific deterioration of social communication features are based on the obvious need of social interactions that any person has *to emit information* about his/her emotions, thoughts, and intentions. He/she needs also to be able *to perceive these categories of information* in others. It is necessary to be aware of others' emotions, thoughts and intentions. Information is transmitted by automatic processes (facial expressions, voice intonations) and by explicit means (language). The capacity to recognize facial expressions has been tested by requiring a subject to label them on photographs of faces, in records of voices, in short movies or along role games [106, 142]. Patients have shown difficulty both in expressing and evaluating emotions in others. Bellack et al. [15] have documented the decrease of sensitivity to positive emotions (pleasure) in line with the supposed anhedonia of patients. But, evaluating negative emotions is difficult also for patients [13]. Interestingly, poor self-monitoring of emotions is coextensive with their poor identification in others, with severe consequences on social interaction [138, 146]. It is necessary to cooperate at work to reach a goal common to several people, without being individually rewarded. Social exchanges replace primary rewards, even in lower animals [49]. But social reinforcement is especially powerful in humans (consider the impact of a smile versus a frown on the behavior of a partner). Having a "theory of mind", i.e. being able to figure out that others think alike ourselves, also helps us to keep doing some specific task, because it implies that every member of a working team knows what his working fellows want to be done. Perturbation of the theory of mind in patients was suspected, much before specific tests were conducted. Patients tended to report autobiographic facts, without being aware that their listener did not dispose of a part of the information needed for understanding them. This has been verified through structured autobiographical interviews (Needs and Resource Assessment, NARA, test) [38, 40]. The patients' interactions with others appeared eroded [132]. The opposite, namely understanding others has been tested, asking the patients to imagine the end of comics or video sketches [36,167], in which this end depended on the intention of the character represented in them (Hinting task). The here over mentioned social cognitive features were not totally altered by the disease. Corrigan et al. [39] have identified four different levels of abstraction in social interactions: *actions, roles, rules and goals*. Let us consider a simplified version of their example: we go out for dinner in a rather smart restaurant. The *rule* consists in waiting for the receptionist whose *role* is to give us an indication by its *action*, of where we have to sit down. Along this process, we have to keep in mind our *aim* and the receptionist's. Using a « Situational Feature Recognition Test » (SFRT), it has been shown that patients misinterpret only the two higher levels of abstraction, i.e. rules and goals.

Patients, as well as schizotypical people, hardly express and identify emotions, thoughts and intentions, when they have heavy thought disorders, and tended to withdraw [70, 185]. It means that the social withdrawal classically attributed to negative symptoms must be clearly distinguished from any other social integration difficulties in humans. In this respect, many conclusions about social interaction in lower animals will remain erroneous.

In terms of neuroanatomy, it is questionable whether the social cognitive properties are sustained by specific brain structures. The fact that lower animals use specific sensory channels for social communication (pheromones -> vomero-nasal organ) would be in favor of some anatomo-functional specificity [101]. Functional brain imaging technique has provided evidence that the right hemisphere is more concerned with social communication, especially some specialized parts or the prefrontal lobe and the temporal lobe. For example the mid prefrontal area is activated even when pleasant feelings are suspected in others, and likewise for the amygdala, for unpleasant events. These preliminary studies have sustained the idea of a "social brain". But the suspected brain areas do not depart clearly from the brain areas activated in general cognitive tasks, being found dysfunctional in patients [117].

PROPOSAL FOR BIOLOGICAL MECHANISMS OF SCHIZOPHRENIA

Genomic Background

The body, in particular its nervous system, is the final results of a juxtaposition of rostro-caudally aligned segments. They differ from each other according to the sequential expression of specific genes, called "Hox" genes [1]. The Hox gene system (Hox A, B, C and D) being quadruple in mammals, there is a broad spectrum of possibilities for phenotypic diversification of each segment. Specialized phenotypes correspond to "function-specific modules". Two examples show that the function, rather than the morphology, may be the common denominator of a selective expression of genes: i) the eyes of insects are different from our own eyes, even though vision in many species share the same genes (called Pax6, Sine Oculis, Optix) [11]; ii) the genes governing the outgrowth of the branchiae in crustaceans are linked to those of the paws (called apterous and pdm), i.e. uptake of oxygen goes with its use [16]. In the nervous system, the segmental structure remains only partially identifiable in the adult because many root neurons migrate far from their birthplace during development. Nevertheless, because neurons are post-mitotic cells, their birth date remains a landmark, even if the functional specializations in the brain are anatomically intermixed. This explains why the functional consequence of a teratogenic accident depends on its date of occurrence, even for the most complex functions.

Highly specialized parts of the body are unable to function independently of each other. How would a millipede move forwards with its many segments, without coherence among them? Studies on mathematical or computational models - interactive automata - show that a globally coherent activity emerges as a result of the interaction of elementary functional modules [166]. Alternately, a leader system connected to all the modules could ensure global coherence. But in both cases, *connectivity is essential.* Neuronal connectivity does not result from the realization of a "ready to work" plan, but from the interplay between genetic and environmental factors. Genetic factors determine which neuron an axon has to contact. It finds its way toward the target neuron stimulated and guided by families of landmark membrane glycoproteins (N-CAMs, N-cadherines, integrins) and gradients of soluble attractive or repellent molecules. Once the target neuron has been contacted, only some neurons survive, others disappear, depending mostly on the influence of neurotrophic factors produced by the target neuron. The resulting synaptic contacts become stabilized or disappear according to their activity. The general idea is that there exists a plan, but its detailed realization depends on the synchronization of pre- with postsynaptic activities [35], that depends itself on their functional utility.

As indicated above, schizophrenia gathers a heterogeneous set of functional alterations. This could result either from the alteration of a global mechanism, for example a neuronal or glial intracellular mechanism, common to many brain areas, or it could also express an alteration of brain connectivity. The first of these hypotheses is beset with the necessity to explain why some brain functions remain preserved. The second hypothesis, the so-called "*dysfunctional connectivity hypothesis*" [75], appeals to an answer to the following two questions: 1) what are the brain areas concerned and how they interact?; 2) what is the nature and the cause of the disconnection? Concerning the nature and cause of the disconnection, it could be no more than a loss of synchrony among action potentials. This would be difficult to observe directly [91], but some predictions about its consequence on the global brain activity could be checked [12, 68]. It could also correspond to a diffuse micro-anatomical or biochemical alteration. Some recent speculations have opened the possibility of a diffuse glial functional deficit or a neuronal cytoskeleton weakness. But for testing these ideas, studies on lower animal models are needed.

MODELS OF SCHIZOPHRENIA USING LOWER ANIMALS

Foreword

Producing schizophrenia in rats (or in any other lower animal) and being able to observe all its manifestations is obviously impossible. Models are only expected to provide explanations for some manifestations of the disease and to offer means to test drugs [79]. For building a model, two aspects have to be considered. First, the animal's brain has to be modified (independent variable of the experimental approach). Second, one or several relevant behavioral criteria have to be tested (dependent variables). The validity of a model is documented either on a theoretical ground (construct validity), on the observation of the modeled feature in patients (face validity), or on the reversibility of any property of the brain by drugs used to attenuate the manifestations of the disease in humans (predictive validity) [188]. It is very difficult to find out whether a specific modification of behavior in humans or lower animals is directly related to the cause of the disease, because of the adaptability of the brain and of the behavior. The reaction to a modification may hide the basic modification. This may reflect an anatomo-functional reorganization or a neuro-psychological substitution of the altered function. Therefore, even if we knew the cause of the disease, its experimental reproduction in an animal would seldom produce a similar phenotypic expression as in humans. We will briefly consider in turn, some classical and more speculative behavioral criteria, and then some means to produce their modification.

Neurobiological and Behavioral Models

1) Prepulse inhibition of the startle reflex and P50: Prepulse inhibition (PPI) refers to the reducing effect of a weak stimulus, called prepulse, on the subsequent startling effect of a strong stimulus, called pulse. Most often, the prepulse is a tone, sometimes a tactile stimulus, and the pulse, a noise or an air-puff. P50 gating also corresponds to a reducing effect of an auditory prepulse on the response to a pulse, the response being assessed using the amplitude of a positive evoked potential, following by 50 ms the pulse. In PPI, the optimum interval between prepulse and pulse is 100 ms and in P50, 500 ms. They were interpreted as *"pre-attentive" filtering mechanisms* and were found deficient in patients, unfortunately not specifically in schizophrenia [17, 60]. My favorite alternate explanation is that the changes observed in such basic reflexes result from a perturbation of the tonic top-down glutamatergic cortico-pontine influence, an expression of the diffuse decreased cerebral connectivity proposed as the primary cause of the disease. Such an idea (deficient top-down control) was already mentioned above about the management of visual or auditory attention processes in patients.

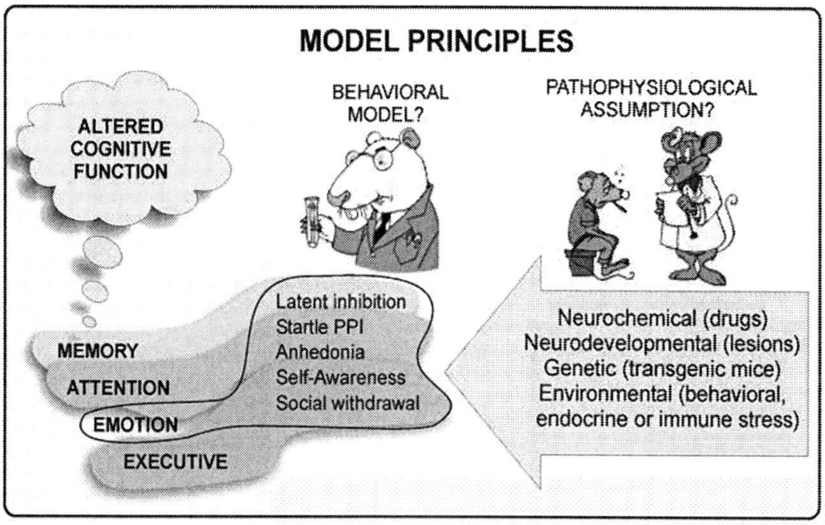

Figure 4.2. Model principles: A model needs to select a relevant cognitive function (left of the figure). A behavior that changes according to specific modifications of this function is required. But, the correspondence between cognitive functions and behaviors are never one-to-one relations. Thus, several behaviors have to be considered together. These behaviors have to be altered by some intervention that is assumed to simulate what happens in the disease. For that, pathophysiological assumptions are needed from researches on patients before being directly or indirectly produced in lower animals (briefly listed at the right of the figure).

In normal conditions, the top down control would serve for the internally driven management of sensory inputs. Indeed, in humans, attention has been shown to modulate PPI in healthy people, a mechanism which is deficient in patients [56, 57].

2) Latent inhibition: Latent inhibition (LI), defined as the "poorer manifestation of learning when a stimulus that announces some relevant event is familiar to the subject rather than being a new one", is absent in acute phases of schizophrenia [127]. But, it has been tested in humans with methods very different from those used in lower animals. There are several interpretations for the suppression of latent inhibition, each one relevant for understanding a specific aspect of schizophrenia. For Lubow, "it would appear that LI represents a biasing of the organism to better process new inputs than older, unimportant ones" [128]. As such, it helps to preserve limited attention resources, providing a defense against processing overload. This is meaningful with respect to the general deficits in attention of patients described in a previous section of this chapter. Another, but not opposite interpretation has been proposed by Weiner and Feldon [186]. "A conflict occurs because the previously non-reinforced stimulus is followed by reinforcement at the stage of conditioning". The brain has to switch the meaning of the stimulus when the conditioning starts; a process that is known to involve dopaminergic neurons and that is altered in patients.

A third explanation places the emphasis on the complex management of cerebral representations of events. The subject is believed to remember the stimulus-no event sequence of events as well as the stimulus-event linkage, a contradictory situation at the retrieval stage of the test that is resolved using complementary information, as for example the sensory-motor context of learning [161]. It explains why LI modifications are so sensitive to minor aspects of the experimental paradigm used. This explanation departs from attention and reminds us of the management difficulties in memories in patients. Appreciable improvement in the understanding of latent inhibition and the meaning of its modification as model of schizophrenia has been brought by an approach based on computational models [24]. A modification of the environment of an animal weakens its influence on memory, if not coextensive with an emotional event or an index of novelty. Each element of the representation serves to estimate novelty. Such models replace the fuzzy concept of "attention" by an operational factor, novelty. Too many novelty signals result in sensory overflow. This constitutes a vicious circle, since bad representation of the world leads to its own worsening, an auto-deteriorating process that requires to be broken as soon as possible.

3) Hyperlocomotion and stereotypy: Most means (drugs, lesions, environmental influences) used to produce changes in PPI and LI, enhance the sensitivity of the animals to amphetamine or apomorphine. Such drugs elicit sustained locomotion or stereotypy (repetitive production of a sequence of gestures) [78,79]. Its measurement is often used to assess predictive validity. No more can be said about its meaning, as it is particularly hard to interpret the cause of the enhanced locomotion. It may correspond to 1) decreased habituation to the environment due to the difficulty in linking its diverse aspects in memory, 2) lack of emotional erosion in a new environment, 3) a modification of vigilance, or 4) the alteration of a general top-down management of motor activity, known to involve glutamatergic and dopaminergic neurons.

4) Social withdrawal: Social withdrawal represents, with anhedonia, the only two aspects of schizophrenia that have been proposed to model negative symptoms [58,59]. As already mentioned above, social withdrawal in humans may reflect a very complex process. It can be elicited by apathy (a negative symptom), drugs, or as a response to social communication difficulties. The observations are often made with animals (mice, rats or monkeys) freely moving in their colony out of any experimental control. A wide field of research could be opened by considering apart each possible interpretation for social withdrawal in humans, and place the animal in a controlled social interaction task. In other words, we should proceed to specific social interaction tests using the complex theoretical frame provided by the ethologists. If we suspect that schizophrenia alters the capacity to express or recognize social signs, that capacity should be evaluated in specific situations (for example in mother-pup, male-female, and resident -intruder interactions).

5) Anhedonia and apathy: Most learning procedures used in lower animals involve reinforcement. An interesting finding was reported by Ellenbroek and Cools [59] about an aspect of experiments in which the animal has to work more and more hard (pressing many times a lever) to obtain a reward, until it stops working: "this is taken to indicate the point where the rewarding value is lower that the effort the animal is willing to make to obtain the reward". This has been considered the best evaluation of hedonic strength. A closely related experimental approach by P. Holland [96], being sustained by a slightly different theoretical background, seems also of great interest for modeling an aspect of negative symptoms. A rat for which the occurrence of food was predicted by the onset of a light, readily explores the food receptacle after the onset of the light. But this tendency is attenuated when disgust to that food has been elicited after the light-food association, in a totally different experimental cage. This experimental design allows only one explanation: the rat changed his representation of the outcome, being then, less incited to explore the food receptacle. This seems to be closer to the cognitive deficit observed in patients, who show lack of initiative, although having normal drive and emotional feelings. The recent finding of the involvement of the frontal lobe of the rat submitted to this experimental situation gives support to this suggestion.

6) Self-awareness: The confusion between being the actor or a passive witness in a situation, leads to differential memories, even in lower animals. Thus, the gate is open to the study of mechanisms by which the animal's brain manages some elementary form of self-awareness. We took the opportunity of employing different means to deliver sucrose in a conditioned taste aversion paradigm to show such a difference [191]. This approach has been proposed for modeling the loss of self-awareness in patients. This is an example of the possibilities that arise as soon as one uses a common theory to bridge the gap between lower animal and human's cognitive processes. Here, it is the parietal cortex that is crucial, rather than the frontal one [73, 74].

Simulating the Putative Cause of the Disease

Two categories of means have been used to produce alterations in the tests mentioned above. Their effect was validated since they were reversed by antipsychotic drugs. One of them is based on the belief that the disease results from a primary disregulation of dopaminergic or glutamatergic neurons in the mesocortico-limbic system. The other considers that the latter is only an indirect consequence of a general loss of connectivity between distant brain areas.

1. Pharmacologically induced abnormal functioning. Psychoactive drugs eliciting or enhancing the acute manifestations of the disease have often been used in adult animal models (amphetamine, cocaine, phencyclidine, ketamine) [5, 94, 129, 150]. PPI is altered by most of them, being reversed by neuroleptic drugs, including some atypical ones [176]. LI is also altered by amphetamine or MK801 (NMDA receptor antagonist like phencyclidine and ketamine), being reversed by neuroleptic drugs [77, 164, 178]. This traditional and coherent presentation of the possibility to model schizophrenia using drugs sustains the DA/Glutamate pathophysiological hypothesis. But, there are numerous other drugs, acting on serotoninergic, GABAergic or cholinergic neurons, which modulate also PPI and/or LI [78, 111]. This requires a brief comment. Those who place emphasis on the dopaminergic pathophysiological hypothesis explain this pharmacological diversity by the broad diversity of neurochemical inputs to the meso-corticolimbic system. With the disconnection hypothesis in mind, this diversity is all but surprising. Any mild perturbation of the normal functioning of the brain interconnections is by definition relevant to study what happens in schizophrenia.

2. Rats with neonatal brain lesions. Lipska and Weinberger [122] have proposed since 1993 to proceed to an injection of ibotenic acid bilaterally into the hippocampus of 7-day-old pups. The drug destroys the neuronal cell bodies and hinders normal brain connectivity along subsequent ontogenesis. As another possible interpretation, a normal construct of the representation of the environment is impossible, because of the early destruction of the ventral hippocampus. It results in locomotion increase and PPI alteration, which only appear after puberty. This may result from abnormal functioning of the meso-cortical system, including decreased frontal cortex reactivity to stress [123].

3. Prenatal interventions. To explore predictions of the neurodevelopmental hypothesis, more direct interventions on brain development were used. They consisted of a global blockade of the brain development at a critical period of life. Injecting metylazoximethanol (MAM) to pregnant female rats, at gestational day 17, the division of germinal neurons was temporarily blocked in their pups [104]. It resulted in modifications of sensitivity of their meso-corticolimbic system, PPI and memory disorders when tested as adults [66]. In other studies, a strong stimulation of the immune system by an injection of a cytokine releaser at gestational day 15, produced hippocampal damage and behavioral abnormalities, including LI perturbations [193]. This is relevant since maternal intoxication or infection enhanced slightly the risk to develop schizophrenia in the child.

4. Transgenic approach. Besides the here over mentioned “risk enhancement factors”, genetic factors have been regularly mentioned. It rests also on epidemiological grounds, as schizophrenic symptoms occur in a number of different genetic diseases (leucodystrophy, Di George disease), and because some symptoms have been found in relatives of patients [51, 187]. A large number of transgenic mice have been proposed for models in the past ten years. Disruption of PPI has been reported in most of them [82]. This diversity expresses perhaps that several different minor neurodevelopmental disorders could result in the same functional disorder (poor neuronal connectivity) and might open the gate to endless genetic proposals. Neurotransmitter – dopamine or glutamate - receptor knock-out works have provided some of them, directly related to the DA/glutamate pathophysiological hypothesis [152]. Studies on spontaneous mutations in rats, for example the so-called APO-SUS, apomorphine susceptible rats, have also been considered of interest [58]. Related to the disconnection hypothesis, the genetic perturbation of maturation of the cytoskeleton in mice deprived of some crucial enzymes for its polymerization can interfere with the establishment of normal neuronal connections [69].

5. Environmental influences. Considering twins (with similar genomes), even when there is one who has schizophrenia, his brother/sister may remain healthy. It means that the neurodevelopmental factor is only one of the factors of the disease. Other factors, like environmental ones, have to be considered and modeled. Isolation rearing of pups produced alterations of PPI and LI in the adulthood of such rats [174, 182]. This has also been observed in pups submitted to intense handling or deprived of maternal care [151].

PROSPECTS

Theories

Several cognitive processes may be altered by schizophrenia. It is a difficult, hazardous and endless job to try to understand each one using specific animal models. It is difficult because it needs a phylogenetic approach of cognition, which would be a new field of research. It is hazardous because the functional alteration under study may have occurred at a phylogenetic step above the species commonly used in models, mice and rats. It could be an endless run after a moving target - like a donkey trying to get a carrot attached to its head - as human studies will continuously provide new observations on cognitive deficits before being able to model them. Things may look considerably different if one *gets a real global theoretical description of the disease and its consequences*. This will probably require much effort but interesting tracks exist. It is necessary to find out the solution to very basic questions, such as how the brain gathers the large amount of information available to produce a conscious representation of the world, and to make phylogenetic speculations on this issue [41].

New means to model the cognitive features of the disease: Cognitive Sciences promote the use of neuronal network or computational models with general explanations. They provide precise predictions. The reduced capacity of patients to create complex mental representations could be simulated by extending the already existing neuronal models. It would be even possible to simulate therapeutic issues [63].

New Therapeutic Strategies

Decreased connectivity invites to try forcing patients to use their remaining brain connections. The process by which this can be done remains to be invented. Another therapeutic possibility consists in stimulating inter-cortical connecting networks. This could be a justification for the transcranial magnetic stimulation (TMS) that has started to be tested in hallucinated patients [90]. Preventive care should also be the focus of research. This requires that clear factors of risk are found, and each cause of disconnection identified. Using specific methods to prevent, or drugs to reduce the loss of neuronal connections would represent a renewal of the therapeutic strategy. Lower animal models need to be used to validate each of these new therapeutic approaches, before its application to humans.

Box 1

Diagnosis

Positive Symptoms

Delusion: It corresponds to an erroneous belief. The distinction between a delusion and a strongly held idea depends on the fact that it is quite impossible to change the patients' mind on their delirious thought, even with clear contradictory evidence. If someone intends to provide a mathematical proof of the existence of God, you do not have to be a psychiatrist to feel that something is going wrong with that person's thought. The belief in being persecuted is very common (*Persecutory delusion*). Another common belief is that the patient gets messages specifically addressed to him *(Referential delusion).* Some patients feel themselves invested with a religious mission *(Religious delusion).* A group of delusions has a particular interest, namely *thought withdrawal or insertion*, and *delusion of control.* The patient believes that someone else controls his/her ideas or his/her movements. Lost of the perception of being the origin of one's thought and actions, is the common point in this case.

Hallucination: defines perceptions that other surrounding people do not share. Even if many forms of hallucinations may exist in patients, they often report hearing voices *(audio-verbal hallucinations).* There can be several voices speaking to each other and to the patient, usually commenting his thoughts and actions. The voices may even speak different languages in multilingual patients. Even patients born deaf may tell that they hear their mother's voice. The strength of the hallucinations, or their frequency of occurrence, varies largely from one patient to another.

Disorganized thinking: It is hard to be sure that someone's mental organization is abnormal. What is actually observed and reported corresponds rather to its behavioral expression, among which the production of speech. Derailments out of the course of the conversation, bizarre intrusions, answers to questions that have not been formulated, tangential construction of the sentences up to totally incoherent phrasing or "word salad" may be the expression of a disorganized thinking activity. Noteworthy, what has been mentioned above, i.e. delusion, hallucination, disorganized thinking and speech, can only be evaluated through conversing with the patient. In other words, the disease seems bound to the verbalization process. Telling this, one should admit that European psychiatrists may not be able to suspect schizophrenia in a Chinese person, which I know not to be true. This means that non-verbal behavioral aspects appear also in patients.

Disorganized behavior: I remember having met in winter, several years ago, a young man sitting on the pavement in underwear (temperature was –5°C), showing a sequence of gestures suggesting that he was picking up flowers. His skin color reflected the effect of the cold temperature but his mind did not. This is representative of the symptom called disorganization. It gathers a broad spectrum of difficulties in performing activities of daily living, even in organizing the basic feeding or dressing activity, maintaining hygiene and appropriate sexual activities. *Catatonic motor activity* belongs also to this set of symptoms. It can consist in total inactivity (*catatonic stupor*), maintaining strange postures (*catatonic posturing*), and fixing postures that resist to attempts to modify them (*catatonic rigidity*).

Negative Symptoms

There are mainly three negative symptoms: *affective flattening, alogia and avolition. Affective flattening* is visible through the patient's face remaining immobile and unresponsive. Patients tell that they feel pleasant or uncomfortable experiences, but this does not appear in their voice tones or corporal expression. In other words, they lose the capacity to communicate their emotions. *Alogia* is manifest by evasive, laconic or empty replies even to precise questions. *Avolition* corresponds to the loss of initiation in goal-directed activities. Apathy has also been evoked, but its meaning is rather similar to that of avolition, and it is used in the description of other severe mental diseases.

Criteria for Diagnosis

At least two symptoms are required for the diagnosis of an *"active phase"* of schizophrenia. *The first active phase occurs mostly in late adolescence* or early adulthood. It happens statistically earlier in men (17-25 years old) than in women (25-30 years old). It is preceded by prodromes, correctly interpreted only retrospectively, once the diagnosis has become obvious. Long before the onset of the first active phase, along childhood, there are minor motor skill alterations [48]. Just before active phases, patients express a variety of odd beliefs and unusual perceptual experiences. Their scholar performances decrease progressively. They tend to withdraw from social interaction and express their affects less than other persons. In other words, they "gradually slip away". Another point of interest is their tendency to become drug addicts, which raises the question of the contribution of the addiction to the disease, or its relation with the disease (self-medication theory). Most patients are heavy smokers and they drink huge amounts of coffee (search of psycho-stimulant drugs). The active phase lasts over one month (this duration criterion has now been challenged by an efficient treatment). Such an active phase tends to recur and, between recurrences, some behavioral disturbances persist. This phase is sometimes reported as *stabilized phase of schizophrenia*. In this report of the time course of the disease, *loss of social interaction* has been mentioned. It is, *per se*, a diagnosis criterion. Rather than a mere consequence of negative symptoms, it is now believed to be the result from the loss of some specific cognitive functions that will be considered in a specific section.

Box 2

Cognitive Sciences, A Unified Model of Brain Function

We shall consider a list of cognitive functions and examine whether each of them is altered or preserved in patients. But before, a short description is needed on how "Cognitive Sciences" model what happens in the brain. It is a theoretical frame that may be applied simultaneously to psychology, neurobiology and computer sciences. The essential idea lies in the belief that the brain manages a coherent internal representation of the actual world. The ongoing sensory-motor experiences feed that representation. The brain is also in charge of holding that representation coherent. Coherency means that memories remain linked to each other according to their sequence, hierarchy and semantic relationship. For example in an Irish coffee, the cream remains above the coffee, itself above the whisky. This is a common example of natural hierarchy, picked up by our eyes. Eischenbaum [55] has proposed that 1) an ordered topographical reference can serve as a prototype for the representation of any other order relationship and 2) that the functional properties of the hippocampus are essential for the coherence of mental representations. Some sensations go often with others, what is an example of externally imposed semantic coherence. Evocation of "winter" goes with the feeling of cold, being surrounded by snow, lack of leaves on the trees, frozen water. If we are actually in winter, the representation is congruent with our environment and new aspects can become linked to the previously stored ones. On the opposite, the lack of congruence would trigger arousal. In our example, this would occur if we read "April" on a calendar. This example means that the representation is continuously compared to the external world (except during deep sleep). Based on the results of the comparison, the representation may be modified (covert action), or the brain may act on the real world (overt action: set the calendar appropriately in the example given above). The representation is also used to simulate actions and their outcomes [121]. To that end, the brain includes a "management" function, called "executive system".

Box 3

A Putative Cause of the Alteration of Attention in Patients

An interesting general description of basic trends of behavior proposed by Dunn has been recently applied to schizophrenia [21]. This model accounts for the feeling that the difficulty of patients to manage their attention is a byproduct of some more general alteration of their sensitivity to the environment. Dunn suggested that two orthogonal, i.e. in some sense independent, behavioral tendencies govern our sensitivity to changes in the environment. One tendency was called "neurological threshold". The other tendency concerns the possibility to "counter the neurological threshold changes". These tendencies were presented in a four quadrant table. Low neurological threshold (supersensitivity to the environment) would elicit an overflow of the brain by sensory information. The opposite, high threshold, would result in a poor actualization of the inner representation of the world. The responses may either be "in accord with the threshold level" or "counteract it". The resultant four quadrants were labeled as follows: 1. Sensory sensitivity => distractibility and irritation/discomfort with the sensation; 2. Sensation avoiding => deliberate behaviors to withdraw from stimuli; 3. Low registration => missing sensory information and under-responsiveness to stimuli; 4. Sensation seeking => pleasure with the pursuit of sensory experiences. A healthy equilibrated personality would stay close to the intersection of these four quadrants. Schizophrenia would result from an excessive attraction towards quadrant 1 (sensory sensitivity). There have indeed been personal reports of patients describing noises as louder, and colors as brighter.

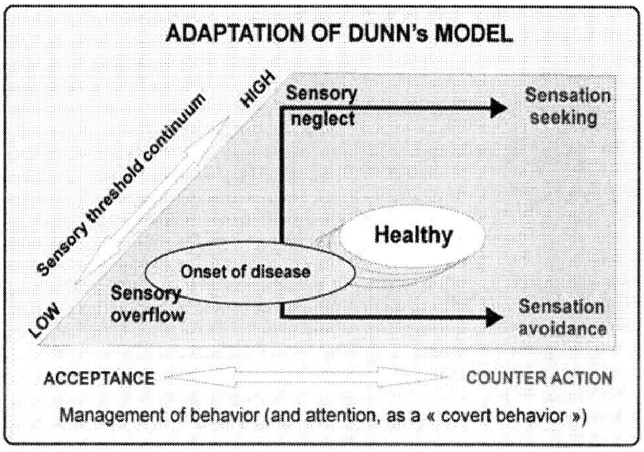

Figure 4A – Adaptation of Dunn's model: The plane plotted on this illustration shows that the brain is more or less sensitive to stimuli (oblique axis) and reacts to any excessive or deficient sensory input (horizontal axis). It is suggested that the two tendencies are balanced in the normal brain at rest (cybernetic model). Dunn tells that, for some unknown reason, the gate to sensory inputs is too much open in schizophrenic patients, at least at a first stage of the disease (yellow ellipse). The brain will react to this imbalance. The yellow arrows show the pathways that the reaction can take: either enhancing the avoidance tendency (reaction), or by closing the door to incoming sensations (gating) that results in global neglect. A secondary avoidance reaction to the down-gating process may result in a sensation seeking attitude.

This is coherent with the sensory gating deficit postulated and simulated in lower animal models of the disease [17, 18] and with the hypersensitivity to the context in visual recognition tasks that would be reduced by a reaction of the brain [145]. As soon as the disease evolves, the subject's brain reaction to the sensory sensitivity may result in an overshoot along the two directions of Dunn's model: on one hand, sensation avoiding, (reminding negative symptoms) and, on the other hand, low registration, predicting the failure to attribute appropriate meanings to stimuli. Another prediction can be drawn, not mentioned by Dunn: when both compensatory mechanisms are active, the overshoot would lead to a sensation seeking activity. This extension of the theory provides an explanation for the tendency of patients to become drug addicts [158].

REFERENCES

[1] Alberts B, Bray D, Lewis J, Raff M, Roberts K, Watson JD. *Molecular Biology of the cell.* 3rd edition. New York: Garland Publishing Inc., 1994.

[2] Aleman A, Hijman R, de Haan EH, Kahn RS. Memory impairment in schizophrenia: a meta-analysis. *Am J Psychiatry* 156:1358-1366, 1999.

[3] Aleman A, Böker KBE, Hijman R, de Haan EHF, Kahn RS. Cognitive basis of hallucinations in schizophrenia: role of top-down information processing. *Schizophr Res* 64:175-185, 2003.

[4] Andreasen NC. Negative and positive schizophrenia: definition and validation. *Arch Gen Psychiatry* 39:789-794, 1982.

[5] Angrist B, Sathananthan G, Wilk S, Gershon S. Amphetamine psychosis: behavioral and biochemical aspects. *J Psychiatry Res* 11:13-23, 1974.

[6] Arango C, Adami H, Sherr JD, Thaker GK, Carpenter WT. Relationship of awareness of diskinesia in schizophrenia to insight into mental illness. *Am J Psychiatry* 156:1097-1099, 1999.

[7] Artiges E, Salame P, Recasens C, Poline JB, Attar-Levy D, De La Raillere A, Paillere-Martinot ML, Danion JM, Martinot JL. Working memory control in patients with schizophrenia: a PET study during a random number generation task. *Am J Psychiatry* 157:1517-1519, 2000.

[8] Baddeley AD. Working memory. *Science* 255:556-559, 1992.

[9] Bacon E, Danion JM, Kauffmann-Muller F, Bruant A. Consciousness in schizophrenia: a metacognitive approach to semantic memory. *Conscious Cogn* 10:473-484, 2001.

[10] Bagary MS, Hutton SB, Symms MR, Barker GJ, Mutsatsa SH, Barnes TRE, Joyce EM, Ron MA. Structural networks subserving oculomotor function in first-episode schizophrenia. *Biol Psychiatry* 56:620-627, 2004.

[11] Balavoine G. A quoi ressemblait l'ancêtre des insectes et des vertébrés ? *La Recherche* 19:46-49, 2005.

[12] Behrendt RP, Young C. Hallucinations in schizophrenia, sensory impairment, and brain disease: a unifying model. *Behav Brain Sci* 27:771-87, 2004.

[13] Bellack AS, Mueser KT, Wade J, Sayers S, Morrison RL. The ability of schizophrenics to perceive and cope with negative affect. *Br J Psychiatry* 160:473-80, 1992.

[14] Berger A, Posner MI. Pathologies of brain attentional networks. *Neurosci Biobehav Rev* 24:3-5, 2000.

[15] Blanchard JJ, Mueser KT, Bellack AS. Anhedonia, positive and negative affect, and social functioning in schizophrenia. *Schizophr Bull* 24:413-424, 1998.

[16] Bonneton F. Comment les ailes sont venues aux insectes. *La Recherche* 19:64-66, 2005.

[17] Braff DL, Geyer MA, Swerdlow NR. Human studies of prepulse inhibition of startle: normal subjects, patient groups, and pharmacological studies. Human studies of prepulse inhibition of startle: normal subjects, patient groups, and pharmacological studies. *Psychopharmacology* (Berl) 156:234-258, 2001.

[18] Braff DL, Light GA. Preattentional and attentional cognitive deficits as targets for treating schizophrenia. *Psychopharmacology* (Berl) 174:75-85, 2004.

[19] Bramon E, Rabe-Hesketh S, Sham P, Murray RM, Frangou S. Meta-analysis of the P300 and P50 waveforms in schizophrenia. *Schizophr Res* 70:315-329, 2004.

[20] Brebion G, Gorman JM, Amador X, Malaspina D, Sharif Z. Source monitoring impairments in schizophrenia: characterisation and associations with positive and negative symptomatology. *Psychiatry Res* 112:27-39, 2002.

[21] Brown C, Cromwell RL, Filion D, Dunn W, Tollefson N. Sensory processing in schizophrenia: missing and avoiding information. *Schizophr Res* 55:187-195, 2002.

[22] Brownstein J, Krastoshevsky O, McCollum C, Kundamal S, Matthysse S, Holzman PS, Mendell NR, Levy DL. Antisaccade performance is abnormal in schizophrenia patients but not in their biological relatives. *Schizophr Res* 63:13-25, 2003.

[23] Burglen F, Marczewski P, Mitchell KJ, van der Linden M, Johnson MK, Danion JM, Salame P. Impaired performance in a working memory binding task in patients with schizophrenia. *Psychiatry Res* 125:247-255, 2004.

[24] Burgos JE. Theoretical note: simulating latent inhibition with selected neural networks. *Behav Processes* 62:183-192, 2003.

[25] Cameron AM, Oram J, Geffen GM, Kavanagh DJ, McGrath JJ, Geffen LB. Working memory correlates of three symtom clusters in schizophrenia. *Psychiatry Res* 110:49-61, 2002.

[26] Cardu B. Neuropsychologie du cerveau, relations catégorielles cerveau-pensée. Paris: De Broeck and Larsier Inc., 1996.

[27] Chan MWC, Yip JTH, Lee TMC. Differential impairment on measures of attention in patients with paranoid and nonparanoid schizophrenia. *J Psychiatry Res* 38:145-152, 2004.

[28] Chan RC, Chen EY, Cheung EF, Chen RY, Cheung HK. Problem-solving ability in chronic schizophrenia. A comparison study of patients with traumatic brain injury. *Eur Arch Psychiatry Clin Neurosci* 254:236-241, 2004.

[29] Chen EYH, Lam LC, Chen RYL, Nguyen DGH, Kwok CL, Au JWY. Neurological signs and sustained attention impairment in schizophrenia. *Eur Arch Psychiatry Clin Neurosci* 251:1-5, 2001.

[30] Chen EYH, Wong AWS, Chen RYL, Au JWY. Stroop interference and facilitation effects in firts-episode schizophrenic patients. *Schizophr Res* 48:29-44, 2001.

[31] Chen WJ, Faraone SV. Sustained attention deficits as markers of genetic susceptibility to schizophrenia. *Am J Med Gen* 97:52-57, 2000.

[32] Chen WJ, Chang C-H, Liu SK, Hwang TJ, Hwu H-G. Sustained attention deficits in nonpsychotic relatives of schizophrenic patients: a recurrent risk ratio analysis. *Biol Psychiatry* 55:995-1000, 2004.

[33] Conklin HM, Curtis CE, Katsanis J, Iacono WG. Verbal memory impairment in schizophrenia patients and their first-degree relatives: evidence from the digit span task. *Am J Psychiatry* 157:275-277, 2000.

[34] Conklin HM, Calkins ME, Anderson CW, Dinzeo TJ, Iacono WG. Recognition memory for faces in schizophrenia patients and their first-degree relatives. *Neuropsychologia* 40:2314-2324, 2002.

[35] Cooper SJ. Donald O. Hebb's synapse and learning rule: a history and commentary. *Neurosci Biobehav Rev* 28:851-874, 2005.

[36] Corcoran R, Mercer G, Frith CD. Schizophrenia, symptomatology and social inference: investigating "theory of mind" in people with schizophrenia. *Schizophr Res*17:5-13, 1995.

[37] Cornblatt BA, Malhotra AK. Impaired attention as an endophenotype for molecular genetic studies in schizophrenia. *Am J Med Gen* 105:11-15, 2001.

[38] Corrigan PW, Buican B, McCracken S. Can severely mentally ill adults reliably report their needs? *J Nerv Ment Dis* 184:523-529, 1996.

[39] Corrigan PW, Garman A, Nelson D. Situational feature recognition in schizophrenic outpatients. *Psychiatry Res* 62:251-257, 1996.

[40] Corrigan PW, McCracken SG, Holmes EP. Motivational interviews as goal assessment for persons with psychiatric disability. *Community Ment Health J* 37:113-122, 2001.

[41] Crick F, Koch C. A framework for consciousness. Nat Neurosci 6:119-126, 2003.

[42] Danion JM, Peretti S, Gras-Vincendon A, Singer L. Memory disorders in schizophrenia. *Encephale* 18:315-328, 1992.

[43] Danion JM, Rizzo L, Bruant A. Functional mechanisms underlying impaired recognition memory and conscious awareness in patients with schizophrenia. *Arch Gen Psychiatry* 56:639-644, 1999.

[44] Danion JM, Meulemans T, Kauffmann-Muller F, Vermaat H. Intact implicit learning in schizophrenia. *Am J Psychiatry* 158:944-948, 2001.

[45] Dankert J, Saoud M, Maruff P. Attention, motor control and motor imagery in schizophrenia: implications for the role of the parietal cortex. *Schizophr Res* 70:241-261, 2004.

[46] Daprati E, Nico D, Franck N, Sirigu A. Being the agent: memory for action events. *Conscious Cogn* 12:670-683, 2003.

[47] Delamillieure P, Constans J-M, Fernandez J, Brazo P, Dollfus S. Relationship between performance on the Stroop test and N-acetylaspartate in the medial prefrontal cortex in deficit and nondeficit schizophrenia:preliminary results. *Psychiatry Res* 132:87-89, 2004.

[48] DeMyer MK, Bryson CQ, Churchill DW. The earliest indicators of pathological development: comparison of symptoms during infancy and early childhood in normal, subnormal, schizophrenic and autistic children. *Res Publ Assoc Res Nerv Ment Dis* 51:298-232, 1973.

[49] De Waal FB. How animals do business. *Sci Am* 292:54-61, 2005.

[50] Dollfus S, Lombardo C, Bénali K, Halbecq I, Abadie P, Marié R-M, Brazo P. Executive/attentional cognitive functions in schizophrenic patients and their parents: a preliminary study. *Schizophr Res* 53:93-99, 2002.

[51] Duchen LW, Eicher EM, Jacobs JM, Scaravilli F, Teixeira F. Hereditary leucodystrophy in the mouse: the new mutant twitcher. *Brain* 103:695-710, 1980.

[52] Duncombe LW. Comparing learning of cooking in home and clinic for people with schizophrenia. *Am J Occup Ther* 58:272-278, 2004.

[53] Egan MF, Goldberg TE, Gscheidle T, Weirich M, Bigelow LB, Weinberger DR. Remative risk of attentional deficits in siblings of patients with schizophrenia. *Am J Psychiatry* 157:1309-1316, 2000.

[54] Egeland J, Rund BR, Sundet K, Landro NI, Asbjornsen A, Lund A, Roness A, Stordal KI, Hugdahl K. Attention profile in schizophrenia compared with depression: differential effects of processing speed, selective attention and vigilance. *Acta Psychiatr Scand* 108:276-284, 2003.

[55] Eichenbaum H. The hippocampus and mechanisms of declarative memory, *Behav Brain Res* 103:123-133, 1999.

[56] Elden A. PhD dissertation, Trontheim, Norway, 2001.

[57] Elden A, Flaten MA. Similar effects of attention directed to acoustic and tactile stimuli on prepulse inhibition of acoustic startle. *Scand J Psychol* 44:363-372, 2003.

[58] Ellenbroek BA, Geyer MA, Cools AR. The behavior of APO-SUS rats in animal models with construct validity for schizophrenia. *J Neurosci* 15:7604-7611, 1995.

[59] Ellenbroek BA, Cools AR. Animal models for the negative symptoms of schizophrenia. *Behav Pharmacol* 11:223-233, 2000.

[60] Ellenbroek BA. Pre-attentive processing and schizophrenia: animal studies. *Psychopharmacology* (Berl) 174:65-74, 2004.

[61] Elvevag B, Weinberger DR, Goldberg TE. The phonological similarity effecti short-term memory serial recal in schizophrenia. *Psychiatry Res* 112:77-81, 2002.

[62] Elvevag B, Kerbs KM, Malley JD, Seeley E, Goldberg TE. Autobiographical memory in schizophrenia: an examination of the distribution of memories. *Neuropsychology* 17:402-409, 2003.

[63] Erdi P. The brain as a hermeneutic device. *Biosystems* 38:179-189, 1996.

[64] Ettinger U, Kumari V, Crawford TJ, Corr PJ, Das M, Zachariah E, Hughes C, Sumich AL, Rabe-Hesketh S, Sharma T. Smooth pursuit and antisaccade eye movements in siblings discordant for schizophrenia. *J Psychiatry Res* 38:177-184, 2004.

[65] Fennig S, Mottes A, Ricter-Levin G, Treves I, Levkovitz Y. Everyday memory and laboratory memory tests: general function predictors in schizophrenia and remitted depression. *J Nerv Ment Dis* 190:677-682, 2002.

[66] Flagstad P, Mork A, Glenthoj BY, van Beek J, Michael-Titus AT, Didriksen M. Disruption of neurogenesis on gestational day 17 in the rat causes behavioral changes relevant to positive and negative schizophrenia symptoms and alters amphetamine-induced dopamine release in nucleus accumbens. *Neuropsychopharmacology* 29:2052-2064, 2004.

[67] Flechtner KM, Steinacher B, Stauer R, Mackert A. Smooth pursuit eye movements of patients with schizophrenia and affective disorder during clinical treatment. *Eur Arch Clin Neurosci* 252:49-53, 2002.

[68] Foucher JR, Otzenberger H, Gounot D. The BOLD response and the gamma oscillations respond differently than evoked potentials: an interleaved EEG-fMRI study. *BMC Neurosci* 4:22, 2003.

[69] Fradley RL, O'Meara GF, Newman RJ, Andrieux A, Job D, Reynolds DS. STOP knockout and NMDA NR1 hypomorphic mice exhibit deficits in sensorimotor gating. *Behav Brain Res* 163:257-264, 2005.

[70] Francis JL, Penn DL. The relationship between insight and social skill in persons with severe mental illness. *J Nerv Ment Dis.* 189:822-829, 2001.

[71] Frank N, Farrer C, Georgieff N, Marie-Cardine M, Daléry J, d'Amato T, Jeannerod M. Defective recognition of one's own actions in patients with schizophrenia. *Am J Psychiatry* 158:454-459, 2001.

[72] Frecska E, Symer C, White K, Piscani K, Kulcsar Z. Perceptional deficits of chronic schizophrenic patients in attentional and intentional tasks. *Psychiatry Res* 126:63-75, 2004.

[73] Fresquet N, Yamamoto J, Sandner G. Frontal lesions do not alter the differential extinction of taste aversion conditioning in rats, when using two methods of sucrose delivery. *Behav Brain Res* 141:25-34, 2003.

[74] Fresquet N, Angst MJ, Sandner G. Insular cortex lesions alter conditioned taste avoidance in rats differentially when using two methods of sucrose delivery. *Behav Brain Res.* 153:357-365, 2004.

[75] Friston KJ, Frith CD. Schizophrenia: a disconnection syndrome? *Clin Neurosci* 3:89-97, 1995

[76] Frith CD, Blakemore S-J, Wolpert DM. Explaining the symptoms of schizophrenia: abnormalities in the awareness of action. *Brain Res Rev* 31:357-363, 2000.

[77] Gaisler-Salomon I, Weiner I. Systemic administration of MK-801 produces an abnormally persistent latent inhibition which is reversed by clozapine but not haloperidol. *Psychopharmacology* (Berl) 166:333-342, 2003.

[78] Geyer MA, Krebs-Thomson K, Braff DL, Swerdlow NR. Pharmacological studies of prepulse inhibition models of sensorimotor gating deficits in schizophrenia: a decade in review *Psychopharmacology* (Berl) 156:117-154, 2001.

[79] Geyer MA, Moghaddam B. Animals models relevant to schizophrenia disorders. In: *Neuropsychopharmacology, The Fifth Generation of Progress.* Eds Davis KL, Charney D, Coyle JT, Nemeroff C. Lippincott Williams and Wilkins, Philadelphia, USA. 703-716, 2002.

[80] Giersch A, Caparos S. Focused attention is not enough to activate discontinuities in lines but scrutiny is. *Conscious Cogn* 27: in press, 2005.

[81] Goel V, Bartolo A, St Clair D, Venneri A. Logical reasoning deficits in schizophrenia. *Schizophr Res* 66:87-88, 2004.

[82] Gogos JA, Morgan M, Luine V, Santha M, Ogawa S, Pfaff D, Karayiorgou M. Catechol-O-methyltransferase-deficient mice exhibit sexually dimorphic changes in catecholamine levels and behavior. *Proc Natl Acad Sci U S A* 95:9991-9996, 1998.

[83] Gold JM, Thaker GK. Current progress in schizophr Res. Cognitive phenotypes of schizophrenia: attention. *J Nerv Ment Dis* 190:638-639, 2002.

[84] Gooding DC, Mohapatra L, Shea HB. Temporal stability of saccadic task performance in schizophrenia and bipolar patients. *Psychol Med* 34:921-932, 2004.

[85] Gras-Vincendon A, Danion JM, Grange D, Bilik M, Willard-Schroeder D, Sichel JP, Singer L. Explicit memory, repetition priming and cognitive skill learning in schizophrenia. *Schizophr Res* 13:117-126, 1994.

[86] Green MF, Nuechterlein KH, Gold JM, Barch DM, Cohen J, Essock S, Fenton WS, Frese F, Goldberg TE, Heaton RK, Keefe RSE, Kern RS, Kraemer H, Stover E, Weinberger DR, Zalcman S, Marder SR. Approaching a consensus cognitive battery for

clinical trials in schizophrenia: the NIMH-MATRICS conference to select cognitive domains and test criteria. *Biol Psychiatry* 56:301-307, 2004.

[87] Grzella I, Müller BW, Oades RD, Bender S, Schall U, Zerbin D, Wolstein J, Sartory G. Novelty-elicited mismatch negativity in patients with schizophrenia on admission and discharge. *J Psychiatry Neurosci* 26:235-246, 2001.

[88] Haggard P, Martin F, Taylor-Clarke M, Jeannerod M, Frank N. Awareness of action in schizophrenia. *Neuroreport* 14:1081-1085, 2003.

[89] Hamera E, Rempfer M, Brown C. Performance in the "Real World": Update on Test of Grocery Shopping Skills (TOGSS). *Schizophr Res.* 78:111-112, 2005.

[90] Haraldsson HM, Ferrarelli F, Kalin NH, Tononi G. Transcranial Magnetic Stimulation in the investigation and treatment of schizophrenia: a review. *Schizophr Res* 71:1-16, 2004.

[91] Hayon G, Abeles M, Lehmann D. A model for representing the dynamics of a system of synfire chains. *J Comput Neurosci* 18:41-53, 2005.

[92] Henik A, Salo R. Schizophrenia and the Stroop effect. *Behav Cogn Neurosci Rev* 3:42-59, 2004.

[93] Henquet C, Krabbendam L, Dautzenberg J, Jolles J, Merckelbach H. Confusing thoughts and speech: source monitoring and psychosis. *Psychiatry Res* 133:57-63, 2005.

[94] Hetem LA, Danion JM, Diemunsch P, Brandt C. Effect of a subanesthetic dose of ketamine on memory and conscious awareness in healthy volunteers. *Psychopharmacology* (Berl)152:283-288, 2000.

[95] Higashima M, Nagasawa T, Kawasaki Y, Oka T, Sakai N, Tsukada T, Koshino Y. Auditory P300 amplitude as a state marker for positive symptoms in schizophrenia: cross-sectional and retrospective longitudinal studies. *Schizophr Res* 59:147-157, 2002.

[96] Holland PC. Relations between Pavlovian-instrumental transfer and reinforcer devaluation. *J Exp Psychol Anim Behav Process* 30:104-117, 2004.

[97] Hong LE, Avila MT, Adami H, Elliot A, Thaker GK. Components of the smooth pursuit function in deficit and nondeficit schizophrenia. *Schizophr Res* 63:39-48, 2003.

[98] Hugdahl K, Rund BR, Lund A, Asbjornsen A, Egeland J, Landro NI, Roness A, Stordal KI, Sundet K. Attentional and executive dysfunctions in schizophrenia and depression: evidence from dichotic listening performance. *Biol Psychiatry* 53:604-616, 2003.

[99] Hutton SB, Crawford TJ, Gibbins H, Cuthbert I, Barnes TRE, Kennard C, Joyce EM, Short and long term effects of antipsychotic medication on smooth pursuit eye tracking in schizophrenia. *Psychopharmacology* (Berl) 157:284-291, 2001.

[100] Hutton SB, Huddy V, Barnes TRE, Robbins TW, Crawford TJ, Kennard C, Joyce EM. The relationship between antisaccades, smooth pursuit, and executive dysfunction in first episode schizophrenia. *Biol Psychiatry* 56:553-559, 2004.

[101] Insel TR, Fernald RD. How the brain processes social information: searching for the social brain. *Annu Rev Neurosci* 27:697-722, 2004.

[102] Izawa R, Yamamoto S. Spatio-temporal disintegration of visual perception in schizophrenia as revealed by a novel cognitive task, the searchlight test. *Schizophr Res* 53:67-74, 2002.

[103] Jeon YW, Polich J. Meta-analysis of P300 and schizophrenia: patients, paradigms, and practical implications. *Psychophysiology* 40:684-701, 2003.

[104] Jongen-Relo AL, Leng A, Luber M, Pothuizen HH, Weber L, Feldon J. The prenatal methylazoxymethanol acetate treatment: a neurodevelopmental animal model for schizophrenia? *Behav Brain Res* 149:159-181, 2004.

[105] Kay SR, Fiszbein A, Opler LA. The positive and negative scale (PANSS) for schizophrenia. *Schizophr Bull* 13:261-276, 1987.

[106] Kee KS, Kern RS, Green MF. Perception of emotion and neurocognitive functioning in schizophrenia: what's the link? *Psychiatry Res* 81:57-65, 1998.

[107] Kircher TJ, Leube DT. Self-conciousness, self-agency, and schizophrenia. *Conscious Cogn* 12:656-669, 2003.

[108] Korn H. Schizophrenia and eye movement - a new diagnostic and therapeutic concept. *Med Hypotheses* 62:29-34, 2004.

[109] Kryukov VI. A model of attention and memory based on the principle of the dominant and the comparator function of the hippocampus. *Neurosci Behav Physiol* 35:235-252, 2005.

[110] Kumari V, Gray JA, Honey GD, Soni W, Bullmore ET, Williams SC, Ng VW, Vythelingum GN, Simmons A, Suckling J, Corr PJ, Sharma T. Procedural learning in schizophrenia: a functional magnetic resonance imaging investigation. *Schizophr Res* 57:97-107, 2002.

[111] Lacroix L, Spinelli S, Broersen LM, Feldon J. Blockade of latent inhibition following pharmacological increase or decrease of GABA(A) transmission. *Pharmacol Biochem Behav* 66:893-901, 2000.

[112] Lastra I, Vazquez-Barquero JL, Herrera Castanedo S, Cuesta MJ, Vazquez-Bourgon ME, Dunn G. The classification of first episode schizophrenia: a cluster-analytical approach. *Acta Psychiatr Scand* 102:26-31, 2000.

[113] Laurent A, Saoud M, Bougerol T, d'Amato T, Anchisi A-M, Biloa-Tang M, Dalery J, Rochet T. Attentional deficits in patients with schizophrenia and in their non-psychotic first degree relatives. *Psychiatry Res* 89:147-159, 1999.

[114] Lee K-H, Williams LM, Haig A, Goldberg E, Gordon E. An integration of 40 Hz gamma and phasic arousal: novelty and routinization processing in schizophrenia. *Clin Neurophysiol* 112:1499-1507, 2001.

[115] Lee K-H, Williams LM, Loughland CM, Davidson DJ, Gordon E. Syndromes of schizophrenia and smooth-pursuit eye movement dysfunction. *Psychiatry Res* 101:11-21, 2001.

[116] Lee K-H, Williams LM, Breakspear M, Gordon E. Synchronous gamma activity: a review and contribution to an integrative neuroscience model of schizophrenia. *Brain Res Rev* 41:57-78, 2003.

[117] Lee K-H, Farrow TFD, Spence SA, Woodruff PWR. Social cognition, brain networks and schizophrenia. *Psychol Med* 34:391-400, 2004.

[118] Lee TMC, Cheung PPY. The relationship between visual-perception and attention in Chinese with schizophrenia. *Schizophr Res* 72:185-193, 2005.

[119] Levy DL, O'Driscoll G, Matthysse S, Cook SR, Holzman PS, Mendell NR. Antisaccade performance in biological relatives of schizophrenia patients: a meta-analysis. *Schizophr Res* 71:113-125, 2004.

[120] Lewis R. Should cognitive deficit be a diagnostic criterion for schizophrenia? *J Psychiatry Neurosci* 29:102-113, 2004.

[121] Lieberman DA. Learning, behavior and cognition. . 3rd edition. Belmont: Wadsworth/Thomson Learning, 2000.

[122] Lipska BK, Weinberger DR. Delayed effects of neonatal hippocampal damage on haloperidol-induced catalepsy and apomorphine induced stereotypic behaviors in the rat. *Brain Res Dev Brain Res* 75:213-222, 1993.

[123] Lipska BK, Weinberger DR. To model a psychiatric disorder in animals: schizophrenia as a reality test. *Neuropsychopharmacology* 23:223-239, 2000.

[124] Liu SK, Chiu C-H, Chang C-J, Hwang T-J, Hwu H-G, Chen WJ. Deficits in sustained attention in schizophrenia and affective disorders: stable versus state-dependent markers. *Am J Psychiatry* 159:975-982, 2002.

[125] Loberg E-M, Jorgensen HA, Hugdahl K. Dichotic listening in schizophrenic patients: effects of previous versus ongoing hallucinations. *Psychiatry Res* 128:167-174, 2004.

[126] Lougland CM, Williams LM, Harris A. Visual scanpath dysfunction in first-degree relatives of schizophrenia probands: evidence for a vulnerability marker? *Schizophr Res* 67:11-21, 2004.

[127] Lubow R, Gewirtz J. Latent inhibition in humans: data, theory and implications for schizophrenia. *Psychol Bull* 117:87-103, 1995.

[128] Lubow RE. Construct validity of the animal latent inhibition model of selective attention deficits in schizophrenia. *Schizophr Bull* 31:139-153, 2005.

[129] Luby ED, Gottlieb JS, Cohen BD, Rosenbaum G, Domino EF. Model psychoses and schizophrenia. *Am J Psychiatry* 119:61-67, 1962.

[130] Lynch G, King JF, Green JF, Byth W, Wilson-Davis K. The effects of haloperidol on visual search, eye movements and psychomotor performance. *Psychopharmacology* (Berl) 133:233-239, 1997.

[131] Lysaker PH, Lancaster RS, Davis LW, Clements CA. Patterns of neurocognitive deficits and unawareness of illness in schizophrenia. *J Nerv Ment Dis* 191:38-44, 2003.

[132] Lysaker PH, Wickett A, Davis LW. Narrative qualities in schizophrenia: associations with impairments in neurocognition and negative symptoms. *J Nerv Ment Dis* 193:244-249, 2005.

[133] Malaspina D, Bruder G, Furman V, Gorman JM, Berman A, Van Heertum R. Schizophrenia subgroups differing in dichotic listening laterality also differ in neurometabolism and symptomatology. *J Neuropsychiatry Clin Neurosci* 12:485-492, 2000.

[134] Manschreck TC, Maher BA, Candela SF, Redmond D, Yurgelun-Todd D, Tsuang M. Impaired verbal memory is associated with impaired motor performance in schizophrenia: relationship to brain structure. *Schizophr Res* 43:21-32, 2000.

[135] Maruff P, Pantelis C, Danckert J, Smith D, Currie J. Deficits in the endogeneous redirection of covert visual attenton in chronic schizophrenia. *Neuropsychologia* 34:079-1084, 1996.

[136] McGurk SR, Mueser KT. Cognitive functioning, symptoms, and work in supported employment: a review and heuristic model. *Schizophr Res* 70:147-173, 2004.

[137] Menon V, Anagnoson, Mathalon DH, Glover GH, Pfefferbaum A. Functional neuroanatomy of auditory working memory in schizophrenia: reation to positive and negative symptoms. *Neuroimage* 13:433-446, 2001.

[138] Mueser KT, Doonan R, Penn DL, Blanchard JJ, Bellack AS, Nishith P, DeLeon J. Emotion recognition and social competence in chronic schizophrenia. *J Abnorm Psychol* 105:271-275, 1996.

[139] Müller N, Riedel M, Eggert T, Straube A. Internally and externally guided voluntary saccades in unmedicated and medicate schizophrenic patients. Part II. Saccadic latency, gain, and fixation suppression errors. *Eur Arch Psychiatry Clin Neurosci* 249:7-14, 1999.

[140] Näätänen R, Michie PT. Early selective attention effects on the evoked potential. A critical review and reinterpretation. *Biol Psychiatry* 8:81-136, 1976.

[141] Nakayama H, Morita K, Mori K, Hirai S, Maeda H. Improvement of exploratory eye movements in schizophrenic patients during recovery period. *Psychiatry Clin Neurosci* 57:169-176, 2003.

[142] Ochsner KN. Current directions in social cognitive neuroscience. *Curr Opin Neurobiol* 14:254-258, 2004.

[143] Ojeda N, Ortuno F, Arbizu J, Lopez P, Marti-Climent JM, Penuelas I, Cervera-Enguix S. Functional neuroanatomy of sustained attention in schizophrenia: contribution of parietal cortices. *Human Brain Mapping* 17:116-130, 2002.

[144] Olichney JM, Iragui VJ, Kutas M, Nowacki R, Jeste DV. N400 Abnormalities in late life schizophrenia and related psychoses. *Biol Psychiatry* 42:13-23, 1997.

[145] Parnas J, Vianin P, Saebye D, Jansson L, Volner-Larsen A, Bovet P. Visual binding abilities in the initial and advances stages of schizophrenia. *Arch Psychiatr Scand* 103:171-180, 2001.

[146] Penn DL, Corrigan PW, Martin J, Ihnen G, Racenstein JM, Nelson D, Cassisi J, Hope DA. Social cognition and social skills in schizophrenia: the role of self-monitoring. *J Nerv Ment Dis* 187:188-190, 1999.

[147] Penn DL, Kohlmaier JR, Corrigan PW. Interpersonal factors contributing to the stigma of schizophrenia: social skills, perceived attractiveness, and symptoms. *Schizophr Res* 45:37-45, 2000.

[148] Pini S, Cassano GB, Dell'Osso L, Amador XF. Insight into illness in schizophrenia, schizoaffective disorder, and mood disorders with psychotic features. *Am J Psychiatry* 158:122-125, 2001.

[149] Posner MI, Snyder CRR, Davidson BJ. Attention and the detection of signals. *J Exp Psychol Gen* 109:160-174, 1980.

[150] Post RM. Cocaine psychoses: a continuum model. *Am J Psychiatry* 132:225-231, 1975.

[151] Pryce CR, Feldon J. Long-term neurobehavioural impact of the postnatal environment in rats: manipulations, effects and mediating mechanisms. *Neurosci Biobehav Rev* 27:57-71, 2003.

[152] Ralph RJ, Varty GB, Kelly MA, Wang YM, Caron MG, Rubinstein M, Grandy DK, Low MJ, Geyer MA. The dopamine D2, but not D3 or D4, receptor subtype is essential

for the disruption of prepulse inhibition produced by amphetamine in mice. *J Neurosci* 19:4627-4633, 1999.

[153] Ramchandran RS, Manoach DS, Cherkasova MV, Lindgren KA, Goff DC, Barton JJS. The relationship of saccadic peak velocity to latency: evidence for a new prosaccadic abnormality in schizophrenia. *Exp Brain Res* 159:99-107, 2004.

[154] Rempfer MV, Hamera EK, Brown CE, Cromwell RL. The relations between cognition and the independent living skill of shopping in people with schizophrenia. *Psychiatry Res* 117:103-112, 2003.

[155] Reuter B, Kathmann N. Using saccade tasks as a tool to analyze executive dysfunctions in schizophrenia. *Acta Psychologica* 115:255-269, 2004.

[156] Riutort M, Cuervo C, Danion JM, Peretti CS, Salame P. Reduced levels of specific autobiographical memories in schizophrenia. *Psychiatry Res* 117:35-45, 2003.

[157] Rizzo L, Danion JM, van der Linden M, Grange D. Patients with schizophrenia remember that an event has occurred, but not when. *Br J Psychiatry* 168:427-431, 1996.

[158] Robinson TE, Berridge KC. The neural basis of drug craving: an incentive-sensitization theory of addiction. *Brain Res Rev* 18:247-291, 1993.

[159] Roff JD, Fultz JM. Childhood antecedents of schizophrenia: developmental sequencing and specificity of problem behavior. *Psychol Rep* 92:793-803, 2003.

[160] Roitman SEL, Mitropoulou V, Keefe RSE, Silverman JM, Serby M, Harvey PD, Reynolds DA, Mohs RC, Siever LJ. Visuospatial working memory in schizotypal personality disorder patients. *Schizophr Res* 41:447-455, 2000.

[161] Rosas JM, Bouton ME. Additivity of the effects of retention interval and context change on latent inhibition: toward resolution of the context forgetting paradox. *J Exp Psychol Anim Behav Process* 23:283-94, 1997.

[162] Ross RG. Early expression of a pathophysiological feature of schizophrenia: saccadic intrusions into smooth-pursuit eye movements in school-age children vulnerable to schizophrenia. *J Am Acad Child Adolesc Psychiatry* 42:468-476, 2003.

[163] Rossi A, Arduini L, Prosperini P, Kalyvoka A, Stratta P, Daneluzzo E. Awareness of illness and outcome in schizophrenia. *Eur Arch Psychiatry Clin Neurosci* 250:73-75, 2000.

[164] Russig H, Kovacevic A, Murphy CA, Feldon J. Haloperidol and clozapine antagonise amphetamine-induced disruption of latent inhibition of conditioned taste aversion. *Psychopharmacology* (Berl) 170:263-270, 2003.

[165] Salgado-Pineda P, Baeza I, Pérez-Gomez M, Vendrell P, Junqué C, Bargallo N, Bernardo M. Sustained attention impairment correlates togray matter decreases in first episode neuroleptic-naïve schizophrenic patients. *Neuroimage* 19:365-375, 2003.

[166] Sandri G. Does computation provide a model for creativity? An epistemological perspective in neuroscience. *J Endocrinol Invest* 27:9-22, 2004.

[167] Sarfati Y, Hardy-Bayle MC, Besche C, Widlocher D. Attribution of intentions to others in people with schizophrenia: a non-verbal exploration with comic strips. *Schizophr Res* 25:199-209, 1997.

[168] Sato Y, Yabe H, Todd J, Michie P, Shinozaki N, Sutoh T, Hiruma T, Nashida T, Matsuoka T, Kaneko S. Impairment in activation of a frontal attention-switch mechanism in schizophrenic patients. *Biol Psychiat* 62:49-63, 2002.

[169] Semkovska M, Stip E, Godbout L, Paquet F, Bedard MA. Behavioral disorganization in schizophrenia during a daily activity: the kitchen behavioral scoring scale. *Brain Cogn* 48:546-553, 2002.

[170] Sereno AB, Holzman PS. Spatial selective attention in schizophrenic, affective disorder, and normal subjects. *Schizophr Res* 20:33-50, 1996.

[171] Simpson J, Done DJ. Analogical reasoning in schizophrenic delusions. *Eur Psychiatry* 19:344-348, 2004.

[172] Smyrnis N, Malogiannis IA, Edvokimidis I, Stefanis NC, Theleritis C, Vaidakis A, Theodoropoulou S, Stefanis CN. Attentional facilitation of response is impaired for antisaccades but noy for saccades in patients with schizophrenia: implications for cortical dysfunction. *Exp Brain Res* 159:47-54, 2004.

[173] Sonntag P, Gokalsing E, Olivier C, Robert P, Burglen F, Kauffmann-Muller F, Huron C, Salame P, Danion JM. Impaired strategic regulation of contents of conscious awareness in schizophrenia. *Conscious Cogn* 12:190-200, 2004.

[174] Stevens KE, Johnson RG, Rose GM. Rats reared in social isolation show schizophrenia-like changes in auditory gating. *Pharmacol Biochem Behav* 58:1031-1036, 1997.

[175] Subotnik KL, Nuechterlein KH, Irzhevsky V, Kitchen CM, Woo SM, Mintz J. Is unawareness of psychotic disorder a neurocognitive or psychological defensive problem? *Schizophr Res* 75:147-157, 2005.

[176] Swerdlow NR, Geyer MA. Using an animal model of deficient sensorimotor gating to study the pathophysiology and new treatments of schizophrenia. *Schizophr Bull* 24:285-301, 1998.

[177] Tonoya Y, Matsui M, Kurachi M, Kurokawa K, Sumiyoshi T. Exploratory eye movements in schizophrenia. Effects of figure size and the instruction on visual search. *Eur Arch Clin Neurosci* 252:255-261, 2002.

[178] Traverso LM, Ruiz G, De la Casa LG. Latent inhibition disruption by MK-801 in a conditioned taste-aversion paradigm. *Neurobiol Learn Mem* 80:140-146, 2003.

[179] Tregellas JR, Tanabe JL, Miller DE, Ross RG, Olincy A, Freedman R. Neurobiology of smooth pursuit eye movements deficits in schizophrenia: an fMRI study. *Am J Psychiatry* 161:315-321, 2004.

[180] Trillenberg P, Lencer R, Heide W. Eye movements and psychiatric disease. *Curr Opin Neurobiol* 17:43-47, 2004.

[181] Tulving E. Memory systems and the brain. *Clin Neuropharmacol* 15:327-328, 1992.

[182] Varty GB, Higgins GA. Examination of drug-induced and isolation-induced disruptions of prepulse inhibition as models to screen antipsychotic drugs. *Psychopharmacology* (Berl) 122:15-26, 1995.

[183] Vauth R, Rusch N, Wirtz M, Corrigan PW. Does social cognition influence the relation between neurocognitive deficits and vocational functioning in schizophrenia? *Psychiatr Res* 128:155-165, 2004.

[184] Vinogradov S, Willis-Shore J, Poole JH, Marten E, Ober BA, Shenaut GK. Clinical and neurocognitive aspects of source monitoring errors in schizophrenia. *Am J Psychiatry* 154:1530-1537, 1997.

[185] Waldeck TL, Miller LS. Social skills deficits in schizotypal personality disorder. *Psychiatry Res* 93:237-246, 2000.

[186] Weiner I, Feldon J. The switching model of latent inhibition: an update of neural substrates. *Behav Brain Res* 88:11-25, 1997.

[187] Williams NM, Owen MJ. Genetic abnormalities of chromosome 22 and the development of psychosis. *Curr Psychiatry Rep* 6:176-182, 2004.

[188] Willner P. The validity of animal models of depression. *Psychopharmacology* (Berl) 83:1-16, 1984.

[189] Wills TJ, Lever C, Cacucci F, Burgess N, O'Keefe J. Attractor dynamics in the hippocampal representation of the local environment. *Science* 308:873-876, 2005.

[190] Woonings FM, Appelo MT, Kluiter H, Slooff CJ, van den Bosch RJ. Learning (potential) and social functioning in schizophrenia. *Schizophr Res* 59:287-296, 2003.

[191] Yamamoto J, Fresquet N, Sandner G. Conditioned taste aversion using four different means to deliver sucrose to rats. *Physiol Behav* 75:387-396, 2002.

[192] Yamashita C, Mizuno M, Nemoto T, Kashima H. Social cognitive problem-solving in schizophrenia: associations with fluency and verbal memory. *Psychiatry Res* 134:123-129, 2005.

[193] Zuckerman L, Weiner I. Maternal immune activation leads to behavioral and pharmacological changes in the adult offspring. *J Psychiatry Res* 39:311-323, 2005.

In: Schizophrenia Research Trends
Editor: Konstance V. Almann, pp. 95-114
ISBN 13: 978-1-60021-746-3

Chapter III

NMDA RECEPTOR HYPOFUNCTION IN SCHIZOPHRENIA: FROM MOUSE TO MAN

Stephen I. Deutsch*,[*,1,2] John Mastropaolo,[1] Barbara L. Schwartz,[1,2] Richard B. Rosse,[1,2] and Brooke Gaskins[1]

[1]Mental Health Service Line, Department of Veterans Affairs Medical Center NW, Washington, DC

[2]Department of Psychiatry, Georgetown University School of Medicine, Washington, DC

ABSTRACT

Glutamate is one of the most abundant neurotransmitters in the brain; it may be responsible for mediating synaptic neurotransmission at 40 percent or more of the brain's synapses. The glutamatergic signal is recognized by both metabotropic and ion channel receptors. The N-methyl-D-aspartic acid (NMDA) receptor is an example of a glutamate-gated ion channel receptor; the binding of glutamate to this receptor increases the likelihood that its channel will transiently assume an open-configuration, allowing the influx of calcium ions. Importantly, there are allosteric modulatory sites, including an obligatory co-agonist site that recognizes glycine, on the NMDA receptor complex that influence glutamate's ability to promote calcium ion conductance. Abnormalities of NMDA receptor-mediated neurotransmission are implicated in a variety of major neuropsychiatric disorders, especially schizophrenia. Specifically, NMDA receptor hypofunction (NRH) is implicated in the pathophysiology of schizophrenia because of the ability of phencyclidine (PCP) to precipitate a schizophreniform psychosis. PCP is a noncompetitive NMDA receptor antagonist that binds to a hydrophobic site within the channel; it is referred to as an open-channel blocker. Descriptively, the PCP-model of schizophrenia is the best pharmacological model of this disorder with symptoms manifest in all of the relevant domains of psychopathology, including positive (e.g.,

[*] Corresponding Author: Stephen I. Deutsch, M.D., Ph.D. Associate Chief of Staff for Mental Health Department of Veterans Affairs Medical Center, 50 Irving Street, NW, Washington, DC 20422; 202 745 8156 (Office); 202 745 8169 (Fax); E-Mail Address: Stephen.Deutsch@med.va.gov

hallucinations), negative (e.g., affective flattening), cognitive (e.g., abnormalities of attention), mood (e.g., dysphoria) and motor symptoms (e.g., posturing).

Because of PCP's pharmacological action as a noncompetitive NMDA receptor antagonist and the PCP-model of schizophrenia, our laboratory has been engaged in characterizing and quantifying behaviors in mice, including genetically-inbred strains, elicited by MK-801 (dizocilpine), a high-affinity analogue of PCP that binds to the same hydrophobic channel domain. Presumably, blockade of the NMDA receptor by MK-801 is a pharmacological strategy for creating NRH in the intact animal. We characterized two behavioral outcome measures: the dose-dependent ability of MK-801 to raise the threshold voltage required for the precipitation of tonic hindlimb extension and elicit irregular episodes of intense jumping behavior (referred to as "popping") in mice. Moreover, 24 hours after mice are forced to swim for up to 10 minutes in cold water, the ability of MK-801 to antagonize electrically precipitated seizures is reduced. Thus, stress affects the endogenous tone of NMDA receptor-mediated neurotransmission. Genetically inbred strains of mice differ in their behavioral sensitivity to MK-801 on these two measures; interestingly, the BALB/c inbred mouse strain is more sensitive than other inbred strains and the NIH Swiss outbred mouse strain. Stress and genetic strain differences interact to affect behavioral sensitivity to MK-801. Importantly, these animal models serve to test the ability of glycinergic interventions to modulate NMDA receptor-mediated neurotransmission in the intact animal. Thus, they are used as screening procedures for NMDA receptor agonist interventional strategies that may be developed as medications for the treatment of schizophrenia. A series of glycinergic interventions have been tested in these models. Also, these paradigms are useful in demonstrating that drugs, whose direct actions are on other neurotransmitter systems, affect NMDA receptor-mediated neurotransmission in the intact animal. Preliminary clinical trials of a few NMDA receptor agonist interventions have been conducted in patients with schizophrenia. In general, the medications are well-tolerated and the results suggest that the adjuvant therapeutic efficacy of specific glycinergic interventions may be influenced by state of illness and the specific antipsychotic medication chosen for maintenance pharmacotherapy (e.g., clozapine). The chapter will concentrate on the results of our laboratory and clinical investigations, whose primary aim was modulation of NMDA receptor-mediated neurotransmission in mice and man.

Key Words: Glutamate, Glycine, NMDA Receptor, Stress, BALB/c Mice, Schizophrenia

Anatomy and Biochemical Pharmacology of the NMDA Receptor Complex

The ion channel that is a part of the N-methyl-D-aspartate (NMDA) receptor complex, a type of glutamate-gated receptor ion channel, has properties of both ligand- and voltage-gating. The channel is named for NMDA, the glutamate analogue that binds preferentially to this receptor. Importantly, a variety of allosteric modulatory sites, covalent modifications of the complex (e.g., phosphorylation and nitrosylation), gene expression, and environmental and developmental factors influence the likelihood that glutamate will be effective in promoting channel opening. The complex regulation of NMDA receptor-gated channel opening makes it both susceptible to pathologic disruption by a variety of mechanisms and affords opportunities for pharmacologic manipulations (Bonhaus et al., 1987; Fagg, 1987; Foster and Wong, 1987).

The channel is comprised of individual polypeptide subunits with multiple transmembranous domains that align themselves to create a channel. The polypeptide receptor subunits are of two types, designated NR1 and NR2. The "obligatory glycine co-agonist site" is located on the NR1 subunit, whereas the site that binds glutamate is on the NR2 subunit. Although these sites are distinct from each other, they interact so that the binding of glycine affects glutamate's affinity for the receptor and the efficiency of coupling between its binding and channel opening. There are four classes of NR2 receptors, designated A through D, that differ in terms of anatomic distribution and their influence on the pharmacological properties of the receptor, including desensitization kinetics and the "modulatory" properties of glycine. Also, subunit expression is regulated by stage of development; in fact, an NR3 subunit appears transiently during development (Deutsch et al., 1998, 2001; Millan, 2005).

Ordinarily, at the resting membrane potential, magnesium ions occupy multiple sites within the channel, obstructing the movement of calcium ions. This magnesium ion blockade is relieved with the depolarization of the membrane, serving as the basis of the voltage-gating of the receptor. Thus, the glutamate-gated activation of NMDA receptors is dependent on membrane depolarization, which may necessitate coordinating the activation of other neurotransmitter receptors with the NMDA receptor. The hydrophobic channel domain possesses binding sites for compounds like phencyclidine (PCP), ketamine and memantine, which are referred to as "open-channel blockers." Interestingly, the functional consequences of blockade or antagonism of the NMDA receptor complex may differ depending upon whether the blockade is due to a competitive (i.e., a compound that binds to glutamate's agonist recognition site on NR2 subunits) or noncompetitive (i.e., a compound that binds to a site within the hydrophobic channel domain) antagonist (Deutsch et al., 1996). Pretreatment with competitive antagonists can prevent channel opening, which is a necessary condition for the action of noncompetitive antagonists.

The complex regulation of channel opening is consistent with the importance of NMDA receptor-mediated neurotransmission to a number of critical processes linked to regions wherein which this receptor is enriched, such as the hippocampus, thalamus and frontal cortex. Moreover, the astrocyte, which enjoys an intimate association with pre-and post-synaptic elements, participates in regulating availability of glutamate, glycine and ligands acting at the so-called Glycine_B co-agonist site (Millan, 2005). In fact, NMDA receptor-mediated neurotransmission is a cogent example of the active participation of glial elements in synaptic transmission.

Glial cells serve as an important potential source of glycine within the area of the synapse; glycine is derived from L-serine by the action of serine hydroxymethltransferase, a key enzyme involved in the regulation of one-carbon metabolism. Further, "excess" glycine is cleared from the synapse by glial cells via several independent, but related mechanisms: glycine-1 transporters (GlyT-1), which transport glycine into the cell in a sodium ion- and chloride ion-dependent manner; small neutral amino acid transporters (SNAT) located on the surface of astrocytes; and the glycine cleavage enzyme system, which is a mitochondrial enzyme complex that oxidatively decarboxylates or "cleaves" glycine such that its alpha carbon enters the one-carbon pool complexed with tetrahydrofolate (Deutsch et al., 1990, 1998; Millan, 2005). D-Serine has been described as a naturally-occurring high-affinity agonist for the $Glycine_B$ co-agonist site. D-Serine is derived from L-serine by the actions of D-serine racemase, an enzyme found within astrocytes in regions of forebrain enriched in NMDA receptors. The clearance of D-serine is via transporters and D-amino acid oxidase, a glial enzyme that deaminates D-serine. Glial cells participate in the "recycling" of glutamate that is released from presynaptic nerve terminals in a depolarization-dependent and calcium ion-dependent manner; in addition to neurons, glial cells possess sodium ion-dependent excitatory amino acid transporters (EAAT) on their surface. The glutamate taken up by glial cells is converted to glutamine, via the action of glutamine synthase, a compound that is released, taken up by neurons, and converted back into glutamate by the action of glutaminase. Glial cells also possess the enzymatic machinery responsible for an alternative pathway for tryptophan metabolism, referred to as the kynurenine pathway (Rosse et al., 1992; Millan, 2005). The kynurenine pathway leads to the formation of kynurenic acid, a competitive antagonist of glycine at the $Glycine_B$ co-agonist binding site, and quinolinic acid, an excitotoxic compound. Conceivably, the synthesis and release of kynurenic acid is a "local" mechanism for regulating NMDA receptor-mediated neurotransmission at the level of the synapse (Rosse et al., 1992).

The surface of astrocytes also regulate levels and availability of N-acetyl-aspartate-glutamate (NAAG), a neurally-active dipeptide that influences presynaptic release of L-glutamate, serves as a potential "local" source of L-aspartate and L-glutamate, two excitatory amino acid neurotransmitters, and is a weak NMDA receptor antagonist. NAAG is a substrate for glutamate carboxypeptidase II and III, which are located on astrocyte plasma membranes and cleave NAAG into L-glutamate and N-acetyl-aspartate (NAA), the source of L-aspartate. There are provocative postmortem data suggesting that elevated levels of NAAG can occur in selected brain regions of schizophrenia patients (i.e., temporal cortex, hippocampus, and frontal cortex), because of reduced activity of glutamate carboxypeptidase II (GCPII), the hydrolytic enzyme enriched on astrocytes responsible for forming NAA and L-glutamate (Coyle, 1996). Importantly, the existence of these glial pathways and mechanisms for modulating the gating efficiency of L-glutamate and NMDA receptor-associated ion channel properties offers platforms for developing medications that can adjust the gain or "fine tune" NMDA receptor-mediated neurotransmission (Millan, 2005). Ideally, these medications would be indicated for a variety of neuropsychiatric disorders, including schizophrenia

Glutamate is a major neurotransmitter employed in intracortical projection pathways, conveying this integrated cortical information along efferent projections to subcortical structures in the midbrain and basal ganglia, and to the hippocampus. Glutamate is prominent within the hippocampus, where it is implicated in the induction of long-term potentiation, an electrophysiological analogue of learning and memory, and thalamus, where it may play a role in "thalamic filtering." Apart from their enrichment in anatomic areas that are linked to the psychopathology of schizophrenia (e.g., frontal cortex and hippocampus), the precipitation of a drug-induced schizophreniform psychosis by PCP in susceptible individuals has focused intense interest on a pathogenetic role of the NMDA receptor in schizophrenia (Deutsch et al., 1989, 2001; Coyle, 1996; Hirsch et al., 1997; Tamminga, 1998). L-Glutamate mediates both "fast" synaptic transmission (i.e., ligand-gated channels) and "slow" synaptic transmission (i.e., "metabotropic" receptors coupled to the synthesis of small, soluble intracellular messengers). There are three "types" of glutamate-gated ion channels, designated NMDA, kainic acid (KA), and *alpha*-amino-3-hydroxy-5-methylisoxazole-4-propionic acid (AMPA) receptors.

A significantly diminished density of dendritic spines on layer III pyramidal neurons has been reported in the cerebral cortex , especially frontal and temporal cortex, of autopsied schizophrenia brains (Hirsch et al., 1997). Importantly, glutamate receptors are located on the dendritic spines of layer III pyramidal cells in the cerebral cortex. Thus, glutamatergic projections "link" anatomic areas that are implicated pathophysiologically or by histopathology in schizophrenia (Coyle, 1996; Farber et al., 1998; Jentsch and Roth, 1999).

Pathophysiology of NMDA Receptor Hypofunction in Schizophrenia

Descriptively, the psychosis caused by PCP resembles naturally-occurring schizophrenia with symptoms manifest in all of the relevant domains of psychopathology, including positive (e.g., hallucinations), negative (e.g., affective blunting), cognitive (e.g., inability to abstract and impairments of attention and working memory), mood (e.g., dysphoria) and motor (e.g., mannerisms) symptoms. In fact, the "PCP model of schizophrenia" is widely considered to be the best drug-induced model of this disorder (Deutsch et al., 1989). Because PCP is a noncompetitive NMDA receptor antagonist that interferes with glutamate's ability to promote calcium ion conductance across the channel, NMDA receptor hypofunction (NRH) or a glutamatergic deficiency has been proposed as a pathophysiological mechanism of this disorder (Deutsch et al., 1989). Further, because of reciprocal connections and complex circuitry, a disturbance or "imbalance" of glutamatergic transmission would affect neurotransmission mediated by dopamine, acetylcholine and gamma aminobutyric acid (GABA), among other neurotransmitters that have been implicated in the pathophysiology of this disorder (Deutsch and Hitri, 1993; Deutsch et al., 1995, 2001, 2002, 2003, 2005; Mastropaolo et al., 2004). NMDA receptors exist on the surface of GABAergic inhibitory neurons within the hippocampus; GABA is the major inhibitory amino acid neurotransmitter within the brain. Given this location, a hypothesized consequence of NRH is a failure to "stimulate" these GABAergic inhibitory interneurons, leading to disinhibition of projections originating downstream from the GABAergic nerve terminal. A heuristic model that has been evoked to explain progressive neurodegeneration in at least a subgroup of patients with schizophrenia and is guiding medication development suggests that NRH leads to disinhibition of glutamatergic projections, whose consequence includes excessive stimulation of the AMPA/KA class of glutamate-gated receptor complexes (Deutsch et al., 2001). Excessive stimulation of AMPA/KA receptors could lead to excitotoxic cell death, a process resulting from disruption of unequal ionic gradients across membranes, depletion of energy reserves as ATP-dependent ion pumps attempt to restore these gradients, generation of reactive oxygen species, and cell death from apoptotic and other mechanisms. The proposed existence of disinhibited glutamatergic neurotransmission and the cascade of excitotoxic events offer many opportunities and suggestions for therapeutic interventions, including facilitation of NMDA receptor-mediated neurotransmission, potentiation of GABAergic neurotransmission, antagonism of AMPA/KA receptors, and "quenching" of locally generated reactive oxygen species (Deutsch et al., 2001).

An anatomical basis exists for defective GABAergic inhibitory mechanisms in schizophrenia that is independent of NRH, but could also contribute to progressive excitotoxicity. Specifically, a significant reduction of GABAergic interneurons in layers II, III, V, and VI of the anterior cingulate has been reported in postmortem brain obtained from schizophrenia patients (Benes et al., 1992; Coyle, 1996; Jentsch and Roth, 1999). Biochemical data also support defective GABAergic inhibitory mechanisms in schizophrenia, including reduced cortical density of reuptake sites for ^{3}H-GABA and a reduction in the binding of ^{3}H-nipecotic acid, a biochemical marker of the sodium-dependent GABA-reuptake site, in medial temporal lobe structures (i.e., left polar temporal cortex, and amygdala and hippocampus bilaterally) and basal ganglia. Reduced activity and levels of mRNA for glutamate decarboxylase (GAD), the synthetic enzyme responsible for GABA production, have been reported that could contribute to diminished GABAergic activity (Benes et al., 1992).

Molecular Genetic and Pharmacological Investigations of NRH and Possible Mechanisms of Progressive Excitotoxicity in Schizophrenia

When levels of mRNA of the alternatively spliced short and long forms of the *gamma*$_2$ subunit of the GABA$_A$ receptor complex were studied in prefrontal cortex from a postmortem cohort of five schizophrenia patients and five controls (Huntsman et al., 1998), the levels of the short form of this subunit were markedly decreased (i.e., 51.7% of control levels) in the schizophrenia patients. The relative overexpression of the long form of the *gamma*$_2$ subunit may result in defective "transduction" of the GABA signal in at least some patients with schizophrenia.

Neurons in the cingulate cortex (posterior cingulate/retrosplenial cortex) and other corticolimbic regions (including piriform cortex, entorhinal cortex, hippocampus and amygdala) are sensitive to toxic intraneuronal vacuolization caused by noncompetitive NMDA receptor antagonists, such as PCP and MK-801 (dizocilpine) (Olney et al., 1989). Benzodiazepine agonists (i.e., drugs related to diazepam), which potentiate GABAergic inhibitory mechanisms, may protect against this PCP/MK-801-induced toxic intraneuronal vacuolization. Females may be more sensitive to PCP/MK-801-induced damage than males, and dendritic spines may be a specific target. Destruction of dendritic spines would lead to a loss of synaptic complexes and disruption of "connectivity". Thus, NRH leads to diminished GABAergic inhibitory tone, whose downstream consequences include toxic intraneuronal vacuolization and destruction of dendritic spines (Coyle, 1996; Farber et al., 1998).

Discrete subgroups of schizophrenia patients may exist with NRH (due to diminished synthesis or altered "ratios" of specific NMDA receptor subunits resulting in fewer heteromeric NMDA receptors or "combination[s]" with diminished sensitivity to L-glutamate) (Jentsch and Roth, 1999; Moghaddam et al., 1997). Reduced genomic expression of NR1, a specific polypeptide subunit of the NMDA receptor complex, was reported in the superior temporal cortex in an autopsy series of schizophrenia brains (Humphries et al., 1996). Moreover, significant associations were found between levels of NR1 mRNA and measures of cognition, including the Global Deterioration Scale, the Mini-Mental State Examination, and the National Adult Reading Test, which provides information about premorbid IQ scores.

In a postmortem study, regional differences in the relative expression of NMDA receptor subunits were found in postmortem brains from schizophrenia patients with "a chronic, nonremitting pattern of illness (n=15)", controls with no evidence of neurological or psychiatric disorders (n=15), and "neuroleptic-treated controls (n=8)" (Akbarian et al., 1996). The schizophrenia cohort showed a relatively selective increase (greater than 50%) in levels of mRNA for the NR2D subunit in the prefrontal cortex, which may be a compensatory response, making these receptors more excitable.

In another postmortem study, data were consistent with an increased density of both the total population of NMDA receptors and NMDA receptors composed of assemblies of NR1 and NR2B subunits in the superior temporal cortex (Grimwood et al., 1999), which were not observed in the premotor cortex. Although these binding data conflict with the molecular data showing reduced levels of NR1 mRNA in a cognitively impaired subgroup of schizophrenia patients, they are consistent with NMDA receptor abnormalities of a neurodevelopmental or compensatory nature in schizophrenia. Thus, differential gene expression and alternative splicing of individual NMDA receptor subunits may represent a genetic mechanism of NRH. There is also a report consistent with the possible bilateral upregulation of NMDA receptors in the orbital frontal cortex of schizophrenia patients (Simpson et al., 1992). Another postmortem study reported an increased density of the strychnine-insensitive glycine binding site in several cortical regions of schizophrenia brain, consistent with upregulation of the NMDA receptor complex (Ishimaru et al., 1994). Inverse relations were suggested in several postmortem brain regions of schizophrenia patients between (elevated) ^{3}H-KA binding and (diminished) ^{3}H-MK-801 binding (for review, see Deutsch et al., 2001).

A variety of postmortem studies of schizophrenia patients report diminished binding (e.g., ^{3}H-KA) and expression of nonNMDA receptor subunits (e.g., GluR1, GluR2, KA2, and GluR6), especially in hippocampus (Jentsch and Roth, 1999), reflecting, perhaps, anomalous development of medial temporal structures in schizophrenia. AMPA receptor binding may be increased in the caudate nucleus of schizophrenia patients, suggesting that pathological changes in binding may be regionally selective (Noga et al., 1997).

Biochemical and Behavioral Studies of NRH

Under certain circumstances, PCP is proconvulsant, which may relate to the ability of acute administration of relatively low, subanesthetic doses of ketamine (i.e., 10 to 30 mg/kg, intraperitoneally), a noncompetitive NMDA receptor antagonist, to cause efflux of L-glutamate in the prefrontal cortex of the rat resulting in behavioral excitation and seizures (Moghaddam et al., 1997). Acute antagonism of NMDA receptor-mediated neurotransmission by administration of ketamine (30 mg/kg, intraperitoneally) to rats increased extracellular levels of dopamine in the prefrontal cortex that was blocked by intracortical infusion of CNQX (6-cyano-7-nitroquinoxaline-2,3-dione; 50 μM), an AMPA/KA receptor antagonist. These data support the role of "nonNMDA" glutamatergic mechanisms in cortical release of dopamine. Also, local blockade of AMPA/KA receptors in the prefrontal cortex of the rat by CNQX attenuated the ability of stress to stimulate the release of dopamine. Behavioral correlates of acutely elevated extracellular levels of L-glutamate include impaired working memory and behavioral activation. Moreover, systemically or locally infused AMPA/KA anatagonists are capable of attenuating the acutely disruptive effects of "low dose" noncompetitive NMDA receptor antagonists such as ketamine (for review, see Deutsch et al., 2001).

MK-801-Elicited Behaviors: Strategies for Studying NRH and its Pharmacological Modulation

The ability of PCP to precipitate a schizophreniform psychosis and its pharmacological action as a noncompetitive NMDA receptor antagonist stimulated interest in the characterization of behaviors elicited in animals by noncompetitive NMDA receptor antagonists, such as PCP and MK-801 (dizocilpine). Ideally, these animal models would serve as useful screening paradigms for the identification of candidate compounds that could attenuate the severity of behavioral consequences linked to NRH and, thus, could serve as potential medications for the treatment of schizophrenia. Also, these animal models could contribute to a fuller understanding of the pathophysiological consequences of NRH, serving, perhaps, as animal models of at least some aspects of schizophrenia itself.

A particularly informative animal behavior that we observed and characterized is the ability of MK-801 (dizocilpine) to elicit irregular episodes of intense jumping behavior in mice that has been referred to as "popping" (Deutsch and Hitri, 1993; Rosse et al., 1995). As noted, MK-801 is an open-channel blocker, whose actions depend on accessibility to a hydrophobic domain within the open channel. Thus, administration of MK-801 is a pharmacological mechanism for creating a condition of NRH; also, a dose response relation was demonstrated for its effectiveness in eliciting popping. A series of experiments showed that the elicitation of popping is unique to noncompetitive NMDA receptor antagonists; thus, popping is a behavioral outcome measure that distinguishes between noncompetitive (e.g., MK-801) and competitive NMDA receptor antagonists (i.e., compounds that bind to glutamate's agonist recognition site). Whereas MK-801 was able to elicit popping in a dose-dependent fashion, a derivative of CGP (2-amino-4-methyl-5-phosphono-3-pentenoic acid), a competitive glutamate antagonist, was unable to do so (Deutsch et al., 1996). Moreover, when mice were pretreated with the CGP derivative, MK-801's ability to elicit popping was blocked. Thus, when glutamate-gated opening of the channel is antagonized competitively by the CGP derivative and fewer channels are able to assume the open configuration, MK-801 cannot gain access to its binding site within the hydrophobic channel domain to elicit popping (Deutsch et al., 1996). Environmental factors influence popping behavior as shown by the fact that mice tested in cages with crushed corn-cob bedding on the floor showed a three-fold greater intensity of MK-801-elicited popping behavior than that of mice tested without this bedding (Deutsch and Hitri, 1993). The intensity of MK-801-elicited popping behavior could be attenuated in dose-dependent fashion by both a conventional (i.e., haloperidol) and atypical (i.e., clozapine) antipsychotic medication (Deutsch and Hitri, 1993; Rosse et al., 1995).

In addition to environmental factors and the ability of pharmacological agents to influence MK-801-elicited popping behavior, the laboratory showed that genetic factors contribute significantly to sensitivity to its elicitation (Deutsch et al., 1997). Specifically, the genetically inbred BALB/c strain of mouse was more sensitive to MK-801-elicited popping than three other inbred strains (i.e., C57BL/6, AKR, and DBA/2) and one outbred strain (NIH Swiss). These data on heightened behavioral sensitivity of the BALB/c strain to MK-801-elicited popping is consistent with work showing that this inbred strain is more sensitive to locomotor stimulating effects of PCP and anticonvulsant effects of MK-801 (Freed et al., 1984). The inheritance of sensitivity to the behavioral effects of MK-801/PCP is complex and likely will be shown to be regulated by multiple genes, each of which contributes a small amount to this sensitivity. The deciphering of the mouse genome and the availability of closely spaced positional markers encourages quantitative trait loci (QTL) analyses to identify loci contributing to "sensitivity" and "resistance." Based on our pharmacological studies, we anticipate that at least some of the genetic strain differences will reflect NMDA receptor subunit combinations that confer differences in binding of glutamate, glycine, and MK-801 as well as differences in the efficiency of coupling the binding of glutamate and glycine with channel opening (Deutsch et al., 1997). However, it is also likely that some of the differences between strains reflect their differences in metabolism, distribution, brain uptake or elimination of MK-801. In any event, the statistical strategies for determining relations between genetic loci and behavioral traits in mice might lead to the identification of homologous loci in the human genome conferring sensitivity to PCP-psychosis in particular, and psychosis and schizophrenia in general.

Using MK-801-elicited mouse popping behavior as a behavioral outcome measure, the laboratory explored the ability of a variety of compounds to attenuate this behavioral effect of MK-801, which is a behavioral reflection of NRH in mice. Because NRH is a hypothesized pathophysiological mechanism of schizophrenia and PCP, a noncompetitive NMDA receptor antagonist, precipitates a drug-induced schizophreniform psychosis with much descriptive similarity to schizophrenia, compounds that attenuate MK-801-elicited mouse popping behavior are potential candidates for development as antipsychotic medications. Also, the ability of a compound that does not act at the NMDA receptor complex directly to attenuate an MK-801-elicited behavior may reveal important functional relationships between neurotransmission mediated by the NMDA receptor and other specific receptors. Thus, blockade of dopamine attenuates MK-801-elicited popping, consistent with the intimate relationship that these two neurotransmitter systems enjoy (Deutsch and Hitri, 1993). To date, based on an evolving preclinical literature, our laboratory has shown that the following compounds, which have very different pharmacological actions, attenuate MK-801-elicited popping behavior: inhibitors of neuronal nitric oxide synthase (i.e., 7-nitroindazole), topiramate, galantamine, and anabasine (Deutsch et al., 1996, 2002, 2003; Mastropaolo et al., 2004). These findings stimulated interest in development and preliminary clinical trials of these, related compounds or related medication strategies as sole or adjuvant approaches for the treatment of schizophrenia (Deutsch et al., 1997, 2003; Drapalski et al., 2001; Rosse et al., 2002). For example, topiramate is of interest because it addresses what may be "downstream" consequences of NRH, such as a dampening of GABAergic inhibitory neurotransmission and excessive stimulation of the AMPA/kainate classes of glutamate receptor. Topiramate is approved for use as an anticonvulsant in the pediatric population; its primary mechanisms of action include antagonism of excitatory amino acid receptors (e.g., kainate receptors) and potentiation of GABAergic neurotransmission in a manner that differs from that of the benzodiazepines. Galantamine is of interest because of its action as a positive allosteric modulator of nicotinic acetylcholine receptors; thus, galantamine would be expected to potentiate cholinergic neurotransmission. In addition to its action as a positive allosteric modulator of nicotinic acetylcholine receptors, galantamine is an inhibitor of acetylcholinesterase and, thus, would be expected to increase and prolong the lifetime of acetylcholine within the synapse. There are very exciting and provocative data suggesting that deficient expression of the alpha7 subtype of nicotinic acetylcholine receptor occurs in schizophrenia. Conceivably, galantamine could target deficits of cholinergic neurotransmission, such as deficient expression of the alpha7 nicotinic acetylcholine receptor. Because of the pathophysiological role attributed to the diminished expression of alpha7 nicotinic acetylcholine receptors in schizophrenia (e.g., impaired sensory inhibition and deficits of voluntary smooth pursuit eye movements), our laboratory examined the ability of anabasine, a direct acting alpha7 nicotinic acetylcholine receptor agonist, to influence MK-801-elicited mouse popping behavior. Anabasine was able to attenuate popping behavior. Unfortunately, the alpha7 nicotinic acetylcholine receptor desensitizes rapidly upon exposure to agonist; thus, anabasine is not likely to be effective when administered chronically, which would be necessary in an illness like schizophrenia (Deutsch et al., 2005). However, our data support consideration of alpha7 nicotinic acetylcholine receptor agonist strategies that would not be limited by the rapid desensitization of this receptor. From a practical clinical perspective, our group has been conducting a pilot investigation of a strategy that combines galantamine, taking advantage of its property as a positive allosteric modulator of nicotinic acetylcholine receptors in general, with a selective alpha7 nicotinic acetylcholine receptor agonist in an effort to overcome the problem with receptor desensitization. Because of agonist-induced receptor desensitization, an alpha7 nicotinic acetylcholine receptor agonist could become a "functional" antagonist when administered for a chronic neuropsychiatric disorder. From a theoretical perspective, it is hoped that galantamine will preserve the receptor in a sensitive, as opposed to refractory, state and enhance the efficiency of coupling between the binding of the selective alpha7 nicotinic acetylcholine receptor agonist and channel opening. Importantly, our animal paradigm of MK-801-elicited popping behavior provided a compelling preclinical rationale for pursuing alpha7 nicotinic acetylcholine receptor agonist strategies for the treatment of schizophrenia. In fact, the MK-801-elicited mouse popping paradigm also provided the preclinical rational for clinical examination of topiramate and galantamine as sole adjuvant medication interventions (Deutsch et al., 2005).

Our laboratory has also investigated MK-801's ability to raise the threshold voltage for the elicitation of tonic hindlimb extension in mice (an antiseizure effect of the drug). This paradigm reflects the endogenous tone of NMDA receptor-mediated neurotransmission.

Moreover, we have used changes in the dose-response relation for antagonizing seizure elicitation with MK-801 to demonstrate the effects of environmental manipulations, pharmacological interventions and genetic factors on NMDA receptor-mediated neurotransmission. These results have immediate relevance and implications for our understanding of the pathophysiology of schizophrenia and development of novel pharmacological interventions that are not dependent directly on the selective antagonism of the dopamine type 2 (D2) receptor. An unexpected early finding that has been replicated several times is the fact that 24 hours after mice are forced to swim for up to 10 minutes in cold water (6^0C), the ability of MK-801 to antagonize electrically precipitated seizures is significantly reduced. These data suggest that 24 hours after exposure of mice to a profound stressor, fewer NMDA receptor-associated channels are in the open configuration and/or channel properties are changed such that MK-801 no longer binds to its site within the hydrophobic domain of the open channel. The latter changes could result from genetic expression, resulting in altered combinations of receptor subunits conferring changed pharmacological properties, covalent modifications of the receptor (such as changes in the state of phosphorylation), or changes in levels of endogenous modulators of the NMDA receptor (e.g., polyamines and neurosteroids), among other mechanisms. Our data support both possibilities: fewer channels in the open configuration and changes in channel properties.

The stress-induced reduction in the ability of MK-801 to antagonize the elicitation of tonic hindlimb extension in mice could be a behavioral manipulation that results in NRH. In order to examine whether or not stress affects "functional" properties of the channel, we tested the ability of a series of open-channel blockers to raise the threshold voltage for the elicitation of tonic hindlimb extension in mice, in addition to MK-801 serving as the comparator control (i.e., PCP, ketamine and memantine), in nonhandled control and stressed mice. Interestingly, a single session of cold water swim stress reduced the antiseizure efficacies of MK-801 and memantine without affecting PCP and ketamine when tested 24 hours later. Thus, there is the possibility that stress affects the charge, size and/or shape characteristics of the channel such that entry to the channel is "denied" to molecules sharing shape and charge distribution characteristics of MK-801 and memantine, whereas entry is permitted to molecules whose features resemble those of PCP and ketamine.

Similar to our findings using the MK-801-elicited mouse popping paradigm, genetic strain differences were observed between four inbred (i.e., BALB/c, C57BL/6, AKR, and DBA/2) and the outbred NIH Swiss mouse strains in terms of the ability of MK-801 to antagonize the electrical precipitation of tonic hindlimb extension. The BALB/c strain was most sensitive to the antiseizure effects of MK-801. Again, the heightened sensitivity of the BALB/c strain could reflect a higher percentage of its NMDA-associated ionophores in the "active" or open configuration, compared with the other strains, or the fact that its channels are constructed from combinations of constituent receptor subunit polypeptides that result in channel domains with relatively greater affinity for MK-801. However, these differences may also be due, in part, to differences between strains in the peritoneal absorption (MK-801 is given intraperitoneally in these experiments), blood-brain barrier penetrability, biodistribution, metabolism or clearance of MK-801. In any event, our data suggest that genetic factors contribute significantly to both seizure proneness and the ability of MK-801 to antagonize seizure elicitation (Deutsch et al., 1998).

Glycinergic agonist interventions have been proposed as a treatment for the presumptive NRH occurring in schizophrenia; it is hoped that agonists for the strychnine-insensitive glycine binding site on the NMDA receptor would "fine tune" or adjust the "gain" of deficient NMDA receptor-mediated neurotransmission. From a theoretical perspective, glycinergic agonist interventions would also be devoid of the potential for excitotxicity that directly-acting glutamatergic interventions would possess. Our laboratory has shown that the effectiveness of glycinergic agonist interventions for enhancing NMDA receptor-mediated neurotransmission is dependent on an interaction of genetic and environmental factors. Specifically, D-serine, a directly-acting glycine agonist, was not able to influence the dose-response relation for MK-801's ability to raise the threshold voltage for the elicitation of electrical seizures in nonhandled and stressed NIH Swiss outbred mice and nonhandled BALB/c genetically-inbred mice. However, D-serine and sarcosine, a glycine reuptake inhibitor, reduced MK-801's antiseizure efficacy in stressed BALB/c mice, the inbred strain with heightened behavioral sensitivity to MK-801. Thus, in the context of acute stress (i.e., subjecting animals to a single session of cold water swim stress 24 hours prior to testing MK-801's antiseizure efficacy), the ability of glycinergic interventions to "antagonize" MK-801's pharmacological-induction of NRH may be dependent on special properties of the genetic substrate. Even in the context of stress, D-serine was ineffective when administered to the NIH Swiss outbred strain, whereas glycinergic interventions were effective in stressed BALB/c genetically inbred mice. With respect to the heuristic value of MK-801's ability to antagonize electrically-precipitated seizures, these data have two practical implications: firstly, the acutely stressed BALB/c mouse strain may be especially valuable for the identification of potentially effective glycinergic interventions and, secondly, the "NMDA receptor pharmacology" of the acutely stressed BALB/c mouse may inform biochemical and pharmacological studies of acutely exacerbated patients with schizophrenia.

Clinical Trials of NRH Modulation

Our group has been involved in the clinical and preclinical investigation of NMDA receptor hypofunction for more than a decade. This research has included investigation of NMDA receptor agonist interventions for schizophrenia, Alzheimer's disease and cognitive function in normal subjects, including healthy elderly adults. The following briefly summarizes some of our studies, including purely cognitive investigations. The latter are relevant because they have led to the inclusion of unique cognitive tasks that may be sensitive to NMDA receptor agonist interventions in general.

We conducted early trials of pharmacologic interventions designed to facilitate NMDA receptor-mediated neural transmission at the level of the strychnine-insensitive glycine binding site in patients with schizophrenia. We examined the use of high dose glycine, milacemide (an acylated "prodrug"of glycine that readily crosses the blood brain barrier and is converted to glycine in the brain), and d-cycloserine (a partial glycine agonist) as adjuvant medications combined with antipsychotic medications (Rosse et al., 1989, 1990, 1991, 1996).

None of the findings from our above mentioned studies suggested significant pharmacotherapeutic utility for these agents at the doses and treatment intervals studied. However, later studies, using higher doses of glycine and d-cycloserine than those employed in our studies did show some promising results (e.g., Javitt et al., 1999; Goff et al., 1999a,b). d-Cycloserine has been shown to improve negative symptoms of schizophrenia when combined with conventional neuroleptics, but it worsens negative symptoms when combined with the atypical antipsychotic clozapine (Goff et al., 1999a,b). It should be noted that in our study, d-cycloserine was given as an adjuvant to the antipsychotic medication molindone, which has been shown to have atypical-like antipsychotic features (e.g., Robertson et al., 1994). In general, the literature on glycinergic interventions is mixed with some studies reporting favorable therapeutic effects. Clearly, dosing issues and the specific antipsychotic medication prescribed in combination with the NMDA receptor agonist intervention influence outcome. The efficacy of these interventions may also be influenced by state (e.g., exacerbated versus remitted state) and chronicity of illness. Finally, the domains of psychopathology or specific symptoms that may be sensitive to NMDA receptor agonist-induced changes are still unclear. Nonetheless, the hypothesis is a compelling one and there are many additional medications that have yet to be explored.

Additionally, we examined the effect of a tryptophan-depletion diet in patients with schizophrenia (Rosse et al., 1992). Tryptophan is a precursor of kynurenic acid, a naturally occurring antagonist that binds to the strychnine-insensitive glycine binding site on the NMDA receptor complex. It is also a precursor to quinolinic acid, a naturally occurring excitotoxin that binds to the NMDA agonist recognition site and has been implicated in the pathogenesis of various neurologic diseases. Thus, depletion of L-tryptophan, by virtue of its ability to diminish centrally available kynurenic and quinolinic acid, might have therapeutic benefit in patients with schizophrenia. After approximately a week on the diet, patients with schizophrenia revealed improved Stroop test performance, but no change in the severity of their symptoms. Other data confirmed the lack of clinical efficacy of tryptophan depletion diets in schizophrenia patients (Sharma et al., 1997).

Cognition and Medication Trials

Our group has demonstrated the effectiveness of drugs that interact with the NMDA-type of glutamate receptor on memory and language measures. We demonstrated in healthy young and older adults that administration of a glycine prodrug (milacemide) facilitated the number of words retrieved and decreased the latency to retrieve those words in a semantic memory task called word retrieval (Schwartz et al., 1991). Milacemide also improved healthy young and older adults' ability to remember the source or context of previously presented information (Schwartz et al., 1992). Remembering source or contextual information is essential to declarative forms of memory such as recall and recognition. In a subsequent study, we observed that the partial glycine agonist, d-cycloserine, improved word retrieval abilities in a priming paradigm in patients with probable Alzheimer's disease (Schwartz et al., 1996).

Our group conducted an open-label investigation to evaluate the therapeutic efficacy, safety, and tolerability of adjuvant topiramate in 12 patients with schizophrenia and schizoaffective disorder (Deutsch et al., 2003; see also case report by Drapalski et al., 2001). An optimal dose of topiramate was determined for each of the 12 patients during a slow four-week titration procedure. Patients were maintained on topiramate and their stable antipsychotic medications for eight weeks, after which topiramate was tapered and discontinued. Patients were followed for an additional four weeks on their stable antipsychotic medications. Clinical measures of efficacy (e.g., Positive and Negative Syndrome Scale), cognitive measures (e.g., recall and recognition, verbal fluency, word retrieval, Trails A and B), and safety measures (e.g., postural sway, weight) were assessed during four phases of the study: baseline, four weeks on adjuvant topiramate (week 4), eight weeks on adjuvant topiramate (week 8), and at follow-up (four weeks after topiramate was discontinued). The results showed that topiramate administration (average dose = 110 mg/day) significantly decreased scores on the Positive and Negative Syndrome Scale. Specifically, total scores at baseline were significantly higher than total scores at week 4 and week 8 on topiramate. After topiramate was discontinued at follow-up, total PANSS scores increased compared with week 8. Scores on the negative subscale of the PANSS showed a similar pattern. Negative symptoms were higher at baseline relative to week 4 and marginally so at week 8 ($P = .06$). After topiramate was discontinued, negative scores at follow-up showed a marginally significant increase compared with those at week 8 ($P = .052$). For the general psychopathology scale, there was a significant difference between baseline and week 8 scores, and between week 8 and follow-up scores. Topiramate did not have a significant effect on scores from the positive symptom subscale of the PANSS, the Quality of Life Scale, or the CGI scale. Adjuvant topiramate did not have global deleterious effects on cognitive function. Consistent with previous reports, topiramate decreased the number of words produced in the verbal fluency test; however, this effect was selective and reversible after the drug was discontinued. There was also a trend for topiramate to decrease working memory measured by the Letter-Number Sequencing Test in the WAIS-III (Wechsler, 1997). It is noteworthy, however, that topiramate did not have a detrimental effect on recall or recognition performance. In fact, an exploratory look at recognition d' scores (measure of recognition discrimination) showed that patients' recognition after eight weeks on topiramate was significantly higher than at baseline. Although topiramate was associated with decreased word finding, these recognition data point to the possibility that adjuvant topiramate might also have salutary effects on cognition in schizophrenia. Because topiramate administration can cause dizziness and unsteadiness, we used a measure of *postural stability* to assess the safety of topiramate. Data collected with the postural stability test revealed that topiramate did not increase instability or balance problems in schizophrenia patients.

In summary, the data are provocative, supporting continued exploration of NMDA receptor agonist strategies for the treatment of schizophrenia. As discussed, the therapeutic efficacy of at least some of these interventions may be influenced by state of illness (e.g., exacerbated versus remitted state) and the specific antipsychotic medication that is co-prescribed. Also, there may be discrete domains of psychopathology or specific symptoms that are sensitive to the therapeutic actions of NMDA receptor agonist interventions.

CONCLUSION

The descriptive studies of the psychosis associated with PCP and the demonstration of stereoselective, saturable binding sites for PCP in the brain led to the unfounded suggestion that a competitive "PCP antagonist" would be a desirable medication strategy for the treatment of schizophrenia. However, in the late 1980's, when it was shown that the PCP binding site was itself located within a hydrophobic channel domain of a glutamate receptor-associated ionophore, it became apparent that a competitive "PCP antagonist" would also be an open-channel blocker; thus, a competitive "PCP antagonist" might also cause NRH, a proposed mechanism of psychosis. The NMDA receptor complex possesses several allosteric modulatory sites that are distinct from the agonist recognition site for glutamate, in addition to a binding site for glycine, the obligatory co-agonist. The existence of these sites represents an opportunity for the development of ligands that are capable of increasing the "potency" of L-glutamate for the promotion of channel opening and calcium ion conductance. Conceivably, positive allosteric modulatory ligands of the NMDA receptor will be developed as medications for treating the presumed NRH in patients with schizophrenia in a manner analogous to the development of benzodiazepine agonists for the treatment of anxiety, seizures, sleep disturbance and muscle spasticity. Benzodiazepine agonists increase the likelihood that GABA will be effective in promoting chloride ion conductance through its associated ionophore; they improve the efficiency of coupling between the binding of GABA and opening of the chloride ion channel.

In the mouse, we have characterized two behaviors that result from the administration of MK-801 (dizocilpine), a noncompetitive NMDA receptor antagonist that causes NRH acutely: MK-801's antagonism of electrically precipitated tonic hindlimb extension and elicitation of mouse popping behavior. Using these animal paradigms, we have shown that environmental stress, pharmacological interventions and genetic factors influence NMDA receptor-mediated neurotransmission. Importantly, these MK-801-elicited behaviors were used successfully to test the ability of drugs to address NRH in the intact animal. These interventions work to enhance NMDA receptor-mediated neurotransmission, potentiate GABAergic neurotransmission, and antagonize nonNMDA excitatory amino acid receptors. Additionally, these procedures support the clinical examination of selective alpha7 nicotinic acetylcholine receptor agonist interventions and inhibitors of neuronal nitric oxide synthase for the treatment of schizophrenia.

It is expected that future medications for the treatment of schizophrenia will target the negative symptom and cognitive domains of psychopathology; they will be less dependent on the antagonism of dopamine for their primary pharmacological mechanism of action. The enhancement of NMDA receptor-mediated neurotransmission and correcting the downstream consequences of NRH, such as dampened GABAergic neurotransmission and excessive and dysregulated stimulation of nonNMDA excitatory amino acid receptors, will guide and serve as the rationale for many of the medication strategies that will be tested in the future. Our work over the past decade represents a useful interchange of experiments and information derived from the mouse and man.

REFERENCES

Akbarian S, Sucher NJ, Bradley D, Tafazzoli A, Trinh D, Hetrick WP, Potkin SG, Sandman CA, Bunney WE Jr., Jones EG. Selective alterations in gene expression for NMDA receptor subunits in prefrontal cortex of schizophrenics. *Journal of Neuroscience* 1996; 16: 19-30.

Benes FM, Vincent SL, Alsterberg G, Bird ED, SanGiovanni JP. Increased GABA receptor binding in superficial layers of cingulated cortex in schizophrenics. *Journal of Neuroscience.* 1992; 12: 924-929.

Billingslea EN, Mastropaolo J, Rosse RB, Bellack AS, Deutsch SI. Interaction of stress and strain on glutamatergic neurotransmission: Relevance to schizophrenia. *Pharmacology Biochemistry and Behavior* 2003; 74(2): 351-356.

Bonhaus SW, Burge BC, McNamara JO. Biochemical evidence that glycine allosterically regulates an NMDA receptor-coupled ion channel. *Eur J Pharmacol* 1987; 142: 489-490.

Coyle JT. The glutamatergic dysfunction hypothesis for schizophrenia. *Harvard Review of Psychiatry* 1996; 3: 241-253.

Deutsch SI, Mastropaolo J, Schwartz BL, Rosse RB, Morihisa JM. A "glutamatergic hypothesis" of schizophrenia: rationale for pharmacotherapy with glycine. *Clinical Neuropharmacology* 1989; 12: 1-13.

Deutsch SI, Deutsch LH, Weizman R. Nonketotic hyperglycinemia: a paradigm for the application of neuroscience to the understanding and treatment of a developmental disorder. In: Deutsch SI, Weizman A, Weizman R, eds. *Application of basic neuroscience to child psychiatry.* New York: Plenum Publishing Corporation, 1990, pp. 165-180.

Deutsch SI, Hitri A: Measurement of an explosive behavior in the mouse induced by MK-801, A PCP analogue. *Clinical Neuropharmacology* 1993; 16(3): 251-257.

Deutsch SI, Park CH, Lukacs LG, Morn C, Koetzner L, Mastropaolo J. MK-801 alters the $GABA_A$ receptor complex and potentiates flurazepam's antiseizure efficacy. *Pharmacology Biochemistry and Behavior* 1995; 51(4): 909-915.

Deutsch SI, Rosse RB, Paul SM, Tomasino V, Koetzner BA, Morn CB, Mastropaolo J. 7-Nitroindazole and metylene blue, inhibitors of neuronal nitric oxide synthase and no-stimulated guanylate cyclase, block MK-801 elicited behaviors in mice. *Neuropsychopharmacology* 1996; 15: 37-43.

Deutsch SI, Rosse RB, Riggs RL, Koetzner L, Mastropaolo J. The competitive NMDA antagonist CPP blocks MK-801-elicited popping behavior in mice. *Neuropsychopharmacology* 1996; 15:329-331.

Deutsch SI, Rosse RB, Paul SM, Riggs RL, Mastropaolo J. Inbred mouse strains differ in sensitivity to popping elicited by MK-801. *Pharmacology Biochemistry and Behavior*; 57(1/2): 315-317.

Deutsch SI, Rosse RB, Schwartz BL, Fay-McCarthy M, Rosenberg P, and Fearing K. Methylene blue adjuvant therapy of schizophrenia. *Clinical Neuropharmacology* 1997; 20(4): 357-363.

Deutsch SI, Mastropaolo J, Riggs RL, and Rosse RB. The antiseizure efficacies of MK-801, phencyclidine, ketamine and memantine are altered selectively by stress. *Pharmacology Biochemistry and Behavior* 1997; 58(3): 709-712.

Deutsch SI, Rosse RB, and Mastropaolo J. Behavioral approaches to the functional assessment of NMDA-mediated neural transmission in intact mice. *Clinical Neuropharmacology* 1997; 20(5):375-384.

Deutsch SI, Rosse RB, Mastropaolo J. Current status of NMDA antagonist interventions in the treatment of nonketotic hyperglycinemia. *Clinical Neuropharmacology* 1998; 21(2): 71-79.

Deutsch SI, Mastropaolo J, Powell DG, Rosse RB, Bachus SE. Inbred mouse strains differ in their sensitivity to an antiseizure effect of MK-801. *Clinical Neuropharmacology* 1998; 21(4): 255-257.

Deutsch SI, Mastropaolo J, Rosse RB. Neurodevelopmental consequences of early exposure to phencyclidine and related drugs. *Clinical Neuropharmacology* 1998; 21(6): 320-332.

Deutsch SI, Rosse RB, Schwartz BL, Powell DG, and Mastropaolo J. Stress and a glycinergic intervention interact in the modulation of MK-801-elicited mouse popping behavior. *Pharmacology Biochemistry and Behavior* 1999; 62(2): 395-398.

Deutsch SI, Rosse RB, Schwartz BL, Mastropaolo J. A revised excitotoxic hypothesis of schizophrenia: therapeutic implications. *Clinical Neuropharmacology* 2001; 24: 43-49.

Deutsch SI, Rosse RB, Billingslea EB, Bellack AS, Mastropaolo J. Topiramate antagonizes MK-801 in an animal model of schizophrenia. *European Journal of Pharmacology* 2002; 449(1): 121-125.

Deutsch SI, Schwartz BL, Rosse RB, Mastropaolo J, Marvel CL, Drapalski AL. Adjuvant topiramate administration: A pharmacological strategy for addressing NMDA receptor or hypofunction in schizophrenia. *Clinical Neuropharmacology* 2003; 26(4): 199-206.

Deutsch SI, Rosse RB, Billingslea EN, Bellack AS, Mastropaolo J. Modulation of MK-801–elicited mouse popping behavior by galantamine is complex and dose-dependent. *Life Sciences* 2003; 73(18): 2355-2361.

Deutsch SI, Rosse RB, Schwartz BL, Weizman A, Chilton M, Arnold DS, Mastropaolo J. Therapeutic implications of selective alpha7 nicotinic receptor abnormality in schizophrenia. *Israel Journal of Psychiatry* 2005; 42(1): 33-44.

Drapalski AL, Rosse RB, Peebles RP, Schwartz BL, Marvel CL, Deutsch SI. Topiramate improves deficit symptoms in a patient with schizophrenia when added to a stable regimen of antipsychotic medication. *Clinical Neuropsychopharmacology* 2001; 24: 290-294.

Fagg GE. Phencyclidine and related drugs bind to the activated N-methyl-D-aspartate receptor-channel complex in rat brain membranes. *Neurosci Lett* 1987; 76: 221-227.

Farber NB, Newcomer JW, Olney JW. The glutamate synapse in neuropsychiatric disorders. *Progress in Brain Research* 1998; 116:421-437.

Foster AC, Wong EHF. The novel anticonvulsant MK-801 binds to the activated state of the N-methyl-D-aspartate receptor in rat brain. *Br J Pharmacol* 1987; 91: 403-409.

Freed WJ, Crump S, Jeste DV. Genetic effects on PCP-induced stimulation in recombinant inbred strains of mice. *Pharmacol Biochem Behav* 1984; 21(1): 159-162.

Gibbs JW, Sombati S, DeLorenzo RJ, Coulter DA. Cellular actions of topiramate: Blockade of kainite-evoked inward currents in cultured hippocampal neurons. *Epilepsia.* 2000; 41 (Suppl. 1): S10-16.

Goff DC, Henderson DC, Evins AE, Amico E. A placebo-controlled crossover trial of D-cycloserine added to clozapine in patients with schizophrenia. *Biological Psychiatry* 1999; 45(4): 512-514.

Goff DC, Tsai G, Levitt J, Amico E, Manoach D, Schoenfeld DA, Hayden DL, McCarley R, Coyle JT. A placebo-controlled trial of D-cycloserine added to conventional neuroleptics in patients with schizophrenia. *Archives of General Psychiatry* 1999; 56: 21-27.

Grimwood S, Slater P, Deakin JFW, et al. NR2B-containing NMDA receptors are up-regulated in temporal cortex in schizophrenia. *NeuroReport* 1999; 10: 461-465.

Hirsch SR, Das I, Garey LJ, deBelleroche J. A pivotal role for glutamate in the pathogenesis of schizophrenia, and its cognitive dysfunction. *Pharmacology Biochemistry and Behavior* 1997; 56: 797-802.

Humphries C, Mortimer A, Hirsch S, de Belleroche J. NMDA receptor mRNA correlation with antemortem cognitive impairment in schizophrenia. *Neuroreport* 1996; 7(12): 2051-2055.

Huntsman, MM, Tran BV, Potkin SG, Bunney WE Jr, Jones EG. Altered ratios of alternatively spliced long and short gamma$_{2,}$ subunit mRNAs of the gamma-amino butyrate type A receptor in prefrontal cortex of schizophrenics. *Proceedings of the National Academy of Sciences USA* 1998; 95: 15066-71.

Ishimaru M, Kurumaji A, Toru M. Increases in strychnine insensitive glycine binding sites in cerebral cortex of chronic schizophrenics: evidence for glutamate hypothesis. *Biological Psychiatry* 1994; 35: 84-95.

Javitt DC, Balla A, Sershen H, Lajtha A. Reversal of phencyclidine-induced effects by glycine and glycine transport inhibitors. *Biological Psychiatry* 1999: 45(6): 668-679.

Jentsch JD, Roth RH. The neuropsychopharmacology of phencyclidine: from NMDA receptor hypofunction to the dopamine hypothesis of schizophrenia. *Neuropsychopharmacology* 1999; 20(3): 201-225.

Jentsch JD, Taylor JR, Roth RH. Subchronic phencyclidine administration increases mesolimbic dopaminergic system responsivity and augments stress- and psychostimulant-induced hyperlocomotion. *Neuropsychopharmacology* 1998: 19: 105-113.

Long KD, Mastropaolo J, Rosse RB, Deutsch SI. Exogenously administered D-serine failed to potentiate the ability of MK-801 to antagonize electrically precipitated seizures in nonhandled control and stressed mice. *European Neuropsychopharmacology*, in the press.

Long KD, Mastropaolo J, Rosse RB, Manaye KF, Deutsch SI. Modulatory effects of D-serine and sarcosine on NMDA receptor-mediated neurotransmission are apparent after stress in the genetically inbred BALB/c mouse strain. *Brain Research Bulletin* 2006; 69: 626-630.

Martin R, Kuznjiecky R, Ho S, Hetherington H, Pan J, Sinclair K, Gilliam F, Faught E. Cognitive effects of topiramate, gabapentin, and lamotrigine in healthy young adults. *Neurology* 1999; 52: 321-327.

Mastropaolo J, Rosse RB, Deutsch SI. Anabasine, a selective nicotinic acetylcholine receptor agonist, antagonizes MK-801 –elicited mouse popping behavior, an animal model of schizophrenia. *Behavioural Brain Research* 2004; 153(2): 419-422.

Millan MJ. N-methyl-D-aspartate receptors as a target for improved antipsychotic agents: novel insights and clinical perspectives. *Psychopharmacology* 2005; 179: 30-53.

Moghaddam B, Adams B, Verma A, Daly D. Activation of glutamatergic neurotransmission by ketamine: a novel step in the pathway from NMDA receptor blockade to dopaminergic and cognitive disruptions associated with the prefrontal cortex. *Journal of Neuroscience* 1997; 17(8): 2921-2927.

Noga JT, Hyde TM, Herman MM, Spurney CF, Bigelow LB, Weinberger DR, Kleinman JE. Glutamate receptors in the postmortem striatum of schizophrenic, suicide, and control brains. *Synapse* 1997; 27: 168-176.

Norris DO, Mastropaolo J, O'Connor DA, Novitzki MR, Deutsch SI. Glycinergic interventions potentiate the ability of MK-801 to raise the threshold voltage for tonic hindlimb extension in mice. *Pharmacology Biochemistry and Behavior* 1992; 43(1): 609-612.

Norris DO, Mastropaolo J, O'Connor DA, Cohen JM, and Deutsch SI. A glycinergic intervention potentiates the antiseizure efficacies of MK-801, flurazepam, and carbamazepine. *Neurochemical Research* 1994; 19(2): 161-165.

Olney JW, Farber NB. Glutamate receptor dysfunction and schizophrenia. *Archives of General* Psychiatry 1995; 52: 998-1007.

Olney JW., Labruyere J, Price MT. Pathological changes induced in cerebrocortical neurons by phencyclidine and related drugs. *Science* 1989; 244: 1360-1362.

Robertson GS, Matsumura H, Fibiger HC.Induction patterns of Fos-like immunoreactivity in the forebrain as predictors of atypical antipsychotic activity. *Journal of Pharmacology and Experimental Therapeutics* 1994; 271(2): 1058-1066.

Rosse RB, Theut SK, Banay-Schwartz M, Leighton M, Scarcella E, Cohen CG, Deutsch SI. Glycine adjuvant therapy to conventional neuroleptic treatment in schizophrenia: an open-label, pilot. *Clinical Neuropharmacology* 1989; 12(5): 416-424.

Rosse RB, Schwartz BL, Leighton MP, Davis RE, Deutsch SI. An open-label trial of milacemide in schizophrenia: An NMDA intervention strategy. *Clinical Neuropharmacology* 1990: 13(4): 348-354.

Rosse RB, Schwartz BL, Davis RE, Deutsch SI. An NMDA intervention strategy in schizophrenia with "low dose" milacemide. *Clinical Neuropharmacology* 1991; 14(3): 268-272.

Rosse RB, Schwartz BL, Zlotolow S, Banay-Schwartz M, Trinidad AC, Peace TD, Deutsch SI. Effects of a low-tryptophan diet as an adjuvant to conventional neuroleptic therapy in schizophrenia. *Clinical Neuropharmacology* 1992; 15(2): 129-141.

Rosse RB, Mastropaolo J, Koetzner L, Morn CB, Sussman DM, Deutsch SI. Computerized measurement of MK-801 – elicited hyperactivity and popping in mice. *Clinical Neuropharmacology* 1995; 18: 448-457.

Rosse RB, McCarthy M, Kendrick K, Deutsch SI. D-Cycloserine adjuvant therapy to molindone in the treatment of schizophrenia. *Clinical Neuropharmacology* 1996; 19(5): 444-450.

Rosse RB, Deutsch SI. Adjuvant galantamine administration improves negative symptoms in a patient with treatment-refractory schizophrenia. *Clinical Neuropharmacology* 2002; 25(5): 272-275.

Schwartz BL, Hashtroudi S, Herting RL, Handerson H, Deutsch SI. Glycine prodrug facilitates memory retrieval in humans. *Neurology* 1991; 41: 1341-1343.

Schwartz BL, Hashtroudi S, Herting RL, Deutsch SI. The effects of milacemide on item and source memory. *Clinical Neuropharmacology* 1992; 15(2): 114-119.

Schwartz BL, Hashtroudi S, Herting RL, Schwartz P, Deutsch SI. D-Cycloserine enhances implicit memory in Alzheimer patients. *Neurology* 1996; 46: 420-424.

Schwartz BL, Hashtroudi S, Herting RL, Fakouhi TD, Deutsch SI. The NMDA receptor complex: enhancement of memory in aging and dementia. In: Herrmann D, McEvoy C, Hertzog C, Hertel P, Johnson M, eds. *Basic and Applied Memory Research: Volume 2, Practical Applications*. Mahwah, New Jersey: Lawrence Erlbaum Associates, Inc., 1996, pp. 423-437.

Schwartz BL, Parker ES, Hovaguimian A, Williams A, Rosse RB, Deutsch SI. Context-dependent memory impairment in schizophrenia: Analysis of the frontal dysfunction hypothesis. International Congress on Schizophrenia Research. March 29- April 2, submitted abstract.

Schwartz BL, Howard DV, Howard JH Jr, Hovaguimian A, Deutsch SI. Implicit learning of visuospatial sequences in schizophrenia. *Neuropsychology* 2003; 17(3): 517-533.

Shank RP, Gardocki JF, Streeter AJ, Maryanoff BE. An overview of the preclinical aspects of topiramate: Pharmacology, pharmacokinetics, and mechanism of action. *Epilepsia* 2000; 41 (Suppl. 1): S3-9.

Sharma RP, Shapiro LE, Kamath SK, Soll EA, Watanabe MD, Davis JM. Acute dietary tryptophan depletion: effects on schizophrenic positive and negative symptoms. *Neuropsychobiology* 1997; 35(1): 5-10.

Simpson MD, Slater P, Royston MC, Deakin JF. Alterations in phencyclidine and sigma binding sites in schizophrenic brains. Effects of disease process and neuroleptic medication. *Schizophrenia Research* 1992; 6: 41-48.

Tamminga CA. Schizophrenia and glutamatergic transmission. *Critical Reviews in Neurobiology* 1998; 12: 21-36.

Weinberger DR, Lipska BK. Cortical maldevelopment, anti-psychotic drugs, and schizophrenia: a search for common ground. *Schizophrenia Research* 1995; 16: 87-110.

In: Schizophrenia Research Trends
Editor: Konstance V. Almann, pp. 115-136

ISBN 13: 978-1-60021-746-3

Chapter IV

EVOLUTION AND SCHIZOPHRENIA

Joseph Polimeni and Jeffrey P. Reiss
University of Manitoba, Winnipeg, Manitoba, Canada

ABSTRACT

This author explores major evolutionary ideas related to schizophrenia, covering four general topics. First, the essential groundwork that justifies the application of evolutionary principles to psychiatric disorders is established. Second, we examine evolutionary theories that frame schizophrenia in its classical orientation, as a disease or accident of normal brain evolution. Third, theories that attribute some evolutionary advantage to schizophrenia are reviewed. Last, a more detailed description of our own hypothesis is presented, suggesting that the origins of schizophrenia may involve shamanism and group selection.

INTRODUCTION

Evolution may be framed as the study of genes through time. Researchers have typically ignored evolutionary perspectives related to psychiatric conditions because the crucial elements, genes and time, are essentially undetermined. The genetic machinations of classic psychiatric disorders have, thus far, been inaccessible and very few systematic psychiatric accounts can be found in the ancient historical record. The scarcity of necessary knowledge in contemporary psychiatry, however, in no way diminishes its potential importance. In medical ailments where the genetics and history are more completely understood such as sickle cell anemia, thalassemia or cystic fibrosis, evolutionary principles form an integral part of our comprehensive appreciation of these conditions [1-3]. Similarly, there is sufficient evidence that many psychiatric conditions rely on genetic instruction in addition to having been around since ancient times. Evolution, therefore, has almost undoubtedly played a prominent role in the configuration of these conditions.

There is almost no doubt that schizophrenia has a significant genetic basis. That schizophrenia tends to aggregate in certain families has long been observed. Through the 1980's, about a dozen major studies with rigorous methodologies confirmed these earlier observations [4]. Collectively, studies show that first-degree relatives of patients with schizophrenia have between 5 and 10 times the risk of being diagnosed compared to control probands [4]. Although shared environmental influences could perhaps explain familial aggregation of schizophrenia, adoption and twin studies implicate a substantive genetic component. Adoption studies demonstrate an appreciable increased risk of schizophrenia in biologic relatives of schizophrenic adoptees [5-7]. Twin studies support the ample role of genetic influence with concordance rates of about 40% in monozygotic twins compared to 15% in dizygotic twins [8].

There are indications that schizophrenia may be a very old phenomenon although no conclusive confirmation exists beyond the last few centuries. Evans et al reviewed Ancient Roman and Greek texts for evidence of schizophrenia and concluded there were no identified cases as defined by DSM-IV [9]. However, all three authors had to be in agreement before a diagnosis could be registered – a method that would certainly create bias in favor of false negatives. The use of stringent modern criteria is perhaps inappropriate for a variety of reasons. Jeste et al outlined six major reasons to explain the scarcity of schizophrenia reports in the historical record including the use of religious rather than medical paradigms to explicate bizarre behaviors and the possibility that modern culture has modified the illness [10]. Despite these inescapable obstacles, several historical accounts of probable schizophrenia exist dating back to Mesopotamia [10-11]. For example, Jeste et al describe a woman conversing with a non-existent person who presented to a London hospital before the year 1189 [10]. Unfortunately, as is typical with historical descriptions, few other psychiatric details accompany the case and therefore a definitive diagnosis of schizophrenia cannot be confirmed.

Dating schizophrenia is currently not possible although it may be attainable once the genetics becomes elucidated. By estimating the rate of mutational changes in DNA, molecular dating techniques can approximate the timing of evolutionary divergence between various genotypes. This, of course, is not yet possible with the classic psychiatric disorders; however, a possible minimum estimate for the age of schizophrenia could be about 60,000 years when Australian aboriginals became effectively isolated from the rest of humankind [12]. Schizophrenia seems to cross all cultures in similar frequencies and has been found in Australian aboriginals and other remote populations[13-15]. This suggests that schizophrenia was well established before the formation of the oldest genetically isolated racial enclaves.

Evolutionary thinking begins with Charles Darwin's theory of natural selection, which explains how species change through time. One necessary component to the theory is that variation exists between individuals of any given species. Organisms with optimal traits produce the greatest number of surviving progeny resulting in "survival of the fittest". This process of "natural selection" transforms species through generations and forms the basis of the theory of evolution. Although published almost 150 years ago, Charles Darwin's well-known book *On the Origins of Species* is still a valuable read for students of evolution [16]. No other single idea has transformed our ability to understand the essence of living organisms and therefore cannot be neglected when establishing biological based concepts.

In 1964, Huxley, Mayr, Osmond and Hoffer [17] were the first to unequivocally apply evolutionary principles to the study of schizophrenia. They identified two characteristics of the illness that were ostensibly incompatible with evolutionary theory. Schizophrenia's considerable prevalence could not be reconciled with its below-average fecundity. In other words, how does schizophrenia, a genetic based phenomenon, persist if those afflicted have fewer progeny? Schizophrenia's 1% prevalence is well above typical mutation rates yet substantially below the full-fledged ubiquity of a successful trait. Furthermore, it appears too discrete an entity to reflect normal variation. Huxley et al proposed that schizophrenia could represent a genetic polymorphism associated with both evolutionary advantageous and disadvantageous characteristics. The net selection pressure upon the condition would be zero, therefore maintaining a stable prevalence figure of 1%. Although the purported advantages provided by Huxley et al (resistance to shock, allergies and infection) have never been substantiated, the formal recognition of the "schizophrenia paradox" was a seminal discovery.

Before proceeding, how axiomatic are the two primary assumptions embedded in the Huxley et al formulation? The first assumption, that schizophrenia represents a high-prevalence condition appears to be valid. The incidence and prevalence of schizophrenia has been studied extensively throughout varied cultures [13,15] and is invariably about 1% – a figure clearly above typical mutation rates by a few orders of magnitude. The possibility does exist, however, that some yet undiscovered high frequency mutagenic phenomenon exclusively related to schizophrenia operates on the genotype.

The second supposition of the Huxley et al paper – that the prevalence rate is stable and accompanied by reduced fecundity – is more tenuous. Over the last half-century, reduced fecundity in schizophrenia has undeniably been a reliable finding [18]. This difference is more pronounced in males. Although some of the divergence may conceivably be attributed to reduced fertility, the lion's share of the disparity is likely related to fewer conjugal relationships and reduced marriage rates [19]. Most studies have originated in the U.S. and Europe although recent studies from Australia and Japan are also in agreement [20-21]. It is not known, however, whether these differences reflect an artifact of modern society, as no accurate estimates of schizophrenia's fecundity exist beyond the last 50 years and no figures have ever been established from traditional societies.

Several studies have attempted to address the question of whether schizophrenia is increasing, fixed or decreasing in incidence. A number of these studies reveal declines in incidence throughout various regions of the Western world (Australia, Denmark, England and Whales, Italy, Ireland, New Zealand and Scotland) while a smaller group show no fluctuations (Croatia, Netherlands and Parts of England) [22-25]. Several possible confounds exist that could give rise to these incongruous observations. Studies typically have used either first-admission rates or national registries with their accompanying limitations to mark the decline of schizophrenia [26-27]. Narrower diagnostic criteria, earlier treatment of psychosis and deinstitutionalization are among many factors that can alter this data through generations [28-29]. Thus, the question of whether the incidence of schizophrenia has changed over the last century remains unresolved.

EVOLUTIONARY THEORIES OF SCHIZOPHRENIA BASED ON DISEASE MODELS

Evolutionary theories related to psychiatry can be broadly divided into those that view psychiatric conditions as adaptive and those that consider them disadvantageous byproducts of ordinary brain evolution. To those who frame schizophrenia as a disadvantageous phenotype, the condition is seen in its traditional perspective as a disorder or disease. This formulation makes schizophrenia analogous to an ailment such as vertebral disc herniation. Any advantage of bipedal locomotion is unfortunately mitigated by vulnerability toward herniated discs, just as schizophrenia may be an unfortunate byproduct of human brain evolution. In this section, we review the four best-known evolutionary theories of schizophrenia based on disease models.

Among the first comprehensive attempts to understand mental illness through evolutionary theory was Farley's hypothesis that schizophrenia could be an extreme variant of normal social behavior [30]. Noting significant variation in human social behavior, he conjectured that social skills must be under polygenic control. The extremes of distribution resulted in persons who were maladjusted, chronically over-aroused and vulnerable to psychotic breakdown. Symptoms such as paranoid delusions and disordered thinking would be considered outliers on a normal continuum. Personality disorder and psychosis would be the toll exacted for the benefit of adaptive social skill genes. The author acknowledged the most prominent flaw in his hypothesis; it "fails to explain why psychosis can so readily be divided into at least two major categories."

An assertion that schizophrenia could be an inevitable consequence of normal brain evolution was also put forth by Randall [31-32]. Specifically, " abnormalities of functional connection between specialized areas in the human brain may underlie the symptoms which constitute the schizophrenia syndrome". In this evolutionary model, novel neural pathways are established randomly, resulting in either advantageous "supernormal connections" or non-adaptive "misconnections". Randall's conclusion; a "biological trial and error of connection would produce a range of behavioral variants", including schizophrenia. Although there may be evidence for modified neural pathways in schizophrenia, the suggestion that neural misconnections occur randomly seems to deny the orderly and specific constellation of symptoms typically observed in any given neuropathological condition. Randall's argument also does not provide a mechanism for the propagation and maintenance of pathology.

Millar used Maclean's concept of the triune brain to speculate on the etiology of schizophrenia [33]. Briefly, the triune concept proposes that the human brain contains the evolutionary remnants of three brains; the reptilian (upper brain stem), paleomammillary (limbic) and neomammillary (cortical). According to this model, each successive brain introduced, incorporates and modifies previous functions. Millar suggested that schizophrenia could reflect "some failure of integration between the limbus and the cortex". Similar concepts outlining the essence of schizophrenia pathology have been formulated such as the "cognitive dysmetria" hypothesis of Andreason et al. [34]. Millar's hypothesis, however, lacks specificity and therefore could be applied to any disease involving cortical function.

Over the last decade, Crow has developed an intricate hypothesis outlining schizophrenia's possible evolutionary pathway [35-40]. A detailed updated version of the hypothesis and an abbreviated review have recently been published [41-42]. Crow believes that the origins of schizophrenia and language are intertwined – the disadvantages associated with psychotic illnesses are permitted to exist because they do not completely counterbalance the evolutionary advantages of language. He views the characteristic lateral asymmetry of language as an obligatory condition for optimum language development and posits that the reduced cerebral asymmetry perhaps associated with schizophrenia reflects a failure of normal brain development. As a result, Crow views schizophrenia and other psychotic illnesses as language problems – or more broadly as communication disorders. Mating characteristics of early man may have produced a sexual selection pressure that ultimately ushered the evolutionary development of language. Consequently, Crow predicts that the brain changes associated with psychosis could be on a gene in a specific homologous region of the X-Y chromosome.

Crow's intricate hypothesis, though interesting, relies on several contentious suppositions. First, Crow suggests that psychosis is intimately linked to language dysfunction. Schizophrenia can certainly be associated with disordered language but the condition also dramatically alters social behavior and executive functions. Furthermore, delusions and hallucinations are usually observed amidst normal syntax. Presumably to counter these sorts of criticisms; Crow has since conceptualized psychosis, not as a language problem per se, but, more broadly as a communication disorder. Second, to bolster the assertion that schizophrenia and language evolved rapidly perhaps on a single gene, Crow utilizes the controversial evolutionary theory of punctuated equilibria – Elridge and Gould's idea that evolution sometimes proceeds at an uncharacteristically velocious rate at speciation [43]. Language, however, may perhaps be one of the most malapropos candidates to be associated with such a theory. This reasoning appears to disregard observations of symbol use in primates and other compelling evidence indicating language probably evolved gradually over several million years [44-45]. Third, Crow's formulation seems to rely on a continuum model of psychosis, suggesting that schizophrenia and bipolar disorder share a common etiology. Without knowing the inner workings of each corresponding disorder, a "continuum" model means nothing more than identifying similarities between two conditions. Kraepelin's categorical model of psychosis is supported by family studies and therefore implicates two disparate entities, albeit with some phenotypic similarity.

Psychiatric Conditions as Evolutionary Advantageous Phenotypes

Introduction

Evolutionary Psychology

Evolutionary Psychology is a recent scientific perspective developed by authors such as Leda Cosmides, John Tooby and Jerome Barkow. The belief that human behavior and cognition can be better appreciated through understanding evolution is fundamental to the field. The specific cognitive capacities of human brains are seen to reflect specialized adaptations to the environmental challenges of ancient hunting and gathering societies during the Pleistocene period. This is not a trivial idea – "to propose a psychological concept that is incompatible with evolutionary biology is as problematic as proposing a chemical reaction that violates the laws of physics" [46]. Evolutionary psychologists view the brain as a myriad of "cognitive modules", each a remnant adaptation to particular problems faced in the Pleistocene environment. In other words, natural selection would have produced a variety of mental rules specialized to contend with a diversity of evolutionary domains such as "cooperation, aggressive threat, parenting, disease avoidance, object permanence, and object movement" [46].

The essential evolutionary developments that characterize modern man are mostly in the cognitive-behavioral domain as opposed to physical transformations. Because Homo sapiens have not appreciably evolved over the last 50,000-100,000 years, almost every extant human adaptive trait has arisen or been modified during the Pleistocene period when hunting and gathering cultures prevailed. An intimate knowledge of hunting and gathering societies can therefore help elucidate early man's environmental challenges and their corresponding cognitive-behavioral adaptations. Identifying universal characteristics between diverse cultures generates a list of candidate adaptations [47]. Of course, not all universal behaviors reflect genotypic adaptation. The use of fire, for example, is so undeniably useful that no genetic blueprint is necessary to maintain the practice. In contrast, other universal human traits such as shame, envy or sexual jealousy are, for the most part, invoked reflexively and typically lack obvious or immediate rewards – therefore, their presence likely requires appreciable genetic input. Another group of human universals such as humor, music, dance, play and perhaps certain psychiatric conditions are more enigmatic and not so easily categorized. At the very least, the potential exists that they could reflect adaptive genotypes.

In the context of modern society and its strict demands on conformity and reliability, psychiatric conditions can truly seem aberrant. To fully understand the possible beneficial role of psychiatric symptoms, one must appreciate how they manifest themselves in traditional hunting and gathering societies. Up until the middle of the 20th century, a few hunting and gathering cultures such as the !Kung, Mbuti Pygmies and Yanomamo had not been tainted by the idiosyncrasies of modern culture and therefore their study provided insight into the natural environment that shaped Homo sapiens' physical, behavioral and cognitive adaptations. Unfortunately, there is a paucity of psychiatric-style descriptions in the original accounts of pioneering anthropologists who first studied these isolated tribes. Thus, many potentially valid ideas related to the possible adaptive qualities of psychiatric conditions are not supported by comprehensive documentation.

Are Some Psychiatric Conditions Better Represented as Phenotypes Instead of Diseases?

The application of evolutionary principles to mental illness perforce prompts researchers to consider potential inherent benefits associated with psychiatric disorders and perhaps discard classic disease models with their implications of broken machinery of the mind. Although Huxley et al, in their landmark paper, were the first to effectively question the classic disease model of schizophrenia, others have since extended the challenge to other psychiatric conditions. Daniel R. Wilson has focused on the implications of evolutionary theory to psychiatric epidemiology, suggesting natural selection may have propagated and shaped bipolar disorder, depression, panic disorder, obsessive-compulsive disorder, sociopathy and dyslexia [48]. Wilson uses the Hardy-Weinberg equation to estimate, for example, that bipolar disorder is three hundred times more common than it should be if the forces of natural selection were inconsequential [49]. Even using conservative parameters, the calculation for schizophrenia yields a similar result.

Another challenge to classic psychiatric disease models involves the example of primary compulsions in obsessive-compulsive disorder (OCD). Checking, washing, counting, needing to confess, requiring precision and hoarding are the six most common compulsions [50] and each one is compelling in its ability to have a potential useful function – especially in hunting and gathering societies [51]. In contrast, veritable pathologies such as stroke, head injury or Trisomy 21 are hardly ever accompanied by symptoms that could conceivably be candidates for utilitarian purposes. Other theories have espoused the potential adaptive qualities of depression, panic disorder, OCD, social phobia, bipolar disorder and attention deficit disorder [52-53]. These disorders are prime candidates for evolutionary study because each one seems genetically bound and simultaneously possesses appreciable prevalence. Paradoxically, schizophrenia, which has been the most intensely studied psychopathology from an evolutionary perspective, may be the least obvious candidate for possessing some useful function.

The boundary between adaptive phenotype and disease can be indistinct and neither definition exclusively precludes the other. For example, dwarfism can be associated with hypopituitarism and this would undoubtedly reflect a non-adaptive bodily malfunction. However, dwarfism associated with African Pygmies seems to be an evolutionary adaptation to the specific challenges of a densely forested environment [54]. Evidence suggests that African Pygmies possess reduced numbers of growth hormone receptors in bodily tissues, however these phenotypic deficits do not truly reflect a disease state [55]. In a similar vein, the erythrocyte-sickling characteristic of sickle cell anemia increases natural mortality but simultaneously protects against malaria [56].

Is Schizophrenia a Disease?

Schizophrenia is clearly a mental disorder with little adaptive benefit to the individual in Western culture, however, no conclusive evidence exists that it is a veritable disease process. Although modern technology has shown neurophysiologic and neuroanatomical differences between groups of patients with schizophrenia and controls, no specific pathological trait or mechanism has yet been delineated. Gliosis and other typical markers of degenerative pathology are conspicuously absent. Furthermore, the multitude of diverse symptoms seemingly implicates some sort of indiscriminant cerebral breakdown, yet schizophrenia is accompanied by a paucity of sensory findings and modest effects on motor systems.

Veritable disease states such as delirium, dementia or temporal lobe epilcpsy can share with schizophrenia such symptoms as hallucinations and paranoid delusions. This fact may be the most bothersome for non-disease models of psychosis, although two plausible explanations exist. First, an adaptive behavior can sometimes reflect a pathological process if it is invoked at inopportune times. The act of vomiting, for example, is an adaptive behavior that expels toxins and infectious elements from the body; however, when caused by a brain tumor it represents pathology. The second explanation relates to the general misconception that evolution spawns near-perfect designs. Although the process of evolution has a remarkable ability to originate complex and effective adaptations, ordinarily this is due to tens or hundreds of millions of years of evolutionary "tinkering". Evolutionary designs with unquestionable deficiencies do exist and are generally due to peculiar historical restraints of defined evolutionary paths. One example is the inessential circuitous route of the laryngeal nerve, whose demarcation is owed to particular transitional steps in the phylogenetic history of the circulatory and nervous systems. Returning to the Pygmy example, a deficit-state such as short stature can be an evolutionary adaptation instead of a disease. If omitting some biological function were adaptive, this would be far more expeditious and therefore probable, compared to the rarity of creating some de novo biological structure. Thus, hallucinations and delusions could be due to some physiological deficit but this does not automatically preclude them from being adaptive in other contexts.

Even if schizophrenia were not accompanied by reduced fecundity, it would still be a perplexing disease from an evolutionary perspective. The problem lies in schizophrenia's relatively high prevalence compared to other diseases known to disable young adults. Catastrophic high-prevalence ailments are much more common in the very young where no significant resource investment has been realized and older people who are evolutionarily dispensable. No organ system is, of course, exempt from low-frequency diseases. This is because no appreciable selective pressure exists to produce, for example, a flawless heart or kidney. In this respect, propagating biological organisms are akin to manufacturing vendibles. Any factory can easily throw out 1 in a thousand widgets without appreciably affecting overall productivity. It would make no sense to invest an enormous effort overhauling a factory to achieve a completely foolproof assembly line. But what if one in ten widgets were defective? Would it then be cost-effective to refurbish the manufacturing process? Getting back to nature, genetic based diseases causing meaningful disability in young adults don't seem to exist at prevalence rates approaching 1%. As a general observation, mammalian organ systems are not usually so shabbily assembled as to require the scrapping of 1 in 100 young adult "widgets". This is just one more reason to contemplate possible advantages associated with psychotic conditions.

The Major Evolutionary Theories of Schizophrenia Positing Evolutionary Advantages

Theories positing the evolutionary advantages of schizophrenia typically focus on 1 of 3 vehicles of selection: individual, kin, or group. Evolutionary adaptation primarily functions at the level of the individual. In other words, individuals compete with each other, with those being most "fit" surviving and populating the next generation with their progeny. Although typically less prominent than individual adaptation, evolutionary competition can occur among other sets such as families or groups. In certain circumstances, a trait disadvantageous to the individual, such as altruism, can exist if the associated kin or corresponding group derives benefit. In humans, competition between tribes presumably resulted in group-level adaptations. Thus, individuals, kin or tribes can be the beneficiaries of adaptive traits.

Individual Advantages

There are only two hypotheses suggesting that some advantage resides inside the individual with schizophrenia that counterbalances its disadvantages – both hypotheses are more for historical interest. The Huxley et al paper has already been introduced. The second hypothesis was formulated by J.M. Kellet in 1973 [57]. It suggested that characteristics associated with schizophrenia could have helped early man's territorial instincts, whereas affective disorders would have assisted negotiating hierarchal tensions. Schizophrenia traits, such as inventiveness and the ability to tolerate low levels of stimulation while remaining alert, would have been advantageous to territorial animals. Kellet's hypothesis, however, addresses only a small component of schizophrenia, providing no evolutionary explanation for psychotic symptoms. Further, the social structure of Homo sapiens lineages is better characterized as hierarchal instead of territorial.

Advantages to Kin

There have been three major hypotheses suggesting that relatives of patients with schizophrenia are the ones that accrue the evolutionary advantages associated with the illness. Studies by Karlsson found superior academic success among relatives of patients with schizophrenia [58]. Accessing records from Iceland's stable population and using diverse methods to measure creative intelligence strengthened confidence in the results. Karlsson explain his results using the balanced polymorphism model – suggesting that creative relatives of schizophrenia patients are super-adaptive heterozygotes. Although not an evolutionary hypothesis per se, Karlsson's work could perhaps explain the persistence of the schizophrenia genotype.

The relationship between insanity and exceptional ability, in afflicted individuals or their relatives, has been a frequent theme through history and in Western culture dates back to Aristotle [59]. Several remarkable personal accounts are known – Isaac Newton became psychotic at age 51 years, and Albert Einstein's son was diagnosed with schizophrenia [60-61]. Other notable examples include Nobel laureate John Nash, who developed schizophrenia in his early 30's and Bertrand Russell, who apparently had several relatives with schizophrenia. Perhaps, a more convincing connection exists with affective disorders [62]. One recent review suggested little evidence exists to link creativity and mental illness [59]. However, the author failed to fully appreciate the discernible bias against making a connection – historical references to mental illness will always be underreported while achievements are without exception widely recognized. The author dismissed even reputable work such as Karlsson's Icelandic study solely because it was of retrospective design. Furthermore, if psychiatric conditions were responsible for only a fraction of all demonstrations of creativity, proving an association would be difficult.

Allen and Sarich [63] postulated that the " schizophrenia advantage is in the somewhat touchy relationship between an individual and his culture and society". Using the balanced polymorphism argument, overt schizophrenia or having no genetic loading for schizophrenia would be non-adaptive. Asymtomatic heterozygotes, perhaps 5%, with some genetic loading for schizophrenia would possess survival advantages by being able to resist the " shared biases and misconceptions of the group". In other words, conforming would not always be advantageous to the individual. The integrity of the group could sustain some betrayal if there were few non-conformists. Allen and Sarich emphasize their hypothesis explains why schizophrenia appears to demonstrate greater prevalence in industrial societies – complex societies can tolerate, sustain and even flourish when some persons possess a greater sense of individuality.

Horrobin [64-65] developed an interesting hypothesis relating neuronal membrane phosholipid metabolism to the evolutionary cerebral changes that created man. Over the last 2 million years, the seemingly greater availability of some essential fatty acids (arachidonic acid and docosahexaenoic acid) combined with phosholipase mutations could have resulted in enhanced neuronal microconnectivity. Amplification of neural connections would generate superior creativity manifested in a variety of ways including schizophrenia, dyslexia and manic-depression. Growing evidence of cerebral phospholipid dysregulation in schizophrenia supports the pathophysiological aspect of this hypothesis. Horrobin emphasizes the possible connection between bipolar disorder and schizophrenia, suggesting psychosis manifests attributes that could have been helpful to early man and is frequently observed to lesser degrees in relatives. For example, mania induces dynamic energy while paranoia results in prudence. Citing Karlsson's work, close relatives of psychotic individuals may have accrued evolutionary advantages through enhanced creativity – a trait that has now permeated all people. Horrobin concluded these neuropsychiatric conditions reflect the foundations of man's creativity.

All kin selection theories of schizophrenia figure that schizophrenia is a disadvantaged phenotype accompanied by low fecundity and that the illness exists because it is evolutionary counterbalanced by exceptional relatives who possess increased fecundity. Although relatives of patients with schizophrenia could perhaps possess special abilities, it is yet undetermined whether these presumed advantages translate to increased fecundity of a magnitude that completely countervails the presumed disadvantages of schizophrenia. A few studies with limited numbers have shown increased fecundity in first-degree relatives but a recent large-scale Finnish study could not establish appreciable differences [66-69]. Nevertheless, as previously mentioned, contemporary fecundity rates may not necessarily reflect those of yesteryear. Another potential pitfall with kin selection theories lies with the balanced polymorphism paradigm. There appear to be few proven cases of balanced polymorphism in nature, presumably because it is not an ideal mechanism for adaptation. The typical examples of balanced polymorphisms in humans, such as sickle cell anemia, Tay-Sachs disease and cystic fibrosis may just be imperfect stopgap measures to counter the abrupt outbreak of pernicious infectious agents [70-72]. Having said this, schizophrenia could perhaps be a befitting example of an imperfect evolutionary adaptation.

Group Advantages

The concept of group selection has an intriguing history – being belittled, disparaged and even ridiculed by evolutionary scientists. Particularly in the 1970's and 80's, to believe in group selection was analogous to admitting to other biologists that one didn't fully understand how evolution worked. Evolutionary theorists were constrained to invoke either individual selection or kin selection models – no matter how inapplicable or contorted the logic. The near complete dismissal of the idea for so long is a testament to how dogmatic and unquestioning the culture of science can be. In 1994, Wilson and Sober's seminal paper, "Reintroducing group selection to the human behavioral sciences" clarified the concept and established group selection as a plausible evolutionary mechanism to explain certain human cognitive-behavioral traits [73]. To those perhaps interested in the topic, the history of the group selection controversy is briefly reviewed in Sober and Wilson's, "Unto Others – the evolution and psychology of unselfish behavior" [74].

Stevens and Price were the first to consider the evolutionary mechanism of group selection to explain the schizophrenia phenotype although their model does not exclude the possible influence of individual and kin selection [53,75]. Their group splitting hypothesis presumes that proliferating tribal communities must eventually split to maintain optimum numbers. Schizotypal traits in certain prominent individuals may be necessary to ensure survival of the offshoot group. Stevens and Price argue that schizotypal traits are frequently found in charismatic leaders; namely Adolph Hitler, Joan of Arc, and Charles Manson. These shaman-like individuals use paranoia, delusions, religious themes and even neologisms, to fraction disaffected individuals and form new groups. They propose that this type of leadership is essentially altruistic and thus maintained by group selection.

Polimeni and Reiss, unaware of the work of Stevens and Price, developed a similar hypothesis although with a distinctly different emphasis – schizophrenia represents a once-adaptive vestigial phenotype that facilitated spiritual rituals conducted by shamans in hunting and gathering societies [76-77]. In our formulation, spirituality and religion are adaptive functions propagated by psychosis-prone shamans. We also question the classic disease model of schizophrenia and view psychosis-prone shamans as group-level adaptive specialists. Analogous to the polyethism of honeybee colonies, schizophrenia could be the most convincing example of behavioral specialization in humans [78]. The two major cornerstones of this hypothesis involve a familiarity with the concepts of group selection and shamanism. In the next section, we review the precursory ideas that led us to this seemingly unusual conclusion.

A Closer Look at Group Selection and Shamanism

Group Selection

Group selected traits exist because they provide some advantage to delimited groups of living organisms competing with other similar groups. The quintessential group selected creatures are ants, bees, wasps and termites. The level of social cooperation in these creatures is astounding and has translated into significant dominance compared to solitary insects occupying similar environmental niches – eusocial insects constitute half of all living insects while only representing 2% of the total number of insect species [79]. The Darwinian benefits of group-selected traits are formidable – so much so that they more than counterbalance the disadvantages created for the individual. The integrity of the group becomes so important that expelled individuals are unable to survive and procreate on their own. Consequently, the colony takes on the characteristic of a self-sustaining organism – sometimes described as a superorganism.

Animals that compete in groups tend to share a set of qualities not readily observed in solitary creatures. Whether a particular trait is best explained by individual, kin or group selection can be scientifically debated, however, the existence of three evolutionary traits – task specialization (also known as division of labor), complex communication and altruism cannot be satisfactorily explained by individual models of selection. Furthermore, these traits are never prominently observed in animals that don't live in close-knit groups. Task specialization is a very prominent trait of eusocial insects. Leafcutter ants, for example, are divided into a number of castes such as foraging workers, gardeners, and soldiers [79]. An example of complex communication is the waggle dance of honeybees. Compared to the behavioral repertoire of solitary insects, waggle dances represent a form of communication unprecedented in complexity – only the communication observed in a few mammals is more sophisticated. As for altruism, soldier ants that risk their lives to protect others or the presence of sterile worker castes in honeybee colonies are two well-known examples.

Extreme genotypic variability within a species is rare. For example, all frogs of the same species tend to be anatomically and behaviorally similar. Genetic variation does exist but typically on a narrow spectrum. Uniform selection pressures tend to homogenize individuals – optimum traits get selected with the greatest frequency . In contrast, group-selected traits can be sizably divergent. For example, some soldier ants can be 300 times heavier than gardener workers of the same species [79]. In addition to anatomical differences, these soldier ants behave differently than their more docile counterparts. The propagation of task specialists seems to be both genetically and environmentally determined [80-81]. It now appears that group level specialization may not be exclusive to insects. In South African mole-rat colonies, two separate castes of breeding females with clear morphological distinctions have recently been discovered [82].

Human beings are similar to eusocial insects in many ways. The various primate ancestors of Homo sapiens have lived in distinct groups for millions of years. Human beings and eusocial insects share several phenotypic traits inadequately explained by mechanisms of individual selection [83]. Examples include, altruism, complex communication, a predisposition for organized warfare and hierarchal social structure. For man, the list of traits poorly explained by individual selection could be extended to incorporate religion[84], ritual, humor and music. Thus, the evolutionary forces of group selection may have shaped the development of many cognitive skills.

The genetics of group selection are essentially unknown. Task specialists could conceivably be maintained by two types of balanced polymorphism – specifically, heterozygote advantage and assortative mating. Using the sickle-cell anemia example, heterozygote advantage could maintain individually disadvantageous traits in the corresponding homozygotes. If the individually disadvantageous trait was altruistic, it would be a group-selected trait ipso facto. Thus, a group selection evolutionary mechanism can work synergistically with a kin selection paradigm. As for assortative mating, Wilson and Dugatkin write, "Assortative interactions can generate highly nonrandom variation among groups, favoring the evolution of altruism and other group level adaptations among genealogically unrelated individuals" [85]. An example would be altruists having a predilection to mate with other non-related altruists and generating a subset of group-selected altruistic individuals. Although generally not the focus of psychiatric epidemiological studies, evidence for assortative mating in psychiatric disorders, including schizophrenia, does exist [86-87].

Shamanism

Shamans are believed to possess spiritual powers resulting in the ability to heal others and communicate with the world beyond. Various forms of shamanism appear to have been universally present in all hunting and gathering societies. Defining characteristics are controversial; some authors emphasizing the presence of voluntary trances while others noting involuntary 'spirit possession" as essential [88-89]. Psychotic-like experiences ostensibly seem to be a salient feature of shamanism as is evident in Michael Winkelman's succinct, yet comprehensive, description[91]:

> "Shamans are selected and trained through a variety of procedures and auguries, including having had involuntary visions, having received signs from spirits, having experienced serious illness, having deliberately undertaken vision quests, and having induced trance states through a variety of procedures, such as hallucinogens, fasting and water deprivation, exposure to temperature extremes, extensive exercise (e.g., dancing and long distance running), various austerities, sleep deprivation, auditory stimuli (e.g. drumming and chanting), and social as well as sensory deprivation. Their trance states are generally labeled as involving soul flight, journeys to the underworld, and/or transformation into animals."(p. 19)

It is believed that shamanism is at least 20,000 years old and was universally present in all traditional hunting and gathering groups. In complex societies, shamanism evolved into societal roles such as medicine man, diviner, witch doctor, medium and healer. These terms are sometimes classified under the general description, magicoreligous practitioner. An analysis of 47 societies throughout the world since 1750 BC revealed that all possessed some form of trance-based magicoreligious practitioner [92]. Therefore, a genetic role in shamanistic behavior must be considered.

The possible connection between shamanism and veritable psychosis has been controversial with a spectrum of varied opinions offered by those studying the topic. Numerous examples exist of shamans experiencing undeniable psychotic episodes. One of the earliest descriptions of shamanism from a Russian 19th century account says, " He who is to become a shaman begins to rage like a raving madman. He suddenly utters incoherent words, falls unconscious, runs through the forests, lives on the bark of trees, throws himself into fire and water, lays hold on weapons and wounds himself, in such wise that his family is obliged to keep watch on him. By these signs it is recognized that he will become a shaman"(Mikhailovsky quoted in Ackerknecht) [93]. Silverman was the first to make a detailed analytical comparison of psychological function between acute schizophrenia and shamanism [94]. He found little difference in several "core psychological factors" but noted a significant contrast in cultural acceptance of aberrant behaviors. Silverman argued that the stigma and futility of mental illness in Western cultures exacerbates psychotic symptoms.

Other anthropologists oppose the idea that psychosis is an integral part of shamanism. For example, Murphy asserted that the Yupik word *nuthkavihak* meaning "being crazy" was not used to describe any of 18 shamans in a Yupik village during fieldwork in 1954-55 [95]. However, Murphy may have only distinguished severe psychosis from its milder forms. A recent analysis of "folk healers" from Indonesian island of Bali found evidence for "initiatory madness" resembling schizophrenia in 18 of 108 [96]. The authors concluded that the phenomenon of psychosis was distinct from shamanism. However, considering these subjects have "priestly functions", the comparison to veritable shamanism may not be entirely appropriate. Besides, a prevalence figure of psychosis in 17% is not trivial and warrants explanation.

We believe that some of the phenotypic discrepancies between traditional shamanism and classic Western psychosis can be reconciled. As Silverman first suggested in 1967, it is certainly possible that the framework of modern society somehow exacerbates psychosis in some unforeseen way [94]. That schizophrenia follows a more severe course in industrialized cultures has been consistently observed although the reasons have not been satisfactorily established [13]. Complex behaviors do not evolve independent of culture – even ones with presumably strong genetic underpinnings. Marked differences in culture can dramatically alter fundamental human behaviors. The varied expression of anger and violence seen in different cultures is just one example.

Perhaps the greatest discrepancy between shamanism and psychosis is that psychosis is viewed as an involuntary experience while shamanistic experiences are considered voluntary or "trance-like". Some human behaviors, however, straddle the spectrum between voluntary and involuntary control. For example, penile erections can be voluntary or involuntary depending on a number of factors such as age, hormone levels, cultural cues, emotional state and cognitive approach. As for psychosis, a Yanomamo shaman's testimony highlights the indistinct margin between voluntary and involuntary hallucinations[97], "After I became a young man, everything in the jungle talked to me...I kept remembering my mother's words: As you learn to control them, they will stop scaring you. How right she was."

Epidemiological characteristics of schizophrenia are generally similar to the basic demographics of shamanism. For example, the onset of schizophrenia in young adulthood and the intensification of symptoms during stressful periods parallels shamanism. The gender bias of males being affected more severely than females is also consistent. Both phenomena seem to share a marked predisposition towards experimentation with psychoactive substances. Schizophrenic patients, for example, abuse many psychoactive substances such as caffeine, cigarettes, alcohol and marijuana significantly above community norms [98-99]. The diversity of substances abused makes it difficult to explain the behavior by some very specific neuropsychiatric mechanism. Similar to shamanism, the desire to experience any altered state-of-mind may be the most parsimonious explanation for psychoactive substance use in schizophrenia. Lastly, schizophrenia's 1% prevalence corresponds well to tribal population densities. Since the average size of hunting and gathering tribes is typically 150-180 individuals [100], a tribe would usually be ensured one psychosis-prone shaman.

Religion appears to have meaningful connections to both shamanism and psychosis, thus supporting the notion that all three phenomena could have common origins. When studied, religious delusions reveal themselves to be a common feature of schizophrenia. For example, one study found significant religious delusions or hallucinations in 15 of 20 schizophrenic patients retrospectively sampled from a state hospital in Hawaii [101]. Another study comparing symptoms of schizophrenia among African cultures, found religious delusions in over 60% of subjects [102]. Similarly, a Greek study showed religious or magical delusions in 56% of schizophrenic patients sampled [103].

In the anthropological record, evidence of religion, along with art, emerges between 30,000-60,000 years ago [104]. The religions of large complex societies have taken a slightly different form compared to hunting and gathering societies. In the latter, concerns about possession or magical spirits are almost universal. A belief in non-physical beings appears to be the most common feature of all religions [105]. Another frequent theme is the assumption that certain people are especially likely to receive supernatural messages from gods or spirits. Two essential points may be derived from these universal findings: 1) religious thoughts resemble some forms of psychosis, and 2) the ubiquity of specific religious cognitive paradigms imparts a potential genetic etiology upon religion. In fact, studies on religious attitudes among monozygotic and dizygotic twins suggest that about 50% of the variation in religious personality is under genetic influence [106].

Experiences of religious exaltation and shamanistic psychosis are comparable and both can be enhanced by hallucinogens. Shamans typically foster hallucinations and trance-like states through a variety of hallucinogenic plants such as Peyote or the mushroom, Amanita muscaria. A myriad of substances can be found in hallucinogenic plants although psilocyban and mescaline are common ingredients. Both these substances can induce hallucinations in non-psychiatric subjects. Neuroreceptors such as GABA, serotonin and dopamine are posited to be of critical importance in both schizophrenia and chemically induced hallucinations. Although less prominent in the major contemporary religions, hallucinogens have a history of being used to achieve ecstatic religious experiences [106]. In Pahnke's famous "Good Friday experiment" conducted in 1962, a hallucinogenic substance was able to intensify mystical feelings in almost all experimental subjects [107]. In a double-blind placebo controlled study, measures of mystical experience were assessed in two groups: ten males received the hallucinogen psilocyban and ten males received placebo. The conclusions were that when used by religiously inclined individuals in a religious setting, psilocyban helped facilitate mystical experiences [107]. Along these lines, a recent PET study implicated the Serotonin 1A receptor in spiritual experiences [108]. For a review of the possible neural substrates of religious experience, see Saver and Rabin [109].

Rituals are an integral part of all cultures and a fundamental activity of both religion and shamanism. In his book *Religions Explained*[110], Pascal Boyer states, "In most human groups people have all sorts of rituals but no good explanation of why they should be performed". Given the amount of time dedicated to ritual by every culture, an adaptive function must be considered. Rituals generally involve the entire relevant group and are typically conducted around life's major events such as birth, marriage, death, spiritual dealings or procurement of sustenance. It is certainly possible that the critical adaptive function of ritual was to foster group cohesion in hunting and gathering societies.

But how do rituals get started and how are they maintained? LaBarre claims, "Every religion in historic fact, began in one man's "revelation" – his dream or fugue or ecstatic trance" [106]. Similarly, in ancient hunting and gathering societies, shamans would be the ones to spearhead spiritual rituals.

To summarize our hypothesis; schizophrenia is viewed as a vestigial phenotype that possesses several adaptive features for hunting and gathering societies. The phenomena known to us, as schizophrenia, would have generated shamans for hunting and gathering tribes through a group selection evolutionary process. Shamanism could perhaps be the most compelling example of cognitive-behavioral task specialization in human beings – analogous to task specialization in honeybees and ants. The primary function of shamanism would be to spearhead magicoreligious rituals. The adaptive function of spiritual rituals would be to homogenize tribal opinion around enigmatic events and foster group cohesion.

In this context, positive symptoms of schizophrenia become evolutionarily beneficial. Delusional or hallucinatory experiences frequently contain magicoreligious or paranoid themes – abstractions of potential importance to hunting and gathering tribes. The dramatic and inscrutable quality of psychotic experiences would cast an indelible impression upon others, thereby reinforcing the notion of unfathomable supernatural forces. The looseness of associations typically observed in psychosis could generate possible creative solutions at times when the integrity of the tribe was critically challenged. Paranoid ideation has its own group-selected advantages. In the anthropological literature, there are examples of paranoid ideation in specific individuals facilitating unprovoked warring raids upon neighboring tribes [97,111]. Although unjustified and horribly brutal, these surprise attacks may nonetheless be an adaptive survival strategy for attacking tribes.

Negative symptoms of schizophrenia such as social withdrawal, avolition and alogia would erode basic human qualities, thereby giving credence to the belief that the afflicted individual was truly a vehicle of supernatural phenomena. Poverty of thought, a pervasive feature of schizophrenia, could attenuate logical analyses of discrepant information and facilitate delusional thinking.

CONCLUSION

Darwin was prescient regarding the possible importance of evolutionary theory to mental conditions [16]:

> "In the distant future I see open fields for far more important researches. Psychology will be based on a new foundation, that of the necessary acquirement of each mental power and capacity by gradation. Light will be thrown on origin of man and his history."(Origin of the Species, 1859)

Evolutionary principles could be relevant to schizophrenia due to its presumed genetic basis and supposed long history. Although neglected prior to the 1960's, a number of evolutionary based hypotheses have since emerged speculating on the possible origins of schizophrenia. Incorporating evolutionary perspectives can only enhance our understanding of schizophrenia.

REFERENCES

[1] Ashley-Koch A, Yang Q, Olney RS. Sickle Homoglobin (Hb S) Allele and Sickle Cell Disease: A HuGE Review. *Am J Epidemiol.* 2000; 151 (9): 839-845.

[2] Flint J, Hill AVS, Bowden DK, et al. High frequencies of a-thalassaemia are the result of natural selection by malaria. *Nature.* 1986; 321: 744-750.

[3] Bertranpetit J, Calafell F. Genetic and geographical variability in cystic fibrosis: evolutionary considerations. In: Chadwick D, Cardew G, eds. *Variation in the human genome.* Wiley: Chichester; 1996: 97-118.

[4] Kendler KS, Diehl SR. Schizophrenia: Genetics. In: Kaplan HI, Sadock BJ, eds. *Comprehensive Textbook of Psychiatry.* 6th ed., Vol I. Baltimore, Md: Williams and Williams; 1995: 942-957.

[5] Kety SS, Wender PH, Jacobsen B, et al. Mental illness in the biological and adoptive relatives of schizophrenic adoptees. Replication of the Copenhagen Study in the rest of Denmark. *Arch Gen Psychiatry.* 1994; 51 (6): 442-455.

[6] Tienari PJ, Wynne LC. Adoption studies of schizophrenia. *Ann Med.* 1994; 26 (4): 233-237.

[7] Tienari P, Wynne LC, Moring J, et al. The Finnish adoptive family study of schizophrenia. Implications for family research. *Br J Psychiatry.* 1994; 23 (Suppl.): 20-26.

[8] Torrey EF, Bowler AE, Taylor EH, Gottesman II. *Schizophrenia and Manic-Depressive Disorder.* New York, NY: Basic Books; 1994.

[9] Evans K, McGrath J, Milns R. Searching for schizophrenia in ancient Greek and Roman literature: a systematic review. *Acta Psychiatr Scand.* 2003; 107 (5): 323-330.

[10] Jeste DV, Del Carmen R, Lohr JB, Wyatt RJ. Did schizophrenia exist before the eighteenth century? *Compr Psychiatry.* 1985; 26 (6): 493-503.

[11] Heinrichs RW. Historical origins of schizophrenia: Two early madmen and their illness. *J Hist Behav Sci.* 2003; 39 (4): 349-363.

[12] Kingdon. *Self Made Man.* New York, NY: John Wiley & Sons; 1993.

[13] Jablensky A, Sartorius N, Ernberg G, et al. Schizophrenia: manifestations, incidence and course in different cultures. A World Health Organization Ten-Country Study. *Psychol Med Monogr Suppl.* 1992; 20: 1-97.

[14] Mowry BJ, Lennon DP, De Felice CN. Diagnosis of schizophrenia in a matched sample of Australian aborigines. *Acta Psychiatr Scand.* 1994; 90 (5): 337-341.

[15] Torrey EF. Prevalence studies in Schizophrenia. *Br J Psychiatry.* 1987; 150: 598-608.

[16] Darwin C. *On the origin of species by means of natural selection.* 2nd ed. London: John Murray; 1859.

[17] Huxley J, Mayer E, Osmond H, Hoffer A. Schizophrenia as a genetic morphism. *Nature.* 1964; 204: 220-221.

[18] Nimgaonkar VL. Reduced fertility in schizophrenia: here to stay? *Acta Psychiatr Scand.* 1998; 98: 348-353.

[19] Haverkamp F, Propping P, Hilger T. Is there an increase of reproductive rates in schizophrenics? *Arch Psychiatr Nervenkr.* 1982; 232: 439-450.

[20] McGrath JJ, Hearle J, Jenner L, Plant K, Drummond A, Barkla JM. The fertility and fecundity of patients with psychoses. *Acta Psychiatr Scand.* 1999; 99 (6): 441-446.

[21] Nanko S, Moridaira J. Reproductive rates in schizophrenic outpatients. *Acta Psychiatr Scand.* 1993; 87: 400-404.

[22] Suvisaari JM, Haukka JK, Tanskanen AJ, Lonnqvist JK. Decline in the Incidence of Schizophrenia in Finnish Cohorts Born From 1954-1965. *Arch Gen Psychiatry.* 1999; 56: 733-740.

[23] Der G, Gupta S, Murray RM. Is schizophrenia disappearing? *Lancet.* 1990; 335: 513-516.

[24] Waddington JL, Youssef HA. Evidence for a Gender-Specific Decline in the Rate of Schizophrenia in Rural Ireland over a 50-Year Period. *Br J Psychiatry.* 1994; 164: 171-176.

[25] Brewin J, Cantwell R, Dalkin T, et al. Incidence of schizophrenia in Nottingham. A comparison of two cohorts, 1978-80 and 1992-94. *Br J Psychiatry.* 1997; 171: 140-144.

[26] Eagles JM. Is Schizophrenia Disappearing? *Br J Psychiatry.* 1991; 158: 834-835.

[27] Jorgensen PM, Mortensen PB. Incidence and Other Aspects of the Epidemiology of Schizophrenia in Denmark, 1971-87. *Br J Psychiatry.* 1992; 161: 489-495.

[28] Kendell RE, Malcolm DE, Adams W. The Problem of Detecting Changes in the Incidence of Schizophrenia. *Br J Psychiatry.* 1993; 162: 212-218.

[29] Stromgren E. Changes in the Incidence of Schizophrenia. *Br J Psychiatry.* 1987; 150: 1-7.

[30] Farley JD. Phylogenetic adaptations and the genetics of psychosis. *Acta Psychiatr Scand.* 1976; 53: 173-192.

[31] Randall PL. Schizophrenia, abnormal connection, and brain evolution. *Med Hypotheses.* 1983; 10: 247-280.

[32] Randall PL. Schizophrenia as a consequence of brain evolution. *Schizophr Res.* 1998; 30: 143-148.

[33] Millar TP. Schizophrenia: an etiological speculation. *Perspect Biol Med.* 1987; 30: 597-607.

[34] Andreasen NC, Paradiso S, O'Leary DS. "Cognitive Dysmetria" as an integrative theory of schizophrenia: a dysfunction in cortical-subcortical-cerebellar circuitry? *Schizophr Bull.* 1998; 24: 203-211.

[35] Crow TJ. The continuum of psychosis and its genetic origins. *Br J Psychiatry.* 1990; 156: 788-797.

[36] Crow TJ. The origins of psychosis and "The Descent of Man". *Br J Psychiatry.* 1991; 159: 14 (Suppl): 76-82.

[37] Crow TJ. Sexual selection, Machiavellian intelligence, and the origins of psychosis. *Lancet.* 1993; 342: 594-598.

[38] Crow TJ. A Darwinian approach to the origins of psychosis. *Br J Psychiatry.* 1995; 167: 12-25.

[39] Crow TJ. Aetiology of schizophrenia: an evolutionary theory. *Int Clin Psychopharmacol.* 1995; 10 (Suppl 3): 49-56.

[40] Crow TJ. Is schizophrenia the price that Homo sapiens pay for language? *Schizophr Res.* 1997; 28: 127-141.

[41] Crow TJ. Schizophrenia as the price that Homo sapiens pays for language: a resolution of the central paradox in the origin of the species. *Brain Res.* Rev 2000; 31: 118-129.

[42] Berlim MT, Mattevi BS, Belmonte-de-Abreu P, Crow TJ. The Etiology of Schizophrenia and the Origin of Language: Overview of a Theory. *Compr Psychiatry.* 2003; 44 (1): 7-14.

[43] Eldredge N, Gould SJ. Punctuated equilibria: an alternative to phyletic gradualism. In: Schopf TJM, ed. *Models in Paleobiology.* San Francisco: Freeman, Cooper and Co.; 1972: 82-115.

[44] Pinker S. *The Language Instinct: How the Mind Creates Language.* New York, NY: William Morrow & Co.; 1994.

[45] Deacon T. *The Symbolic Species.* New York and London: WW Norton & Company; 1997.

[46] Barkow JH, Cosmides L, Tooby J. *The Adapted Mind: Evolutionary Psychology and the Generation of Culture.* New York, NY: Oxford University Press, Inc; 1992.

[47] Brown DE. *Human Universals.* New York, NY: McGraw-Hill (and Temple University Press); 1991.

[48] Wilson DR. Evolutionary epidemiology and manic depression. *Br J Med Psychol.* 1998; 71: 375-395.

[49] Baron-Cohen S, ed. *The Maladapted Mind: Classic Readings in Evolutionary Psychopathology.* East Sussex, UK: Psychology Press; 1997.

[50] Rasmussen SA, Eisen JL. The epidemiology and clinical features of obsessive compulsive disorder. *Psychiatr Clin North Am.* 1992; 15 (4): 743-758.

[51] Polimeni J, Reiss J, Sareen J. *Could Obsessive-Compulsive Disorder have Originated as a Group-Selected Trait in Hunting and Gathering Societies?* 2004. In submission.

[52] McGuire M, Troisi A. *Darwinian Psychiatry.* New York, NY: Oxford University Press; 1998.

[53] Stevens A, Price J. *Evolutionary Psychiatry: A New Beginning.* 2nd ed. London, UK: Routledge; 2000.

[54] Shea BT, Bailey RC. Allometry and adaptation of body proportions and stature in African pygmies. *Am J Phys Anthropol.* 1996; 100 (3): 311-340.

[55] Baumann G, Shaw MA, Merimee TJ. Low levels of high-affinity growth hormone-binding protein in African pygmies. *N Eng J Med.* 1989; 320 (26): 1705-1709.

[56] Clegg JB, Weatherall DJ. Thalassemia and Malaria: new insights into an old problem. *Proc Assoc Am Physicians.* 1999; 111 (4): 278-282.

[57] Kellett JM. Evolutionary theory for the dichotomy of the functional psychoses. *Lancet.* 1973; 1(7808): 860-863.

[58] Karlsson JL. Inheritance of schizophrenia. *Acta Psychiatr Scand.* 1974; 247(suppl.): 77-88.

[59] Waddell C. Creativity and mental illness: is there a link? *Can J Psychiatry.* 1998; 43: 166-172.

[60] Jeste DV, Harless KA, Palmer BW. Chronic late-onset schizophrenia-like psychosis that remitted: revisiting Newton's psychosis? *Am J Psychiatry.* 2000; 157:3: 444-449.

[61] Andreasen NC, Paradiso S, O'Leary DS. "Cognitive Dysmetria" as an integrative theory of schizophrenia: a dysfunction in cortical-subcortical-cerebellar circuitry? *Schizophr Bull.* 1998; 24(2): 203-211.

[62] Post F. Creativity and psychopathology: a study of 291 world-famous men. *Br J Psychiatry.* 1994; 165: 22-34.

[63] Allen J S, Sarich VM. Schizophrenia in an evolutionary perspective. *Perspect Biol Med.* 1988; 32,1: 132-153.

[64] Horrobin DF. Schizophrenia: the illness that made us human. *Med Hypotheses.* 1998; 50: 269-288.

[65] Horrobin DF. Lipid metabolism, human evolution and schizophrenia. *Prostaglandins, Leukot Essent Fatty Acids.* 1999; 60 (5-6): 431-437.

[66] Fananas L, Bertranpetit J. Reproductive rates in families of schizophrenic patients in a case-control study. *Acta Psychiatr Scand.* 1995; 91(3): 202-204.

[67] Waddington JL, Youssef HA. Familial-genetic and reproductive epidemiology of schizophrenia in rural Ireland: age at onset, familial morbid risk and parental fertility. *Acta Psychiatr Scand.* 1996; 93(1): 62-68.

[68] Srinivasan TN, Padmavati R. Fertility and schizophrenia: evidence for increased fertility in the relatives of schizophrenic patients. *Acta Psychiatr Scand.* 1997; 96(4): 260-264.

[69] Haukka J, Suvisaari J, Lonnqvist J. Fertility of patients with schizophrenia, their siblings, and the general population: a corhort study from 1950-1959 in Finland. *Am J Psychiatry.* 2003; 162(3): 460-463.

[70] Aluoch JR. Higher resistance to Plasmodium falciparum infection in patients with homozygous sickle cell disease in western Kenya. *Trop Med Int Health.* 1997; 2(6): 568-571.

[71] Spyropoulos B. Tay-Sachs carriers and tuberculosis resistance. *Nature.* 1988; 331(6158): 666.

[72] Rodman DM, Zamudio S. The Cystic Fibrosis Heterozygote – Advantage in Surviving Cholera? *Med Hypotheses.* 1991; 36: 253-258.

[73] Wilson DS, Sober E. Reintroducing group selection to the human behavioral sciences. *Behav Brain Sci.* 1994;17: 585-654.

[74] Sober E, Wilson DS. *Unto Others: The Evolution and Psychology of Unselfish Behavior.* Cambridge, Ma: Harvard University Press; 1998.

[75] Stevens A, Price J. *Prophets, Cults, and Madness.* London, UK: Gerald Duckworth & Co. Ltd; 2000.

[76] Polimeni J, Reiss JP. How shamanism and group selection may reveal the origins of schizophrenia. *Med Hypotheses.* 2002; 58(3): 244-248.

[77] Polimeni J, Reiss JP. Evolutionary Perspectives on Schizophrenia. *Can J Psychiatry.* 2003; 48 (1): 34-39.

[78] Wilson EO. *Sociobiology: The New Synthesis.* Cambridge, Ma: Belknap Press; 1975, 2000.

[79] Holldobler B, Wilson EO. *Journey to the Ants: A Story of Scientific Exploration.* Cambridge, Ma: Belknap Press; 1994.

[80] Oldroyd BP, Sylvester HA, Siriwat W, Rinderer TE. Task specialization in a wild bee, Apis florea (Hymenoptera: Apidae), revealed by RFLP banding. *Behav Ecol Sociobiol.* 1994; 34(1): 25-30.
[81] Page RE Jr, Robinson GE. The genetics of division of labor in honey bee colonies. *Advances in Insect Physiology.* 1991; 23: 117-169.
[82] O'Riain MJ, Jarvis JUM, Alexander R, Buffenstein R, Peeters C. Morphological castes in a vertebrate. *Proc Natl Acad Sci U S A.* 2000; 97(24); 13194-13197.
[83] Ridley M. *Evolution.* Cambridge, Ma: Blackwell Science Inc.; 1996.
[84] Wilson DS. *Darwin's Cathedral: Evolution, Religion, and the Nature of Society.* Chicago: The University of Chicago Press; 2002.
[85] Wilson DS, Dugatkin LA. Group selection and assortative interactions. *Am Nat.* 1997; 149(2): 336-351.
[86] Parnas J. Assortative mating in schizophrenia: results from the Copenhagen High-Risk Study. *Psychiatry.* 1988; 51(1): 58-64.
[87] Mathews CA, Reus VI. Assortative mating in the affective disorder: a systematic review and meta-analysis. *Compr Psychiatry.* 2001; 42(4): 257-262.
[88] Bourguignon E. Trance and shamanism: What's in a name? *J Psychoactive Drugs.* 1989; 21(1): 9-15.
[89] Noll R. What has really been learned about shamanism? *J Psychoactive Drugs.* 1989; 21(1): 47-50.
[90] Wright PA. The nature of the shamanistic state of consciousness: a review. *J Psychoactive Drugs.* 1989; 21(1): 25-33.
[91] Winkelman MJ. A cross-cultural study of shamanistic healers. *J Psychoactive Drugs.* 1989; 21 (1): 17-24.
[92] Winkelman MJ. Shamans and other "magico-religious" healers: a cross-cultural study of their origins, nature, and social transformations. *Ethos.* 1990; 18(3): 308-352.
[93] Ackerknecht EH. Psychopathology, Primitive Medicine and Primitive Culture. *Bull Hist Med.* 1943; 14: 30-67.
[94] Silverman J. Shamans and acute schizophrenia. *Am Anthropol.* 1967; 69: 21-31.
[95] Murphy JM. Psychiatric labeling in cross-cultural perspective. *Science.* 1976; 191: 1019-1028.
[96] Stephen M, Suryani LK. Shamanism, Psychosis and Autonomous Imagination. *Cult Med Psychiatry.* 2000; 24(1): 5-40.
[97] Ritchie MA. *Spirit of the Rainforest: A Yanomamo Shaman's Story.* Chicago: Island Lake Press; 1996.
[98] Selzer JA, Lieberman JA. Schizophrenia and Substance Abuse. *Psychiatr Cl North Am.* 1993; 16(2): 401-412.
[99] Degenhardt L, Hall W. Cannabis and psychosis. *Curr Psychiatry Rep.* 2002; 4(3): 191-196.
[100] Bownds DM. *The Biology of Mind.* Bethesda, Md: Fitzgerald Science Press; 1999.
[101] Brewerton T. Hyperreligiosity in psychotic disorders. *J Nerv Ment Dis.* 1994; 182 (5): 302-304.

[102] Maslowski J, Jansen van Rensburg D, Mthoko N. A polydiagnostic approach to the differences in symptoms of schizophrenia in different cultural and ethnic populations. *Acta Psychiatr Scand.* 1998; 98: 41-46.

[103] Vlachos IO, Beratis S, Hartocollis P. Magico-Religious Beliefs and Psychosis. *Psychopathology.* 1997; 30(2): 93-99.

[104] Mithen S. *The Prehistory of the Mind.* London: Thames and Hudson; 1996.

[105] Boyer P. *The Naturalness of Religious Ideas.* Berkeley, Ca: University of California Press; 1994.

[106] Spilka B, Hood, RW, Hunsberger B, Gorsuch R. *The Psychology of Religion: An Empirical Approach.* 3rd ed. New York, NY: Guilford Press; 2003.

[107] Doblin R. Pahnke's "Good Friday Experiment": A Long-Term Follow-Up and Methodological Critique. *The Journal of Transpersonal Psychology.* 1991; 23(1): 1-28.

[108] Borg J, Andree B, Soderstrom H, Farde L. The Serotonin System and Spiritual Experiences. *Am J Psychiatry.* 2003; 160(11): 1965-1969.

[109] Saver JL, Rabin J. The neural substrates of religious experience. *J Neuropsychiatry Clin Neurosci.* 1997; 9(3): 498-510.

[110] Boyer P. *Religion Explained: The Evolutionary Origins of Religious Thought.* New York, NY: Basic Books; 2001.

[111] Bogoraz-Tan VG. *The Chukchee: Material Culture (part 1), Religion (part 2), Social Organization (part 3).* New York, NY: E.J. Brill, Ltd; G.E. Stechert and Co.; 1904 (part 1), 1907 (part 2), 1909 (part 3). As seen in the eHRAF Collection of Ethnography on the Web, (January 7, 2004).

In: Schizophrenia Research Trends
Editor: Konstance V. Almann, pp. 137-161
ISBN 13: 978-1-60021-746-3

Chapter V

LATENT INHIBITION AND LEARNED IRRELEVANCE PARADIGMS: A CONVENIENT WAY TO ASSESS INFORMATION PROCESSING DEFICITS IN SCHIZOPHRENIA

A. Orosz[1,2], *K. Cattapan-Ludewig*[2], *G. Gal*[3], *J. Feldon*[1]
1 Laboratory of Behavioral Biology, ETH Zürich, Switzerland
2 University Hospital of Psychiatry, Bern, Switzerland
3 Mental Health Epidemiology and Psychosocial Aspects of Illness, Gertner Institute for Epidemiology and Health Policy Research, Sheba Medical Center, Tel Hashomer, Israel

ABSTRACT

One of the key features of schizophrenia is the inability to filter out irrelevant stimuli which consequently leads to stimulus overload. There are different paradigms which aim at investigating these deficient filter mechanisms; one of these is latent inhibition (LI). LI refers to the retardation of associative learning that normally occurs when the to-be-conditioned stimulus (CS) is previously preexposed without reinforcement. It is based on a form of selective attention and reflects the ability of normal individuals to ignore irrelevant external and internal stimuli. In schizophrenia, the LI effect is disrupted. This LI disruption is due to faster learning of the CS-US (unconditioned stimulus) association which results in better performance of preexposed schizophrenic subjects compared to healthy controls. Because of this, attenuated LI has become an important tool to model cognitive and attentional deficits in schizophrenia.

In recent studies a newly developed visual learned irrelevance (LIrr) paradigm has been applied. Learned irrelevance is yet another attentional paradigm related to latent inhibition. In contrast to LI, in a LIrr test procedure both the CS and the US are preexposed in an unrelated manner. LIrr has been shown to retard associative learning even more than LI.

In the following chapter the advantages of LI and LIrr, respectively, in schizophrenia research are discussed. Moreover, the differences between the currently applied LI paradigms will be presented as well as the LI modulations in healthy controls, first-episode and chronic schizophrenia patients.

INTRODUCTION

The Core Symptoms of Schizophrenia

Schizophrenia is a very heterogeneous disorder encompassing a variety of different symptoms. These are usually clustered in positive and negative symptoms as well as several cognitive dysfunctions. Cognitive deficits are core symptoms of schizophrenia and serve as specific markers of that disorder. There are various cognitive functions, such as memory, learning, planning and attention, an impairment of which results in the reduced ability to cope with everyday life. The cognitive deficits thought to be the most central to schizophrenia are information processing and attention abnormalities (1-4).

Information Processing and Attentional Deficits

Disturbances in attention and pre-attentive information processing are considered to be key features of schizophrenia (1) and are hypothesized to be strongly associated with its clinical and functional impairments (5-7). Because of these deficits, schizophrenics cannot adequately process sequentially presented stimuli (8) and are therefore vulnerable to be overloaded by external and internal stimuli (9). As a result they suffer from cognitive fragmentation and thought disorder (6;10-12).

The phenomenon of latent inhibition (LI) is based on a form of selective attention which enables normal individuals not to attend to and to filter out irrelevant stimuli (13-15) in order to protect themselves from stimulus overload. Therefore, experiments measuring LI are appropriate to quantify information processing deficits in schizophrenia.

Latent Inhibition

LI refers to the retardation of associative learning, for example classical conditioning – the formation of an association between a conditioned stimulus (CS) and an unconditioned stimulus (US) (Fig. 1) - that normally occurs if the CS is previously preexposed without reinforcement (16;17). Schizophrenic patients fail to show LI. Because of this, disrupted LI has become an important tool to model cognitive and attentional deficits in schizophrenia and might even be treated as a state marker of it (18). Disrupted or reduced LI means that people with schizophrenia learn a CS-US association faster than healthy controls and perform better on the various tasks involved in LI paradigms (19;20). Thus, factors such as general deficits in intellectual ability, medication side effects or lack of motivation of schizophrenia patients can almost be excluded from being responsible for LI disruption, i.e. faster learning following preexposure (19;21).

Another advantageous property of LI is that it can be similarly demonstrated in humans and animals. Actually, LI was first studied in animals of different species (for a review see (22)) and then translated to paradigms which could be performed in humans (23). There are only a few paradigms which can be used in both animals and humans. Such paradigms that can be applied to various species are very useful because the effects of manipulations (e.g. pharmacological, physiological, environmental) can be compared across species and may give clues to elementary questions. Experiments with rats and mice especially allow one to analyze the neural and neurochemical basis of LI and have provided evidence for the central elements in the pathophysiology of schizophrenia (24-28). A thorough investigation of human LI data has led to the conclusion that LI is the same phenomenon in humans and animals, and that the processes underlying LI are analogous across species (17).

How to test LI – the basic procedure

Classical conditioning, also referred to as Pavlovian conditioning, involves learning about the association of two or more stimuli. In a conditioning procedure, the paired presentation of a CS and US leads to a CS-US association in which the CS becomes a signal for the US. Latent inhibition refers to a CS-preexposure effect which results from the non-reinforced presentation of the CS alone prior to the conditioning procedure (Fig. 1). All LI test paradigms share a basic procedure (28) involving two or three distinct stages: preexposure, conditioning and, in some paradimgs, a test phase. As all animal and most human LI paradigms apply a between-subject design, two groups, a "stimulus preexposed" (PE) and a "non-preexposed" (NPE) group, are formed. At the preexposure stage, subjects in the PE group are repeatedly exposed to the CS, which is not followed by any consequences, while subjects in the NPE group do not encounter the CS. When preexposure is completed, all subjects enter into the conditioning stage in which the CS is paired with a reinforcer (US) over a number of trials. The resulting conditioned response (CR), i.e. the rate of conditioning, is quantified either during the conditioning stage, or in a separate test phase in which the CS is presented alone. The LI effect is measured by comparing the performance of the PE to that of the NPE group.

Latent Inhibition in Animals

Animal LI test paradigms

There are three test paradigms commonly used to assess LI in rats and mice. These are conditioned taste aversion (CTA), conditioned emotional response (CER) and two-way active avoidance. Classical eyeblink conditioning is a further paradigm that has a long history of testing the neural substrates of LI and which is predominantly applied to rabbits.

Conditioned taste aversion (CTA)

In CTA, the PE animals are preexposed to water flavored with sucrose (CS), while the NPE animals receive pure water only (29-31). In the conditioning phase, both groups have access to flavored water which is now paired with the US, nausea caused by LiCl injection. LI is measured by the different volume intake of flavored water by the PE and NPE animals in the test phase after conditioning.

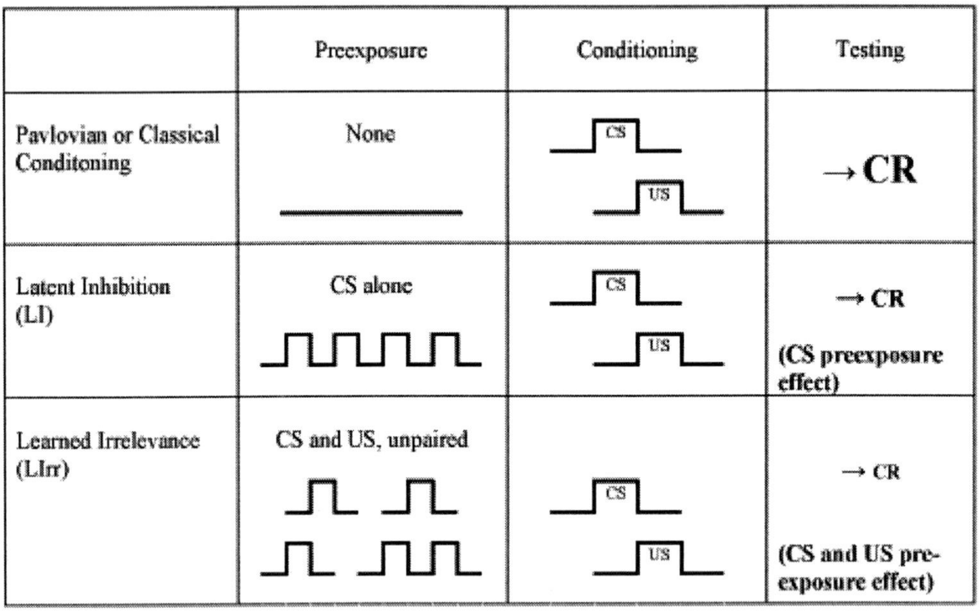

Figure 1: Schematic presentation of the test procedures of Pavlovian conditioning, latent inhibition and learned irrelevance. In Pavlovian conditioning the presentation of a CS is paired with a US, resulting in the learning of a CS-US association. As a consequence, the CS alone elicits a conditioned response (CR) in the test phase which is the same as the natural response to the US alone.
In order to obtain a latent inhibition effect, the CS is preexposed several times prior to the conditioning procedure. Because of the familiarity with the CS, the learning of the CS-US association is retarded and the CR is attenuated. In the preexposure stage of a learned irrelevance test procedure, the US is presented too, but with no correlation to the CS. After conditioning, the learning is even more reduced than in LI.

Conditioned emotional response (CER)

A conditioned emotional response is commonly measured by a conditioned lick suppression procedure (32-34). During the preexposure stage, a tone (CS) is presented several times to the PE animals. In the conditioning phase the tone is presented to both the NPE and the PE group and is paired with a foot shock (US). In the test phase the animals of both groups, which had been all on a water deprivation schedule before, had free access to water. After a specific number of licks, the tone is presented again. The variable of interest is the amount of time that is required to complete a certain number of licks after the onset of the tone. The LI effect is typically quantified by the between-group difference in the suppression ratio computed by A/(A+B), whereby A is the time period before tone onset, and B refers to the period of time needed for a specific number of responses (licks) during tone presentation in the test phase.

Two-way active avoidance

The two-way active - or shuttle - avoidance task is performed in a so-called shuttle box; a box divided in two compartments by a low barrier. Mild electric shocks can be delivered in either compartment through a grid floor. Animals are tested separately, i.e. there is only one animal in the box at any given time. PE animals are placed in the box and preexposed to an auditory (tone) or visual (light) stimulus (CS). During conditioning, the stimulus is paired with a foot shock (US). NPE animals quickly learn to jump over the barrier as soon as the stimulus is presented, in order to avoid the foot shock. As PE animals are retarded in associating the stimulus with the shock, they stay more often or longer in the "dangerous" compartment after CS onset.

Eyeblink conditioning

In a classical eyeblink conditioning procedure a neutral stimulus (CS) such as a tone or light is paired either with an air puff to the cornea or a periorbital electric shock (US) which both elicit a reflexive eyeblink response to protect the cornea (35;36). As a result of CS preexposure, PE animals fail to produce an anticipatory eyeblink response to the CS in the subsequent test phase.

ANIMAL MODELS OF SCHIZOPHRENIA

How to model schizophrenia in animals

As has been previously discussed, LI is important in schizophrenia research because it serves as a measure of deficient information processing. Schizophrenia is a disease restricted to human beings, therefore, it is necessary to induce schizophrenic symptoms in animals in order to perform schizophrenia research. In other words, an animal model of schizophrenia has to be created which can be done pharmacologically, environmentally, developmentally or by lesions of specific brain structures.

The amphetamine animal model of schizophrenia

It has been suggested that the neurotransmitter dopamine (DA) plays a major role both in schizophrenia as well as in the LI phenomenon. Amphetamine, an indirect DA agonist, causes behavioral disturbances in rats which are similar to human psychosis (37-40). In addition, it disrupts latent inhibition (32;41-45) which indicates information processing dysfunctions. Amphetamine has therefore become the preferred drug to mimic schizophrenia (25;46).

Furthermore, amphetamine induced LI disruption can be reversed by both typical (i.e. chloropromazine, haloperidol) and atypical (i.e. clozapine) antipsychotics (47). Moreover, typical as well as atypical antipsychotic drugs (APDs) enhance LI in normal rats when administered on their own (29;32;48).

The switching model

Further investigation aimed to find out at which stage (preexposure or conditioning) amphetamine and APDs exert their effect on LI. As LI is assumed to be a consequence of learned inattention to the preexposed, non-reinforced stimulus, both kinds of drugs were thought to show their impact in the preexposure phase (28). But, Weiner et al. (46;49) reported that rats receiving amphetamine only during preexposure, showed intact LI. Similarly, rats preexposed under haloperidol, while conditioned without it, showed normal LI (50). These results indicate that both kinds of drugs do not act on the ability to learn to ignore irrelevant stimuli during preexposure (28). Rather it seems that they affect the ability to continue to respond to a stimulus as irrelevant as soon as it is reinforced during conditioning. The switching model, formulated by Weiner (47), does not reject the assumption that learning of irrelevance occurs during preexposure. But, it adds that the irrelevance of a stimulus is manifested and expressed during the conditioning stage (28). According to the switching model, a CS-noUS association is learnt in the preexposure stage, whereas the CS-US association is learnt during conditioning (19;28;47). These two associations compete for expression during conditioning (28). Normally, behavior in the conditioning stage is controlled by the CS-noUS association. In order to express the CS-US association, the subject has to *switch* to it from the formerly dominant CS-noUS association (19;28). Applied to the effects of amphetamine and APDs, the switching model proposes that amphetamine disrupts LI by promoting excessive switching of responses, whereas APDs retard it (28).

LI and glutamate

Besides DA, the excitatory neurotransmitter glutamate is also shown to be involved in schizophrenia, as well as in LI. Pharmacological blockade of the NMDA glutamate receptors produces behavioral effects relevant to schizophrenic symptomatology (28;51). Especially negative and cognitive symptoms which express themselves as impairments in social interaction and behavioral inflexibility can be mimicked by NMDA antagonists in rats (51;52). On LI, the NMDA antagonist MK-801 has the opposite effect as amphetamine: it leads to abnormally persistent LI (28;51). The LI effect can be considered as a specific balance between the number of preexposures and conditioning trials. Thus, the LI effect is normally disrupted after a specific number of paired CS-US presentations in the conditioning phase. Applying the switching theory, this occurs as soon as the subject has switched from the CS-noUS to the CS-US association. MK-801 treated rats show persistent LI even after a number of conditioning trials which disrupts LI in normal rats. This indicates that they are still inhibited in expressing the CS-US association. In other words, NMDA antagonists impair the ability to switch between behaviors (53).

The finding that glutamate depletion might be responsible for deficient behavioral switching is in accordance with the theory proposing that NMDA receptor hypofunction is involved in the negative symptomatology of schizophrenia.

LATENT INHIBITION IN HUMANS

Animal LI paradigms applied to humans

Only a few paradigms used to assess LI in animals can be directly transferred to humans. These are CTA and classical eyeblink conditioning. The CTA has been applied to humans using cranberry juice as CS and apomorphine induced nausea as US (54;55). Eyeblink conditioning studies investigating LI in humans have been conducted by several groups (35;56). The basic procedure for humans is the same as that applied to animals, but with a weaker corneal air puff.

Additionally, there is also a modified human paradigm which applies conditioned suppression (57). In this paradigm both the PE and the NPE subjects have to perform the Tower of Toronto puzzle which requires the subjects to arrange four discs in a specific order by translocating them over three vertical pegs. The task is repeated several times in order to achieve a problem-solving routine with constant times per move. After the training trials, the PE, but not the NPE group is preexposed to a pure tone (CS) while completing the puzzle. During the conditioning stage, the CS is paired with a loud burst of white noise (US) for both groups increasing the duration of the hand movement. The LI effect is measured by the different degrees of suppression of ongoing motor activity (time per move) due to the noise burst in the PE compared to the NPE group.

Paradigms designed especially for human LI measurements

In addition to paradigms adopted from animal LI testing procedures, there are some that are designed specially for humans. These are Pavlovian conditioning of autonomic responses (58), instrumental learning to criterion (23;59), and the recently introduced visual LI paradigms (60-62).

Pavlovian conditioning of autonomic responses

In paradigms employing Pavlovian conditioning of autonomic responses, reactions of the autonomic nervous system are measured for LI assessment. The recorded variables are skin conductance, vasomotor activity and heart rate. The conditioning task typically involves a tone as CS and an aversive (electric shock) or non-aversive (reaction time task, noise burst) US (58). Indications of the LI effect are expressed as the differences in the autonomic responses between the subjects of the PE and NPE group during conditioning.

Instrumental learning to criterion

In an instrumental learning to criterion task, the PE group is preexposed to a visual (63) or auditory CS (13;20;23;64;65). In the conditioning stage, this CS becomes the signal for the subjects to respond to, i.e. to perform a specific task (17). Subjects are reinforced when they respond in the presence of the CS. The dependent variable is the CR which is the number of trials to reach criterion, usually constituted by a specific number of consecutive correct (reinforced) responses. LI is measured by the different performance of the PE and the NPE subjects.

Most experiments (13;20;66) using instrumental learning procedures are replications of the experimental setup of Ginton et al. 1975 (23). In the original procedure, the CS, a short burst of white noise, is presented to PE subjects in the preexposure stage, whilst the subjects of the NPE group do not hear such noise bursts. Subsequently, in the conditioning stage, all subjects hear the noise burst which now signals the increment of a score on a counter. All subjects are instructed to decrease this score by pressing a button every time they anticipate that it will rise. If they respond correctly in the presence of the CS, they are reinforced by a decrement of the score. If, however, they respond in the absence of the CS or fail to respond in the presence of the CS, the score is raised. As soon as the subject presses the button several times consecutively during CS presentation, the test is terminated. PE subjects preexposed to the CS are less likely to learn the association between the noise burst and the score increment and need more trials to reach the criterion that indicates a LI effect.

Visual LI paradigms

One of the recently developed LI paradigms (60;67) uses a visual search procedure in which the subjects' task is to search for a unique target shape embedded between a number of homogeneous distractor elements. They are required to indicate the presence or absence of the target by pressing corresponding keys (0= target absent, 1= target present). Later on, the preexposed distractor element becomes the target, while the target serves as a new distractor. In addition to that, novel elements are introduced on occasion and serve first as target and in a later stage as distractor or vice versa.

Preexposure occurs in those trials in which the subject has to look for a target which was a distractor before and which is presented among distractors consisting of a former target shape. NPE trials are those in which a novel target is presented with familiar distractor elements.

In sum, two kinds of CS are involved, preexposed (a target that was a distractor before) and a non-preexposed (novel target) stimuli allowing preexposure and non-preexposure to take place in one and the same individual, i.e. a within-subject study design is applied. The US consists of the target which commands the subjects to respond. As the dependent variable the time to find the target, i.e. the response time (RT) is measured.

In another new visual LI paradigm (61;62) subjects are preexposed to a colored rectangular field that contains six small windows (preexposed "PE-CS"). In the conditioning phase, one of the windows is shaded by a black square which changes its position every trial. The subjects are instructed to try to predict the position of the square (US) by pressing one of six keys which represent the six windows. One specific position is indicated by a field stained with the preexposed color, while another distinct position is predicted by a field of a different color (non-preexposed "NPE-CS"). The remaining four positions are not predicted at all and the black square appears on a blank background. The dependent variables are the CR and the time to predict the black square's position (RT) in the trials with colored (PE and NPE) backgrounds.

Response time as the dependent variable

It is unique that these visual LI paradigms measure the response time (RT) as the dependent variable and not the conditioned response as instrumental learning to criterion paradigms. The conditioned responses (number of correct responses) are measured as well, but they do not indicate a LI effect (61;62). This is thought to be because the associations of the multiple CS and the US are much harder to learn than those in the instrumental learning tasks, e.g. in the paradigm of Ginton et al. (23). In the visual LI paradigms the subjects only scarcely learn the rule underlying the task and, therefore, do not reach the criterion of a specific number of consecutive correct responses. However, it is debatable whether this new generation of paradigms takes us away from those used in animal LI studies. They might make it more difficult to compare and contrast the results obtained with physiological and pharmacological manipulations across species (21).

The masking task

Human LI paradigms can be divided into two groups: paradigms that require a masking task (MT) to produce a LI effect and paradigms that do not. While CTA and Pavlovian conditioning of autonomic responses can obtain a LI effect without an additional task, instrumental learning to criterion as well as eyeblink conditioning and visual LI paradigms need masking (17;58).

A MT is a simple task administered to all subjects in the preexposure phase or in both the preexposure and the conditioning phase. In the frequently replicated paradigm of Ginton et al. (23), the MT involves a recording of a list of nonsense syllables which is played several times to PE as well as NPE subjects during preexposure and conditioning. In the preexposure phase, subjects are instructed to pick one specific syllable and to count how many times it is repeated. For the PE group, the noise bursts (CS) are interspersed with the syllables, while the NPE group hears only the syllables. For both groups the syllables are played also during conditioning, but then the subjects are no longer required to perform the counting task.

Several studies have shown that a MT is necessary to obtain a LI effect in humans (23;56;62;63;68). The original motivation to use a masking task was to reduce the subjects' awareness to the change of stages (56;68), i.e. the transition from the preexposure to the conditioning phase. However, as mentioned in the example above, LI is also obtained if the MT stimuli are presented in the preexposure and the conditioning stage, but the task only has to be completed during preexposure (20;23;66). Moreover, if the MT is applied only during preexposure a LI effect can be yielded as well. (69). These findings suggest that a MT does not affect the transition between phases, but rather the preexposure stage itself (70). Thus, the MT serves to "mask" the significance of the CS and prevents the subjects from focusing their full attention onto the preexposed CS (17). In other words, a masking task consumes attentional resources and therefore allows an attention decline towards the CS (63). Needless to say, a MT has never been necessary to produce LI in non-human animals (17).

The reason why instrumental learning to criterion, conditioned eyeblink and visual LI paradigms need a MT is that the measured responses are outputs of skeletal behaviors which can be voluntarily controlled and modulated by attentional processes (17). On the other hand, LI paradigms applying conditioned autonomic responses or conditioned taste aversion do not require a masking task because they measure more elementary autonomic responses which are involuntary and relatively insensitive to controlled attentional processes (17).

Within-subject and between-subject study designs

All human LI paradimgs presented above, with the exception of the new visual LI paradigms, use a between-subject test paradigm involving a PE and a NPE subject group. The formation of two groups is one of the main problems of a between-subject study design. It requires the recruiting of twice as many subjects than a within-subject study (19) which in turn leads to many problems in matching subjects (71). Another limitation is that a between-subject design cannot provide an individual index of LI for each subject, because only group comparisons can be made (19;71). The urgent need for a within-subject task arose when LI research with patient groups was promoted (71). As LI is assumed to reflect the operation of attentional mechanisms (70;72), its assessment has gained great interest in disorders which show modulation of attention (e.g. schizophrenia, Parkinson's disease, attention deficit hyperactivity disorder, obsessive compulsive disorder) (71).

The advantage of a within-subject study design is that it involves only one group as the same subject undergoes preexposure as well as non-preexposure to a CS. Applying a within-subject task reduces time and effort (58), especially in studies involving patient groups because it is often difficult to recruit and motivate the patients needed for experiments. Moreover, LI can be indexed for each individual. Thus, in clinical populations, the correlations between LI and clinical variables such as symptomatology or medication can be investigated more directly than by applying a between-subject paradigm (21;73).

The metamorphosis of a between-subject LI paradigm

The first attempt to design a within-subject LI experiment was made Lubow and Moore in 1959 in goats and sheep (16). Unfortunately, they obtained only a small LI effect. Subsequently, only between-subject LI experiments were conducted until 1995 when Gray et al. (73) transformed the original between-subject LI paradigm of Ginton et al. (23) to a within-subject procedure. They used two different CSs - a burst of white noise as the preexposed CS (PE-CS) and a tone as the non-preexposed CS (NPE-CS). During preexposure the white noise is presented in the background of the MT (21;73), whereas during conditioning both, the PE-CS and the NPE-CS are paired with the US, which consists of an increment of the score.

Requirements for within-subject LI paradigms

In a within-subject paradigm two different stimuli are used, one for the PE and another one for the NPE condition, instead of two separate groups, as in between-subject studies (18;73). However, there are some factors which have to be considered when replacing a between-subject paradigm with a within-subject LI procedure. Gray et al. (21) elaborated on two major requirements: first, the LI effect has to be of a similar magnitude, regardless which of the two stimuli is preexposed and second, the magnitude of the LI effect obtained by the within-subject paradigm must be comparable to that produced by the corresponding between-subject paradigm. Concurrently, they investigated if the within-subject version of the paradigm of Ginton et al. (23) met these requirements. For this purpose, they compared the LI effect produced by the original between-subject paradigm to that produced by the within-subject variation. In order to support the first requirement, they counterbalanced the two stimuli, i.e. some subjects were preexposed to the white noise, while others were preexposed to the tone. This way it can be investigated if the two stimuli have specific properties which influence the speed of learning. The authors succeeded in showing a similar LI effect with both stimuli as the preexposed CS. Moreover, they were able to show a significant within-subject LI in terms of slower learning of the PE-CS – US association (21). However, the LI effect was notably smaller than the one produced by the corresponding between-subject procedure (21). Consistently, Lubow had reported before that between-subject designs provide larger LI effects (70).

Two different CS – a sticking point

It was speculated that the within-subject LI effect was weaker because the two stimuli were of the same kind (both auditory) and therefore too similar. As a consequence, learning about one stimulus could have facilitated the learning about the other stimulus (21) leading to an overall faster learning. A solution to this problem would be the involvement of stimuli of different modalities, e.g. one auditory, the other visual. But this would in turn raise the issue if they differed in their salience. A stimulus which is more salient than the other is easier conditioned (21). Hence, there is faster learning on salient stimuli.

The new visual LI paradigms introduced above both apply a within-subject design but do not encounter such problems because the task is quite complex - there are several PE- as well as NPE-CS which even change roles within a test session (60;71;74).

Disrupted LI as a Marker of Schizophrenia

Comparable to animals, intoxication with amphetamine elicits psychosis like symptoms (75) and disrupts LI (18;76-79) in healthy human individuals. Additionally, amphetamine also exacerbates psychosis in schizophrenia patients in remission (80). As acute schizophrenia is thought to be primarily due to a current hyperdopaminergic state (20), LI is expected to be absent in acute schizophrenia patients. Actually, there are many studies supporting the notion that LI is disrupted in acute schizophrenics (9;20;73;81;82) while it is robustly present in healthy subjects (76;78). However, there are also findings reporting normal (13;64;65;83) or potentiated (84) LI in schizophrenia.

Concerning antipsychotic drugs, it is assumed that they enhance LI in healthy controls (85). Inconsistently, Williams and colleagues reported that the typical APD haloperidol abolished auditory LI in healthy volunteers (65). This group also found disrupted LI in medicated acute schizophrenics. This result had already been found by Baruch et al. (20) before.

LI is disrupted in acute, but not in chronic schizophrenia

In chronic schizophrenia patients constantly medicated with APDs, LI is suggested to be reinstated (20;58;81). Baruch et al. (20) considered that the difference between acute and chronic schizophrenia is a result of distinct situations of antipsychotic medication. It was shown that LI is also intact in unmedicated and still symptomatic chronic schizophrenia patients (73). It was suggested that illness duration rather than neuroleptic medication is responsible for LI normalization in chronic schizophrenia (73). Support for this is provided by Rascle and collaborators (81) who found enhanced LI in chronic schizophrenia patients. Moreover, they report that the LI effect did not depend on the drug treatment status (drug-free, atypical or typical neuroleptics). Based on these findings, LI disruption might be treated as a state rather than a trait marker of acute schizophrenia (18). Cohen and co-workers (84) suggest that LI stabilization might be correlated with the composition of symptom types. In acute schizophrenia positive symptoms are more prevalent than in chronic schizophrenia. These are attributed to the currently increased DA level (86) which is also responsible for LI disruption. Therefore, the shift of symptomatology away from positive symptoms towards negative symptoms may lead to LI reinstatement in chronic schizophrenia.

It should, however, be pointed out that there are also data showing disrupted LI in chronic schizophrenia regardless of medication or illness duration (83).

Potential confounding factors

However, for the inconsistencies between the results in LI experiments a range of confounding factors might be responsible. First of all, it has to be taken into account that some LI modulations, such as drug effects or the impact of specific symptoms on LI may be task specific (65). Williams et al. (65) obtained different results with the same subjects, depending on whether they used an auditory or a visual LI paradigm.

Second, the fact that the involved patient groups show great differences in illness duration (first-episode, acute or chronic) and/or medication (drug-naive, recent recommencement of medication or constantly medicated) might be an explanation for the heterogeneous results.

Third, it was mentioned above that it is also relevant to the magnitude of the LI effect if a between-subject or within-subject paradigm is used.

LEARNED IRRELEVANCE

A phenomenon closely related to LI

There is a phenomenon closely related to LI called learned irrelevance (LIrr). In contrast to LI, LIrr is obtained by the uncorrelated preexposure of both the CS and the US (Fig. 1). Thus, the only difference between LI and LIrr is that in a LIrr paradigm the US is also presented during preexposure. In this context it is important to note that the presentation of the US alone in the preexposure phase is also able to retard learning of the CS-US association during conditioning (87-89). This latter phenomenon is known as the US preexposure effect. It has been the subject of many animal studies to find out whether LIrr is simply the sum of LI (CS preexposure effect) and the US preexposure effect or whether it is a phenomenon in its own right (90-96).

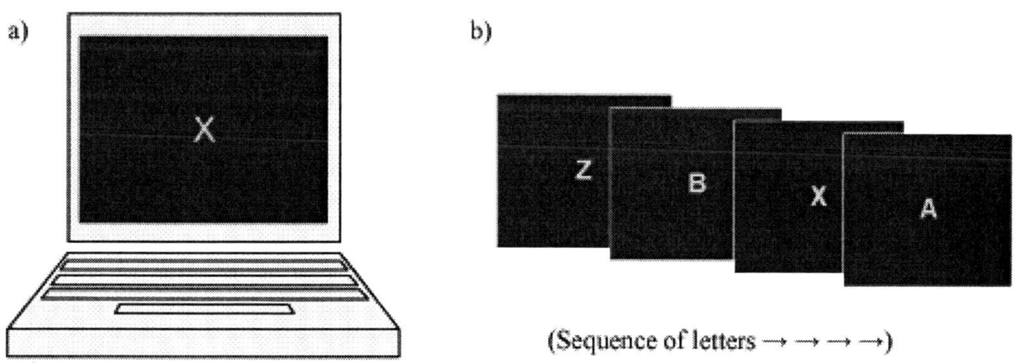

Figure 2: a) A schematic presentation of the LIrr test set-up. Latin letters are presented in yellow on a blue background. b) Letters change in a one second rate without any inter-trial intervals. "X" is the target and, in this example, "B" is the preceding CS.

LIrr retards associative learning more than LI

Baker and Mackintosh (91) conditioned rats to lick water in the presence of a tone after various types of preexposure: water alone (US), tone alone (CS), and uncorrelated presentations of tone and water. They found that the effect of unpaired CS and US presentation was dramatically stronger in retarding subsequent conditioning than the preexposure of either CS or US alone (92). There are further studies showing that the retardation of learning resulting from LIrr is stronger than that produced by LI (35;90;94;97). A potential explanation for the stronger learning retardation by LIrr is based on the theory of context dependence of LI (92;96). It has been shown that the LI effect is context dependent (70). This means that if the preexposure and the conditioning take place in different contexts, LI might be reduced or even abolished (98). These contexts can be spatial (test room, environment) or temporal (time of day) (30). In a basic LI procedure the context changes between the preexposure and the conditioning phase, as in the latter phase the US is presented, while in the former it is not (19). This change of context might contribute to LI reduction. In contrast, in LIrr paradigms the US is part of the context in which the preexposure takes place (19) and it is also presented during conditioning. Thus, there is no context change what might produce a stronger LI effect. However, this would mean that LIrr and LI are the same phenomenon (19;99).

LIrr paradigms might be more sensitive for individual variables

Regardless of whether LIrr constitutes a separate phenomenon, it is definitively worthwhile to introduce LIrr in psychiatric research. It is assumed that LIrr might produce stronger effects than LI in humans as well (35) and can be therefore useful in situations where LI tasks have produced results which are difficult to interpret (19). Moreover, Young et al. (97) revealed in a fMRI study that brain activity during a LIrr paradigm overlaps the regions which are activated by a LI paradigm. These findings indicate that results obtained by LIrr paradigms can be compared with those produced with LI paradigms (19) and might deliver supplementary or complementary insights into the underlying mechanisms.

A Novel Continuous within-Subject LIrr Paradigm

The essential in a nutshell

In a handful recent studies (97;100) a new within-subject LIrr paradigm (developed by A.M. Young and coworkers) has been applied. The paradigm has been further adapted by G. Gal (101; 102). It is a short and simple computerized visual letter recognition task and is therefore manageable even for pathological groups. The pioneering properties of this new test are: first, it does not require a masking task, second, it is continuous, i.e. preexposure and conditioning have not to be performed separately, and third, it allows repeated measurements (102).

As it is characteristic for a within-subject LI paradigm, this LIrr task also involves two different kinds of CSs, preexposed CSs (PE-CS) and non-preexposed CSs (NPE-CS).

General description

The paradigm involves a visual target detecting task in which the subject is instructed to press a key on the computer keyboard as soon as the target, the letter X, appears on the screen. In addition to the target, there are 10 different characters constituting the test. These non-target characters are divided in two groups, NPE and PE, containing five capital Latin letters each. In the studies of Orosz et al. the five vowels (A, E, I, O and U) are assigned to be the NPE letters, while a selection of five consonants (B, D, T, Y and Z) form the PE character group (101; 102).

All characters are yellow and are presented on a blue background which covers the entire computer screen (Fig. 2). The letters are all of the same size and are positioned in the center of the screen. Each letter persists for one second and changes directly without any interstimulus interval to the subsequent characters. A test session consists of 450 letters, hence the test duration is 450 seconds which is equal to 7.5 minutes.

Composition of a test session

There are 75 targets in a test session which are presented according to the schedules of three different conditions. These are preexposed (PE), non-preexposed (NPE) and random (R). The three conditions, in turn, are segmented in five blocks each. Thus, there is a total of 15 blocks in a test session. Regardless of the condition, all blocks contain 30 characters: five targets, 5 CSs, and 20 filler letters. Depending on the condition, the CS letters consist of characters from either the NPE or the PE group and they are always presented immediately before the target. Because of their specific role they are also called target predictor letters or cues. Filler letters consist of characters of the PE group shown in a pseudorandom order. They serve to “fill” the intertrial intervals between the CS-target contingencies. On average, there are four filler letters between a target and the next CS, whereas the range is between one and eight. Filler letters never predict the target.

While the target and the filler letters always involve the same characters, the predictor letters (CSs) are different across the three conditions (Fig. 3):

NPE

In the NPE condition, letters of the NPE group (A, E, I, O and U) serve as CSs. In a NPE block the target is preceded five times by the same NPE-CS, e.g. five times by A. Each letter is used only in one block as target predictor in a test session. Consequently, the five different letters of the NPE group are distributed to the five NPE blocks. Note that NPE letters appear only as target predictors in the NPE blocks and are not presented elsewhere in the test.

PE

In the PE condition blocks, PE letters (B, D, T, Y and Z) act as CS. Comparable to the NPE condition, in the PE condition, each letter of the PE group predicts the target five consecutive times in one particular block.

R

For the CSs in R, also letters of the PE group are used. But, unlike in the PE condition, in R, the target is preceded five times by a different PE letter. This means that every PE letter appears once in each of the five R blocks in a test session. In an R block, the target is predicted once by each of the five PE letters. (Remember that in a PE block one particular PE letter is presented five times before the target)

In summary, letters of the PE character group are used for three different purposes: first, as CS in the PE condition, second, as the CS in the R condition and, third, as filler letters.

R block: **Y B X T D Z B Z T D X Y D Y Z X T B T Y X Z B D B Y T X Z D**

PE block: **Z D X B T Y Z T B D X Y B Z Y T D X B Z D X Y T B Z T D X Y**

NPE block: **T I X D B Y Z D Y I X T Y I X B D Z B T I X Y Z D I X Z B T**

Black: randomly presented PE-letters (filler letters)
Red: target
Light green: target predictor, PE (D) or NPE (I)

Figure 3: Examples of blocks of the three different conditions. PE letters are B, D, T, Y, and Z, whereas NPE letters are constituted by A, E, I, O, and U. In an R block, the target "X" is preceded once by each PE letter. In this example of a PE block, the PE-CS "D" predicts the target five times. In the NPE block presented in this example, NPE letter "I" serves as target predictor. There are four more R, PE and NPE blocks in a test session. R blocks are similar throughout the session, while the PE and the NPE blocks use the remaining four PE and NPE letters as target predictors.

Thus, the 450 letters of a test session are composed of a total of 75 targets, 25 NPE characters and 350 PE letters which serve as PE-CS (25), R-CS (25) and filler letters (300).

Blocks

The blocks of the three different conditions alternate in a pseudorandom order, whereby the first block of a test session is always an R-block and blocks of the same condition are never presented successively. The order of the blocks is conserved: R, PE, NPE, R, NPE, PE, R, PE, NPE, R, NPE, PE, R, PE, NPE.

The task

The subjects are told that they are going to perform a reaction time task and that they have to press a certain key as quickly as they can when the target appears. They are instructed to observe the other letters as well, because they might give hints on the appearance of the target. For an accurate completion of the test, subjects are required, at least rudimentary, to learn associations between the CS letters and the target. The dependent variable is the reaction time (in ms) to the target, i.e. the time measured between the target onset and the pressing of the key. Differences in reaction times across the condition blocks indicate the degree of learning in the specific conditions.

The LIrr effect

In case of LIrr, performance on the reaction time task is the fastest in the NPE, relatively slower in the PE and the slowest in the R condition blocks. There are total of 25 NPE letters surrounded by 350 PE letters in a test session. Therefore, NPE letters attract more attention than the letters of the PE group which can be seen regularly throughout the test. Moreover, subjects learn that NPE letters always predict the target. As a consequence, they are more attentive when a NPE-CS appears and are already prepared to respond before the target is presented.

The formation of an equivalent association between PE-CSs and the target is reduced. The reasons are the R blocks as well as the filler letters. In the R blocks, the target seems to appear without any rules as it is predicted five times by a different letter of the PE group. Thus, in the R blocks the subjects learn that PE characters are not necessarily followed by the target (unlike NPE letters). Moreover, filler letters which consist of PE letters are never succeeded by the target.

However, as in a PE block the target is preceded five times by the same PE-CS, subjects begin to learn the association between the current PE-CS and the target. That is why the reaction times become lower within the PE blocks and are on average lower than in the R. But, the formation of an association, as with NPE-CSs, is disrupted for the PE characters because of the repeated occurrence of the R blocks and the filler letters.

Advantages of the new test

Because of the complexity of the task - the rule underlying the X appearance is impossible to learn - no masking task is required to divert the subjects' attention from the CS. Furthermore, it is also because of the complexity that repeated measurements can be carried out. Subjects do not learn the rule underlying the task and thereforc they cannot apply it to possible follow-up testing.

RESULTS OBTAINED BY THIS NEW LIRR PARADIGM

LIrr in first-episode and acute schizophrenia

To date, there are two published reports (97;100) and an abstract (101) of studies that apply the new LIrr paradigm ((97; 100):version of A.M.Young, (101): version of G.Gal) to healthy controls as well as schizophrenia patients. All groups yielded robust LIrr in healthy control subjects. Concerning the patient groups, there were some differences between the studies.

Young and collaborators found disrupted LIrr in acute schizophrenia patients who were drug-free or within 14 days of recommencement of antipsychotic treatment. As comparable results were produced by LI experiments (20;60;73;81), they reasoned that very similar processes may underlie the phenomena of LI and LIrr (97). Furthermore, the found in their fMRI study that the LIrr paradigm gives rise to activation in brain areas, e.g. the hippocampal formation, which has been shown to be activated also in LI experiments (97).

In addition, Gal and coworkers (100) and the group of Orosz (101) tested never medicated first-episode acute schizophrenia patients in order to investigate if disrupted LIrr is already present at the onset of the illness. Both research groups measured disrupted LIrr endorsing the paradigm to be a reliable tool to assess attentional dysfunctions in acute schizophrenia.

LIrr in Chronic Schizophrenia

However, there were some conflicting outcomes concerning the performance of chronic schizophrenia patients. While Gal and colleagues (100) reported disrupted LIrr also in chronic schizophrenia patients, Young et al. (97) failed to show any learning of the CS-US association under either PE or NPE conditions. Young at al. have interpreted these findings as the result of a general failure of associative learning as it was already reported by Martins et al. (83). However, various LI studies have shown that LI is reinstated in chronic schizophrenia (20;58;73). It has to be noted that the chronic schizophrenia patients involved in the Gal et al. (100) study were tested during an acute phase, whereas the patients of Young et al. (97) were in a stable "steady" state. Thus, the LIrr disruption measured by Gal et al. might be due to the current acute phase. This might indicate that, as LI disruption (18), LIrr abolition might be seen as a state marker of acute schizophrenia. On the other hand, the failure of the LIrr paradigm to detect possible slight modulations of associative learning in chronic schizophrenia could also be a limitation on the applicability of this new paradigm which is more useful in studies of acute schizophrenia (97).

Conclusion

LIrr paradigms are appropriate to assess information processing deficits in schizophrenia

Latent inhibition has become an important concept in schizophrenia research in animals as well as in humans. To date, several human LI studies have been carried out, but have yielded conflicting results and have been afflicted with various methodological problems.

The new LIrr paradigm introduced in this chapter seems to offer a useful tool to assess associative and attentional learning deficits in humans. It offers many advantages and achievements compared to the commonly used LI paradigms: the task is short, simple and continuous and the paradigm is within-subject. Moreover, no masking task is required and it is possible to test the same subject repeatedly. Last but not least, there is also a variation of the test paradigm which is suitable for fMRI (97).

As LIrr is very closely related to LI, it has been expected that the same results are obtained by this LIrr paradigm as by previous LI experiments. Indeed, studies applying the LIrr paradigm produced the same results with healthy controls and acute and first-episode schizophrenia patients as a predominant number of former LI studies. But there are inconsistencies concerning the findings in chronic schizophrenia, indicating the necessity of further investigation. Possible confounding factors are differences in medication, illness duration and symptomatology. Furthermore, it must be taken into consideration that schizophrenia patients might not understand or might be incapable of following the instructions which are necessary to obtain a LIrr effect.

Although the necessity of the instructions is a limitation, the LIrr paradigm provides many results which are similar to those obtained by LI paradigms, indicating that LIrr can be equally used in schizophrenia research.

References

[1] Nuechterlein KH, Dawson ME. Information processing and attentional functioning in the developmental course of schizophrenic disorders. *Schizophr Bull* 1984; 10(2):160-203.

[2] Braff DL, Swerdlow NR. Neuroanatomy of schizophrenia. *Schizophr Bull* 1997; 23(3):509-512.

[3] Gray JA, Feldon J, Rawlins JNP, Hemsley DR, Smith AD. The neuropsychology of schizophrenia. *Behav Brain Sci* 1991; 14:1-84.

[4] Perry W, Braff DL. Information-processing deficits and thought disorder in schizophrenia. *Am J Psychiatry* 1994; 151(3):363-367.

[5] Braff DL. Psychophysiological and information processing approaches to schizophrenia. In: Charney DS, Nestler E, Bunney BS, editors. *Neurobiological Foundation of Mental Illness.* New York: Oxford University Press, 1999: 258-271.

[6] McGhie A, Chapman J. Disorders of attention and perception in early schizophrenia. *Br J Med Psychol* 1961; 34:103-116.

[7] Green MF. What are the functional consequences of neurocognitive deficits in schizophrenia? *Am J Psychiatry* 1996; 153(3):321-330.

[8] Geyer MA, Swerdlow NR, Mansbach RS, Braff DL. Startle response models of sensorimotor gating and habituation deficits in schizophrenia. *Brain Res Bull* 1990; 25(3):485-498.

[9] Vaitl D, Lipp O, Bauer U, Schuler G, Stark R, Zimmermann M et al. Latent inhibition and schizophrenia: Pavlovian conditioning of autonomic responses. *Schizophr Res* 2002; 55(1-2):147-158.

[10] Braff DL, Geyer MA. Sensorimotor gating and schizophrenia. Human and animal model studies. *Arch Gen Psychiatry* 1990; 47(2):181-188.

[11] Perry W, Geyer MA, Braff DL. Sensorimotor gating and thought disturbance measured in close temporal proximity in schizophrenic patients. *Arch Gen Psychiatry* 1999; 56(3):277-281.

[12] Venables PH. The effects of auditory and visual stimulation on the skin potential response of schizophrenics. *Brain* 1960; 83:77-92.

[13] Leumann L, Feldon J, Vollenweider FX, Ludewig K. Effects of typical and atypical antipsychotics on prepulse inhibition and latent inhibition in chronic schizophrenia. *Biol Psychiatry* 2002; 52(7):729-739.

[14] Bleuler E. Dementia praecox oder die Gruppe der Schizophrenien. In: Achaffenburg G, editor. Handbuch der Psychiatrie. Leipzig, Wien: Franz Deuticke Verlag, 1911.

[15] Braff DL. Information processing and attention dysfunctions in schizophrenia. *Schizophr Bull* 1993; 19(2):233-259.

[16] Lubow RE, MOORE AU. Latent inhibition: the effect of nonreinforced pre-exposure to the conditional stimulus. *J Comp Physiol Psychol* 1959; 52:415-419.

[17] Lubow RE, Gewirtz JC. Latent inhibition in humans: data, theory, and implications for schizophrenia. *Psychol Bull* 1995; 117(1):87-103.

[18] Swerdlow NR, Stephany N, Wasserman LC, Talledo J, Sharp R, Auerbach PP. Dopamine agonists disrupt visual latent inhibition in normal males using a within-subject paradigm. *Psychopharmacology (Berl)* 2003; 169(3-4):314-320.

[19] Gray NS, Snowden RJ. The relevance of irrelevance to schizophrenia. *Neurosci Biobehav Rev* 2005; 29(6):989-999.

[20] Baruch I, Hemsley DR, Gray JA. Differential performance of acute and chronic schizophrenics in a latent inhibition task. *J Nerv Ment Dis* 1988; 176(10):598-606.

[21] Gray NS, Snowden RJ, Peoples M, Hemsley DR, Gray JA. A demonstration of within-subjects latent inhibition in the human: limitations and advantages. *Behav Brain Res* 2003; 138(1):1-8.

[22] Lubow RE. Latent inhibition. *Psychol Bull* 1973; 79(6):398-407.

[23] Ginton A, Urca G, Lubow RE. The effects of preexposure to a nonattended stimulus on subsequent learning: Latent inhibition in adults. *Bull Psychonomic Soc* 1975; 5:5-8.

[24] Weiner I, Feldon J. The switching model of latent inhibition: an update of neural substrates. *Behav Brain Res* 1997; 88(1):11-25.

[25] Gray JA, Moran PM, Grigoryan G, Peters SL, Young AM, Joseph MH. Latent inhibition: the nucleus accumbens connection revisited. *Behav Brain Res* 1997; 88(1):27-34.

[26] Gray JA, Joseph MH, Hemsley DR, Young AM, Warburton EC, Boulenguez P et al. The role of mesolimbic dopaminergic and retrohippocampal afferents to the nucleus accumbens in latent inhibition: implications for schizophrenia. *Behav Brain Res* 1995; 71(1-2):19-31.
[27] Moser PC, Hitchcock JM, Lister S, Moran PM. The pharmacology of latent inhibition as an animal model of schizophrenia. *Brain Res Brain Res Rev* 2000; 33(2-3):275-307.
[28] Weiner I. The "two-headed" latent inhibition model of schizophrenia: modeling positive and negative symptoms and their treatment. *Psychopharmacology (Berl)* 2003; 169(3-4):257-297.
[29] Russig H, Kovacevic A, Murphy CA, Feldon J. Haloperidol and clozapine antagonise amphetamine-induced disruption of latent inhibition of conditioned taste aversion. *Psychopharmacology (Berl)* 2003; 170(3):263-270.
[30] Moron I, Manrique T, Molero A, Ballesteros MA, Gallo M, Fenton A. The contextual modulation of conditioned taste aversions by the physical environment and time of day is similar. *Learn Mem* 2002; 9(5):218-223.
[31] Ellenbroek BA, Knobbout DA, Cools AR. The role of mesolimbic and nigrostriatal dopamine in latent inhibition as measured with the conditioned taste aversion paradigm. *Psychopharmacology (Berl)* 1997; 129(2):112-120.
[32] Weiner I, Shadach E, Tarrasch R, Kidron R, Feldon J. The latent inhibition model of schizophrenia: further validation using the atypical neuroleptic, clozapine. *Biol Psychiatry* 1996; 40(9):834-843.
[33] Lawrence NS, Sharp T, Peters SP, Gray JA, Young AM. GABA transmission in the ventral pallidum is not involved in the control of latent inhibition in the rat. *Neuroscience* 2003; 122(1):267-275.
[34] Carlton PL, Vogel JR. Habituation and conditioning. *J Comp Physiol Psychol* 1967; 63(2):348-351.
[35] Allen MT, Chelius L, Masand V, Gluck MA, Myers CE, Schnirman G. A comparison of latent inhibition and learned irrelevance pre-exposure effects in rabbit and human eyeblink conditioning. *Integr Physiol Behav Sci* 2002; 37(3):188-214.
[36] Gormezano I, Schneiderman N, Deaux E, Fuentes I. Nictitating membrane: classical conditioning and extinction in the albino rabbit. *Science* 1962; 138:33-34.
[37] Angrist B, Sathananthan G, Wilk S, Gershon S. Amphetamine psychosis: behavioral and biochemical aspects. *J Psychiatr Res* 1974; 11:13-23.
[38] Angrist B, Rotrosen J, Gershon S. Responses to apomorphine, amphetamine, and neuroleptics in schizophrenic subjects. *Psychopharmacology (Berl)* 1980; 67(1):31-38.
[39] Janowsky DS, Davis JM. Methylphenidate, dextroamphetamine, and levamfetamine. Effects on schizophrenic symptoms. *Arch Gen Psychiatry* 1976; 33(3):304-308.
[40] Hall RC, Popkin MK, Beresford TP, Hall AK. Amphetamine psychosis: clinical presentations and differential diagnosis. *Psychiatr Med* 1988; 6(1):73-79.
[41] Killcross AS, Robbins TW. Differential effects of intra-accumbens and systemic amphetamine on latent inhibition using an on-baseline, within-subject conditioned suppression paradigm. *Psychopharmacology (Berl)* 1993; 110(4):479-489.

[42] Bakshi VP, Geyer MA, Taaid N, Swerdlow NR. A comparison of the effects of amphetamine, strychnine and caffeine on prepulse inhibition and latent inhibition. *Behav Pharmacol* 1995; 6(8):801-809.

[43] Moran PM, Fischer TR, Hitchcock JM, Moser PC. Effects of clozapine on latent inhibition in the rat. *Behav Pharmacol* 1996; 7(1):42-48.

[44] Weiner I, Bernasconi E, Broersen LM, Feldon J. Amphetamine-induced disruption of latent inhibition depends on the nature of the stimulus. *Behav Pharmacol* 1997; 8(5):442-457.

[45] Weiner I, Tarrasch R, Bernasconi E, Broersen LM, Ruttimann TC, Feldon J. Amphetamine-induced disruption of latent inhibition is not reinforcer-mediated. *Pharmacol Biochem Behav* 1997; 56(4):817-826.

[46] Weiner I, Lubow RE, Feldon J. Disruption of latent inhibition by acute administration of low doses of amphetamine. *Pharmacol Biochem Behav* 1988; 30(4):871-878.

[47] Weiner I. Neural substrates of latent inhibition: the switching model. *Psychol Bull* 1990; 108(3):442-461.

[48] Solomon PR, Crider A, Winkelman JW, Turi A, Kamer RM, Kaplan LJ. Disrupted latent inhibition in the rat with chronic amphetamine or haloperidol-induced supersensitivity: relationship to schizophrenic attention disorder. *Biol Psychiatry* 1981; 16(6):519-537.

[49] Weiner I, Lubow RE, Feldon J. Abolition of the expression but not the acquisition of latent inhibition by chronic amphetamine in rats. *Psychopharmacology (Berl)* 1984; 83(2):194-199.

[50] Weiner I, Feldon J, Katz Y. Facilitation of the expression but not the acquisition of latent inhibition by haloperidol in rats. *Pharmacol Biochem Behav* 1987; 26(2):241-246.

[51] Gaisler-Salomon I, Weiner I. Systemic administration of MK-801 produces an abnormally persistent latent inhibition which is reversed by clozapine but not haloperidol. *Psychopharmacology (Berl)* 2003; 166(4):333-342.

[52] Moghaddam B, Adams B, Verma A, Daly D. Activation of glutamatergic neurotransmission by ketamine: a novel step in the pathway from NMDA receptor blockade to dopaminergic and cognitive disruptions associated with the prefrontal cortex. *J Neurosci* 1997; 17(8):2921-2927.

[53] Carlsson M, Carlsson A. The NMDA antagonist MK-801 causes marked locomotor stimulation in monoamine-depleted mice. *J Neural Transm* 1989; 75(3):221-226.

[54] Arwas S, Rolnick A, Lubow RE. Conditioned taste aversion in humans using motion-induced sickness as the US. *Behav Res Ther* 1989; 27(3):295-301.

[55] Cannon DS, Best MR, Batson JD, Feldman M. Taste familiarity and apomorphine-induced taste aversions in humans. *Behav Res Ther* 1983; 21(6):669-673.

[56] Schnur P, Ksir CJ. Latent inhibition in human eyelid conditioning. *J Exp Psychol* 1969; 80(2):388-389.

[57] Salgado JV, Vidal M, Oberling P, Graeff FG, Danion JM, Sandner G. Associative learning and latent inhibition in a conditioned suppression paradigm in humans. *Behav Brain Res* 2000; 117(1-2):53-60.

[58] Vaitl D, Lipp OV. Latent inhibition and autonomic responses: a psychophysiological approach. *Behav Brain Res* 1997; 88(1):85-93.

[59] Lubow RE, Ingberg-Sachs N, Zalstein-Orda N, Gerwirtz JC. Latent inhibition in low and high "psychotic-prone" normal subjects. *Pers Indiv Diff* 1992; 13:563-572.

[60] Lubow RE, Kaplan O, Abramovich P, Rudnick A, Laor N. Visual search in schizophrenia: latent inhibition and novel pop-out effects. *Schizophr Res* 2000; 45(1-2):145-156.

[61] Lubow RE, De la CG. Latent inhibition as a function of schizotypality and gender: implications for schizophrenia. *Biol Psychol* 2002; 59(1):69-86.

[62] De la Casa LG, Lubow RE. Latent inhibition with a response time measure from a within-subject design: effects of number of preexposures, masking task, context change, and delay. *Neuropsychology* 2001; 15(2):244-253.

[63] Braunstein-Bercovitz H, Lubow RE. Are high-schizotypal normal participants distractible or limited in attentional resources? A study of latent inhibition as a function of masking task load and schizotypy level. *J Abnorm Psychol* 1998; 107(4):659-670.

[64] Swerdlow NR, Braff DL, Hartston H, Perry W, Geyer MA. Latent inhibition in schizophrenia. *Schizophr Res* 1996; 20(1-2):91-103.

[65] Williams JH, Wellman NA, Geaney DP, Cowen PJ, Feldon J, Rawlins JN. Reduced latent inhibition in people with schizophrenia: an effect of psychosis or of its treatment. *Br J Psychiatry* 1998; 172:243-249.

[66] Lubow RE, Weiner I, Schlossberg A, Baruch I. Latent inhibition and schizophrenia. *Bull Psychonomic Soc* 1987; 25:464-467.

[67] Lubow RE, Kaplan O. Visual search as a function of type of prior experience with target and distractor. *J Exp Psychol Hum Percept Perform* 1997; 23(1):14-24.

[68] Spence KW. Cognitive and drive factors in the extinction of the conditioned eye blink in human subjects. *Psychol Rev* 1966; 73(5):445-458.

[69] Lubow RE, Caspy T, Schnur P. Latent inhibition and learned helplessness in children: Similarities and differences. *Journal of Experimental Child Psychology* 1982; 34:231-256.

[70] Lubow RE. *Latent inhibition and condition attention theory.* New York: Cambridge University Press, 1989.

[71] Lubow RE. Latent inhibition as a measure of learned inattention: some problems and solutions. *Behav Brain Res* 1997; 88(1):75-83.

[72] Pearce JM, Hall G. A model for Pavlovian learning: variations in the effectiveness of conditioned but not of unconditioned stimuli. *Psychol Rev* 1980; 87(6):532-552.

[73] Gray NS, Pilowsky LS, Gray JA, Kerwin RW. Latent inhibition in drug naive schizophrenics: relationship to duration of illness and dopamine D2 binding using SPET. *Schizophr Res* 1995; 17(1):95-107.

[74] Lubow RE, Dressler R, Kaplan O. The effects of target and distractor familiarity on visual search in de novo Parkinson's disease patients: latent inhibition and novel pop-out. *Neuropsychology* 1999; 13(3):415-423.

[75] Lieberman JA, Kane JM, Alvir J. Provocative tests with psychostimulant drugs in schizophrenia. *Psychopharmacology (Berl)* 1987; 91(4):415-433.

[76] Thornton JC, Dawe S, Lee C, Capstick C, Corr PJ, Cotter P et al. Effects of nicotine and amphetamine on latent inhibition in human subjects. *Psychopharmacology (Berl)* 1996; 127(2):164-173.

[77] Salgado JV, Hetem LA, Vidal M, Graeff FG, Danion JM, Sandner G. Reduction of latent inhibition by D-amphetamine in a conditioned suppression paradigm in humans. *Behav Brain Res* 2000; 117(1-2):61-67.

[78] Gray NS, Pickering AD, Hemsley DR, Dawling S, Gray JA. Abolition of latent inhibition by a single 5 mg dose of d-amphetamine in man. *Psychopharmacology (Berl)* 1992; 107(2-3):425-430.

[79] Kumari V, Cotter PA, Mulligan OF, Checkley SA, Gray NS, Hemsley DR et al. Effects of d-amphetamine and haloperidol on latent inhibition in healthy male volunteers. *J Psychopharmacol* 1999; 13(4):398-405.

[80] Janowsky DS, el Yousel MK, Davis JM, Sekerke HJ. Provocation of schizophrenic symptoms by intravenous administration of methylphenidate. *Arch Gen Psychiatry* 1973; 28(2):185-191.

[81] Rascle C, Mazas O, Vaiva G, Tournant M, Raybois O, Goudemand M et al. Clinical features of latent inhibition in schizophrenia. *Schizophr Res* 2001; 51(2-3):149-161.

[82] Gray NS, Hemsley DR, Gray JA. Abolition of latent inhibition in acute, but not chronic schizophrenia. *Neurol Psychiatr Brain Res* 1992; 1:83-89.

[83] Martins SA, Jones SH, Toone B, Gray JA. Impaired associative learning in chronic schizophrenics and their first-degree relatives: a study of latent inhibition and the Kamin blocking effect. *Schizophr Res* 2001; 48(2-3):273-289.

[84] Cohen E, Sereni N, Kaplan O, Weizman A, Kikinzon L, Weiner I et al. The relation between latent inhibition and symptom-types in young schizophrenics. *Behav Brain Res* 2004; 149(2):113-122.

[85] Williams JH, Wellman NA, Geaney DP, Cowen PJ, Feldon J, Rawlins JN. Antipsychotic drug effects in a model of schizophrenic attentional disorder: a randomized controlled trial of the effects of haloperidol on latent inhibition in healthy people. *Biol Psychiatry* 1996; 40(11):1135-1143.

[86] Laruelle M, Abi-Dargham A, Gil R, Kegeles L, Innis R. Increased dopamine transmission in schizophrenia: relationship to illness phases. *Biol Psychiatry* 1999; 46(1):56-72.

[87] Kremer EF. Truly random and traditional control procedures in CER conditioning in thc rat. *J Comp Physiol Psychol* 1971; 76(3):441-448.

[88] Randich A, LoLordo VM. Associative and nonassociative theories of the UCS preexposure phenomenon: implications for Pavlovian conditioning. *Psychol Bull* 1979; 86(3):523-548.

[89] Meyer U, Chang dL, Feldon J, Yee BK. Expression of the CS- and US-pre-exposure effects in the conditioned taste aversion paradigm and their abolition following systemic amphetamine treatment in C57BL6/J mice. *Neuropsychopharmacology* 2004; 29(12):2140-2148.

[90] Bennett CH, Maldonado A, Mackintosh NJ. Learned irrelevance is not the sum of exposure to CS and US. Q *J Exp Psychol* B 1995; 48(2):117-128.

[91] Baker AG, Mackintosh NJ. Excitatory and inhibitory conditions following uncorrelated presentations of CS and US. *Animal Learning and Behavior* 1977; 5:315-319.

[92] Baker AG, Mackintosh NJ. Preexposure to the CS alone, US alone, or CS and US uncorrelated: Latent Inhibition, blocking by context, or learned irrelevance? *Learning and Motivation* 1979; 10:278-294.

[93] Bonardi C, Yann OS. Learned irrelevance: a contemporary overview. Q *J Exp Psychol* B 2003; 56(1):80-89.

[94] Matzel LD, Schachtman TR, Miller RR. Learned irrelevance exceeds the sum of CS-preexposure and US-preexposure deficits. *Journal of Experimental Psychology* 1988; *Animal Behavior Processes* 14:311-319.

[95] Bennett CH, Wills SJ, Oakeshott SM, Mackintosh NJ. Is the context specificity of latent inhibition a sufficient explanation of learned irrelevance? Q *J Exp Psychol* B 2000; 53(3):239-253.

[96] Bonardi C, Hall G. Learned irrelevance: no more than the sum of CS and US preexposure effects? *Journal of Experimental Psychology* 1996; *Animal Behavior Processes* 22:183-191.

[97] Young AM, Kumari V, Mehrotra R, Hemsley DR, Andrew C, Sharma T et al. Disruption of learned irrelevance in acute schizophrenia in a novel continuous within-subject paradigm suitable for fMRI. *Behav Brain Res* 2005; 156(2):277-288.

[98] Lipp O. *Latente Inhibition: Hemmung klassisch konditionierter autonomer Reaktionen durch Vorerfahrung mit dem zu konditionierenden* Reiz. Regensburg: S.Roderer Verlag, 1989.

[99] Hall G. *Perceptual and Associative Learning.* Oxford Science Publications, 1991.

[100] Gal G, Mendlovic S, Bloch Y, Beitler G, Levkovitz Y, Young AM et al. Learned irrelevance is disrupted in first-episode but not chronic schizophrenia patients. *Behav Brain Res* 2005; 159(2):267-275.

[101] Orosz AT, Feldon J, Gal G, Ludewig K. Deficient latent inhibition in unmedicated first-episode schizophrenia. *Eur Arch.Psychiatry Clin Neurosci.* 254[Supplement 1], I/32. 2004. Ref Type: Abstract

[102] Orosz AT, Feldon J, Gal G, Simon A, Cattapan-Ludewig K. Repeated measurements of learned irrelevance by a novel within-subject paradigm in humans. *Behav Brain Res.*, 2007 Jun 4;180(1):1-3.

In: Schizophrenia Research Trends
Editor: Konstance V. Almann, pp. 163-182
ISBN 13: 978-1-60021-746-3

Chapter VI

THE ASSOCIATION OF VERBAL LEARNING DEFICITS WITH UNAWARENESS OF MENTAL DISORDER: IMPLICATIONS FOR PSYCHOLOGICAL TREATMENTS IN SCHIZOPHRENIA

Marek Nieznański[2], *Agnieszka Chojnowska*[2], *Witold Duński*[2], *Monika Czerwińska*[2] *and Sławomir Walczak*[2]
[1]Institute of Psychology, University of Cardinal Stefan Wyszyński, Warsaw, Poland
[2]Institute of Psychiatry and Neurology, Warsaw, Poland

ABSTRACT

In recent decades, evidence has accumulated that cognitive impairments are a central feature of schizophrenic disorder. Many research findings have indicated that cognitive impairments limit the rate of improvement in various kinds of psychological interventions for schizophrenic patients. The lack of awareness of mental disorder is another important correlate of patients' response to treatment, compliance and prognosis. In our study we hypothesized that schizophrenic patients' ability to be aware of the illness is dependent on more basic ability to directly acquire verbal information, in particular information given throughout treatment interventions. Twenty-seven outpatients with long illness duration were rated on the Scale to Assess Unawareness of Mental Disorder (SUMD) and assessed on verbal learning and memory test. We obtained several significant correlations indicating the presence of the relationship between "learning potential" and insight about psychosis. Afterwards, some of the patients participated in 12 sessions of cognitive training and/or 12 sessions of psychoeducation. The

[2] Corresponding author's address: Marek Nieznański, Ph.D.; Al. KEN 26 m. 181; 02-797 Warszawa, POLAND
E-mail: mnieznanski@wp.pl

effectiveness of these interventions on illness awareness was assessed and the influence of verbal learning abilities on insight change was explored and discussed.

INTRODUCTION

Many research findings have reported stable and significant memory deficits in schizophrenia [cf. Aleman et al., 1999]. These deficits appear to encompass various memory systems and components, including sensory, short-term (or working), long-term, declarative, and procedural memory, etc. [cf. Schröder et al., 1996; Stip and Lussier, 1996]. Relationships between memory impairments and other aspects of psychopathology in schizophrenia have been intensively studied in recent decades. The findings of these research are often inconsistent but mostly they suggest that verbal memory is connected with negative and disorganization symptoms but not with hallucinations and delusions. Moreover, recent meta-analysis have pointed out the role of moderating factors, especially illness duration and gender, that can substantially affect relationships between symptoms and memory [Nieznański, 2004].

The unawareness of illness has been regarded as a crucial factor in schizophrenia by many clinicians and researchers. It seems to be the most common symptom of schizophrenia, and it occurs more often in schizophrenia than in other psychotic disorders. It is estimated that between 50 and 80 % of individuals with schizophrenia have poor insight regarding the fact that they have a mental disorder [cf. Amador and Gorman, 1998; Cuesta and Peralta, 1994; Mintz, Dobson, and Romney, 2003]. In the last two decades, many research have been focused on understanding, defining, and measuring the unawareness of illness in psychotic disorders. Most authors have concluded that it is a multidimensional phenomenon which includes at least three components: awareness of illness, awareness of the need for treatment, and recognition of signs of illness. The ability to attribute symptoms to disorder and to understand the social consequences of mental illness are often added to these dimensions [cf. Amador and David 1998; Cuesta and Peralta, 1994; David, 1990; Mintz, Dobson, and Romney, 2003].

Unawareness of illness is assumed to have deleterious effects on treatment compliance and prognosis [cf. Lamot and Grzywa, 1997; McEvoy et al., 1989b; Smith et al., 1999a]. The findings regarding association between symptoms and insight are mixed. Some investigations have demonstrated positive or inverse relationships between awareness of illness and depressive symptoms [Carroll et al., 1999; Collins et al., 1997, Schwartz, 2001; Smith et al., 2000]. Other reports have suggested no significant association between insight and any symptom group, especially acute psychopathology [Cuesta and Peralta, 1994; Kemp and David, 1996; McEvoy 1989a; Michalakeas et al., 1994]. However, many studies have shown that poorer insight is related to more severe positive symptoms [Carroll et al., 1999; Collins et al., 1997, Kim et al., 1997; Lysaker et al., 1998; for review see: Mintz, Dobson, and Romney, 2003].

AWARENESS OF ILLNESS AND NEUROCOGNITION IN SCHIZOPHRENIA

Three main theories are most often described in the literature regarding the etiology of poor insight in schizophrenia. Firstly, according to the psychodynamic approach, poor insight is a denial of illness, it is a defense mechanism protecting against low self-esteem. Secondly, "clinical" hypotheses have been proposed that unawareness of mental disorder is a manifestation of other groups of symptoms or, alternatively, it is an independent basic symptom arising directly from the illness process. Finally, the neuropsychological view has been developed which assumes that poor insight is a function of neurocognitive deficits [cf. Carroll et al., 1999; Cuesta and Peralta, 1994; Macpherson, Jerrom, and Hughes, 1996; Smith et al., 2000].

The neuropsychological theory draws a parallel between unawareness of illness in schizophrenia and poor insight described in some neurological conditions. Lack of insight has been evidenced in lesions in the frontal lobe of right hemisphere. Many authors have also pointed out a clinical resemblance of the syndrome of "anosognosia" in parietal lobe disorder and lack of insight in schizophrenia [e.g., Cuesta and Peralta, 1994; Cuesta et al., 1995; Lele and Joglekar, 1998]. Some studies have searched for the relationship between unawareness of illness and neuroanatomical measures. Flashman et al. [2000], using a structural magnetic resonance imaging, have found that patients with schizophrenia who were unaware of their symptoms had smaller brain size and intracranial volume than patients with schizophrenia with good insight, however, these results have been not confirmed by Rossell et al. [2003].

Most investigators focused on associations between lack of insight and frontal dysfunction indexed by Wisconsin Card Sorting Test (WCST). However, these studies have yielded inconsistent findings, with number of studies which found [e.g., Lysaker et al., 1998, 2002; Marks et al., 2000; Mohamed et al., 1999; Rossell et al., 2003; Smith et al., 2000; Voruganti, Heslegrave, and Awad, 1997; Young et al., 1998; Young, Davila, and Scher, 1993] and which did not find [e.g., Arduini, Kalyvoka, and Stratta, 2003; Collins et al., 1997; Cuesta et al., 1995; McEvoy et al., 1996] significant relationship between performance on WCST and insight scores [cf. Drake and Lewis, 2003].

A group of studies has found a modest association between general cognitive ability and awareness of illness [e.g., Rossell et al., 2003; Young et al., 1998; cf. Kemp and David, 1996; Macpherson, Jerrom, and Hughes, 1996b]. Some reports have investigated relationship between insight and memory impairments in patients with schizophrenia. They found no significant relationship between insight scores and Rivermead Behavioural Memory Test [Carroll et al., 1999], memory score from Luria Nebraska Neuropsychological Battery [McCabe et al., 2002], California Verbal Learning Test [Smith et al. 2000], measures of working memory [Rossell et al., 2003], and a global memory index based on Hopkins Verbal Learning Test (HVLT) and two subtests from Wechsler Memory Scale-Revised [Lysaker et al., 1998]. Significant relationships were found only in two studies, that is in a study by Marks et al. [2000], between worse performance on immediate recall in HVLT and denial of presence of illness and, in opposite direction, between better performance on immediate recall and lack of insight in study conducted by Cuesta and Peralta [1994].

The contrasting results from studies regarding association between various cognitive deficits and lack of insight in schizophrenia are due to many factors. Some authors [e.g., Carroll et al., 1999; Collins et al., 1997; Kemp and David, 1996] have suggested that this association is present in a subgroup of more chronically disabled patients with long illness duration. Moreover, there are important variations in study design, sample composition (i.e. patients' clinical and demographical characteristics), and methods of cognitive deficit assessment across investigations [Kemp and David, 1996; Macpherson, Jerrom, and Hughes, 1996b]. Another source of inconsistencies are differences in definitions and measures of insight. As Kemp and David [1996] have stated, insight is not a unitary concept, hence only certain aspects may be associated with cognitive deficits [see also Smith et al., 2000].

Study 1: Unawareness of Illness and Verbal Learning Deficit

Study 1 tested the hypothesis that impaired insight in schizophrenia is associated with verbal memory and learning deficit. Specifically, it was assumed that one's ability to be aware of the illness is partly dependent on more basic ability to retrieve verbal information, and on the ability to add and adjust new information to the already existing knowledge. According to Green et al. [2000], a capacity for learning, termed "learning potential", is an important mediator between basic neurocognition and patient's ability to acquire and perform instrumental life skills (see Woonings et al., 2002 for opposite suggestions). We hypothesized, that verbal learning abilities may be also a requisite for the ability to acquire the information about illness and to modify some concepts concerning mental disorder. The postulated association between verbal learning and insight may be restricted only to some aspects of illness awareness, it is probably connected with beliefs and knowledge about one's own illness rather than with the personal attitudes and emotions or the willingness to co-operate with medical staff, however, all these aspects are to some extent connected with each other. This hypothesis is consistent with a model proposed by Macpherson, Jerrom, and Hughes [1996], they postulated that a high level of cognitive functioning, as measured by various intelligence tests connected with educational background, is required to understand and assimilate complex concepts of mental illness and treatment. In their study patients' awareness of illness was significantly predicted by the length of education.

Method

Subjects

Our sample consisted of 27 subjects representing chronic outpatients with a history of many hospitalizations. The mean age for the group was 44.8 ± 9.6 years, 14 subjects were women. Four patients had primary, 5 technical, 12 secondary, and 6 university level of education. Twenty one patients met ICD-10 [WHO, 1992] criteria for schizophrenia (F 20.0, F 20.5), five for schizoaffective disorders (F 25.0, F 25.1) and one for persistent delusional disorder (F 22.0). The diagnoses were made by psychiatric staff of the treatment unit. No subject with a history of previous electroconvulsive therapy, evidence of organic brain syndrome or mental retardation was included in the study. Four patients with suspected alcohol-abuse problems were not excluded from the study. All participants were treated at community outpatient unit at the Institute of Psychiatry and Neurology in Warsaw and were receiving antipsychotic medication at fixed doses at the time of testing. Sixteen of the patients were receiving atypical neuroleptics in a standard therapeutic range, and 11 were maintained on typicals. The majority of patients, especially those on conventional neuroleptics, were also receiving anticholinergic drugs. Several participants were treated with antidepressants or mood stabilizers in addition to antipsychotics.

Clinical Assessment

All patients were rated on the Positive and Negative Syndrome Scale (PANSS) [Kay, Fiszbein, and Opler, 1987], which is a 30-item scale with 7 items measuring positive, 7 negative, and 16 items measuring general aspects of psychopathology. The second clinical scale used in our study was the Scale to Assess Unawareness of Mental Disorder (SUMD), developed by Amador and Strauss [Amador et al., 1993]. The scale samples discrete and global aspects of insight, it follows recent conceptualizations of insight as a multidimensional phenomenon. The first three general items assess, in succession, the patient's general awareness of a mental disorder, awareness of the effects of medication on the disorder, and a general understanding of the consequences of the illness. Subscales 4 to 20 pertain to specific symptoms. Awareness is assessed in the aspect of recognition of signs or symptoms of illness and attribution of the cause or source of these symptoms. We computed two overall insight scores: symptoms awareness and symptoms attribution, which were the means of scores patients received in the symptoms subscales. During the assessment of unawareness of mental disorder some symptom subscales were not rated, i.e. in the cases when a subject had not exhibited a particular symptom. In the analyses we used rates of current and past illness awareness. All item scores range from 1 to 5. Higher scores indicate poorer awareness or attribution. In order to be rated on PANSS and SUMD subjects were interviewed by an experienced psychiatrist of the treatment unit (A.Ch. or W.D.). Information from patient's psychologist or therapist and current medical documentation were also taken into consideration.

Assessment of Verbal Learning Ability

Subjects were presented orally with a list of 15 common words and then were immediately requested to recall as many of the words as they could remember. The procedure consisted of three such consecutive trials and one trial after a 10-minute delay. Three parameters of memory and learning were determined: 1) the total number of words recalled in immediate trials, 2) the sum of all words remembered in the delayed trial as a measure of long term retrieval, and 3) an index of "learning potential" defined as the difference between the number of words recalled in the third and first trial. Patients were tested individually by a psychologist (M.N. or M.C.) who was blind to the insight and symptoms ratings.

Results

The group showed a mild overall level of psychopathology with prevalent negative symptoms. Scores on the SUMD indicated that majority of subjects were aware of their illness. Only several patients received maximum ratings indicating full unawareness of mental disorder. Mean ratings for patients' unawareness of current and past illness are presented in Table 1. Exploratory analyses were undertaken to determine the influence of gender, level of education, illness duration, and medication type (atypical vs. traditional neuroleptics) on insight scores. The only significant results were the positive associations of illness duration with unawareness of the effects of medication, unawareness of past symptoms, and misattribution of current symptoms (see Table 3).

Table 1. The Means and Standard Deviations of the Verbal Learning Test and Clinical Variables (n=27)

SUMD* General items		**PANSS**	
Awareness of mental disorder: current	2.6±1.2	PANSS positive	14.7±3.6
Awareness of mental disorder: past	2.5±1.1	PANSS negative	20.7±5.3
Awareness of effects of medication: current	2.1±1.2	PANSS total	72.0±140
Awareness of effects of medication: past	2.4±1.4		
Awareness of social consequences: current	2.0±1.3	**Illness duration** (years)	18.0±8.7
Awareness of social consequences: past	2.0±1.3		
SUMD Overall scores		**Verbal Learning**	
Symptoms awareness: current	2.9±1.0	Immediate recall	12.7±4.3
Symptoms awareness: past	2.8±1.1	Delayed recall	3.1±2.0
Symptoms attribution: current (n=23)	2.6±1.0	Learning potential	1.9±2.0
Symptoms attribution: past (n=24)	2.5±1.1		

* Higher scores on the SUMD items indicate worse insight

Table 2. Spearman Rank Correlations between Verbal Learning and Insight Scores (n=27)

SUMD	Immediate recall	Delayed recall	Learning potential
General items			
Awareness of mental disorder: current	.15	-.25	-.40*
Awareness of mental disorder: past	.33**	-.25	-.21
Awareness of effects of medication: current	-.06	-.22	-.38*
Awareness of effects of medication: past	.05	-.17	-.34**
Awareness of social consequences: current	.04	-.22	-.26
Awareness of social consequences: past	-.04	-.22	-.30
Overall scores			
Symptoms awareness: current	.27	-.17	-.20
Symptoms awareness: past	.24	-.19	-.22
Symptoms attribution: current (n=23)	.31	.24	-.23
Symptoms attribution: past (n=24)	.23	-.00	-.21

one-tailed, * $p<.03$; ** $p<.05$

Table 2 presents Spearman rank correlation coefficients between verbal memory and learning test performance and insight scores. We found no statistically significant correlations between delayed recall and SUMD scores. Better immediate recall was significantly related only with unawareness of past mental disorder SUMD item. Better learning potential was significantly associated with better awareness of current mental disorder and both awareness of current and past achieved effects of medication.

Significant correlations were found between severity of negative symptoms and awareness of current and past mental disorder and with overall awareness of current and past symptoms. The PANSS positive symptoms scores correlated significantly with all SUMD scores except awareness of social consequences of mental disorder (see Table 3).

Table 3. Spearman Rank Correlations between Severity of Symptoms, Illness Duration, and Insight Scores (n=27)

SUMD	PANSS negative	PANSS positive	Illness duration
General items			
Awareness of mental disorder: current	.53[f]	.56[g]	.24
Awareness of mental disorder: past	.33[a]	.69[i]	.20
Awareness of effects of medication: current	.14	.55[g]	.39[c]
Awareness of effects of medication: past	.22	.73[i]	.50[e]
Awareness of social consequences: current	.29	.26	.00
Awareness of social consequences: past	.31	.29	.08
Overall scores			
Symptoms awareness: current	.50[e]	.77[i]	.29
Symptoms awareness: past	.44[d]	.71[i]	.36[b]
Symptoms attribution: current (n=23)	.19	.46[d]	.40[c]
Symptoms attribution: past (n=24)	.32	.62[h]	.27

one-tailed; [a] $p<.05$, [b] $p<.04$, [c] $p<.03$, [d] $p<.02$, [e] $p<.006$, [f] $p<.004$, [g] $p<.003$, [h] $p<.002$, [i] $p<.000$

Discussion

The subjects participating in our study displayed an unusually good awareness. It may be due to the fact that patients with good insight into illness are more probable to agree to participate in the research and it is consistent with the observation that outpatients have more insight than inpatients [Young et al., 1998]. As expected, schizophrenic patients with high ratings of learning potential were more aware of mental disorder and achieved effects of medication than patients with low learning potential. However, it was the only memory and learning index which was connected with insight scores in the hypothesized direction. It indicates a specific character of learning potential as a cognitive variable associated with outcome in schizophrenia. We suppose that capacity to recall new words after repeated trials is dependent on basic verbal memory functioning, and as our results suggested, it mediates the awareness of illness, probably by determining the ability to assimilate information about illness [see Green et al., 2000]. We would like to mention, that there is some similarity between learning potential, measured by the progress in word list recall, and "cognitive flexibility" measured by WCST. When learning a list of words subjects have to adjust their responses in consecutive trials after the feedback from the experimenter reading the same list before each trial. In the WCST subjects are instructed to sort cards according to a particular rule. The experimenter is telling them whether their sort was correct. After a set of sorts the criterion for matching is changed and subject must adjust their responses [cf. Woonings et al., 2002; Drake and Lewis, 2003]. This common feature, that is an ability to change reaction and gain from the feedback, may be connected with some aspects of illness awareness.

Contrary to our hypotheses lack of insight was connected with better immediate recall. This result replicates that of Cuesta and Peralta [1994] study, however this association remains unclear and needs further investigation. The potential role of mechanisms of denial have to be considered in this context. It is possible that patients with their working memory functioning better are also more capable of using some kind of self-deception [cf. Startup, 1996].

Among sample describing variables the illness duration seems to have the most impact on insight scores. It was indicated that patients who had longer illness duration were less aware of their illness. This supports the view that mechanisms of the relationship between insight and cognition may differ in subgroups of chronically disabled patients and patients with short illness duration. This result does not correspond with findings reported by Thompson, McGorry, and Harrigan [2001] that first-episode patients with schizophrenia are less aware of having mental illness than multiple-episode patients. They suggested that multiple-episode patients may appear to have good insight because they are more skilled in using medical terms, and they acquired appropriate language to explain their illness. However, our sample included mostly multiple-episode patients, and illness duration and number of episodes are related but not identical indicators of illness course.

Our findings are in line with other reports which have shown a relationship between schizophrenia symptoms and unawareness of illness. Severity of negative symptoms was significantly correlated with unawareness of mental disorder and unawareness of symptoms. Severity of positive symptoms was connected with unawareness of mental disorder, effects of medication and both unawareness and misattribution of symptoms.

Study 2: Verbal Learning Ability and Insight Improvement after Psychological Intervention

Cognitive Impairment as 'Rate-Limiting' Factor in Rehabilitation of Patients with Schizophrenia

Many studies have demonstrated that level of cognitive functioning is among the most significant predictors of acquisition of new social skills and improvement in vocational functioning after psychiatric rehabilitation interventions [e.g., Bell and Bryson, 2001; Cook and Razzano, 2000; Hoffmann et al., 2003; Kern, Green, and Satz, 1992]. Sometimes, in order to make psychiatric rehabilitation more effective, it is started with cognitive skills training, like in the Integrated Psychological Therapy developed by Brenner et al. [1994]. In other approaches, the rehabilitation outcome is optimized by reducing the cognitive burden on patients. To achieve this, for example, Kern et al. [2002, 2003] used special learning method (ie. "errorless learning"), and Velligan et. al. [1996, 2000] designed various environmental adaptations and compensatory strategies.

Among cognitive impairments limiting effectiveness of rehabilitation interventions verbal memory and attention are being mentioned most often. For example, Kern, Green, and Satz [1992] designed skills training modules to improve patients' knowledge and awareness of their psychiatric condition. They showed that verbal memory, sustained attention, and freedom from distractibility had the highest correlation with this training outcome. Similarly, in study reported by Silverstein, Hitzel, and Schenkel [1998] attentiveness and verbal memory were critical for patients' ability to benefit from social skills training. Moreover, some studies indicated that severity of symptoms contributed less than cognitive impairment to rehabilitation outcome [e.g., Bell and Bryson, 2001; Lysaker and Bell, 1995; Smith, et al., 1999b].

Cognitive Training and Psychoeducational Intervention: Modifiability of Illness Unawareness

In the past decade cognitive impairments have become the target of many rehabilitation programs. Several studies have yielded promising findings, for example in Wexler et al.'s [1997] study most patients practicing sustained perceptual, memory and motor tasks achieved performance levels equal to or greater than high functioning healthy control subjects. In another successful program, Bellack et al. [2001] trained two groups of patients on two different neurocognitive tasks. Both groups showed large improvements on the trained test and moderate improvement on the untrained test, while a control group failed to exhibit improvement on either test. In Wykes et al.'s [1999] study patients with schizophrenia participated in an intensive cognitive remediation program aimed at improving executive functioning. In comparison with a control group attending occupational therapy, experimental group significantly more reduced deficits in cognitive flexibility and memory domains. Similarly, Medalia et al. [1998] have demonstrated that schizophrenic patients receiving computerized attention training made significantly greater progress than the control group. Patients participating in the training became more vigilant and less distractible, moreover, these effects further generalized on severity of their symptomatology. However, there is also much skepticism concerning the effects of direct remediation of cognitive deficits in schizophrenia, especially their generalizability and durability [cf. Bellack, 1992; Nieznański, 2000a]. A group of studies did not find any evidence that cognitive rehabilitation has grater impact on outcome than conventional interventions [e.g., Benedict et al., 1994; Lewis et al., 2003; Medalia, Revheim, and Casey, 2000]. In recent meta-analysis of several randomized controlled trials, Pilling et al. [2002] have concluded that cognitive remediation does not appear to give reliable benefits for patients with schizophrenia. Similarly, Suslow, Schonauer, and Ardt [2001] in their review of the literature have drawn the inference that there is a weak evidence that attention training is effective in schizophrenia. Nevertheless, cognitive deficit remains one of the most important targets of rehabilitation in schizophrenia and studies searching for successful rehabilitation methods are still growing.

Psychoeducation is a widely used method aimed at helping people with schizophrenia to manage their illness more effectively. This kind of intervention mostly increases patients' knowledge but rather does not affect their behavior [Mueser et al., 2002]. However, in the literature it is recommended as a method reducing risk of relapse, preventing noncompliance and optimizing compliance [e.g., Chładzińska-Kiejnia, Górna, and Bąk, 1997; Merinder, 2000; Tafliński, 1998; Rund et al., 1994; Weiden, 1997]. Some studies have demonstrated improvements of insight in patients with schizophrenia after participation in educational programs [Carroll et al., 1999; Kemp et al., 1996; Macpherson, Jerrom, and Hughes, 1996]. As Mueser et al. [2002, p. 1274] have concluded, "psychoeducation remains important because access to information about mental illness is crucial to people's ability to make informed decisions about their own treatment, and psychoeducation is the foundation for more comprehensive programs".

The aim of Study 2 was to evaluate the influence of cognitive rehabilitation and psychoeducational intervention on various aspects of illness awareness in outpatients with schizophrenia spectrum disorders. It was hypothesized that both interventions may improve patients' insight. In cognitive training group this improvement may be achieved indirectly by improving cognitive functions potentially connected with insight into illness. We can assume this because we have found the applied method of training effective in improving patients' various cognitive skills [Nieznański, Walczak, and Chojnowska, 2000; Nieznański et al., 2004]. For psychoeducational intervention it may be expected to directly improve patients' knowledge about symptoms and effects of medication, which may make easier for them to understand and manage the illness. The second aim of this study was to investigate if verbal learning abilities, which we showed in Study 1 that correlated with insight scores, may also predict patients' improvement in insight scores after participation in psychological intervention.

Method

Subjects

We invited subjects from Study 1 to participate in psychoeducation or cognitive training. The courses were conducted alternately, therefore patients could participate in both interventions (in psychoeducation - cognitive training sequence or opposite, cognitive training - psychoeducation sequence). Twenty three out of 27 patients agreed to participate, among them 10 participated in both offered interventions, 4 patients participated solely in cognitive training and 9 solely in psychoeducation. Therefore we were able to assess 14 subjects before and after cognitive training ("cognitive training group"), and 19 before and after psychoeducation ("psychoeducational group"). For those subjects who participated in both interventions the post-test from the first intervention was a pre-test of the second intervention.

Cognitive Skills Training

Patients participating in cognitive training received one 40-50 minutes session per week for 12 weeks. They were divided into 2-3 persons subgroups, they were joined according to the similar level of cognitive abilities. During a typical training session, subjects were practicing 5-8 cognitive tasks, each demanding various combinations of cognitive abilities. For example, during one of the sessions patients were engaged in practicing: 1) sorting of cards with geometrical figures, according to their color and/or number and/or shape; 2) giving words connected with the word "book" and categorizing gathered associations into various classes; 3) searching for words containing letter "b" in a given text; 4) copying complex figures and than drawing them again from memory; 5) making analogies between pairs of objects; 6) assembling a story from fragmented sentences. Specifically for this project, a training manual was developed [Nieznański, 2000b], containing over 70 cognitive tasks, designed to exercise a wide range of cognitive abilities impaired in schizophrenia, among them various aspects of attention, verbal and nonverbal learning and memory, long-term and short-term memory, executive functioning, conceptual thinking etc. The tasks were adopted from other cognitive trainings [e.g., Brenner et al., 1994] and selected from various cognitive tests described in the literature on methods of testing intellectual abilities [e.g., Guilford, 1967; Matczak, 1994]. Activities were graded with respect to their complexity, with easier versions of tasks given to subgroups of less-skilled patients. Detailed results concerning the influence of our cognitive training on cognitive functioning and symptom severity have been presented elsewhere [Nieznański et al., 2004].

Psychoeducational Treatment

During 12 sessions patients had got acquainted with a range of topics on the nature and treatment of mental disorder, and the need for maintaining medication to prevent or delay relapse was stressed by the psychiatrist leading the sessions. Patients were divided into two subgroups (9 or 10 persons in each) and participated in the sessions once a week. Materials from a program of relapse prevention "PRelapse" and earlier experiences with educating patients about their illness were used during the sessions.

Statistical Methods of Outcome Prediction

Two logistic multiple-regression analyses were carried out, using stepwise backward regression based on the Wald statistic, with improvement of awareness of current (first analysis) and past (second analysis) illness as the dependent variable. Patients who achieved a better score on at least one SUMD general item in the post-test were classified as improving insight (n=10), those whose SUMD scores did not improve or deteriorated were classified as not improving (n=16); seven patients were not classified because all their pre-test SUMD scores were maximally good, so they could not improve. We entered significant variables outlined in the correlational analyses of Study 1 into analyses, for the first analysis they included: illness duration, severity of negative symptoms, severity of positive symptoms, and learning potential. In the second analysis we entered one more variable - immediate recall. Two other independent variables potentially important for insight improvement were also entered: the kind of intervention (cognitive training versus psychoeducation) and the phase of treatment (i.e. improvement achieved in first intervention versus in second intervention). These two variables, as well as dependent variables, were coded as "dummy variables" [see: Glantz and Slinker, 2001].

Results

The improvements in illness awareness were found in both groups. In the psychoeducational group significant changes were found on SUMD items of mental disorder awareness and awareness of effects of medication, as well as on overall awareness of symptoms, and overall attribution scores. In the cognitive training group patients improved significantly on overall score of symptom awareness (see Table 4).

Table 4. Changes in Insight Scores after Psychoeducation (n=14) and Cognitive Training (n=19)

	Cognitive training		Psychoeducation	
SUMD	Pre-test	Post-test	Pre-test	Post-test
General items				
Awareness of mental disorder: current	2.50 ±1.40	2.14±1.40	2.42[a]±1.02	2.21[a]±1.03
Awareness of mental disorder: past	2.57±1.28	2.14±1.23	2.47[b]±1.28	2.32[b]±1.11
Awareness of effects of medication: current	1.79±1.42	2.0±1.57	2.11[b]±1.20	1.89[b]±1.20
Awareness of effects of medication: past	1.93±1.38	1.93±1.33	2.32[a]±1.11	2.11[a]±1.15
Awareness of social consequences: current	2.21±1.48	2.07±1.54	1.74±1.10	1.68±1.11
Awareness of social consequences: past	2.07±1.54	2.07±1.54	1.74±1.10	1.63±1.12
Overall scores				
Symptoms awareness: current	2.71[c]±1.23	2.35[c]±1.44	2.79[d]±0.91	2.53[d]±0.96
Symptoms awareness: past	2.58[c]±1.21	2.27[c]±1.31	2.65[e]±0.94	2.43[e]±0.95
Symptoms attribution: current	2.41±1.21	2.04±1.19	2.67[d]±1.05	2.43[d]±1.06
Symptoms attribution: past	2.39±1.27	2.0±1.18	2.69[f]±1.16	2.38[f]±1.07

Matched-pairs signed-ranks test, one-tailed; [a] $z=1.82$ $p<.04$, [b] $z=1.60$ $p=.05$, [c] $z=1.68$ $p<.05$, [d] $z=2.67$ $p<.004$; [e] $z=2.77$ $p<.003$; [f] $z=2.58$ $p<.005$

The first logistic multiple-regression analysis was conducted with improvement of awareness of current illness as the dependent variable. This analysis showed that pre-treatment learning potential, illness duration, and phase of treatment contributed most to the prediction of insight improvement, while pre-treatment severity of negative and positive symptoms, and kind of psychological intervention (cognitive training vs. psychoeducation) made nonsignificant contributions. The second stepwise backward regression analysis was conducted with improvement of awareness of past illness as the dependent variable. Only two variables significantly explained insight improvement, that is: immediate recall and learning potential. The kind of intervention, phase of treatment, illness duration and pre-treatment severity of positive and negative symptoms did not contribute significantly to improvement of awareness of past mental disorder (see Table 5).

Table 5. Significant Predictors of Improvement in SUMD General Items after Psychological Intervention (n=26)

Dependent variable	Independent variables	B	SE	Wald	p (df=1)	R
Improvement of awareness of current illness	Constant	5.29	4.29	1.52	.217	
	Phase of treatment	3.80	1.73	4.81	.028	.28
	Learning potential	.81	.40	4.11	.043	.25
	Illness duration	-.55	.31	3.20	.074	-.19
Improvement of awareness of past illness	Constant	2.52	1.53	2.71	.10	
	Immediate recall	-.29	.12	5.35	.02	-.31
	Learning potential	.41	.25	2.70	.10	.14

Discussion

Both applied interventions improved patients' awareness of the illness. The influence was more prevalent in the psychoeducational group than in the cognitive training group. However, it must be noted that in the cognitive training group the sample size was smaller (n=14) than in psychoeducational group (n=19) and some comparable improvements appeared not large enough to reach significance. It is possible that patients improved their insight scores not due to a change in their attitudes and beliefs about illness but rather because they became more skilled in verbalizing and explaining their illness. However, we believe that this change in patients' knowledge about mental illness is also a valuable treatment effect which may contribute to improvements in patients' compliance or quality of life. Our Study 2 lacked a group without any intervention, therefore it cannot be excluded that improvement in insight was due to a spontaneous change, however this possibility seems to be very improbable in chronic, clinically stable outpatients.

The first logistic regression analysis showed that the improvement in awareness of current illness was more probable after participation in the second intervention and for patients with higher learning potential, and shorter illness duration. The second analysis showed that an improvement in awareness of past illness was predicted by higher learning potential and worse immediate recall. Both analyses suggested that it was not important what kind of intervention (psychoeducation vs. cognitive training) the patient received, the positive and negative symptom severity also had no significant predictive value. These results of multiple-regression analyses we consider only preliminary because of inadequate sample size. However, they support our hypothesis that learning potential may be an important predictor of patients' ability to improve their insight after participation in psychological intervention.

These results have some clinical implications. They suggest that poor learning potential, but not poor ability to retrieve information, may be a rate-limiting factor for interventions aimed at insight improvement. This finding is consistent with results of Wiedl's [1999] study, which have shown that cognitive modifiability is an important predictor of readiness for rehabilitation. Moreover, it seems that various forms of rehabilitation may lead to improvements in insight. Our study showed that psychoeducation and, to a lesser degree, cognitive training improve patients' awareness of illness, while Lysaker and Bell [1995] have observed improvements following participation in vocational rehabilitation. It also seems that psychological interventions may be more successful for patients with shorter illness duration, and, when two consecutive interventions are given, for patients participating in the second intervention.

CONCLUSION

- Our findings support the hypothesis that impaired insight in schizophrenia is associated with low learning capacity. It was demonstrated in Study 1, where unawareness of mental disorder and unawareness of effects of medication correlated significantly with low learning potential, and in Study 2, where patients with low learning potential were less able to improve insight scores after participation in psychological intervention.
- General ability to retrieve verbal information appeared to be unrelated to illness awareness. Moreover, the relation between the immediate recall and awareness of past mental disorder seemed opposite to the expected one. This finding remains unclear and requires further investigation.
- This study also pointed out the importance of illness duration as a variable affecting patients' insight. It was showed that patients with shorter illness duration are both more aware of the illness and more prone to improve their awareness after psychological intervention.
- The data from this study suggest that the relationship between symptoms and insight is rather a correlational than cause-effect relationship. Study 1 indicated that negative and positive symptom severity are correlated with unawareness of illness, however in Study 2 the severity of symptoms did not predict insight changes after psychological intervention. It is consistent with other studies that have found no association between changes in psychopathology and changes in insight in patients recovering from acute psychotic episode [Armstrongh, Chandrasekaran, and Perme, 2002; Cuesta, Peralta, and Zarzuela, 2000].
- The multidimensional nature of illness awareness was pointed out in both conducted studies. It was especially apparent in case of the dimension of understanding of the social consequences of illness. This variable did not correlate with any of the studied variables and did not change after psychological interventions. It is possible that this component is related to patients' emotions and social experiences, while other insight dimensions are more connected with patients' knowledge about illness, and more liable to improvement following psychological intervention.
- The main limitation of this study is small sample size, therefore most of our results should be considered as exploratory. Moreover, we have to emphasize that our inferences are mostly restricted to a population of outpatients with schizophrenia spectrum disorders in the remission phase of the illness, and could not be generalized on acute patients.

ACKNOWLEDGEMENTS

We gratefully acknowledge the encouragement and support given by Professor Jacek Wciórka to our initiative on cognitive rehabilitation. We would also like to thank our colleagues, therapists from the community outpatient unit (Zespół Leczenia Środowiskowego IPiN), Grażyna Blaszyńska, Stefan Czyżewicz, Ewa Jankowska and Bogdan Krzystoszek for their help in the arrangement of cognitive training. We are also very obliged to all the patients who trusted us and participated in our research.

REFERENCES

Aleman, A., Hijman, R., de Haan, E. H. F., and Kahn, R. (1999). Memory impairment in schizophrenia: A meta-analysis. *American Journal of Psychiatry*, 156, 1358-1366.

Amador, X. F., and David, A. S. (Eds.), (1998). *Insight and Psychosis*. New York: Oxford University Press.

Amador, X. F., and Gorman, J. M. (1998). Psychopathologic domains and insight in schizophrenia. *Psychiatric Clinics of North America*, 21, 27-42.

Amador, X. F., Strauss, D. H., Yale, S. A., Flaum, M. M., Endicott, J., and Gorman, J. M. (1993). Assessment of insight in psychosis. *American Journal of Psychiatry*, 150, 873-879.

Arduini, L., Kalyvoka, A., and Stratta, P. (2003). Insight and neuropsychological function in patients with schizophrenia and bipolar with psychotic features. *Canadian Journal of Psychiatry,* 48, 338-341.

Armstrongh, K. P. L., Chandrasekaran, R., and Perme, B. (2002). Insight, psychopathology and schizophrenia. *Indian Journal of Psychiatry*, 44, 332-336.

Bell, M. D., and Bryson, G. (2001). Work rehabilitation in schizophrenia: Does cognitive impairment limit improvement? *Schizophrenia Bulletin*, 27, 269-279.

Bellack, A. S. (1992). Cognitive rehabilitation for schizophrenia: Is it possible? Is it necessary? *Schizophrenia Bulletin*, 18, 43-50.

Bellack, A. S., Weinhardt, L. S., Gold, J. M., and Gearon, J. S. (2001). Generalization of training effects in schizophrenia. *Schizophrenia Research*, 48, 255-262.

Benedict, R. H. B., Harris, A. E., Markow, T., McCormick, J. A., Neuchterlein, K. H., and Asarnow, R. F. (1994). Effects of attention training on information processing in schizophrenia. *Schizophrenia Bulletin*, 20, 537-546.

Brenner, H. D., Roder, V., Hodel, B., Kienzle, N., Reed, D., and Liberman, R. P. (1994). *Integrated psychological therapy for schizophrenic patients* (IPT). Seattle: Hogrefe and Huber Publishers.

Carroll, A., Fattah, S., Clyde, Z., Coffey, I., Owens, D. G. C., and Johnstone, E. C. (1999). Correlates of insight and insight change in schizophrenia. *Schizophrenia Research*, 35, 247-253.

Chładzińska-Kiejnia, S., Górna, R., and Bąk, O. (1997). Psychoedukacja w zapobieganiu nawrotom schizofrenii [Psychoeducation in relapse prevention of schizophrenia]. *Psychiatria Polska*, 31, 595-606.

Collins, A. A., Remington, G. J., Coulter, K., and Birkett, K. (1997). Insight, neurocognitive function and symptom clusters in chronic schizophrenia. *Schizophrenia Research*, 27, 37-44.

Cook, J. A., and Razzano, L. (2000). Vocational rehabilitation for persons with schizophrenia: Recent research and implications for practice. *Schizophrenia Bulletin*, 26, 87-103.

Cuesta, M. J., and Peralta, V. (1994). Lack of insight in schizophrenia. *Schizophrenia Bulletin*, 20, 359-366.

Cuesta, M. J., Peralta, V., Caro, F., and de Leon, J. (1995). Is poor insight in psychotic disorders associated with poor performance on the Wisconsin Card Sorting Test? *American Journal of Psychiatry*, 152, 1380-1382.

Cuesta, M. J., Peralta, V., and Zarzuela, A. (2000). Reappraising insight in psychosis: Multi-scale longitudinal study. *British Journal of Psychiatry*, 177, 233-240.

David, A. S. (1990). Insight and psychosis. *British Journal of Psychiatry*, 156, 798-805.

Dębowska, G., Grzywa, A., and Kucharska-Pietura, K. (1998). Insight in paranoid schizophrenia - its relationship to psychopathology and premorbid adjustment. *Comprehensive Psychiatry*, 39, 255-260.

Drake, R. J., and Lewis, S. W. (2003). Insight and neurocognition in schizophrenia. *Schizophrenia Research*, 62, 165-173.

Flashman, L. A., McAllister, T. W., Andreasen, N. C., and Saykin, A. J. (2000). Smaller brain size associated with unawareness of illness in patients with schizophrenia. *American Journal of Psychiatry*, 157, 1167-1169.

Glantz, S. A., and Slinker, B. K. (2001). *Applied regression and analysis of variance* (2nd ed). New York: McGraw-Hill.

Green, M. F., Kern, R. S., Braff, D. L., and Mintz, J. (2000). Neurocognitive deficits and functional outcome in schizophrenia: Are we measuring the "right stuff"? *Schizophrenia Bulletin*, 26, 119-136.

Guilford, J. P. (1967). *The nature of human intelligence*. New York: McGraw-Hill.

Hoffmann, H., Kupper, Z., Zbinden, M., and Hirsbrunner, H.-P. (2003). Predicting vocational functioning and outcome in schizophrenia outpatients attending a vocational rehabilitation program. *Social Psychiatry and Psychiatric Epidemiology*, 38, 76-82.

Kay, S. R., Fiszbein, A., and Opler, L. A. (1987). The Positive and Negative Syndrome Scale (PANSS) for schizophrenia. *Schizophrenia Bulletin*, 13, 261-276.

Kemp, R., and David, A. (1996). Psychological predictors of insight and compliance in psychotic patients. *British Journal of Psychiatry*, 169, 444-450.

Kemp, R., Hayward, P., Applewhaite, G., Everitt, B., and David, A. (1996). Compliance therapy in psychotic patients: Randomised controlled trial. *BMJ*, 312, 345-349.

Kern, R. S., Green, M. F., Mintz, J., and Liberman, R. P. (2003). Does 'errorless learning' compensate for neurocognitive impairments in the work rehabilitation of persons with schizophrenia? *Psychological Medicine*, 33, 433-442.

Kern, R. S., Green, M. F., and Satz, P. (1992). Neuropsychological predictors of skills training for chronic psychiatric patients. *Psychiatry Research*, 43, 223-230.

Kern, R. S., Liberman, R. P., Kopelowicz, A., Mintz, J., and Green, M. F. (2002). Applications of errorless learning for improving work performance in persons with schizophrenia. *American Journal of Psychiatry*, 159, 1921-1927.

Kim, Y., Sakamoto, K., Kamo, T., Sakamura, Y., and Miyaoka, H. (1997). Insight and clinical correlates in schizophrenia. *Comprehensive Psychiatry*, 38, 117-123.

Lamot, G., and Grzywa, A. (1997). Wgląd a choroba psychiczna [Insight and psychotic illness]. *Psychiatria Polska*, 31, 97-110.

Lele, M. V. and Joglekar, A. S. (1998). Poor insight in schizophrenia: Neurocognitive basis. *Journal of Postgraduate Medicine*, 44, 50-55.

Lewis, L., Unkefer, E. P., O'Neal, S. K., Critii, C. J., and Fultz, J. (2003). Cognitive rehabilitation with patients having persistent, severe psychiatric disabilities. *Psychiatric Rehabilitation Journal*, 26, 325-331.

Lysaker, P. H., and Bell, M. D. (1995). Work rehabilitation and improvements in insight in schizophrenia. *Journal of Nervous and Mental Disease*, 183, 103-106.

Lysaker, P. H., Bell, M. D., Bryson, G. J., and Kaplan, E. (1998). Neurocognitive function and insight in schizophrenia: Support for an association with impairments in executive function but not with impairments in global function. *Acta Psychiatrica Scandinavica*, 97, 297-301.

Lysaker, P. H., Bryson, G. J., Lancaster, R. S., Evans, J. D., and Bell, M. D. (2002). Insight in schizophrenia: Associations with executive function and coping style. *Schizophrenia Research*, 59, 41-47.

Macpherson, R., Jerrom, B., and Hughes, A. (1996). A controlled study of education about drug treatment in schizophrenia. *British Journal of Psychiatry*, 168, 709-717.

Marks, K. A., Fastenau, P. S., Lysaker, P. H., and Bond, G. R. (2000). Self-Appraisal of Illness Questionnaire (SAIQ): Relationship to researcher-rated insight and neuropsychological function in schizophrenia. *Schizophrenia Research*, 45, 203-211.

Matczak, A. (1994). *Diagnoza intelektu* [Diagnosis of intellect]. Warszawa: Instytut Psychologii PAN.

McCabe, R., Quayle, E., Beirne, A. D., and Duane, M. M. A. (2002). Insight, global neuropsychological functioning, and symptomatology in chronic schizophrenia. *Journal of Nervous and Mental Disease,* 190, 519-525.

McEvoy, J. P., Apperson, L. J., Appelbaum, P. S., Ortlip, P., Brecosky, J., Hammil, K., Geller, J. L., and Roth, L. (1989). Insight in schizophrenia: Its relationship to acute psychopathology. *Journal of Nervous and Mental Disease*, 177, 43-47.

McEvoy, J. P., Freter, S., Everett, G., Geller, J. L., Appelbaum, P., Apperson, L. J., and Roth, L. (1989). Insight and the clinical outcome of schizophrenic patients. *Journal of Nervous and Mental Disease*, 177, 48-51.

McEvoy, J. P., Hartman, M., Gottlieb, D., Godwin, S., Apperson, L. J., and Wilson, W. (1996). Common sense, insight, and neuropsychological test performance in schizophrenia patients. *Schizophrenia Bulletin*, 22, 635-641.

Medalia, A., Aluma, M., Tryon, W., and Merriam, A. E. (1998). Effectiveness of attention training in schizophrenia. *Schizophrenia Bulletin*, 24, 147-152.

Medalia, A., Revheim, N., and Casey, M. (2000). Remediation of memory disorders in schizophrenia. *Psychological Medicine*, 30, 1451-1459.

Merinder, L. B. (2000). Patient education in schizophrenia: A review. *Acta Psychiatrica Scandinavica*, 102, 98-106.

Michalakeas, A., Skoutas, C., Charalambous, A., Peristeris, A., Marinos, V., Keramari, E., and Theologou, A. (1994). Insight in schizophrenia and mood disorders and its relation to psychopathology. *Acta Psychiatrica Scandinavica*, 90, 46-49.

Mintz, A. R., Dobson, K. S., and Romney, D. M. (2003). Insight in schizophrenia: A meta-analysis. *Schizophrenia Research*, 61, 75-88.

Mohamed, S., Fleming, S., Penn, D. L., and Spaulding, W. (1999). Insight in schizophrenia: Its relationship to measures of executive functions. *Journal of Nervous and Mental Disease*, 187, 525-531.

Mueser, K. T., Corrigan, P. W., Hilton, D. W., Tanzman, B., Schaub, A., Gingerich, S., Essock, S. M., Tarrier, N., Morey, B., Vogel-Scibilia, S., and Herz, M. I. (2002). Illness management and recovery: A review of the research. *Psychiatric Services*, 53, 1272-1284.

Nieznański, M. (2000a). Trening umiejętności poznawczych - możliwości i ograniczenia nowej formy rehabilitacji w schizofrenii [Cognitive training - prospects and limitations of the new form of rehabilitation in schizophrenia]. *Psychiatria Polska*, 34, 267-274.

Nieznański, M. (2000b). *Materiały do prowadzenia treningu umiejętności poznawczych* [Materials for management of cognitive skills training]. Unpublished manuscript, Warszawa: ZLŚ IPiN.

Nieznański, M. (2004). Metaanaliza wyników badań nad związkami nasilenia objawów schizofrenii z zaburzeniami pamięci werbalnej [Relationship between schizophrenic symptoms and verbal memory impairment: A meta-analysis]. *Studia Psychologica*, 5, 313-332.

Nieznański, M., Czerwińska, M., Chojnowska, A., Walczak, S., and Duński, W. (2004). Effectiveness of cognitive skills training in schizophrenia. *Archives of Psychiatry and Psychotherapy*, 6, 33-45.

Nieznański, M., Walczak, S., and Chojnowska, A. (2000). Rehabilitacja umiejętności poznawczych w schizofrenii - doniesienie wstępne [Cognitive rehabilitation in schizophrenia: Preliminary report]. *Wiadomości Psychiatryczne*, 3, 79-84.

Pilling, S., Bebbington, P., Kuipers, E., Garety, P., Geddes, J., Martindale, B., Orbach, G., and Morgan, C. (2002). Psychological treatments in schizophrenia: II. Meta-analyses of randomized controlled trials of social skills training and cognitive remediation. *Psychological Medicine*, 32, 783-791.

Rossell, S. L., Coakes, J., Shapleske, J., Woodruff, P. W. R., and David, A. S. (2003). Insight: Its relationship with cognitive function, brain volume and symptoms in schizophrenia. *Psychological Medicine*, 33, 111-119.

Rund, B. R., Moe, L., Sollien, T., Fjell, A., Borchgrevink, T., Hallert, M., and Næss, P. O. (1994). The Psychosis Project: Outcome and cost-effectiveness of a psychoeducational treatment programme for schizophrenic adolescents. *Acta Psychiatrica Scandinavica*, 89, 211-218.

Schröder, J., Tittel, A., Stockert, A., and Karr, M. (1996). Memory deficits in subsyndromes of chronic schizophrenia. *Schizophrenia Research*, 21, 19-26.

Schwartz, R. C. (2001). Self-awareness in schizophrenia: Its relationship to depressive symptomatology and broad psychiatric impairments. *Journal of Nervous and Mental Disease,* 189, 401-403.

Silverstein, S. M., Hitzel, H., and Schenkel L. (1998). Identifying and addressing cognitive barriers to rehabilitation readiness. *Psychiatric Services*, 49, 34-36.

Smith, T. E., Hull, J. W., Goodman, M., Hedayat-Harris, A., Willson, D. F., Israel, L. M., and Munich, R. L. (1999a). The relative influences of symptoms, insight, and neurocognition on social adjustment in schizophrenia and schizoaffective disorder. *Journal of Nervous and Mental Disease*, 187, 102-108.

Smith, T. E., Hull, J. W., Israel, L. M., and Willson, D. F. (2000). Insight, symptoms, and neurocognition in schizophrenia and schizoaffective disorder. *Schizophrenia Bulletin*, 26, 193-200.

Smith, T. E., Hull, J. W., Romanelli, S., Fertuck, E., and Weiss, K. A. (1999b). Symptoms and neurocognition as rate limiters in skills training for psychotic patients. *American Journal of Psychiatry,* 156, 1818-1819.

Startup M. (1996). Insight and cognitive deficits in schizophrenia: Evidence for a curvilinear relationship. *Psychological Medicine*, 26, 1277-1281.

Stip, E., and Lussier, I. (1996). The heterogeneity of memory dysfunction in schizophrenia. *Canadian Journal of Psychiatry*, 41 (supl. 1), S14-S20.

Suslow, T., Schonauer, K., and Arolt, V. (2001). Attention training in the cognitive rehabilitation of schizophrenic patients: A review of efficacy studies. *Acta Psychiatrica Scandinavica,* 103, 15-23.

Tafliński, T. (1998). Edukacja pacjentów i ich rodzin jako element oddziaływań psychospołecznych w leczeniu schizofrenii [Schizophrenic patients' and their families' education as a part of psychosocial influence in schizophrenia treatment]. *Psychoterapia*, 1 (104), 33-42.

Thompson, K. N., McGorry, P. D., and Harrigan, S. M. (2001). Reduced awareness of illness in first-episode psychosis. *Comprehensive Psychiatry*, 42, 498-503.

Velligan, D. I., Bow-Thomas, C. C., Huntzinger, C., Ritch, J., Ledbetter, N., Prihoda, T.J., and Miller, A.L. (2000). Randomized controlled trial of the use of compensatory strategies to enhance adaptive functioning in outpatients with schizophrenia. *American Journal of Psychiatry,* 157, 1317-1323.

Velligan, D. I., Mahurin, R. K., True J. E., Lefton, R. S., and Flores, C. V. (1996). Preliminary evaluation of cognitive adaptation training to compensate for cognitive deficits in schizophrenia. *Psychiatric Services*, 47, 415-417.

Voruganti, L. N. P., Heslegrave R. J., and Awad, A. G. (1997). Neurocognitive correlates of positive and negative syndromes in schizophrenia. *Canadian Journal of Psychiatry*, 42, 1066-1071.

Weiden, P. J. (1997). Psychosocial management of noncompliance. *Journal of Practical Psychiatry and Behavioral Health*, 3, 169-175.

Wexler, B. E., Hawkins, K. A., Rounsaville, B., Anderson, M., Sernyak, M. J., and Green, M. F. (1997). Normal neurocognitive performance after extended practice in patients with schizophrenia. *Schizophrenia Research*, 26, 173-180.

Wiedl, K. H. (1999). Cognitive modifiability as a measure of readiness for rehabilitation. *Psychiatric Services*, 50, 1411-1419.

Woonings, F. M. J., Appelo, M. T., Kluiter, H., Slooff, C. J., and van den Bosch, R. J. (2002). Learning (potential) and social functioning in schizophrenia. *Schizophrenia Research*, 59, 287-296.

World Health Organization. (1992). *The ICD-10 classification of mental and behavioral disorders: Clinical descriptions and diagnostic guidelines*. Geneva: WHO. (Polish translation edited by S. Pużyński and J. Wciórka).

Wykes T., Reeder C., Corner J., Williams C., and Everitt B. (1999). The effects of neurocognitive remediation on executive processing in patients with schizophrenia. *Schizophrenia Bulletin*, 25, 291-307.

Young, D. A., Davila, R., and Scher, H. (1993). Unawareness of illness and neuropsychological performance in chronic schizophrenia. *Schizophrenia Research*, 10, 117-124.

Young, D. A., Zakzanis, K. K., Bailey, C., Davila, R., Griese, J., Sartory, G., and Thom, A. (1998). Further parameters of insight and neuropsychological deficit in schizophrenia and other chronic mental disease. *Journal of Nervous and Mental Disease*, 186, 44-50.

In: Schizophrenia Research Trends
Editor: Konstance V. Almann, pp.183-247

ISBN 13: 978-1-60021-746-3

SPECIAL BOOK BIBLIOGRAPHY ON SCHIZOPHRENIA

100 questions & answers about schizophrenia: painful minds / Lynn E. DeLisi. Published/Created: Sudbury, Mass.: Jones and Bartlett Publishers, c2006. Description: xv, 141 p.: ill.; 23 cm. ISBN: 0763736546 (pbk.: alk. paper) 9780763736545 (pbk.: alk. paper).

A casebook of cognitive behaviour therapy for command hallucinations: a social rank theory approach / Sarah Byrne ... [et al.]. Published/Created: Hove, East Sussex; New York, NY: Routledge, 2006. Description: p.; cm. Projected Publication Date: 0601 ISBN: 1583917853 (hbk)

A Clinical guide for the treatment of schizophrenia / edited by Alan S. Bellack. Published/Created: New York: Plenum Press, c1989. Description: xiv, 329 p.; 24 cm. ISBN: 0306430649

A comparative investigation of the performance of childhood schizophrenics and non-schizophrenic children on the Wechsler intelligence scale for children. Published/Created: [Garden City, N.Y.,] 1957. Description: 64 l. diagrs., tables. 29 cm.

A comparison of formal and content factors in the diagnostic testing of schizophrenia.

A comparison of normal and schizophrenic subjects in level of aspiration, frustration, aggression. Published/Created: New York, New York University, 1952. Description: 12 p. illus. 23 cm.

A follow-up investigation of schizophrenic children treated in residence. Published/Created: [New York, Jewish Board of Guardians, 1970] Description: 71 p. 23 cm.

A Harry Stack Sullivan case seminar: treatment of a young male schizophrenic / with comment, twenty-five years later, by John C. Dillingham ... [et al.]; Robert G. Kvarnes, editor, Gloria H. Parloff, assistant editor. Edition Information: 1st ed. Published/Created: New York: Norton, c1976. Description: xvii, 241 p.; 22 cm. ISBN: 0393011305

A home for the heart. Edition Information: [1st ed.] Published/Created: New York, Knopf, 1974. Description: x, 461 p. illus. 25 cm. ISBN: 0394483774

A new approach to schizophrenia. Published/Created: New York, Merlin Press, 1956. Description: 195 p. 22 cm.

A New concept in psychiatric management [Motion picture] Published/Created: [n.p.] E. R. Squibb and Sons, 1967. Made by Sturgis-Grant Productions. Description: p. 39 min. sd. color. 16 mm.

A new psychotherapy in schizophrenia; relief of frustrations by symbolic realization. Published/Created: New York, Grune & Stratton, 1956. Description: 199 p. 23 cm.

A pebble in Newcomb's Pond / Marianna Dengler; illustrated by Kathleen Garry-McCord. Published/Created: New York: Holt, Rinehart and Winston, c1979. Description: 160 p.: ill.; 22 cm. ISBN: 0030446414

A portrait of Pia / Marisabina Russo. Published/Created: Orlando: Harcourt, 2007. Description: p. cm. Projected Publication Date: 0704 ISBN: 9780152055776

A promise of sanity / Carolyn Pearl Owens with Melody Beattie. Published/Created: Wheaton, Ill.: Tyndale House Publishers, c1982. Description: 179 p.; 21 cm. ISBN: 0842349014 (pbk.)

A psychotherapy of schizophrenia: direct analysis. Including an appendix by Arthur Auerbach. With a foreword by O. Spurgeon English, and a pref. by Lawrence S. Kubie. Published/Created: Springfield, Ill., Thomas [1961] Description: 279 p. illus. 24 cm.

A schizophrenic patient's response in art therapy to changes in the life of the psychotherapist Published/Created: Bethesda, Md., U. S. Dept. of Health, Education, and Welfare, Public Health Service, National Institutes of Health [1960] Description: 30 p. illus. 24 cm.

A solitary dance: a novel / by Robert Lane. Edition Information: 1st ed. Published/Created: Winnebago, Wisc.: Serrell & Simons, 1983. Description: 224 p.: ill.; 23 cm. ISBN: 0943104823: 0943104831 (pbk.)

A study of conceptual behavior in reactive and process schizophrenics. Published/Created: [n.p., n.d.] Description: 38 l. illus.

A time to heal; corrective socialization: a treatment approach to childhood schizophrenia, by William Goldfarb, Irving Mintz, and Katherine W. Stroock. Published/Created: New York, International Universities Press [c1969] Description: ix, 148 p. 23 cm.

A user's guide to capitalism and schizophrenia: deviations from Deleuze and Guattari / Brian Massumi. Edition Information: A Swerve ed. Published/Created: Cambridge, Mass.: MIT Press, c1992. Description: 229 p.; 24 cm. ISBN: 0262132826 (hc) 0262631431 (pbk)

A way to the soul of the mentally ill. Edition Information: Authorized English ed. by Rudolf Ekstein and Bernard H. Hall. Foreword by Frieda Fromm-Reichmann. Published/Created: New York, International Universities Press [1954] Description: 158 p. 23 cm.

Abnormalities in parents of schizophrenics: a review of the literature and an investigation of communication defects and deviances / by Steven R. Hirsch and Julian P. Leff. Published/Created: London; New York: Oxford University Press, 1975. Description: 200 p.: ill.; 26 cm. ISBN: 0197121446

Adaptation in schizophrenia: the theory of segmental set / David Shakow. Published/Created: New York: Wiley, c1979. Description: xvii, 245 p.; 24 cm. ISBN: 0471057568

Advances in the neurobiology of schizophrenia / edited by J.A. den Boer, H.G.M. Westenberg, and H.M. van Praag. Published/Created: Chichester; New York: Wiley, c1995. Description: x, 469 p.: ill.; 24 cm. ISBN: 0471952877

Affective and schizophrenic disorders: new approaches to diagnosis and treatment / edited by Michael R. Zales. Published/Created: New York: Brunner/Mazel, c1983. Description: xvii, 291 p.: ill.; 24 cm. ISBN: 0876303246

Against the tide; Edition Information: [1st ed.] Published/Created: New York, Exposition Press [1966] Description: p. cm.

All my children, by Jacqui Lee Schiff with Beth Day. Published/Created: [New York] M.Evans; distributed in association with Lippincott, Philadelphia [1970] Description: 233 p. 22 cm.

America fooled: the truth about antidepressants, antipsychotics, and how we've been deceived / Timothy Scott. Published/Created: Victoria, Tex.: Argo Pub., c2006. Description: 523 p.; 24 cm. ISBN: 9780977307500 (hardcover: alk. paper) 0977307506 (hardcover: alk. paper)

Amines and schizophrenia; [papers] edited by Harold E. Himwich, Seymour S. Kety [and] John R. Smythies. Edition Information: [1st ed.] Published/Created: Oxford, New York, Symposium Publications Division, Pergamon Press [1967] Description: ix, 290 p. illus. 24 cm.

An anthropological physiology of schizophrenia and its sociofamilial context, by L. I. Jacobs. Edition Information: [1st ed.] Published/Created: New York, Vantage Press [c1966] Description: 96 p. illus. 21 cm.

An atlas of schizophrenia / Martin Stefan, Mike Travis and Robin M. Murray. Published/Created: New York: Parthenon Pub. Group, c2002. Description: 98 p. ill. (chiefly col.); 30 cm. ISBN: 1850700745 (alk. paper)

An evaluation of an intensive group living program with schizophrenic patients, by Meyer Williams [and others]. Published/Created: [Washington] American Psychological Association, 1962. Description: 25 p. 26 cm.

An experimental study of certain aspects of paranoid schizophrenic mosaic field organization and their interrelationships. Published/Created: Washington, Catholic University of America Press, 1954. Description: 55 p. illus., tables. 23 cm.

An Inquiry into schizophrenia and depression / volume editors, P. Simon, P. Soubrié D. Widlocher. Published/Created: Basel; New York: Karger, c1988. Description: 212 p.: ill.; 25 cm. ISBN: 3805547579

Analysis of parergasia, by Gladys C. Terry and Thomas A. C. Rennie, with introduction by Adolf Meyer. Published/Created: New York, Nervous and Mental Disease Monographs, 1938. Description: 4 p. l., 3-202 p. incl. tables. fold. diagr. 24 cm.

Annotated bibliography of childhood schizophrenia and related disorders, Published/Created: New York, Basic Books [1956] Description: p. cm.

Annotated bibliography on childhood schizophrenia, 1955-1964 [by] James R. Tilton, Marian K. DeMyer [and] Lois Hendrickson Loew. Published/Created:

New York, Grune & Stratton [1966] Description: v, 136 p. 25 cm.

Annual review of the schizophrenic syndrome. Published/Created: New York, Brunner/Mazel. Description: 4 v. ill. 24 cm. v. 2-5; 1972-1976/77. ISSN: 0090-287X

Anti-Oedipus: capitalism and schizophrenia / by Gilles Deleuze and Félix Guattari; translated from the French by Robert Hurley, Mark Seem, and Helen R. Lane. Published/Created: New York: Viking Press, 1977. Description: xxiv, 400 p.; 25 cm. ISBN: 0670129410

Anti-Oedipus: capitalism and schizophrenia / by Gilles Deleuze and Felix Guattari; translated from the French by Robert Hurley, Mark Seem, and Helen R. Lane; preface by Michel Foucault. Published/Created: Minneapolis: University of Minnesota Press, c1983. Description: xxiv, 400 p.: ill.; 22 cm. ISBN: 0816612250 (pbk.)

Approaches to insanity; a philosophical & sociological study. Published/Created: New York, Wiley [1973] Description: ix, 170 p. 23 cm. ISBN: 0470177403

Armstrong circle theatre. Man in shadow / a Talent Associates production; NBC Television presents; directed by William Corrigan; executive producer, David Susskind; produced by Robert Costello; television play by David Padwa. Published/Created: United States: NBC Television Network, 1956-03-06; United States: NBC Television Network, 1956-07-10. Description: 2 reels of 2 (ca. 2160 ft.): sd.; 16 mm. neg trk. 2 reels of 2 (ca. 2160 ft.): sd.; 16 mm. neg trk (copy 2)

As it happeneth to the fool: a study of withdrawal and depression, with examples from autism and schizoid states. Published/Created: London, Guild of Pastoral Psychology, 1969. Description: 30 p. 19 cm. ISBN: 0852660049

Assessing schizophrenic thinking: a clinical and research instrument for measuring thought disorder / Mary Hollis Johnston, Philip S. Holzman. Edition Information: 1st ed. Published/Created: San Francisco: Jossey-Bass, c1979. Description: xvi, 310 p.: ill.; 24 cm. ISBN: 0875894348

Attention and schizophrenia: neurobiological bases / Robert D. Oades. Published/Created: Boston: Pitman Advanced Pub. Program, c1982. Description: 343 p.: ill.; 25 cm. ISBN: 0273084909

Autobiography of a schizophrenic. Published/Created: [Bristol? Eng.] 1951. Description: 64 p. 19 cm.

Aversive maternal control: a theory of schizophrenic development [by] Alfred B. Heilbrun, Jr. Published/Created: New York, Wiley [1973] Description: xiii, 323 p. 23 cm. ISBN: 0471368954

Basic mechanisms of psychotherapeutic significance: three examples of one kind of analysis / by Erik Gotlind. Published/Created: Stockholm: Almqvist & Wiksell International, 1974. Description: 90 p.; 22 cm. ISBN: 9122000011

Behavioral treatment for substance abuse in people with serious and persistent mental illness: a handbook for mental health professionals / Alan S. Bellack, Melanie E. Bennett, Jean S. Gearon. Published/Created: New York, NY: Routledge, 2007. Description: p.; cm. Projected Publication Date: 1111 ISBN: 0415952832 (pb: alk. paper)

Benedict Nta TankaÊ¾s Commentary and dramatized ideas on "Disease and witchcraft in our society": a Schreber case from Cameroon annotated autobiographical notes by an African on his mental illness / Alexander Boroffka. Published/Created: Frankfurt a.M.; Bern; Cirencester/U.K.: Lang, 1980. Description: 150 p.: maps; 21 cm. ISBN: 382046901X

Beyond symptom suppression: improving long-term outcomes of schizophrenia / formulated by the Committee on Psychopathology, Group for the Advancement of Psychiatry. Edition Information: 1st ed. Published/Created: Washington, DC: American Psychiatric Press, c1992. Description: x, 117 p.; 24 cm. ISBN: 0873182022 (alk. paper)

Beyond the double bind: communication and family systems, theories, and techniques with schizophrenics / edited by Milton M. Berger. Published/Created: New York: Brunner/Mazel, c1978. Description: xix, 264 p.; 24 cm. ISBN: 0876301847

Biochemistry, schizophrenias, and affective illnesses / edited by Harold E. Himwich. Published/Created: Huntington, N.Y.: R. E. Krieger Pub. Co., 1977, c1971. Description: xiv, 500 p.: ill.; 24 cm. ISBN: 0882755242

Biochemistry, schizophrenias, and affective illnesses. Edited by Harold E. Himwich. Published/Created: Baltimore, Williams & Wilkins, 1970 [c1971] Description: xiv, 500 p. illus. 24 cm. ISBN: 0683040278

Biological aspects of schizophrenia and addiction / edited by Gwynneth Hemmings. Published/Created: Chichester [Sussex]; New York: Wiley, c1982. Description: xv, 277 p.: ill.; 24 cm. ISBN: 0471101176

Biological mechanisms of schizophrenia and schizophrenia-like psychoses / by Hisatoshi Mitsuda and Tetsuo Fukuda. Published/Created: Stuttgart: Thieme; Tokyo: Igaku Shoin, 1975. Description: xx, 341 p.: ill.; 27 cm. ISBN: 3135215016

Biological perspectives of schizophrenia: report of the Dahlem Workshop on Biological Perspectives of Schizophrenia, Berlin 1986, October 26-31 / rapporteurs, T.J. Crow ... [et al.]; program advisory committee, H. Helmchen ... [et al.]. Published/Created: Chichester; New York: Wiley, 1987. Description: xiii, 354 p.; 24 cm. ISBN: 0471916838

Biological psychiatry: a review of recent advances [by] J. R. Smythies with the collaboration of Alec Coppen and Norman Kreitman. Published/Created: London, Heinemann Medical, 1968. Description: viii, 112 p. illus. 22 cm.

Biological psychiatry; a review of recent advances [by] J. R. Smythies with the collaboration of Alec Coppen and Norman Kreitman. Published/Created: [New York] Springer-Verlag New York [1968] Description: viii, 112 p. illus. 22 cm.

Biological research in schizophrenia; report of a WHO Scientific Group. Published/Created: Geneva, World Health Organization, 1970. Description: 35 p. 24 cm.

Biology of schizophrenia and affective disease / edited by Stanley J. Watson. Edition Information: 1st ed. Published/Created: Washington, D.C.: American Psychiatric Press, c1996. Description: xvii, 535 p.: ill.; 24 cm. ISBN: 0880487461

Borderline phenomena and the Rorschach test / edited by Jay S. Kwawer ... [et al.].

Published/Created: New York, NY: International Universities Press, c1980. Description: xvii, 505 p.; 24 cm. ISBN: 0823605779

Brain biochemistry and brain disorders / Philip G. Strange. Published/Created: Oxford; New York: Oxford University Press, 1992. Description: xi, 342 p.: ill.; 26 cm. ISBN: 0198542593 (hbk.): 0198547757 (pbk.)

Brain dopaminergic systems: imaging with positron tomography: proceedings of a workshop held in Caen, France, within the framework of the European Community medical and public health research / edited by J.C. Baron ... [et al.]. Published/Created: Dordrecht; Boston: Kluwer Academic Publishers, 1991. Description: xii, 198 p.: ill.; 25 cm. ISBN: 079231476X (hb: alk. paper)

Brain electrical potentials and psychopathology: proceedings of the VII International Symposium on Clinical Neurophysiological Aspects of Psychiatric Conditions, held September 7-8, 1985, in Philadelphia, Pennsylvania / editors, Charles Shagass, Richard C. Josiassen, Richard A. Roemer. Published/Created: New York: Elsevier, c1986. Description: xiv, 398 p.: ill.; 24 cm. ISBN: 0444011277

Breakthroughs in antipsychotic medications: a guide for consumers, families, and clinicians / Peter J. Weiden ... [et al.]. Published/Created: New York: W. W. Norton, c1999. Description: 207 p.: ill. (some col.); 25 cm. ISBN: 0393703037 (pbk.)

Bûchner and madness: schizophrenia in Georg Bûchner's Lenz and Woyzeck / James Crighton. Published/Created: Lewiston, N.Y.: E. Mellen Press, c1998. Description: x, 318 p.; 24 cm. ISBN: 0773413529

Bunretsubyö no genshögaku. Published/Created: 50 [1975] Description: 3, 375 p.; 22 cm.

Bunretsubyö no ronrigakuteki seishin byöri. Published/Created: 1977. Description: vi, 321, 7 p.: ill.; 22 cm.

Can a virus cause schizophrenia?: facts and hypotheses / Bradley D. Pearce. Published/Created: Boston, Mass.: Kluwer Academic Pub., c2003. Description: x, 144 p.: ill.; 24 cm. ISBN: 1402073003 (alk. paper)

Can schizophrenia be localized in the brain? / edited by Nancy C. Andreasen. Published/Created: Washington, DC: American Psychiatric Press, c1986. Description: x, 87 p.; 22 cm. ISBN: 088048084X (alk. paper)

Capitalism and schizophrenia in the later novels of Louis-Ferdinand Céline: d'un ... l'autre / Greg Hainge. Published/Created: New York: P. Lang, c2001. Description: ix, 276 p.; 24 cm. ISBN: 0820451959 (alk. paper)

Case studies in schizophrenia: based on the readings of Edgar Cayce / David McMillin. Published/Created: Virginia Beach, Va.: A.R.E. Press, 1997. Description: xvi, 195 p.; 21 cm. ISBN: 0876043821 (pbk.)

Case studies in schizophrenia [by] Clarence G. Schulz and Rose K. Kilgalen. Published/Created: New York, Basic Books [1970, c1969] Description: xxi, 265 p. 25 cm.

Catecholamines and schizophrenia: [proceedings of the third international Symposium on Catecholamines,

Strasbourg, France, May 18-21, 1973] / edited by Steven W. Matthysse and Seymour S. Kety. Edition Information: 1st ed. Published/Created: Oxford; New York: Pergamon Press, 1975. Description: xix, 369 p., [6] leaves of plates: ill.; 26 cm. ISBN: 0080182429

Causal thought in schizophrenic children. Published/Created: Johannesburg, Rand Afrikaans University, 1972. Description: 87 p. 21 cm. ISBN: 0869700065

Celebrate the morning. Edition Information: [1st ed.] Published/Created: New York, Atheneum, 1972. Description: 177 p. 22 cm.

Chaosophy / Félix Guattari; edited by Sylvère Lotringer. Published/Created: New York, N.Y.: Semiotext(e): Distributed by MIT Press, c1995. Description: 252 p.; 18 cm. ISBN: 1570270198

Charles Darwin in cyberspace: a novel / written & illustrated by Claire Burch. Published/Created: Oakland, Calif.: Regent Press, c2005. Description: ix, 339 p.: ill.; 21 cm. ISBN: 1587901161 (pbk.)

Childhood intellectual development in schizophrenia. [Sound recording] [By] George W. Albee. Published/Created: Fort Lee, N.J., Sigma Inforation [1972] Description: 1 cassette. 2 1/2 x 4 in.

Childhood schizophrenia / Sheila Cantor. Published/Created: New York: Guilford Press, c1988. Description: viii, 193 p.: ill.; 24 cm. ISBN: 0898627133

Childhood schizophrenia. Published/Created: Cambridge, Mass., Published for the Commonwealth Fund by Harvard University Press, 1961. Description: 216 p. 22 cm.

Children at risk for schizophrenia: a longitudinal perspective / edited by Norman F. Watt ... [et al.]. Published/Created: Cambridge [Cambridgeshire]; New York: Cambridge University Press, 1984. Description: xvii, 658 p.: ill.; 24 cm. ISBN: 0521248884

Children with autism and other pervasive disorders of development & behavior: therapy through activities / David L. Nelson. Published/Created: Thorofare, NJ: Slack, c1984. Description: 263, [38] p.: ill.; 24 cm. ISBN: 0913590959

Children with emerald eyes: histories of extraordinary boys & girls / by Mira Rothenberg; foreword by Peter A. Levine. Published/Created: Berkeley, Calif.: North Atlantic Books; Lyons, Colo.: Ergos Institute, 2002. Description: xiii, 293 p.: ill.; 23 cm. ISBN: 1556434480 (pbk.)

Children with emerald eyes: histories of extraordinary boys & girls / Mira Rothenberg. Published/Created: New York: Dial Press, c1977. Description: 293 p.; 24 cm. ISBN: 0803713770

Children without childhood; a study of childhood schizophrenia [by] Benjamin B. Wolman. Published/Created: New York, Grune & Stratton [1970] Description: ix, 236 p. 23 cm.

Chronic schizophrenia [by] Thomas Freeman, John L. Cameron [and] Andrew McGhie. Pref. by Anna Freud. Foreword by T. Ferguson Rodger. Published/Created: New York, International Universities Press [1958] Description: x, 158 p. 23 cm.

Chronic schizophrenia and adult autism: issues in diagnosis, assessment, and psychological treatment / Johnny L. Matson, editor. Published/Created: New

York: Springer Pub. Co., c1989. Description: x, 342 p.; 24 cm. ISBN: 0826160204

Chronic schizophrenia; explorations in theory and treatment. Edited by Lawrence Appleby, Jordan M. Scher, and John Cumming. With a foreword by Karl Menninger. Published/Created: Glencoe, Ill., Free Press [1960] Description: xv, 368 p. illus., diagrs., tables. 22 cm.

Clinical and other uses of the Hoffer-Osmond diagnostic test / [contributors, R. Glen Green ... et al.]; editors, Abram Hoffer, Harold Kelm, Humphry Osmond. Published/Created: Huntington, N.Y.: R. E. Krieger Pub. Co., 1975. Description: xvi, 237 p.; 24 cm. ISBN: 0882752944

Clinical practice for people with schizophrenia: a humanistic and empathetic encounter / Kam-Shing Yip. Published/Created: New York: Nova Science Publishers, c2006. Description: p.; cm. Projected Publication Date: 0604 ISBN: 1600210732

Clinical research in schizophrenia: a multidimensional approach / [authored and] edited by Roy R. Grinker, Sr. and Martin Harrow. Published/Created: Springfield, Ill., U.S.A.: Thomas, c1987. Description: xvii, 418 p.; 26 cm. ISBN: 0398053235

Clinical trials with methylperidol on psychotic, especially paranoid patients. By Henry Mjônes, Carl-Otto Jonsson [and] Lars-Gôran Allgén. Published/Created: Stockholm, 1966. Description: 10 p. illus., (13) pages of tables. 30 cm.

Cognition in schizophrenia: impairments, importance, and treatment strategies / edited by Tonmoy Sharma and Philip Harvey. Published/Created: Oxford; New York: Oxford University Press, 2000. Description: x, 363 p.: ill.; 24 cm. ISBN: 019262993X (pbk.)

Cognition in schizophrenia and paranoia: the integration of cognitive processes / Peter A. Magaro. Published/Created: Hillsdale, N.J.: L. Erlbaum Associates, 1980. Description: xii, 339 p.: ill.; 24 cm. ISBN: 0898590280

Cognitive dysfunction in schizophrenia. Published/Created: Copenhagen: Munksgaard, c2001. Description: 91 p.: ill.; 28 cm. ISBN: 8716164644

Cognitive synthesis test / P.P. Abraham, L.A. Okoniewski, M. Lehman; with a foreword by L. Bellak. Published/Created: Berlin; New York: Springer-Verlag, c1987. Description: vii, xii p.: col. ill.; 30 cm. ISBN: 0387173307 (U.S.: pbk.)

Cognitive therapy of schizophrenia / David G. Kingdon, Douglas Turkington. Published/Created: New York: Guilford Press, c2005. Description: xvi, 219 p.: ill.; 26 cm. ISBN: 1593851049 (alk. paper)

Cognitive therapy with schizophrenic patients / Carlo Perris. Published/Created: New York: Guilford Press, c1989. Description: xiii, 240 p.: ill.; 24 cm. ISBN: 0898627370

Cognitive therapy with schizophrenic patients: the evolution of a new treatment approach / edited by Marco C.G. Merlo, Carlo Perris, Hans D. Brenner. Published/Created: Seattle: Hogrefe & Huber Publishers, c2002. Description: xvi, 218 p.: ill.; 24 cm. ISBN: 0889372535

Cognitive-behavioral therapy of schizophrenia / David G. Kingdon, Douglas Turkington; foreword by Aaron T. Beck.

Published/Created: New York: Guiford Press, c1994. Description: xii, 242 p.: ill.; 24 cm. ISBN: 0898623359 (acid-free paper)

Cognitive-behavioural therapy with delusions and hallucinations: a practice manual / Hazel E. Nelson. Edition Information: 2nd ed. Published/Created: Cheltenham, U.K.: Nelson Thornes, 2005. Description: ix, 339 p.: ill.; 24 cm. ISBN: 0748792562 (pbk.)

Collected papers on schizophrenia and related subjects, by Harold F. Searles. With a pref. by Robert P. Knight. Published/Created: New York, International Universities Press, 1965. Description: 797 p. 23 cm.

Common errors in the psychopharmacologic treatment of schizophrenia. [Sound recording] By] Ivan K. Goldberg. Published/Created: Fort Lee, N.J., Sigma Information [1973] Description: p. 1 cassette. 2 1/2 x 4 in.

Common questions on schizophrenia and their answers / Abram Hoffer. Published/Created: New Canaan, Conn.: Keats Pub., c1987. Description: 213 p.: ill.; 21 cm. ISBN: 0879833785 (pbk.)

Communication and the mentally ill patient: developmental and linguistic approaches to schizophrenia / edited by Jenny France and Niki Muir. Edition Information: 2nd ed. Published/Created: Philadelphia; London: Jessica Kingsley Publishers, 2000. Description: p. cm. Projected Publication Date: 0002

Communication and the mentally ill patient: developmental and linguistic approaches to schizophrenia / edited by Jenny France and Niki Muir. Published/Created: London; Bristol, PA: Jessica Kingsley, c1997. Description: 195 p.: ill.; 24 cm. ISBN: 1853024147

Communication therapy in childhood schizophrenia: an auditory monitoring approach / Elaine Yudkovitz, Nancy Lewison, Judy Rottersman. Published/Created: New York: Grune & Stratton, c1976. Description: xiii, 209 p.; 24 cm. ISBN: 0808909932

Communication, family, and marriage, edited by Don D. Jackson. Published/Created: Palo Alto, Calif., Science and Behavior Books [1968] Description: x, 289 p. 22 cm.

Community and schizophrenia; an epidemiological analysis [by] H. Warren Dunham. Published/Created: Detroit, Wayne State University Press, 1965. Description: xxv, 312 p. illus., maps. 24 cm.

Complex theory of schizophrenia. [Sound recording] Published/Created: [S.l.]: Big Sur Recordings, [1972] Description: 1 cassette.

Comprehensive treatment of schizophrenia: linking neurobehavioral findings to psychosocial approaches / H. Kashima ... [et al.] (eds.). Published/Created: Tokyo; New York: Springer, c2002. Description: xvii, 404 p.: ill.; 24 cm. ISBN: 4431702989 (hard: alk. paper)

Conceptual breadth in process and reactive schizophrenia. Published/Created: [n.p., n.d.] Description: 38 l. illus.

Conceptual thinking in schizophrenic children.

Conflict and reconciliation; a study in human relations and schizophrenia. Published/Created: New York, Science House, 1969. Description: xi, 267 p. 22 cm. ISBN: 0876680252

Conflict and reconciliation; a study in human relations and schizophrenia. Published/Created: Garden City, N.Y., Anchor Books, 1969. Description: xi, 267 p. 19 cm.

Confronting hallucinations. [Sound recording] Published/Created: [S.l.]: Big Sur Recordings, [1968] Description: 2 cassettes.

Congruent therapy. [Sound recording] Published/Created: Orlando, Fla., American Academy of Psychotherapists [196-] Description: p. cm.

Conquering schizophrenia: a father, his son, and a medical breakthrough / Peter Wyden. Published/Created: New York: Knopf: Distributed by Random House, Inc., 1998. Description: viii, 335 p.: ill.; 25 cm. ISBN: 0679446710 (alk. paper)

Consciousness: East and West / Kenneth R. Pelletier and Charles Garfield. Published/Created: New York: Harper & Row, 1976. Description: x, 307 p.; 21 cm. ISBN: 0060903864

Contemporary diagnosis and management of the patient with schizophrenia / Henry A. Nasrallah and Donald J. Smeltzer. Published/Created: Newtown, Pa.: Handbooks in Health Care Co., c2002. Description: 248 p.: ill.; 18 cm. ISBN: 1931981027

Contemporary issues in schizophrenia / edited by Alan Kerr, Philip Snaith; with the assistance of Stanley Thorley (indexing) Alison Campbell. Published/Created: London: Gaskell; [Washington, D.C.]: Distributed in North America by American Psychiatric Press, c1986. Description: xii, 483 p.: ill.; 25 cm. ISBN: 0880482281

Contemporary issues in the treatment of schizophrenia / edited by Christian L. Shriqui, Henry A. Nasrallah. Edition Information: 1st ed. Published/Created: Washington, DC: American Psychiatric Press, c1995. Description: xxvi, 863 p.: ill.; 24 cm. ISBN: 0880486813 (alk. paper)

Contemporary theories of schizophrenia: review and synthesis / Sue A. Shapiro. Published/Created: New York: McGraw-Hill, c1981. Description: xii, 289 p.; 24 cm. ISBN: 007056423X

Contributions to the psychopathology of schizophrenia: selected reprints, with new commentaries, from Progress in experimental personality Research / edited by Brendan A. Maher. Published/Created: New York: Academic Press, 1977. Description: ix, 382 p.: ill.; 23 cm. ISBN: 0124652506

Controversies in schizophrenia: changes and constancies: proceedings on the 74th Annual Meeting of the American Psychopathological Association, New York City, March 1-3, 1984 / edited by Murray Alpert. Published/Created: New York: Guilford Press, c1985. Description: ix, 432 p.: ill.; 24 cm. ISBN: 0898626579

Coping with mental illness / Barbara Moe. Edition Information: 1st ed. Published/Created: New York: Rosen Pub. Group, 2001. Description: 138 p.; 24 cm. ISBN: 0823932052 (lib. bdg.)

Coping with schizophrenia / Evelyn B. Kelly. Edition Information: 1st ed. Published/Created: New York: Rosen Pub., 2001. Description: 106 p.: ill.; 24 cm. ISBN: 0823928535 (lib. bdg.)

Coping with schizophrenia: a guide for families / Kim T. Mueser, Susan

Gingerich; foreword by Harriet P. Lefley. Published/Created: Oakland, Calif.: New Harbinger Pub., c1994. Description: xvii, 355 p.: ill.; 23 cm. ISBN: 1879237784 (pbk.) 1879237792

Coping with schizophrenia: a survival manual for parents, relatives, and friends / by Mona Wasow; [with forewords by Shirley Starr & Werner Mendel]. Published/Created: Palo Alto, Calif.: Science and Behavior Books, c1982. Description: xviii, 160 p.; 23 cm. ISBN: 0831400625 (pbk.)

Countertransference and related subjects: selected papers / by Harold F. Searles. Published/Created: New York: International Universities Press, 1979. Description: xi, 625 p.; 24 cm. ISBN: 0823610853

Creative, psychotic & ecstatic states. [Sound recording] Published/Created: [S.l.]: Big Sur Recordings, [1969] Description: 4 cassettes.

Crime and schizophrenia: causes and cures / Adrian Raine, editor. Published/Created: New York: Nova Science Publishers, c2006. Description: x, 342 p.: ill. (some col.); 26 cm. ISBN: 1594546096

Critical issues in the treatment of schizophrenia / Workshop on Critical Issues in the Treatment of Schizophrenia, Florence, March 10-12, 1995; volume editors, N. Brunello ... [et al.]. Published/Created: Basel; New York: Karger, 1995. Description: vi, 205 p.: ill.; 25 cm. ISBN: 3805561997 (hardcover: acid-free paper)

Crossing the borders: psychotherapy of schizophrenia / Svein Haugsgjerd ... [et al.]; edited by Jens Bolvig Hansen. Published/Created: Ludvika, [Sweden]: Dualis: Nordic Association for Psychotherapy of Psychoses, [1993] Description: 128 p.; 21 cm. ISBN: 9187852136

Cross-national study of the symptomatology of schizophrenia: an Anglo-Americo-Egyptian comparison / by Refaat Mahfouz Mahmoud; supervisor, M.S. Abdel-Gawad; introduction by Y.T. el-Rakhawy. Published/Created: Cairo: Dar el-Ghad Scientific Publications, 1977. Description: ii, 167, 3, 18 p.: graphs; 29 cm.

Cross-walk of national schizophrenia guidelines / editors, Molly T. Finnerty, John P. Docherty, J.B. Goss. Published/Created: Clifton Park, NY: RTP PUb. Group, c2000. Description: 82 p.: ill. (some col.); 28 cm. ISBN: 0937317039

Cultura e schizofrenia. Published/Created: [Torino], Minerva medica, 1967. Description: 69 p. 22 cm.

Current issues in the psychopharmacology of schizophrenia / Alan Breier ... [et al.]. Published/Created: Philadelphia: Lippincott Williams & Wilkins, c2001. Description: xviii, 579 p.: ill.; 24 cm. ISBN: 0781724228

Current problems in neuropsychiatry: schizophrenia, epilepsy, the temporal lobe; edited by R. N. Herrington. Published/Created: London, Published [for] the Royal Medico-Psychological Association by Headley Bros, 1969. Description: v, 184 p. 7 plates, illus. 25 cm. ISBN: 0900443022

Dante's cure: a journey out of madness / by Daniel Dorman. Published/Created: New York: Other Press, c2003. Description: xi, 266 p.; 23 cm. ISBN: 1590511018 (hbk.: alk. paper)

Deinstitutionalized residential care for the mentally disordered: the Soteria House approach / Holly Skodol Wilson. Published/Created: New York: Grune & Stratton, c1982. Description: xx, 138 p.; 24 cm. ISBN: 0808914278

Deleuze and Guattari: an introduction to the politics of desire / Philip Goodchild. Published/Created: London; Thousand Oaks, Calif.: SAGE, 1996. Description: ix, 226 p.; 24 cm. ISBN: 0803976003 0803976011 (pbk.)

Deleuze and Guattari's Anti-Oedipus: introduction to schizoanalysis / Eugene W. Holland. Published/Created: London; New York: Routledge, 1999. Description: xii, 161 p.: ill.; 24 cm. ISBN: 0415113180 (hbk) 0415113199 (pbk.)

Dementia prÃ¦cox and paraphrenia, Published/Created: Edinburgh, E. & S. Livingstone, 1919. Description: 1 p. l., x. 331 p. illus. (incl. facsims.) diagrs. 23 cm.

Dementia praecox and paraphrenia. Translated by R. Mary Barclay. Edited by George M. Robertson. Published/Created: Huntington, N.Y., R. E. Krieger Pub. Co., 1971. Description: xxiv, 331 p. illus., facsims. 23 cm.

Dementia praecox, the past decade's work and present status: a review and evaluation. Foreword by Winfred Overholser. Published/Created: New York, Grune & Stratton, 1948 [c1947] Description: xv, 456 p. diagrs. 24 cm.

Depression and schizophrenia: a contribution on their chemical pathologies / H. M. van Praag. Published/Created: New York: Spectrum Publications, c1977. Description: 260 p.: ill.; 24 cm. ISBN: 0893350028

Depression in schizophrenia / edited by Lynn E. DeLisi. Edition Information: 1st ed. Published/Created: Washington, DC: American Psychicatric Press, c1990. Description: xiii, 162 p.: ill.; 22 cm. ISBN: 088048196X (alk. paper)

Depression in schizophrenics / edited by Richard Williams and J. Thomas Dalby. Published/Created: New York: Plenum Press, c1989. Description: vii, 263 p.: ill.; 26 cm. ISBN: 0306432404

Destiny and disease in mental disorders, with special reference to the schizophrenic psychoses, by C. Macfie Campbell. Edition Information: "First edition." Published/Created: New York, Norton [c1935] Description: 207 p. 21 cm.

Developmental neuropathology of schizophrenia / edited by Sarnoff A. Mednick ... [et al.]. Published/Created: New York: Plenum Press, c1991. Description: viii, 247 p.: ill.; 26 cm. ISBN: 0306440814 (hardbound)

Diagnosis: Schizophrenia, a comprehensive resource for patients, families, and helping professionals / [edited by] Rachel Miller and Susan E. Mason. Published/Created: New York: Columbia University Press, c2002. Description: xviii, 192 p.: ill.; 24 cm. ISBN: 0231126247 (cloth: alk. paper) 0231126255 (pbk.: alk. paper)

Diagnostic criteria for functional psychoses / P. Berner ... [et al.]. Edition Information: 2nd ed. Published/Created: Cambridge [England]; New York, NY, USA: Cambridge University Press, 1992. Description: xvi, 268 p.: ill.; 24 cm. ISBN: 0521423155 (hardback)

Diagnostic criteria for schizophrenic and affective psychoses / P. Berner ... [et al.].

Published/Created: [London?]: World Psychiatric Association; [S.l.]: Distributed by American Psychiatric Press, c1983. Description: viii, 183 p.: ill.; 21 cm.

Dialogue with Sammy: a psychoanalytical contribution to the understanding of child psychosis / Joyce McDougall and Serge Lebovici. Published/Created: London: Free Association Books, 1989. Description: x, 278 p.: ill.; 22 cm. ISBN: 1853431095

Differential patterns in schizophrenia on the Weschler-Bellevue intelligence test. Published/Created: Allahabad, U.P., India, Allahabad Christian Press, 1950. Description: vi, 71 p. tables (part fold.) 22 cm.

Differential treatment and prognosis in schizophrenia, by Robert D. Wirt [and] Werner Simon, in collaboration with Anne L. Wirt [and others] Published/Created: Springfield, Ill., C. C. Thomas [1959] Description: 198 p. illus. 24 cm.

Direct analysis and schizophrenia; clinical observations and evaluations [by] O. Spurgeon English [and others] Published/Created: New York, Grune & Stratton [1961] Description: vii, 128 p. 23 cm.

Discontinuity of spiral aftereffect duration trends in acute schizophrenia, by Alf L. Andersson, Gôran Franzén and Egil Ruuth. Published/Created: [Lund] Lund University, 1971. Description: 20 p. 30 cm.

Disembodied spirits and deanimated bodies: the psychopathology of common sense / by Giovanni Stanghellini. Published/Created: Oxford; New York: Oxford University Press, c2004. Description: 225 p.: ill.; 24 cm. ISBN: 0198520883 (hard) 0198520891 (pbk.)

Disordered thinking and schizophrenic psychopathology / by Martin Harrow and Donald Quinlan. Published/Created: New York: Gardner Press, c1985. Description: xviii, 461 p.; 24 cm. ISBN: 0898760992

Disordered thought in schizophrenia [by] Loren J. Chapman [and] Jean P. Chapman. Published/Created: New York, Appleton-Century-Crofts [1973] Description: xi, 359 p. illus. 25 cm. ISBN: 0390184934

Disorders of synaptic plasticity and schizophrenia / edited by John Smythies. Published/Created: San Diego, Calif.: Elsevier Academic Press, 2004. Description: xvi, 542 p.: ill.; 24 cm. ISBN: 0123668603

Disorders of the schizophrenic syndrome / edited by Leopold Bellak. Published/Created: New York: Basic Books, c1979. Description: ix, 629 p.: ill.; 24 cm. ISBN: 0465016758

Disorders of volition / edited by Natalie Sebanz and Wolfgang Prinz. Published/Created: Cambridge, Mass.: MIT Press, c2006. Description: vii, 493 p.: ill. (some col.); 24 cm. ISBN: 0262195402 (hc: alk. paper)

Don D. Jackson: selected essays at the dawn of an era / Wendel A. Ray, editor. Published/Created: Phoenix, Ariz.: Zeig, Tucker, & Theisen, c2005. Description: xxviii, 370 p.: ill.; 23 cm. ISBN: 1932462201 978193246220X 9781932462203

Doris: the story of a disfigured deaf child. Translated by Harold A. Basilius. Published/Created: Detroit, Wayne State

University Press, 1974. Description: 129 p. illus. 24 cm. ISBN: 0814314953

Double bind: the foundation of the communicational approach to the family / edited by Carlos E. Sluzki, Donald C. Ransom. Published/Created: New York: Grune & Stratton; London: distributed in the United Kingdom by Academic Press, c1976. Description: xix, 359 p.; 24 cm. ISBN: 0808909509

Drug and social therapy in chronic schizophrenia. Edited by Milton Greenblatt [and others] Contributing authors: Dexter M. Bullard, Jr. [and others] Published/Created: Springfield, Ill., C.C. Thomas [1965] Description: xiii, 238 p. illus. 24 cm.

Drug maintenance strategies in schizophrenia / edited by John M. Kane. Published/Created: Washington, D.C.: American Psychiatric Press, c1984. Description: xv, 90 p.: ill.; 21 cm. ISBN: 0880480548 (pbk.)

Drug therapy and schizophrenia / by Shirley Brinkerhoff. Published/Created: Philadelphia: Mason Crest Publishers, c2004. Description: [128] p.: col. ill.; 25 cm. ISBN: 1590845749 (lib. bdg.) 1590845595 (series)

Drugs for mental illness: a revolution in psychiatry / Marvin E. Lickey, Barbara Gordon. Published/Created: New York: W.H. Freeman, c1983. Description: viii, 349 p.: ill.; 24 cm. ISBN: 0716714574 0716714582 (pbk.)

Dual diagnosis: schizophrenia and other psychotic disorders and developmental disabilities / by Kathleen M. Olson, Jessica A. Hellings, and Patricia A. Black. Published/Created: Baltimore: Paul H. Brookes, c2003. Description: vii, 47 p.; 23 cm. ISBN: 1557666237

Dynamics of character: self-regulation in psychopathology / David Shapiro. Published/Created: New York: Basic Books, c2000. Description: xii, 172 p.; 24 cm. ISBN: 0465095712

Early clinical intervention and prevention in schizophrenia / edited by William S. Stone, Stephen V. Faraone, Ming T. Tsuang. Published/Created: Totowa, N.J.: Humana Press, c2004. Description: xiv, 374 p.: ill.; 24 cm. + 1 CD-ROM (4 3/4 in.) ISBN: 1588290018 (acid-free paper)

Early intervention in psychotic disorders / edited by Tandy Miller ... [et al.]. Published/Created: Dordrecht; Boston, MA: Kluwer Academic Pub., 2001. Description: xiii, 289 p.: ill.; 25 cm. ISBN: 0792367499 (hardbound: alk. paper) 0792367502 (pbk.: alk. paper)

Edward the "Crazy Man" / by Marie Day. Published/Created: Toronto; New York: Annick Press; Buffalo, NY: Distributed in the U.S.A. by Firefly Books, c2002. Description: 1 v. (unpaged): col. ill.; 28 cm. ISBN: 1550377205 (pbk.) 1550377213 (bound)

Ego functions in schizophrenics, neurotics, and normals; a systematic study of conceptual, diagnostic, and therapeutic aspects [by] Leopold Bellak, Marvin Hurvich [and] Helen K. Gediman. With the assistance of Patricia Crawford and David Jacobs. Published/Created: New York, Wiley [1973] Description: xii, 571 p. illus. 23 cm. ISBN: 0471064130

Ego structure in paranoid schizophrenia: a new method of evaluating projective material. Published/Created: Springfield,

Ill., Thomas [1958] Description: x, 186 p. illus., diagrs., tables. 23 cm.

Emotional disorders / M. Nikki Goldman. Published/Created: New York: M. Cavendish, c1994. Description: 96 p.: ill.; 27 cm. ISBN: 1854356194

Essays in schizophrenia / Bernard H. Shulman. Edition Information: 2nd ed. Published/Created: Chicago, Ill.: Alfred Adler Institute, 1984, c1980. Description: xv, 195 p.; 22 cm. ISBN: 0918560292 (pbk.)

Essays in schizophrenia [by] Bernard H. Shulman. Published/Created: Baltimore, Williams & Wilkins, 1968. Description: xv, 206 p. 24 cm.

Essential psychopharmacology of antipsychotics and mood stabilizers / Stephen M. Stahl. Published/Created: Cambridge, UK; New York, NY: Cambridge University Press, 2002. Description: ix, 142 p.: ill. (some col.); 25 cm. ISBN: 0521890748 (pbk.)

Estrangement and relationship; experience with schizophrenics [by] Francis A. Macnab. Published/Created: Bloomington, Indiana, University Press [1966, c1965] Description: xviii, 299 p. illus. 22 cm.

Etiopathogenetic hypotheses of schizophrenia: the impact of epidemiological, biochemical, and neuromorphological studies / edited by C.L. Cazzullo ... [et al.]. Published/Created: Lancaster; Boston: MTP Press, c1987. Description: xii, 190 p.: ill.; 24 cm. ISBN: 0852008430

Evaluation of programs for the treatment of schizophrenia: a health economic prespective / prepared by Ron Goeree for Mental Health Division, Health Services Directorate, Health Programs and Services Branch, Health Canada. Published/Created: [Ottawa]: Health Canada, c1994. Description: i, 30 p.: ill.; 28 cm. ISBN: 0662223896

Everything you need to know about schizophrenia / Michelle S. Friedman. Published/Created: New York: Rosen Pub. Group, c2000. Description: 64 p.: ill. (some col.); 24 cm. ISBN: 0823930912 (lib. bdg.)

EWI: manual for the clinical use of the experiential world inventory, by A. Moneim El-Meligi and Humphry Osmond. Published/Created: [New York] Mens Sana Pub. [c1970] Description: xix, 173, [1] p. illus. 23 cm.

Experiences of schizophrenia: an integration of the personal, scientific, and therapeutic / Michael Robbins. Published/Created: New York: Guilford Press, c1993. Description: xvi, 511 p.: ill.; 25 cm. ISBN: 0898629977 (acid-free paper)

Experimental studies of schizophrenia, by Carmi Schooler and Solomon E. Feldman. Published/Created: Goleta, Calif., Psychonomic Press [1967] Description: iv, 260 p. 28 cm.

Exploring the self: philosophical and psychopathological perspectives on self-experience / edited by Dan Zahavi. Published/Created: Amsterdam; Philadelphia: J. Benjamins Pub. Co., 2000. Description: vi, 299 p.: ill.; 22 cm. ISBN: 1556196660 (alk. paper)

Families helping families: living with schizophrenia / by Families of the Mentally Ill Collective; Nona Dearth ... [et al.]. Edition Information: 1st ed. Published/Created: New York: W.W. Norton, c1986. Description: xx, 163 p.; 22 cm. ISBN: 039302301X

Family and multi-family work with psychosis / Gerd-Ragna Bloch Thorsen, Trond GrÃ¸nnestad, Anne Lise Ã˜xnevad. Published/Created: New York: Routledge, 2006. Description: p.; cm. Projected Publication Date: 0610 ISBN: 9781583917268 (hbk) 1583917268 (hbk) 9781583917275 (pbk.) 1583917276 (pbk.)

Family care of schizophrenia: a problem-solving approach to the treatment of mental illness / Ian R.H. Falloon, Jeffrey L. Boyd, Christine W. McGill. Published/Created: New York: Guilford Press, c1984. Description: xii, 451 p.: ill.; 24 cm. ISBN: 089862049X

Family involvement in the treatment of schizophrenia / edited by Marion Zucker Goldstein. Published/Created: Washington, D.C.: American Psychiatric Press, c1986. Description: x, 135 p.: ill.; 21 cm. ISBN: 0880480971 (pbk.: alk. paper)

Family management of schizophrenia: a study of clinical, social, family, and economic benefits / Ian R.H. Falloon and others. Published/Created: Baltimore: Johns Hopkins University Press, c1985. Description: xiii, 207 p.: ill.; 24 cm. ISBN: 080182429X (alk. paper)

Family therapy in schizophrenia / edited by William R. McFarlane; foreword and afterword by C. Christian Beels. Published/Created: New York: Guilford Press, c1983. Description: xii, 355 p.: ill.; 24 cm. ISBN: 0898620422

Fetal neural development and adult schizophrenia / edited by Sarnoff A. Mednick ... [et al.]. Published/Created: Cambridge; New York: Cambridge University Press, 1991. Description: xi, 244 p.: ill.; 24 cm. ISBN: 052139158X (hardcover)

Fish's schizophrenia. Edition Information: 2nd ed. / edited by Max Hamilton. Published/Created: Bristol: J. Wright, 1976. Description: xv, 212 p.: ill.; 23 cm. ISBN: 0723603340

Foreign sperm: the cause of sexually transmitted diseases, cancers, autoimmune diseases, alzheimers, schizophrenia, and kuru / by Donald E. Tyler. Published/Created: Ontario, OR: Discovery Books, c2004. Description: 155 p.; 23 cm. ISBN: 1884981097

Fragments from the diary of a madman. Published/Created: London, Gryf Publications, 1972. Description: 87 p. 22 cm. ISBN: 0901342130

From the mental patient to the person / Peter Barham and Robert Hayward. Published/Created: London; New York: Travistock/Routledge, 1991. Description: viii, 162 p.; 22 cm. ISBN: 0415041201

Frontal lobes and schizophrenia; second lobotomy project of Boston Psychopathic Hospital. Edited by Milton Greenblatt and Harry C. Solomon. Published/Created: New York, Springer Pub. Co., 1953. Description: xi, 425 p. illus. 24 cm.

Frontline. Broken minds / a D.L. Sage production for Frontline; produced and written by DeWitt Sage, Jr. Published/Created: United States: WETA-TV, 1990-10-30; United States: WETA-TV, 1993-12-28. Description: 1 videocassette of 1 (ca. 60 min.): sd., col.; 3/4 in. viewing copy. 1 videocassette of 1 (ca. 60 min.): sd., col.; 3/4 in. viewing copy (copy 2)

Genetic and environmental factors in schizophrenia: a study of schizophrenic twins and their families. Published/Created: Copenhagen, Munksgaard, 1973. Description: 156 p. 25 cm. ISBN: 8716012232

Genetic factors in "schizophrenia." Compiled and edited by Arnold R. Kaplan. With forewords by Arnold Sorsby and Newton E. Morton. Published/Created: Springfield, Ill., Thomas [1972] Description: xxvi, 698 p. illus. 27 cm. ISBN: 0398023271

Genetics, environment and psychopathology / editors, Sarnoff A. Mednick ... [et al]. Published/Created: Amsterdam: North-Holland Pub. Co.; New York: American Elsevier, 1974. Description: xiv, 346 p.: ill.; 24 cm. ISBN: 0444106928 (American Elsevier)

Getting your life back together when you have schizophrenia / Roberta Temes; foreword by Rita Seiden. Published/Created: Oakland, CA: New Harbinger, c2002. Description: vi, 172 p.; 23 cm. ISBN: 1572242736 (pbk.)

Good food, milk free, grain free / Hilda Cherry Hills; introd. by Beatrice Trum Hunter. Edition Information: Health science ed. Published/Created: New Canaan, Conn.: Keats Pub., 1980. Description: xx, 154 p.; 22 cm. ISBN: 0879832010 (pbk.) 0879832002

Group therapy for schizophrenic patients / Nick Kanas. Published/Created: Washington, DC: American Psychiatric Press, c1996. Description: xxi, 157 p.; 22 cm. ISBN: 0880481722 (alk. paper)

Growth and change of schizophrenic children; a longitudinal study. Published/Created: Washington, Winston; [distributed by Halsted Press, New York] 1974. Description: xv, 271 p. 24 cm. ISBN: 0470311029

Guidelines for neuroleptic relapse prevention in schizophrenia: proceedings of a consensus conference held April 19-20, 1989, in Bruges, Belgium / edited by Werner Kissling. Published/Created: Berlin; New York: Springer-Verlag, c1991. Description: viii, 166 p.: ill.; 24 cm. ISBN: 3540539859 (alk. paper) 0387539859 (alk. paper)

Handbook of social functioning in schizophrenia / edited by Kim T. Mueser, Nicholas Tarrier. Published/Created: Boston: Allyn & Boston, c1998. Description: xix, 455 p.: ill.; 25 cm. ISBN: 0205164447

Handbook of studies on schizophrenia / edited by Graham D. Burrows, Trevor R. Norman, and Gertrude Rubinstein. Published/Created: Amsterdam; New York: Elsevier; New York, NY, USA: Sole distributors for the USA and Canada, Elsevier Science Pub. Co,m 1986. Description: 2 v.: ill.; 23 cm. ISBN: 0444807160 (U.S.: pt. 1) 0444807268 (U.S.: pt. 2)

Harry [sound recording]. Published/Created: Orlando, Fla.: American Academy of Psychotherapists, [196-] Description: 1 sound tape reel (35 min.): 3 3/4 ips; 7 in. + 1 script (21 p.; 28 cm.)

Hearing voices: embodiment and experience / Lisa Blackman. Published/Created: London; New York: Free Association Books, 2001. Description: ix, 266 p.; 23 cm. ISBN: 1853435341 (hbk.) 1853435333 (pbk.)

High school students who later became schizophrenic [by] Eli M. Bower [and others] With an introd. by Daniel Blain.

Published/Created: [Sacramento, 1960] Description: vii, 157 p. illus. 23 cm.

Homo schizo / by Alfred de Grazia. Edition Information: Limited 1st ed. Published/Created: Princeton, N.J.: Metron Publications, c1983. Description: 2 v.; 21 cm. ISBN: 0940268019 (v. 1) 0940268027 (v. 2)

Hospitalised schizophrenics: their socio-sexual life and rehabilitation / R.K. Upadhyay. Published/Created: Delhi, India: Mittal Publications, 1987. Description: xi, 215 p.; 23 cm. ISBN: 8170990181

How to become a schizophrenic: the case against biological psychiatry / John Modrow. Edition Information: 2nd ed. Published/Created: Everett, Wash.: Apollyon Press, c1995. Description: xv, 295 p.: ill.; 24 cm. ISBN: 096326267X

How to become a schizophrenic: the case against biological psychiatry / John Modrow. Published/Created: Everett, Wash.: Apollyon Press; Traverse City, Mich.: Distributed by Publisher's Distribution Center, c1992. Description: xi, 291 p.: ill.; 23 cm. ISBN: 0963262629 (pbk.)

How to live with schizophrenia / by Abram Hoffer and Humphry Osmond; with a foreword by Nolen D.C. Lewis. Edition Information: New rev. ed. Published/Created: New York: Carol Pub. Group, c1992. Description: 222 p.; 23 cm. ISBN: 0806513829

How to live with schizophrenia / by Abram Hoffer and Humphry Osmond; with a foreword by Nolen D. C. Lewis. Published/Created: Secaucus, N.J.: University Books, [1974] Description: 224 p.; 24 cm. ISBN: 0821600044

How to live with schizophrenia, by Abram Hoffer and Humphry Osmond. With a foreword by Nolan D. C. Lewis. Published/Created: New Hyde Park, N.Y., University Books [1966] Description: xi, 177 p. 24 cm.

Humming whispers / by Angela Johnson. Published/Created: New York: Orchard Books, c1995. Description: 121 p.; 22 cm. ISBN: 0531068986 0531087484 (lib. bdg.)

If your adolescent has schizophrenia: an essential resource for parents / Raquel E. Gur and Ann Braden Johnson. Published/Created: Oxford; New York: Oxford University Press, 2006. Description: x, 163 p.; 22 cm. ISBN: 0195182111 (9780195182118) 019518212X (9780195182125) 9780195182118 9780195182125

Imaging of the brain in psychiatry and related fields / Konrad Maurer (ed.). Published/Created: Berlin; New York: Springer-Verlag, c1993. Description: xix, 375 p.: ill. (some col.); 25 cm. ISBN: 3540547851 (alk. paper) 0387547851 (New York: alk. paper)

Immunological alterations in psychiatric diseases: international symposium, Reisenburg, September 22-23, 1995 / volume editors, A. Henneberg, W.P. Kaschka. Published/Created: Basel; New York: Karger, 1997. Description: p. cm. Projected Publication Date: 1111 ISBN: 3805563841 (hardcover: alk. paper)

In search of a response [by] Leida Berg [and] Harold Steinberg. Published/Created: New York, Tiresias Press [1973] Description: xi, 10, 354, 613 p. 26 cm. ISBN: 0913292001

In search of madness: schizophrenia and neuroscience / R. Walter Heinrichs. Published/Created: Oxford; New York: Oxford University Press, 2001. Description: x, 347 p.: ill.; 24 cm. ISBN: 0195122194 (alk. paper)

Innovations in the psychological management of schizophrenia: assessment, treatment, and services / edited by Max Birchwood, Nicholas Tarrier. Published/Created: Chichester [West Sussex, England]; New York: Wiley, c1992. Description: xii, 326 p.: ill.; 24 cm. ISBN: 0471929352

Inside out / Terry Trueman. Edition Information: 1st ed. Published/Created: New York: HarperTempest, c2003. Description: 117 p.; 19 cm. ISBN: 0066239621 006623963X (lib. bdg.)

Insight and psychosis / edited by Xavier F. Amador and Anthony S. David. Edition Information: 2nd ed. Published/Created: Oxford; New York: Oxford University Press, 2004. Description: 402 p.: ill.; 24 cm. ISBN: 0198525680 (pbk.)

Institutionalism and schizophrenia; a comparative study of three mental hospitals 1960-1968 [by] J. K. Wing and G. W. Brown. With a chapter by the physician superintendents of the three hospitals. Published/Created: Cambridge [Eng.] University Press, 1970. Description: xiii, 260 p. illus. 23 cm. ISBN: 0521078822

Integrated psychological therapy for schizophrenic patients (IPT) / Hans D. Brenner ... [et al.]. Published/Created: Seattle: Hogrefe & Huber, c1994. Description: 174 p.: ill.; 24 cm. + 1 computer disk (3 1/2 in.) ISBN: 0889370850

Intensive psychotherapy of schizephrenia. [Sound recording] Published/Created: New York, Psychotherapy Tape Library, p1978. Description: 3 cassettes.

Interpretation of schizophrenia / Silvano Arieti. Edition Information: 2nd ed. Published/Created: Northvale, N.J.: Jason Aronson, 1994. Description: xvii, 756 p.: ill.; 23 cm. ISBN: 1568212097

Interpretation of schizophrenia. Edition Information: 2d ed., completely rev. and expanded. Published/Created: New York, Basic Books [1974] Description: xvii, 756 p. illus. 25 cm. ISBN: 0465034292

Interpretation of schizophrenia. Published/Created: New York, R. Brunner, 1955. Description: 522 p. illus. 22 cm.

Intrapsychic and interpersonal dimensions of treatment: a clinical dialogue / Robert Langs and Harold F. Searles. Published/Created: New York: Jason Aronson, c1980. Description: xi, 323 p.; 24 cm. ISBN: 0876684045

Is this kid "crazy"?: understanding unusual behavior / Margaret O. Hyde. Edition Information: 1st ed. Published/Created: Philadelphia: Westminster Press, c1983. Description: 96 p.; 21 cm. ISBN: 0664327079

Issues and controversies in the psychotherapy of schizophrenia / edited by John G. Gunderson, Loren R. Mosher. Edition Information: 1st softcover ed. Published/Created: Northvale, N.J.: J. Aronson, 1994. Description: xlii, 441 p.: ill.; 22 cm. ISBN: 1568213972

Jordi / by Theodore Isaac Rubin. Edition Information: 1st Collier Books ed. Published/Created: New York: Collier

Books, 1988, c1960. Description: 73 p.; 18 cm. ISBN: 0020535805 (pbk.)

Journal of autism and childhood schizophrenia. Published/Created: New York [etc.] Plenum Press [etc.] Description: 8 v. 23 cm. v. 1-8; Jan./Mar. 1971-Dec. 1978. ISSN: 0021-9185

Journal of schizophrenia. Published/Created: [Margate, N.J.]: Elias Publications, 1967- Description: 2 v.; 22 cm. Began publication with: Vol. 1, no. 1 (1967); ceased with Vol. 2 (1968).

Juvenile-onset schizophrenia: assessment, neurobiology, and treatment / edited by Robert L. Findling and S. Charles Schulz. Published/Created: Baltimore: Johns Hopkins University Press, c2005. Description: xiv, 311 p.: ill.; 24 cm. ISBN: 0801880181 (hardcover: alk. paper)

King of the pygmies / Jonathon Scott Fuqua. Edition Information: 1st ed. Published/Created: Cambridge, Mass.: Candlewick Press, 2005. Description: 246 p.; 22 cm. ISBN: 0763614181

Lack of discretion of judgment because of schizophrenia: doctrine and recent rotal jurisprudence / Raymond L. Burke. Published/Created: Roma: Pontificia Università Gregoriana, 1986. Description: 254 p.; 23 cm.

Lafayette Clinic Studies on schizophrenia. Edited by Garfield Tourney and Jacques S. Gottlieb. Published/Created: Detroit, Wayne State University Press, 1971. Description: 532 p. illus. 24 cm. ISBN: 0814314317

Language and thought in schizophrenia; collected papers presented at the meeting of the American Psychiatric Association, May 12, 1939, Chicago, Illinois and brought up to date. Edited by J.S. Kasanin ... With a preface by Nolan D.C. Lewis ... Published/Created: Berkeley, Los Angeles, University of California Press, 1944. Description: xiv, 133 p. diagrs. 21 cm.

Late onset schizophrenia / edited by Robert Howard, Peter V. Rabins, David J. Castle. Published/Created: Petersfield, UK; Philadelphia, USA: Wrightson Biomedical Pub., c1999. Description: ix, 278 p.: ill.; 24 cm. ISBN: 1871816394 (hard cover)

Laterality and psychopathology / editors, Pierre Flor-Henry and John Gruzelier. Published/Created: Amsterdam; New York: Elsevier Science Publishers; New York: Sole distributors for the USA and Canada, Elsevier Science Pub. Co., 1983. Description: ix, 648 p.: ill.; 25 cm. ISBN: 0444804811

Learning in dementia precox, by Edwin G. Boring ... a study from the Psychological laboratory of the Government hospital for the insane, Washington, D. C., with an introduction by Shepherd Ivory Franz. Published/Created: Princeton, N.J., Lancaster, Pa., Psychological review company [1913] Description: 2 p. l., 101 p. incl. tables. diagrs. 25 cm.

Lectures in psychiatry: the functional psychoses: the schizophrenias and major affective disorders / by Ken Reed. Published/Created: St. Louis, Mo., U.S.A.: W.H. Green, c1985. Description: ix, 292 p.: ill.; 23 cm. ISBN: 0875273394

Lenz / Georg Bûchner; translated by Richard Sieburth. Edition Information: 1st ed. Published/Created: New York, N.Y.: Archipelago Books, c2004. Description: 199 p.; 16 cm. ISBN: 0974968021

Levels of schizophrenia / by Albert E. Scheflen. Published/Created: New York, N.Y.: Brunner/Mazel, c1981. Description: xvii, 171 p.; 24 cm. ISBN: 0876302525

Libido and delusion ... Edition Information: Enl. 2d ed. Published/Created: Washington, Mental therapy publications [1946] Description: xi, 259 p. illus. 24 cm.

Lisa & David; Jordi: two extraordinary tales of troubled children struggling to find their places in the real world / by Theodore Isaac Rubin. Published/Created: New York: Collier Books; Toronto: Collier Macmillan Canada; New York: Maxwell Macmillan International, c1990. Description: 157 p.; 18 cm. ISBN: 0020535759

Live company: psychoanalytic psychotherapy with autistic, borderline, deprived, and abused children / Anne Alvarez. Published/Created: London; New York: Tavistock/Routledge, 1992. Description: xv, 246 p.; 25 cm. ISBN: 0415060966 (hb) 0415060974 (pbk)

Living and working with schizophrenia / by M.D. [i.e. M.V.] Seeman ... [et al.]. Published/Created: New York: New American Library, [1984] c1982. Description: xiii, 146 p.; 21 cm. ISBN: 0452255414 (pbk.)

Living and working with schizophrenia / M.V. Seeman ... [et al.]. Published/Created: Toronto; Buffalo: University of Toronto Press, c1982. Description: xiii, 146 p.; 22 cm. ISBN: 0802064744

Living outside mental illness: qualitative studies of recovery in schizophrenia / Larry Davidson; foreword by John S. Strauss. Published/Created: New York: New York University Press, c2003. Description: xii, 227 p.: ill.; 24 cm. ISBN: 0814719422 (acid-free paper) 0814719430 (pbk.: acid-free paper)

Living with schizophrenia / Alexander P. Hyde. Published/Created: Chicago: Contemporary Books, c1980. Description: x, 133 p.; 22 cm. ISBN: 0809277069

Living with schizophrenia / by the relatives. Published/Created: Surbiton: National Schizophrenia Fellowship, [1975] Description: [1], 54 p.; 30 cm. ISBN: 0904854000

Living with schizophrenia / Stuart Emmons ... [et al.]. Published/Created: Washington, DC: Accelerated Development, c1997. Description: xx,,195 p.: ill.; 24 cm. ISBN: 1560325569 (paper: alk. paper)

Loretta. [Sound recording] Published/Created: Orlando, Fla., American Academy of Psychotherapists [196-] Description: p. cm.

Lost girls & love hotels: a novel / Catherine Hanrahan. Edition Information: 1st ed. Published/Created: New York: HarperPerennial, c2006. Description: 208, 16 p.; 21 cm. ISBN: 0060846844

LSD psychosis and acute schizophrenia: a follow-up study / Wayne J. Lavender. Published/Created: New York: Distributed by Dabor Science Publications, [1977] Description: p. cm. ISBN: 0895610027

Mad in America: bad science, bad medicine, and the enduring mistreatment of the mentally ill / Robert Whitaker. Published/Created: Cambridge, MA: Perseus Pub., c2002. Description: xviii, 334 p.; 24 cm. ISBN: 0738203858

Mad in America: bad science, bad medicine, and the enduring mistreatment of the mentally ill / Robert Whitaker. Published/Created: Cambridge, MA: Perseus Pub., c2002 (2003 printing). Description: xviii, 334 p.; 21 cm. ISBN: 0738207993

Madness and modernism: insanity in the light of modern art, literature, and thought / Louis A. Sass. Published/Created: New York, NY: BasicBooks, c1992. Description: x, 595 p.: ill.; 24 cm. ISBN: 0465043127

Madness on the couch: blaming the victim in the heyday of psychoanalysis / Edward Dolnick. Published/Created: New York: Simon & Schuster, c1998. Description: 368 p.: ill.; 25 cm. ISBN: 0684824973

Madwives: schizophrenic women in the 1950s / Carol A.B. Warren. Published/Created: New Brunswick: Rutgers University Press, c1987. Description: xii, 283 p.; 24 cm. ISBN: 0813512255

Magic and schizophrenia. Posthumously edited by Warner Muensterberger, with the assistance of S. H. Posinsky. Foreword by Sandor Lorand. Published/Created: New York, International Universities Press [1955] Description: viii, 230 p. 23 cm.

Marijuana and madness: psychiatry and neurobiology / edited by David Castle, Robin Murray. Published/Created: New York: Cambridge University Press, 2004. Description: xvi, 218 p.: ill.; 26 cm. ISBN: 0521819407 (hb) 0521525462 (pbk)

Marriage and fertility of women suffering from schizophrenia or affective disorders, by Barbara C. Stevens. Published/Created: London, New York, Oxford U.P., 1969. Description: ix, 188 p. forms, map. 26 cm. ISBN: 0197121411

Masked schizophrenia, diagnosis and a unified method of treatment / Margaret Olds Strahl. Published/Created: New York: Springer Pub. Co., c1980. Description: ix, 230 p.; 24 cm. ISBN: 0826128203 0826128211 (pbk.)

Maternal dependency and schizophrenia: mothers and daughters in a therapeutic group, a group-analytic study [by] Joseph Abrahams [and] Edith Varon. Published/Created: New York, International Universities Press [c1953] Description: 240 p. 23 cm.

Medical illness and schizophrenia / edited by Jonathan M. Meyer, Henry A. Nasrallah. Edition Information: 1st ed. Published/Created: Washington, DC: American Psychiatric Pub., c2003. Description: xii, 242 p.: ill.; 23 cm. ISBN: 1585621064 (alk. paper)

Medicating schizophrenia: a history / Sheldon Gelman. Published/Created: New Brunswick, N.J.: Rutgers Unviversity Press, c1999. Description: ix, 274 p.; 24 cm. ISBN: 0813526426 (alk. paper) 0813526434 (pbk.: alk. paper)

Medicine and mental illness: the use of drugs in psychiatry / Marvin E. Lickey and Barbara Gordon. Published/Created: New York: Freeman & Co., c1991. Description: xi, 459 p.: ill.; 25 cm. ISBN: 0716721953 (hard) 0716721961 (soft)

Megavitamin therapy: in reply to the American Psychiatric Association Task Force report on megavitamins and orthomolecular psychiatry / A. Hoffer, H. Osmond. Published/Created: Regina, Sask.: Canadian Schizophrenia Foundation, [1976] Description: 123 p.: ill.; 26 cm.

Mending minds: a guide to the new psychiatry of depression, anxiety, and other serious mental disorders / Leonard L. Heston. Published/Created: New York: W.H. Freeman, c1992. Description: xi, 233 p.; 24 cm. ISBN: 0716721589: 0716721678 (pbk.)

Mental disease in history: a selection of translated readings / edited by J. Thomas Dalby. Published/Created: New York: Peter Lang, 1996. Description: xix, 264 p.; 24 cm. ISBN: 0820430560 (alk. paper)

Mental disorder in urban areas; Published/Created: Chicago, University of Chicago Press [1965, c1939] Description: xxxviii, 260 p. maps. 21 cm.

Mental disorder in urban areas; Published/Created: New York, Hafner Pub. Co., 1960 [c1939] Description: xxxviii, 270 p. maps, diagrs., tables. 22 cm.

Mental health and aging / compiled by Michael A. Smyer, Boaz Kahana. Published/Created: Washington, D. C.: Association for Gerontology in Higher Education, 1992. Description: 10 leaves; 28 cm.

Milieu therapy in schizophrenia. Foreword by Dexter M. Bullard. Introd. by David McK. Rioch. Published/Created: New York, Grune & Stratton, 1962. Description: 169 p. illus. 23 cm.

Mind, brain, and schizophrenia / Peter Williamson. Published/Created: Oxford; New York: Oxford University Press, c2006. Description: xii, 278 p.: ill.; 25 cm. ISBN: 0195176375 (alk. paper)

Models of madness: psychological, social and biological approaches to schizophrenia / edited by John Read, Loren R. Mosher, Richard P. Bentall. Edition Information: 1st ed. Published/Created: New York, NY: Brunner-Routledge, 2004. Description: p.; cm. Projected Publication Date: 0404 ISBN: 1583919058 (hbk) 1583919066 (pbk)

Modern psychoanalysis of the schizophrenic patient: theory of the technique / Hyman Spotnitz. Edition Information: 2004 2nd ed. Published/Created: New York: YBK Publishers, 2004. Description: x, 238 p.; 24 cm. ISBN: 0970392362 (pbk.)

Modern psychoanalysis of the schizophrenic patient: theory of the technique / Hyman Spotnitz. Edition Information: 2nd ed. Published/Created: Northvale, NJ: J. Aronson, c1999. Description: 337 p.; 23 cm. ISBN: 076570157X (alk. paper)

Modern psychoanalysis of the schizophrenic patient: theory of the technique / Hyman Spotnitz. Edition Information: 2nd ed. Published/Created: New York, N.Y.: Human Sciences Press, c1985. Description: 337 p.; 22 cm. ISBN: 0898852501

Modern psychoanalysis of the schizophrenic patient; theory of the technique. Published/Created: New York, Grune & Stratton [1969] Description: vi, 234 p. 23 cm.

Molecular and cell biology of neuropsychiatric diseases / edited by Frank Owen and Ruth Itzhaki. Edition Information: 1st ed. Published/Created: London: Chapman & Hall, 1994. Description: x, 201 p.: ill.; 25 cm. ISBN: 0412478005 (acid-free paper)

Mother-daughter relationships and social behavior; a study of some aspects of mother-daughter relationships and the social participations of a selected group of schizophrenic patients treated in St. Elizabeths Hospital in Washington, D.C.

Published/Created: Washington, Catholic University of America Press, 1955. Description: xiii, 369 p. 23 cm.

Mr. Vac. [Sound recording] Published/Created: Orlando, Fla., American Academy of Psychotherapists [196-] Description: p. cm.

Mr. Vac. [Sound recording] Published/Created: Orlando, Fla., American Academy of Psychotherapists [196-?] Description: p. cm.

Multiple personality, allied disorders, and hypnosis / Eugene L. Bliss. Published/Created: New York: Oxford University Press, 1986. Description: ix, 271 p.; 25 cm. ISBN: 0195036581

Murals of the mind: image of a psychiatric community [by] Jay Harris and Cliff Joseph. Published/Created: New York, International Universities Press [1973] Description: 274 p. illus. 22 cm. ISBN: 0823634906

My divided brain / by W.R. Baker. Published/Created: Santa Barbara, Calif.: Fithian Press, c1999. Description: 78 p.; 22 cm. ISBN: 1564742989 (alk. paper)

My sister, then and now / by Virginia L. Kroll; illustrations by Mary Worcester. Published/Created: Minneapolis: Carolrhoda Books, c1992. Description: 1 v. (unpaged): ill.; 20 cm. ISBN: 087614718X

Mythology of the soul: a research into the unconscious from schizophrenic dreams and drawings, by H. G. Baynes. Edition Information: [New ed.]. Published/Created: London, Rider, 1969. Description: xxii, 980 p. illus. (some col.). 23 cm. ISBN: 0090987403

Mythology of the soul; a research into the unconscious from schizophrenic dreams and drawings, by H. G. Baynes. Published/Created: London, Baillière, Tindall and Cox, 1940. Description: xii, 939 p. front., illus., plates (part col.) 25 cm.

Natural healing for schizophrenia: a compendium of nutritional methods / Eva Edelman. Published/Created: Eugene, Or.: Borage Books, c1996. Description: vi, 201 p.: ill.; 29 cm. ISBN: 0965097625

Natural healing for schizophrenia: and other common mental disorders / Eva Edelman. Edition Information: 3rd ed., [rev., updated, expanded]. Published/Created: Eugene, Or.: Borage Books, c2001. Description: x, 238 p.: ill.; 28 cm. ISBN: 0965097676

Natural healing for schizophrenia: and other common mental disorders / Eva Edelman. Edition Information: 2nd ed., [completely rev., updated, and expanded]. Published/Created: Eugene, Or.: Borage Books, c1998. Description: x, 238 p.: ill.; 29 cm. ISBN: 0965097668

Negative schizophrenic symptoms: pathophysiology and clinical implications / edited by John F. Greden, Rajiv Tandon. Edition Information: 1st ed. Published/Created: Washington, DC: American Psychiatric Press, c1991. Description: xxix, 290 p.: ill.; 22 cm. ISBN: 0880481927 (alk. paper)

Negative symptom and cognitive deficit treatment response in schizophrenia / edited by Richard S.E. Keefe, Joseph P. McEvoy. Edition Information: 1st ed. Published/Created: Washington, DC: American Psychiatric Press, c2001. Description: xiv, 201 p.: ill.; 24 cm. ISBN: 0880487852 (alk. paper)

Negative versus positive schizophrenia / A. Marneros, N.C. Andreasen, M.T. Tsuang, eds.; contributors, N.C. Andreasen ... [et al.]. Published/Created: Berlin; New York: Springer-Verlag, c1991. Description: ix, 466 p.: ill.; 25 cm. ISBN: 3540543880 (Berlin: alk. paper): 0387543880 (New York: alk. paper)

Nekotorye toksicheskie osobennosti krovi pri shizofrenii. Published/Created: 1967. Description: 59 p. 20 cm.

Neural development and schizophrenia: theory and research / edited by Sarnoff A. Mednick, J. Meggin Hollister. Published/Created: New York: Plenum Press, c1995. Description: x, 262 p.: ill.; 26 cm. ISBN: 030644996X

Neurochemical and immunologic components in schizophrenia: proceedings of a conference held at the University of Texas Medical Branch, October 28-31, 1976 / sponsored by the National Foundation-March of Dimes, co-sponsored by the Multidisciplinary Research Program in Mental Health of the University of Texas Medical Branch; editors, Daniel Bergsma, Allan L. Goldstein; scientific editors, Bernard Haber, Geraldine H. Cohen; associate editor, Natalie W. Paul; assistant editor, Jeanne Mudge. Published/Created: New York: A. R. Liss, c1978. Description: xvi, 431 p.: ill.; 24 cm. ISBN: 0845110195

Neurochemistry of schizophrenia & depression / Aman U. Khan. Published/Created: Clovis, Calif.: A.J. Publisher, 1998. Description: 366 p.: ill.; 24 cm. ISBN: 0963410512

Neurodevelopment & adult psychopathology / edited by Matcheri S. Keshavan and Robin M. Murray. Published/Created: Cambridge; New York: Cambridge University Press, 1997. Description: xvi, 282 p.: ill.; 26 cm. ISBN: 052148104X (hardback) 0521485657 (pbk.)

Neurodevelopment and schizophrenia / edited by Matcheri S. Keshavan, James L. Kennedy, and Robin M. Murray. Published/Created: Cambridge, U.K.; New York, NY, USA: Cambridge University Press, 2004. Description: xviii, 488 p.: ill.; 26 cm. ISBN: 0521823315 (hardback)

Neurodevelopmental mechanisms in psychopathology / edited by Dante Cicchetti, Elaine F. Walker. Published/Created: Cambridge, UK; New York: Cambridge University Press, 2003. Description: xii, 558 p.: ill.; 25 cm. ISBN: 0521802253 0521002621 (pb.)

Neuroleptics: neurochemical, behavioral, and clinical perspectives / editors, Joseph T. Coyle, S.J. Enna. Published/Created: New York: Raven Press, c1983. Description: x, 331 p.: ill.; 24 cm. ISBN: 0890047359

Neuropsychology, psychophysiology, and information processing / editors, S.R. Steinhauer, J.H. Gruzelier, J. Zubin. Published/Created: Amsterdam; New York: Elsevier, 1991. Description: xi, 687 p.: ill.; 25 cm. ISBN: 0444812679

Neurotransmitter receptors in actions of antipsychotic medications / edited by Michael S. Lidow. Published/Created: Boca Raton: CRC Press, c2000. Description: 256 p.: ill. (some col.); 26 cm. ISBN: 0849307449 (alk. paper)

Neurotransmitters in neuronal plasticity and psychiatric disorders: proceedings of the Tenth Workshop on Neurotransmitters and Diseases, Tokyo, June 5, 1993 / editor, Michio Toru; organizing committee, Ichiro Kanazawa ... [et al.].

Published/Created: Amsterdam, Netherlands: Excerpta Medica: Elsevier Science Publishers, 1993. Description: vii, 103 p.: ill.; 25 cm. ISBN: 0444818065

New biological vistas on schizophrenia / edited by Jean-Pierre Lindenmayer, Stanley R. Kay. Published/Created: New York: Brunner/Mazel, c1992. Description: xiii, 299 p.: ill.; 24 cm. ISBN: 0876306547

New developments in interventions with families of schizophrenics / Michael J. Goldstein, editor. Published/Created: San Francisco: Jossey-Bass, c1981. Description: 99 p.; 23 cm. ISBN: 0875898491 (pbk.)

New directions in drug treatment for schizophrenia / guest editors William T. Carpenter, Jr., Nina R. Schooler. Published/Created: Rockville, Md.: U.S. Dept. of Health and Human Services, Public Health Service, Alcohol, Drug Abuse, and Mental Health Administration, National Institute of Mental Health, 1984. Description: 64 p.; 27 cm.

New family interventions and associated research in psychiatric disorders: Gedenkschrift in honor of Michael J. Goldstein / Annette Schaub (ed.). Published/Created: Wien; New York: Springer, c2002. Description: vi, 281 p.: ill., port.; 23 cm. ISBN: 3211837000 (pbk.)

New perspectives in schizophrenia / edited by Alistair Forrest, James Affleck. Published/Created: Edinburgh; New York: Churchill Livingstone; New York: distributed by Longman Inc., 1975. Description: vii, 259 p.; 23 cm. ISBN: 0443012474

New perspectives in schizophrenia / edited by Morton N. Menuck and Mary V. Seeman. Published/Created: New York: Macmillan, c1985. Description: xviii, 234 p.: ill.; 24 cm. ISBN: 0023808004

Nicotinic acid in the treatment of schizophrenias; Canadian Mental Health Association collaborative study [by] Thomas A. Ban. Published/Created: [Toronto] Canadian Mental Health Association [1971- Description: v. 28 cm. ISBN: 0919104010 (v. 1)

NMR spectroscopy in psychiatric brain disorders / edited by Henry A. Nasrallah and Jay W. Pettegrew. Edition Information: 1st ed. Published/Created: Washington, DC: American Psychiatric Press, c1995. Description: xx, 260 p.: ill.; 22 cm. ISBN: 0880484837 (alk. paper)

Nosology, epidemiology, and genetics of schizophrenia / editors, Ming T. Tsuang, John C. Simpson. Published/Created: Amsterdam; New York: Elsevier; New York, NY: Sole distributor for the USA and Canada, Elsevier Science Pub. Co., 1988. Description: xiv, 623 p.: ill.; 25 cm. ISBN: 0444904662 (U.S.)

Not made of wood: a psychiatrist discovers his own profession / [by] Jan Foudraine; translated [from the Dutch] by Herbert H. Hoskins. Published/Created: London: Quartet Books, 1974. Description: xxi, 417 p.; 22 cm. ISBN: 0704320215. 0704330164

Not made of wood; a psychiatrist discovers his own profession. Translated by Hubert H. Hoskins. Published/Created: New York, Macmillan [1974] Description: 414 p. 24 cm. ISBN: 0025402005

Novel antipsychotic drugs / editor, Herbert Y. Meltzer. Published/Created: New York:

Raven Press, c1992. Description: xvii, 267 p.: ill.; 24 cm. ISBN: 0881678937

Nursing care of the schizophrenic patient / Monica Frost; foreword by David Goldberg. Published/Created: London: Kimpton, 1974. Description: 95 p.; 22 cm. ISBN: 0853137854

Occupational therapy in forensic psychiatry: role development and schizophrenia / Victoria P. Schindler. Published/Created: New York: Haworth Press, c2004. Description: xvi, 181 p.: ill.; 23 cm. ISBN: 0789021242 (hard cover: alk. paper) 0789021250 (soft cover: alk. paper)

Office treatment of schizophrenia / edited by Mary V. Seeman, Stanley E. Greben. Edition Information: 1st ed. Published/Created: Washington, DC: American Psychiatric Press, c1990. Description: xiv, 208 p.; 22 cm. ISBN: 0880481919 (alk. paper)

Olfaction and the brain / edited by Warrick J. Brewer, David Castle and Christos Pantelis; with a foreword by Peter Doherty. Published/Created: Cambridge: Cambridge University Press, c2006. Description: xvi, 365 p., [2] leaves of plates: ill. (some col.); 26 cm. ISBN: 0521849225 9780521849227

On an(archy) & schizoanalysis / Rolando Perez. Published/Created: Brooklyn, N.Y.: Autonomedia, c1990. Description: 144 p.: ill.; 23 cm. ISBN: 093675639X

On prognosis and rehabilitation in schizophrenic and paranoid psychoses. A comparative follow-up study of two series of patients first admitted to hospital in 1950 and 1960 respectively, by K. A. Achté. Published/Created: Copenhagen, Munksgaard, 1967. Description: 217 p. 24 cm.

Origins and development of schizophrenia: advances in experimental psychopathology / edited by Mark F. Lenzenweger and Robert H. Dworkin. Published/Created: Washington, DC: American Psychological Association, c1998. Description: xxvii, 557 p.: ill.; 24 cm. ISBN: 1557984972 (cloth: alk. paper)

Orthomolecular psychiatry: treatment of schizophrenia, edited by David Hawkins and Linus Pauling. Published/Created: San Francisco, W. H. Freeman [1973] Description: xix, 697 p. illus. 26 cm. ISBN: 0716708981

Out the back wards' door [by] Marsha Kincheloe [and] Lorraine Hagar. Published/Created: [n.p., 1974] Description: 90 p. 21 cm.

Outcome and innovation in psychological treatment of schizophrenia / edited by Til Wykes, Nick Tarrier, and Shôn Lewis. Published/Created: Chichester; New York: John Wiley, c1998. Description: ix, 291 p.: ill.; 23 cm. ISBN: 0471976598 0471978426 (pbk.)

Papers of Nolan Don Carpentier Lewis, 1897-1978 (bulk 1922-1958). Description: 4,900 items. 14 containers. 5.6 linear feet.

Paresis and plunder: the models of madness in psychiatry and anti-psychiatry / [by] Thomas Szasz. Published/Created: [Colchester]: University of Essex, [1977] Description: [2], 17 p.; 21 cm. ISBN: 0901726133

Passage through madness. [Sound recording] Published/Created: Orlando, Fla., American Academy of Psychotherapists [197-] Description: p. cm.

Pathologies of the modern self: postmodern studies on narcissism, schizophrenia, and depression / David Michael Levin, editor. Published/Created: New York: New York University Press, c1987. Description: xvii, 548 p.: ill.; 24 cm. ISBN: 0814750265

Personal therapy for schizophrenia and related disorders: a guide to individualized treatment / Gerard E. Hogarty. Published/Created: New York: Guilford Press, c2002. Description: xiv, 338 p.: ill.; 24 cm. ISBN: 157230782X (alk. paper)

Personality dimensions associated with positive reaction to placebo. Published/Created: Washington, Catholic University of America Press, 1959. Description: 33 p. tables. 23 cm.

Perspectives in schizophrenia research / editors, Claude F. Baxter, Theodore Melnechuk. Published/Created: New York: Raven Press, 1980. Description: xvii, 445 p.: ill.; 25 cm. ISBN: 0890044902 0890045178 (jacket)

Pharmacologic treatment of schizophrenia / Robert R. Conley, Deanna L. Kelly. Edition Information: 1st ed. Published/Created: Caddo, OK: Professional Communications, c2000. Description: 192 p.: ill.; 19 cm. ISBN: 1884735568 (pbk.: alk. paper)

Phenomenology and Lacan on schizophrenia: after the decade of the brain / Alphonse de Waelhens, Wilfried Ver Eecke. Published/Created: Leuven, Belgium: Leuven University Press, 2001. Description: 337 p.; 24 cm. ISBN: 9058671607

Phenomenology and treatment of schizophrenia / edited by William E. Fann ... [et al.]. Published/Created: Jamaica, N.Y.: Spectrum Publications, c1978. Description: 551 p.: ill.; 24 cm. ISBN: 089335032X

Phenomenology, language & schizophrenia / Manfred Spitzer ... [et al.], editors. Published/Created: New York: Springer-Verlag, c1992. Description: viii, 389 p.: ill.; 24 cm. ISBN: 0387979506 (New York: acid-free paper) 3540979506 (Berlin: acid-free paper)

Phil and me / by Amanda Tetrault. Published/Created: [London?]: Trolley Books, 2004. Description: 1 v. (unpaged): chiefly ill., ports. (some col.); 22 x 29 cm. ISBN: 190456304X

Philosophy and psychopathology / Manfred Spitzer, Brendan A. Maher, editors. Published/Created: New York: Springer-Verlag, c1990. Description: xii, 247 p.; 24 cm. ISBN: 0387973036 (alk. paper)

Poems from the madhouse / Sandy Jeffs. Edition Information: 2nd ed. Published/Created: North Melbourne, Vic.: Spinifex, 2000. Description: viii, 88 p.: ill.; 19 cm. ISBN: 1876756039

Politics as experience. [Sound recording] Published/Created: [S.l.: s.n., 1967] Description: 1 cassette.

Portrait of a schizophrenic nurse. Foreword by Maurice Partridge. Published/Created: London, Hammond, Hammond [1965] Description: 207 p. 23 cm.

Positive and negative symptoms in psychosis: description, research, and future directions / edited by Philip D. Harvey, Elaine F. Walker. Published/Created: Hillsdale, N.J.: L. Erlbaum Associates, 1987. Description: x, 341 p.: ill.; 24 cm. ISBN: 089859880X

Positive and negative syndromes in schizophrenia: assessment and research /

Stanley R. Kay. Published/Created: New York: Brunner/Mazel, c1991. Description: xv, 283 p.; 23 cm. ISBN: 0876306083

Positron-emission tomography in schizophrenia research / edited by Nora D. Volkow, Alfred P. Wolf. Published/Created: Washington, DC: American Psychiatric Press, c1991. Description: xvii, 124 p.: ill. (some col.); 24 cm. ISBN: 0880481951 (alk. paper)

Poverty and schizophrenia; an examination of the relationship between environmental factors and the schiophrenia discharge rate: the development of a predictive formula. Research team: Gillian Lomas [and others] Published/Created: London, Psychiatric Rehabilitation Association, 1973. Description: [3], 27 leaves. illus. 30 cm. ISBN: 0900980095

Practice guideline for the treatment of patients with schizophrenia. Edition Information: 1st ed. Published/Created: Washington, DC: American Psychiatric Association, c1997. Description: xi, 146 p.: ill.; 28 cm. ISBN: 0890423091 (alk. paper)

Precarious haven / Juniper Wiley. Published/Created: Boulder, Colo.: Westview Press, 1996. Description: viii, 152 p.; 25 cm. ISBN: 0813327458 (hardcover: alk. paper)

Predictors of relapse in schizophrenia / edited by Jeffrey A. Lieberman, John M. Kane. Published/Created: Washington, D.C.: American Psychiatric Press, c1986. Description: xiii, 153 p.: ill.; 21 cm. ISBN: 0880481250 (soft: alk. paper)

Prenatal exposures in schizophrenia / edited by Ezra S. Susser, Alan S. Brown, Jack M. Gorman. Edition Information: 1st ed. Published/Created: Washington, DC: American Psychiatric Press, c1999. Description: xix, 275 p.: ill.; 24 cm. ISBN: 0880484993

Preventive intervention in schizophrenia: are we ready?: proceedings of a conference held at the University of California, Los Angeles, May 15-16, 1980 / compiled and edited by Michael J. Goldstein. Published/Created: Rockville, Md. (5600 Fishers Lane, Rockville 20857): U.S. Dept. of Health and Human Services, Public Health Service, Alcohol, Drug Abuse, and Mental Health Administration, National Institute of Mental Health, [1982] Description: xiii, 310 p.: ill.; 24 cm.

Primary prevention of schizophrenia in high-risk groups: report on a working group, Copenhagen, 9-12 June, 1975. Published/Created: Copenhagen: Regional Office for Europe, World Health Organization, 1977. Description: 97 p.; 21 cm.

Primitive internalized object relations: a clinical study of schizophrenic, borderline, and narcissistic patients / Vamik D. Volkan. Published/Created: New York: International Universities Press, c1976. Description: xxiii, 344 p.; 23 cm. ISBN: 0823649954

Principles of experimental psychopathology: essays in honor of Brendan A. Maher / edited by Mark F. Lenzenweger and Jill M. Hooley. Edition Information: 1st ed. Published/Created: Washington, DC: American Psychological Association, c2003. Description: xviii, 305 p.: ill.; 26 cm. ISBN: 1557989281 (alk. paper)

Problems of interdisciplinary longitudinal research on psychiatric patients: a controlled seven year study of endocrine and other indices in drug treated chronic schizophrenics, by Nathan S. Kline [and others] Published/Created: Copenhagen, Munksgaard, 1968. Description: 75 p. 24 cm.

Progress in schizophrenia research / Janet E. Pletson, editor. Published/Created: New York: Nova Science Publishers, c2005. Description: ix, 218 p.: ill.; 27 cm. ISBN: 1594541833 (hardcover

Progress in the functional psychoses / [edited by] Robert Cancro, Lester E. Shapiro, and Martin Kesselman. Published/Created: New York: SP Medical & Scientific Books, c1979. Description: 192 p.: ill.; 24 cm. ISBN: 0893350729

Propranolol and schizophrenia: proceedings of a conference sponsored by the Kroc Foundation, held December 1976, at its headquarters in the Santa Ynez Valley, California / editors, Eugene Roberts, Peter Amacher. Published/Created: New York: A. R. Liss, 1978. Description: viii, 152 p.: ill.; 24 cm. ISBN: 0845103008

Psychiatry and anti-psychiatry, by David Cooper. Published/Created: London, New York [etc.] Tavistock Publications, 1967. Description: xiii, 128 p. diagr. 23 cm.

Psychiatry and biological factors / edited by Edouard Kurstak. Published/Created: New York: Plenum Medical Book Co., c1991. Description: xx, 311 p.: ill.; 24 cm. ISBN: 0306436213

Psychiatry in dissent: controversial issues in thought and practice / Anthony Clare; foreword by Michael Shepherd. Published/Created: Philadelphia: Institute for the Study of Human Issues, 1979, c1976. Description: xxvi, 438 p.: ill.; 20 cm. ISBN: 0915980924

Psychiatry in dissent: controversial issues in thought and practice / Anthony Clare; foreword by Michael Shepherd. Published/Created: London: Tavistock Publications, 1976. Description: xvii, 438 p.: ill.; 21 cm. ISBN: 0422745901: 0422746002

Psychoanalysis and family therapy: selected papers / Helm Stierlin. Published/Created: New York: J. Aronson, c1977. Description: 355 p.; 22 cm. ISBN: 0876682573

Psychoanalytic treatment of schizophrenic and characterological disorders, by L. Bryce Boyer and Peter L. Giovacchini. With a contribution by Edward D. Hoedemaker. Published/Created: New York, Science House [1967] Description: 379 p. 22 cm.

Psychoanalytic treatment of schizophrenic, borderline, and characterological disorders / by L. Bryce Boyer and Peter L. Giovacchini. Edition Information: 2d ed. rev. and expanded. Published/Created: New York: J. Aronson, c1980. Description: xxv, 422 p.: ill.; 23 cm. ISBN: 0876684088

Psychobiology of schizophrenia: in memory of C. and O. Vogt and M. Hayashi: proceedings of a satellite symposium to the 8th International Congress of Pharmacology, Gifu, Japan, 27-29 July 1981 / editors, M. Namba and H. Kaiya. Edition Information: 1st ed. Published/Created: Oxford [Oxfordshire]; New York: Pergamon Press, 1982. Description: xix, 323 p.: ill.; 26 cm. ISBN: 0080280072

Psychobiology of the striatum / edited by A. R. Cools, A. H. M. Lohman, and J. H. L. van den Bercken. Published/Created: Amsterdam; New York: North-Holland Pub. Co., 1977. Description: 197 p.: ill.; 25 cm. ISBN: 0720406331

Psychodiagnosis in schizophrenia [by] Irving B. Weiner. Published/Created: New York, Wiley [1966] Description: xiv, 573 p. illus. 24 cm.

Psychodynamic approach to group-therapy and to psychotherapy of psychotics, by R. Battegay and G. Benedetti. Published/Created: Copenhagen, Munksgaard, 1971. Description: 40 p. 24 cm.

Psychoeducational groups for patients with schizophrenia: a guide for practitioners / Haya Ascher-Svanum, Audrey A. Krause. Published/Created: Gaithersburg, Md.: Aspen Publishers, 1991. Description: 1 v. (loose-leaf): ill.; 26 cm. ISBN: 0834201976

Psychological changes during the first year following prefrontal lobotomy, by I. W. Scherer [and others. Published/Created: Washington] American Psychological Association, 1953. Description: 24 p. 26 cm.

Psychological management of schizophrenia / edited by Max Birchwood and Nicholas Tarrier. Published/Created: Chichester; New York: Wiley, c1994. Description: x, 165 p.: ill.; 23 cm. ISBN: 0471950564 (paper)

Psychological processes in the schizophrenic adaptation [by] Samuel J. Beck. With a chapter by H. B. Molish, and a chapter by Jum C. Nunnally. Published/Created: New York, Grune & Stratton [1965] Description: viii, 421 p. illus. 24 cm.

Psychology and schizophrenia / Janet E. Pletson (editor). Published/Created: New York: Nova Science Publishers, 2006. Description: p. cm. Projected Publication Date: 0603 ISBN: 1594548676

Psychoneuroimmunology: hypotheses and current research / Expert Meeting of Psychoimmunology, Innsbruck, January 21-22, 2000; volume editors, B. Sperner-Unterweger, W.W. Fleischhacker, W.P. Kaschka. Published/Created: Basel; New York: Karger, 2001. Description: viii, 140 p.: ill.; 25 cm. ISBN: 380557262X (hard cover: alk. paper)

Psychoneurosis & schizophrenia. Edited and with a foreword by Gene L. Usdin. Authors: Hilde Bruch [and others] Published/Created: Philadelphia, J.B. Lippincott [1966] Description: 192 p. illus. 25 cm.

Psychopathic personalities. Published/Created: New York, Philosophical Library [1957] Description: 179 p. 22 cm.

Psychopathology: the evolving science of mental disorder / edited by Steven Matthysse ... [et al.]. Published/Created: Cambridge [England]; New York, NY, USA: Cambridge University Press, 1996. Description: xiv, 633 p.: ill.; 24 cm. ISBN: 0521444691 (hardback)

Psychopathology and child development: research and treatment / edited by Eric Schopler and Robert J. Reichler. Published/Created: New York: Plenum Press, c1976. Description: xvi, 395 p.: ill.; 24 cm. ISBN: 0306308703

Psychopathology and psychopharmacology. Edited by Jonathan O. Cole, Alfred M. Freedman, and Arnold J. Friedhoff. Published/Created: Baltimore, Johns Hopkins University Press [1973] Description: x, 298 p. illus. 24 cm. ISBN: 0801814820

Psychopathology of schizophrenia, ed. by Paul H. Hoch and Joseph Zubin.

Published/Created: New York, Grune & Stratton, 1966. Description: xii, 582 p. ill.

Psychopathology of schizophrenia. [Sound recording] Published/Created: New York, J. Norton Publishers [1974?] Description: p. cm.

Psychopharmacology: current trends / editors, Daniel E. Casey, A. Vibeke Christensen. Published/Created: Berlin; New York: Springer-Verlag, c1988. Description: viii, 212 p.: ill.; 25 cm. ISBN: 038718693X (U.S.)

Psychophysiology and experimental psychopathology: a tribute to Samuel Sutton / edited by David Friedman and Gerard Bruder. Published/Created: New York, N.Y.: New York Academy of Sciences, 1992. Description: xii, 287 p.: ill. (some col.); 24 cm. ISBN: 089766647X (cloth: alk. paper) 0897666488 (pbk.: alk. paper)

Psychoses of the schizophrenic spectrum in twins: a discussion of the nature-nurture debate in the etiology of "endogenous" psychoses / Ernst Franzek, Helmut Beckmann. Published/Created: Wien; New York: Springer, 1999 Description: ix, 147 p.; 23 cm. ISBN: 321183298X

Psychoses, affective disorders, and dementia / [edited by] John E. Helzer, Samuel B. Guze. Published/Created: New York: Basic Books; Philadelphia: Lippincott, c1986. Description: xviii, 372 p.: ill.; 27 cm. ISBN: 0397508115 (Lippincott)

Psychosis: understanding and treatment / edited by Jane Ellwood. Published/Created: London; Bristol, Pa.: Jessica Kingsley Publishers, 1995. Description: 186 p.: ill.; 23 cm. ISBN: 1853022659

Psychosis in the inner city: the Camberwell first episode study / David J. Castle ... [et al.]. Published/Created: Hove, East Sussex, UK: Psychology Press, c1998. Description: xiii, 209 p.: ill.; 24 cm. ISBN: 0863775160

Psychosocial approaches to deeply disturbed persons / Peter R. Breggin, E. Mark Stern, editors. Published/Created: New York: Haworth Press, c1996. Description: 231 p.: ill.; 23 cm. ISBN: 1560248416 (acid-free paper)

Psychosocial intervention in schizophrenia: an international view / edited by H. Stierlin, L.C. Wynne, M. Wirsching. Published/Created: Berlin; New York: Springer-Verlag, 1983. Description: xi, 251 p.: ill. (some col.); 25 cm. ISBN: 0387121951 (U.S.: pbk.)

Psychosocial treatment of chronic mental patients: milieu versus social-learning programs / Gordon L. Paul and Robert J. Lentz. Published/Created: Cambridge, Mass.: Harvard University Press, 1977. Description: 528 p.: graphs; 26 cm. ISBN: 0674721128

Psychosocial treatment of schizophrenia / editors, Marvin I. Herz, Samuel J. Keith, John P. Docherty. Published/Created: Amsterdam; New York: Elsevier; New York, NY, U.S.A.: Sole distributors for the USA and Canada, Elsevier Science Pub. Co., 1990. Description: xiv, 419 p.; 24 cm. ISBN: 0444812504 (U.S.)

Psychosocial treatment of schizophrenia: multidimensional concepts, psychological, family, and self-help perspectives / John S. Strauss, Wolfgang Bôker, and Hans D. Brenner, editors. Published/Created: Toronto; Lewiston, N.Y.: Huber, c1987. Description: 221 p.: ill.; 23 cm. ISBN: 0920887104

Psychotherapeutic intervention in schizophrenia / Lewis B. Hill. Edition Information: 1994 ed. Published/Created: Northvale, N.J.: J. Aronson, 1994. Description: viii, 216 p.; 21 cm. ISBN: 1568213131

Psychotherapeutic intervention in schizophrenia / Lewis B. Hill. Edition Information: 5th impression / with a new introd. by Jarl E. Dyrud. Published/Created: Chicago: University of Chicago Press, 1973, c1955. Description: xv, 216 p.; 21 cm. ISBN: 0226336492. 0226336506

Psychotherapeutic intervention in schizophrenia. Published/Created: [Chicago] Univ. of Chicago Press [1955] Description: vii, 215 p.

Psychotherapy for the whole family; case histories, techniques, and concepts of family therapy of schizophrenia in the home and clinic [by] Alfred S. Friedman [and others] Published/Created: New York, Springer Pub. Co. [1965] Description: vii, 354 p. illus., form. 24 cm.

Psychotherapy of chronic schizophrenic patients. Edition Information: [lst ed.] Published/Created: Boston, Little, Brown [1958]. Description: ix, 219 p. illus. 22 cm.

Psychotherapy of preoedipal conditions: schizophrenia and severe character disorders / by Hyman Spotnitz. Published/Created: New York: J. Aronson, c1976. Description: 396 p.; 24 cm. ISBN: 0876682425

Psychotherapy of schizophrenia / by Gaetano Benedetti. Edition Information: 1995 softcover ed. Published/Created: Northvale, N.J.: J. Aronson, 1995. Description: xxiv, 244 p.: ill.; 21 cm. ISBN: 1568217560 (alk. paper)

Psychotherapy of schizophrenia / edited by John G. Gunderson and Loren R. Mosher. Published/Created: New York: J. Aronson, [1975] Description: xlii, 441 p.: ill.; 24 cm. ISBN: 0876682085

Psychotherapy of schizophrenia / Gaetano Benedetti. Published/Created: New York: New York University Press, c1987. Description: xx, 244 p.: ill.; 24 cm. ISBN: 0814710875

Psychotherapy of schizophrenia: proceedings of the 6th International Symposium on Psychotherapy of Schizophrenia, Lausanne, September 28-30, 1978 / edited by Christian Mûller; sponsored by the Swiss National Research Fund. Published/Created: Amsterdam: Excerpta Medica; New York: sole distributors for the USA and Canada, Elsevier North-Holland, 1979. Description: 307 p.; 25 cm. ISBN: 0444900764 (Elsevier North-Holland)

Psychotherapy of schizophrenia: the treatment of choice / Bertram P. Karon, Gary R. VandenBos. Published/Created: New York: J. Aronson, c1981. Description: xv, 504 p.; 24 cm. ISBN: 0876684444

Psychotherapy of schizophrenia; proceedings of the fourth international symposium, Turku, Finland, August 4-7, 1971. Edited by David Rubinstein and Yrjô O. Alanen. Published/Created: Amsterdam, Excerpta Medica, 1972. Description: xv, 347 p. 25 cm. ISBN: 9021901897

Psychotherapy of schizophrenic and manic-dcpressive states. Contributions of basic sciences to psychiatry; definitive statements and future problems. Edited by Hassan Azima [and] Bernard C. Glueck,

Jr. Published/Created: [Washington] American Psychiatric Assoication, 1963. Description: 175 p. illus. 23 cm.

Psychotherapy of the psychoses / edited by Arthur Burton. Published/Created: Huntington, N.Y.: R. E. Krieger Pub. Co., 1976, c1961. Description: x, 385 p.; 24 cm. ISBN: 0882754130

Psychotherapy with schizophrenics, a reappraisal. Joseph G. Dawson, Herbert K. Stone [and] Nicholas P. Dellis, editors. Published/Created: Baton Rouge, Louisiana University Press [c1961] Description: xii, 156 p. 23 cm.

Psychotic continuum / A. Marneros, N.C. Andreasen, M.T. Tsuang, eds.; contributors, N.C. Andreasen ...[et al.]. Published/Created: Berlin; New York: Springer-Verlag, c1995. Description: x, 167 p.: ill.; 25 cm. ISBN: 3540588205 0387588205 (New York)

Publication. Published/Created: [New York] [n.d.] Description: no. 23 cm.

R.D. Laing: contemporary perspectives / Salman Raschid, editor. Published/Created: London: Free Association Books, 2005. Description: 325 p.: ill., port.; 24 cm. ISBN: 1853437018

Rational emotive cognitive therapy in the treatment of schizophrenia. [Sound recording] Published/Created: [n.p.] BMA Audio Cassettes, p1978. F214. Description: 1 cassette.

Reactive & process schizophrenia [by] Robert E. Kantor [and] William G. Herron. Published/Created: Palo Alto, Calif., Science and Behavior Books [1966] Description: vii, 184 p. 23cm.

Recent advances in schizophrenia / A. Kales, C.N. Stefanis, J.A. Talbott, editors; with a foreword by Lewis L. Judd. Published/Created: New York: Springer-Verlag, c1990. Description: xxv, 416 p.: 23 ill.; 25 cm. ISBN: 038797024X (U.S.: hard cover) 0387972218 (U.S.: soft cover) 354097024X (Germany: hard cover) 3540972218 (Germany: soft cover)

Recent advances in the biology of schizophrenia, by Thomas A. Ban. Published/Created: Springfield, Ill., Thomas [1973] Description: ix, 119 p. illus. 24 cm. ISBN: 0398025711

Recent developments in schizophrenia, a symposium; edited by Alec Coppen and Alexander Walk. Published/Created: Ashford (Kent), Published by authority of the Royal Medico-Psychological Association by Headley, 1967 [1969] Description: [5], 158 p. 25 cm.

Recent research on schizophrenia, edited by Philip Solomon and Bernard C. Glueck, Jr. Published/Created: [Washington] American Psychiatric Association, 1964. Description: 205 p. illus. 23 cm.

Reconceiving schizophrenia / edited by Man Cheung Chung, K.W.M. (Bill) Fulford and George Graham. Published/Created: Oxford; New York: Oxford University Press, 2007. Description: x, 341 p.; 24 cm. ISBN: 019852613X (pbk: alk. paper) 9780198526131 (pbk: alk. paper)

Reconstructing schizophrenia / edited by Richard P. Bentall. Published/Created: London; New York: Routledge, 1992. Description: xvii, 308 p.: ill.; 22 cm. ISBN: 041501574X (hbk.) 0415075246 (pbk.)

Recovery from schizophrenia: an international perspective / editors, Kim Hopper ... [et al.]. Published/Created: Madison, Conn.: PsychoSocial Press, 2003. Description: p. cm. Projected Publication Date: 0306 ISBN: 1887841393

Recovery from schizophrenia: an international perspective--results from the WHO-coordinated international study of schizophrenia (ISoS) / edited by Kim Hopper ... [et al.]. Published/Created: Oxford; New York: Oxford University Press, 2007. Description: p.; cm. Projected Publication Date: 0701 ISBN: 9780195313673 (cloth: alk. paper) 0195313674 (cloth: alk. paper)

Recovery from schizophrenia: psychiatry and political economy / Richard Warner. Edition Information: 3rd ed. Published/Created: Hove; New York: Brunner-Routledge, c2004. Description: xiii, 408 p.: ill.; 25 cm. ISBN: 0415212669 0415212677 (pbk.)

Recovery from schizophrenia: psychiatry and political economy / Richard Warner. Edition Information: 2nd ed. Published/Created: London; New York: Routledge, 1994. Description: xii, 366 p.: ill.; 24 cm. ISBN: 0415092604 (hbk) 0415092612 (pbk)

Recovery from schizophrenia: psychiatry and political economy / Richard Warner. Published/Created: London; Boston: Routledge & Kegan Paul, 1985. Description: x, 380 p.: ill.; 24 cm. ISBN: 0710099797

Recovery from schizophrenia; the Roland method. Published/Created: Springfield, Ill., Thomas [1957] Description: 162 p. illus. 24 cm.

Redefining treatment-resistant schizophrenia: highlights of a scientific symposium at the 1999 Annual Meeting of the American Psychiatric Association, Washington DC. Published/Created: [United States?]: [Health Learning Systems?], c2000. Description: 13 p.: ill.; 28 cm.

Reflections on modern psychiatry / edited by David J. Kupfer. Published/Created: Washington, DC: American Psychiatric Press, c1992. Description: xv, 143 p.: ill.; 24 cm. ISBN: 0880485167 (acid-free paper)

Regressive therapy; therapeutic regression of schizophrenic children, adolescents, and young adults [by] Richard H. Cox and Truman G. Esau. Published/Created: New York, Brunner/Mazel [1974] Description: xiv, 154 p. 22 cm.

Reparenting schizophrenics: the cathexis experience: schizophrenics in treatment, an ethnographic study of ritual healing an symbolic action / by Elaine Childs-Gowell. Published/Created: North Quincy, Mass.: Christopher Pub. House, c1979. Description: ix, 262 p.: ill.; 25 cm. ISBN: 0815803729

Report of the international pilot study of schizophrenia. Published/Created: Geneva, 1973- Description: v. illus. 24 cm.

Research and the complex causality of the schizophrenias / formulated by the Committee on Research, Group for the Advancement of Psychiatry. Published/Created: New York: Brunner/Mazel, c1984. Description: xv, 85 p.; 23 cm. ISBN: 0876303734 (pbk.)

Research in dementia precox / Nolan D. C. Lewis. Published/Created: New York: Arno Press, 1980, c1936. Description: xi, 320 p.; 24 cm. ISBN: 0405119259

Research in schizophrenia, National Institute of Mental Health. Published/Created:

Bethesda, Maryland: U.S. Dept. of Health, Education, and Welfare, Public Health Service, National Institutes of Health, National Institute of Mental Health; [for sale by the Superintendent of Documents, U.S. Govt. Print. Off., 1964] Description: v, 18 p.; 28 cm.

Research in the schizophrenic disorders: the Stanley R. Dean award lectures / edited by Robert Cancro, Stanley R. Dean. Published/Created: New York: SP Medical & Scientific Books, c1985- Description: xii, 287 p.: ill.; 24 cm. ISBN: 089335211X (v. 1) 0893352128 (v. 2)

Research on the tiology of schizophrenia. Published/Created: New York, Consultants Bureau [1961] Description: 195 p. illus. 24 cm.

Research techniques in schizophrenia. Published/Created: [Washington] 1956. Description: 153 p. ill.

Return from madness: psychotherapy with people taking the new anti-psychotic medications and emerging from severe, lifelong, and disabling schizophrenia / Kathleen Degen and Ellen Nasper. Published/Created: Northvale, N.J.: Aronson, c1996. Description: xiv, 242 p.: ill.; 22 cm. ISBN: 1568216254 (alk. paper)

Ricky. [Sound recording] Published/Created: Orlando, Fla., American Academy of Psychotherapists [196-] Description: p. cm.

Risk and protective factors in the development of psychopathology / edited by Jon Rolf ... [et al.]. Published/Created: Cambridge; New York: Cambridge University Press, 1990. Description: xv, 554 p.: ill.; 25 cm. ISBN: 0521350999

Rose and Thorn. Published/Created: New York, N.Y.: DC Comics, c2004. Description: 6 v.: chiefly col. ill.; 26 cm. No. 1 (Feb. 2004)-no. 6 (July 2004). ISSN: 1556-2220

Sanity plea: schizophrenia in the novels of Kurt Vonnegut / by Lawrence R. Broer. Published/Created: Ann Arbor: UMI Research Press, c1989. Description: 216 p.; 24 cm. ISBN: 0835718859 (alk. paper)

Sanity plea: schizophrenia in the novels of Kurt Vonnegut / Lawrence R. Broer. Edition Information: Rev. ed. Published/Created: Tuscaloosa, AL: University of Alabama Press, 1994. Description: xiv, 241 p.; 23 cm. ISBN: 0817307524

Sanity, madness and the family [by] R. D. Laing [and] A. Esterson. Edition Information: 2nd ed. Published/Created: London, Tavistock Publications, 1970- Description: v. 23 cm. ISBN: 0422734608

Sanity, madness, and the family: families of schizophrenics / R.D. Laing and A. Esterson. Published/Created: London; New York: Routledge, 1999. Description: xii, 272 p.; 23 cm. ISBN: 0415198216

Sanity, madness, and the family [by] R. D. Laing [and] A. Esterson. Published/Created: New York, Basic Books [1965, c1964- Description: v. 22 cm.

Sanity, madness, and the family, by R. D. Laing and A. Esterson. Edition Information: [2nd ed.] Published/Created: Harmondsworth, Penguin, 1970- Description: v. 18 cm. ISBN: 0140211578 (v. 1)

Sanity, madness, and the family; families of schizophrenics [by] R. D. Laing [and] A. Esterson. Edition Information: 2d

[American] ed. Published/Created: New York, Basic Books [1971, c1964] Description: xii, 272 p. 22 cm. ISBN: 0465071759

Schizofrénia; problémy schizofrénie z hładiska etiologichého, laboratórneho, psychologického, terapeutického a súdneho. Published/Created: Bratislava, Vydavatełstvo Slovenskej akadeémie vied, 1959. Description: 297 p. diagrs., tables. 25 cm.

Schizophrenia / by Douglas W. Smith. Published/Created: New York: F. Watts, c1993. Description: 95 p., [16] p. of plates: ill.; 24 cm. ISBN: 0531125149

Schizophrenia / by Melissa Abramovitz. Published/Created: San Diego, Calif.: Lucent Books, c2002. Description: 112 p.: ill.; 24 cm. ISBN: 1560069082 (hbk.: lib. bdg.)

Schizophrenia / Christopher D. Frith and Eve C. Johnstone. Published/Created: Oxford; New York: Oxford University Press, 2003. Description: 199 p.: ill.; 18 cm. ISBN: 0192802216

Schizophrenia / edited by M. Moscarelli, A. Rupp, N. Sartorius. Published/Created: Chichester; New York: Wiley, c1996. Description: xxiii, 546 p.: ill.; 26 cm. ISBN: 0471961086 (acid-free paper)

Schizophrenia / edited by Mario Maj, Norman Sartorius. Edition Information: 2nd ed. Published/Created: Chichester; Hoboken, N.J.: Wiley, c2003. Description: xvi, 498 p.; 24 cm. ISBN: 0470849649

Schizophrenia / edited by Mario Maj, Norman Sartorius. Published/Created: Chichester; New York: Wiley, c1999. Description: xvi, 492 p.; 24 cm. ISBN: 0471999067 (cased)

Schizophrenia / edited by Steven R. Hirsch and Daniel R. Weinberger; foreword by Timothy J. Crow. Published/Created: Oxford; Cambridge, Mass., USA: Blackwell Sciene, 1995. Description: xiv, 740 p.: ill.; 26 cm. ISBN: 0632032766

Schizophrenia / edited by Steven R. Hirsch, Daniel R. Weinberger. Edition Information: 2nd ed. Published/Created: Malden, Mass.: Blackwell Science, c2003. Description: xvi, 748 p.: ill.; 29 cm. ISBN: 0632063882 (hardback)

Schizophrenia / Elaine Landau. Published/Created: New York: F. Watts, c2004. Description: 80 p.; 23 cm. ISBN: 0531122158 (lib. bdg.) 0531166147 (pbk.)

Schizophrenia / Heather Barnett Veague; foreword by Pat Levitt. Published/Created: New York NY: Chelsea House, c2007. Description: p. cm. Projected Publication Date: 0707 ISBN: 9780791085448 0791085449

Schizophrenia / Jane E. Phillips and David P. Ketelsen. Published/Created: Berkeley Heights, NJ: Enslow Publishers, c2003. Description: 112 p.: ill.; 24 cm. ISBN: 0766018962

Schizophrenia / John M. Neale, Thomas F. Oltmanns. Published/Created: New York: Wiley, c1980. Description: xiv, 554 p.: ill.; 24 cm. ISBN: 0471630861

Schizophrenia / John S. Strauss and William T. Carpenter. Published/Created: New York: Plenum Medical Book Co., c1981. Description: xi, 220 p.: ill.; 24 cm. ISBN: 0306407043

Schizophrenia / Patrick Young; introduction by C. Everett Koop. Published/Created: New York: Chelsea House Publishers, c1988. Description: 114 p.: ill.; 24 cm. ISBN: 0791000524

Schizophrenia / Peter B. Jones, Peter F. Buckley; with contributions by David Kessler. Published/Created: [Edinburgh; New York]: Churchill Livingstone/Elsevier, 2006. Description: 167 p.: col. ill.; 21 cm. ISBN: 0443102503 (pbk.)

Schizophrenia / Richard Warner, Giovanni de Girolamo. Published/Created: Geneva: World Health Organization, 1995. Description: x, 139 p.: ill.; 24 cm. ISBN: 9241561718

Schizophrenia / Scott Barbour, editor. Published/Created: San Diego, CA: Greenhaven Press, c2002. Description: 191 p.; 24 cm. ISBN: 0737706368 (pbk.: alk. paper) 0737706376 (lib.: alk. paper)

Schizophrenia / Steven M. Silverstein, William D. Spaulding, and Anthony A. Menditto. Published/Created: Cambridge, MA: Hogrefe, c2006. Description: viii, 84 p.; 26 cm. ISBN: 0889373159

Schizophrenia: a developmental analysis / Sidney J. Blatt, Cynthia M. Wild. Published/Created: New York: Academic Press, 1976. Description: xii, 274 p.; 24 cm. ISBN: 0121050505

Schizophrenia: a disease or some ways of being human? / F. A. Jenner ... [et al.]; foreword by Anthony Clare. Published/Created: Sheffield, England: Sheffield Academic Press, c1993. Description: 164 p.; 25 cm. ISBN: 1850754012

Schizophrenia: a fresh approach / Gwen Howe. Published/Created: Newton Abbot; North Pomfret, Vt.: David & Charles, c1986. Description: 174 p.; 22 cm. ISBN: 0715388711 (pbk.)

Schizophrenia: a guide for sufferers and their families / by Jacqueline M. Atkinson. Published/Created: Wellingborough, Northamptonshire: Turnstone Press; New York, N.Y.: Distributed by Sterling Pub. Co., 1985. Description: 144 p.; 22 cm. ISBN: 0855002166 (pbk.)

Schizophrenia: a life-course developmental perspective / edited by Elaine F. Walker. Published/Created: San Diego: Academic Press, c1991. Description: xiv, 337 p.: ill.; 24 cm. ISBN: 0127320806 (acid-free paper)

Schizophrenia: a neuropsychological perspective / edited by Christos Pantelis, Hazel E. Nelson, and Thomas R.E. Barnes. Published/Created: Chichester; New York: J. Wiley, c1996. Description: xi, 470 p.: ill.; 24 cm. ISBN: 0471966444

Schizophrenia: a new guide for clinicians / edited by John G. Csernansky. Published/Created: New York: Marcel Dekker, c2002. Description: xiii, 334 p.; 23 cm. ISBN: 0824706420 (alk. paper)

Schizophrenia: a philosophical reflection on Lacan's structuralist interpretation / Alphonse de Waelhens; translated, with introd., notes, and bibliography by W. Ver Eecke. Published/Created: Pittsburgh: Duquesne University Press; Atlantic Highlands, N.J.: distributed by Humanities Press, c1978. Description: xiv, 261. p.; 24 cm. ISBN: 0391006584

Schizophrenia: a scientific delusion? / Mary Boyle. Edition Information: 2nd ed. Published/Created: London; New York: Routledge, 2002. Description: xi, 362 p.: ill.; 25 cm. ISBN: 0415227178 (hbk.) 0415227186 (pbk.)

Schizophrenia: a scientific delusion? / Mary Boyle. Published/Created: London; New

York: Routledge, 1990. Description: viii, 248 p.: ill.; 24 cm. ISBN: 0415040965

Schizophrenia: advances in diagnosis and treatment / by Arthur Henley. Edition Information: 1st ed. Published/Created: New York, N.Y.: Public Affairs Committee, 1987. Description: 24 p.: col. ill.; 18 cm. ISBN: 0882911198 (pbk.)

Schizophrenia: an integrated approach to research and treatment / M.J. Birchwood, S.E. Hallett, M.C. Preston. Published/Created: New York: New York University Press, 1989. Description: viii, 403 p.; 24 cm. ISBN: 0814711251

Schizophrenia: an international follow-up study / World Health Organization. Published/Created: Chichester [Eng.]; New York: Wiley, c1979. Description: xvii, 438 p.: ill.; 24 cm. ISBN: 0471996238

Schizophrenia: an introduction to research and theory / Glenn Shean. Edition Information: 2nd ed. Published/Created: Lanham: University Press of America, c1987. Description: ix, 273 p.; 23 cm. ISBN: 0819164763 (pbk.: alk. paper)

Schizophrenia: an introduction to research and theory / Glenn Shean. Published/Created: Cambridge, Mass.: Winthrop Publishers, c1978. Description: ix, 255 p.; 24 cm. ISBN: 0876267975

Schizophrenia: biological and psychological perspectives / edited by Gene Usdin. Published/Created: New York: Brunner/Mazel, [1975] Description: xvi, 144 p.: ill.; 22 cm. ISBN: 0876301103

Schizophrenia: breaking down the barriers / edited by S.G. Holliday, R.J. Ancill, and G.W. MacEwan. Published/Created: Chichester; New York: John Wiley, c1996. Description: xiii, 248 p.: ill.; 24 cm. ISBN: 0471967033 (acid-free paper)

Schizophrenia: comprehensive treatment and management / Marvin I. Herz, Stephen R. Marder. Published/Created: Philadelphia: Lippincott Williams & Wilkins, c2002. Description: xii, 308 p.: ill.; 26 cm. ISBN: 0683307096

Schizophrenia: concepts and clinical management / Eve C. Johnstone ... [et al.]. Published/Created: Cambridge, U.K.; New York, NY: Cambridge University Press, 1999. Description: xiv, 271 p.: ill. (some col.); 23 cm. ISBN: 0521580846 (hardback)

Schizophrenia: concepts, vulnerability, and intervention / Eckart R. Straube, Kurt Hahlweg, (eds.). Published/Created: Berlin; New York: Springer-Verlag, c1990. Description: ix, 244 p.: ill.; 24 cm. ISBN: 0387505733 (U.S.: alk. paper)

Schizophrenia: empirical research and findings / by Eckart R. Straube and Robert D. Oades. Published/Created: San Diego: Academic Press, c1992. Description: xiii, 637 p.: ill.; 24 cm. ISBN: 0126730105 (acid-free paper)

Schizophrenia: exploring the spectrum of psychosis / edited by R.J. Ancill, S. Holliday, and J. Higenbottam. Published/Created: Chichester; New York: Wiley, c1994. Description: xvii, 376 p.: ill.; 24 cm. ISBN: 0471952559

Schizophrenia: from mind to molecule / edited by Nancy C. Andreasen. Edition Information: 1st ed. Published/Created: Washington, DC: American Psychiatric Press, c1994. Description: xv, 278 p.: ill. (some col.); 24 cm. ISBN: 0880489502 (alk. paper)

Schizophrenia: from neuroimaging to neuroscience / edited by Stephen M. Lawrie, Daniel R. Weinberger and Eve C. Johnstone. Published/Created: Oxford; New York: Oxford University Press, 2004. Description: xiv, 405 p., [12] p. of plates: ill. (some col.); 25 cm. ISBN: 0198525966 (alk. paper) l

Schizophrenia: innovations in diagnosis and treatment / Colin A. Ross. Published/Created: New York: Haworth Maltreatment and Trauma Press, 2004. Description: xviii, 288 p.; 23 cm. ISBN: 0789022699 (hard: alk. paper) 0789022702 (soft: alk. paper)

Schizophrenia: its origins and need-adapted treatment / Yrjô O. Alanen; foreword, Stephen Fleck; introduction, Murray Jackson; translated by Sirkka-Liisa Leinonen. Published/Created: London: Karnac Books, 1997. Description: xix, 312 p.: ill.; 23 cm. ISBN: 1855751569

Schizophrenia: losing touch with reality / Daniel E. Harmon. Published/Created: Philadelphia: Chelsea House, c2000. Description: 93 p.: ill.; 23 cm. ISBN: 0791049531

Schizophrenia: medical & psychological subject index with bibliography / Harold Pietre Drummond. Edition Information: 1st ed. Published/Created: Washington, D.C.: ABBE Publishers Association, c1987. Description: 163 p.; 29 cm. ISBN: 088164496X: 0881644978 (pbk.)

Schizophrenia: new directions for clinical research and treatment / editors, Charles A. Kaufmann, Jack M. Gorman. Published/Created: Larchmont, NY: M.A. Liebert, c1996. Description: viii, 253 p.: ill.; 26 cm. ISBN: 0913113743

Schizophrenia: origins, processes, treatment, and outcome / edited by Rue L. Cromwell, C.R. Snyder. Published/Created: New York: Oxford University Press, 1993. Description: x, 373 p.: ill.; 26 cm. ISBN: 0195069226 (cloth: acid-free paper)

Schizophrenia: pathophysiological mechanisms: proceedings of the Nobel Symposium 111 on schizophrenia, held in Stockholm, Sweden on October 1-3, 1998 / edited by G. Sedvall and L. Terenius. Edition Information: 1st ed. Published/Created: Amsterdam; New York: Elsevier, 2000. Description: vii, p. 105-404: ill. (some col.); 28 cm. ISBN: 0444503153

Schizophrenia: pharmacotherapy and psychotherapy / Lester Grinspoon, Jack R. Ewalt, Richard I. Shader. Published/Created: Huntington, N.Y.: Krieger, 1977, c1972. Description: xxii, 290 p.: ill.; 24 cm. ISBN: 0882756036

Schizophrenia: positive and negative symptoms and syndromes / volume editor, Nancy C. Andreasen. Published/Created: Basel; New York: Karger, c1990. Description: viii, 210 p.: ill.; 25 cm. ISBN: 3805550502

Schizophrenia: questions and answers / prepared by Schizophrenia Research Branch; David Shore, editor. Published/Created: Rockville, Md.: U.S. Dept. of Health and Human Services, Public Health Service, Alcohol, Drug Abuse, and Mental Health Administration, National Institute of Mental Health: Public Inquiries Branch [distributor], [1986] Description: 25 p.; 22 cm.

Schizophrenia: recent biosocial developments / edited by Costas N. Stefanis and Andreas D. Rabavilas. Published/Created:

New York, N.Y.: Human Sciences Press, c1988. Description: 286 p.: ill.; 22 cm. ISBN: 0898853451

Schizophrenia: report of a CSAG committee on schizophrenia / chaired by Professor Andrew Sims. Published/Created: London: HMSO, 1995. Description: 2 v.; 30 cm. ISBN: 0113219296 (v. 1) 0113219229 (v. 2)

Schizophrenia: science and practice / edited by John C. Shershow. Published/Created: Cambridge, Mass.: Harvard University Press, 1978. Description: 248 p.: ill.; 24 cm. ISBN: 0674791126

Schizophrenia: scientific progress / edited by S. Charles Schulz and Carol A. Tamminga. Published/Created: New York: Oxford University Press, 1989. Description: xv, 418 p.: ill.; 24 cm. ISBN: 0195055276

Schizophrenia: selected papers / David Shakow. Published/Created: New York; International Universities Press, c1977. Description: xvii, 354 p.; 24 cm. ISBN: 0823660028; 0823660036

Schizophrenia: straight talk for family and friends / Maryellen Walsh. Edition Information: 1st ed. Published/Created: New York: Morrow, c1985. Description: 264 p.; 24 cm. ISBN: 0688041787

Schizophrenia: symptoms, causes, treatments / Kayla F. Bernheim, Richard R. J. Lewine. Edition Information: 1st ed. Published/Created: New York: Norton, c1979. Description: xii, 256 p.; 21 cm. ISBN: 0393011747. 0393090175

Schizophrenia: the bearded lady disease / compiled by J. Michael Mahoney. Edition Information: Rev. ed. Published/Created: Bloomington, IN: 1stBooks, c2005. Description: xvi, 507 p.; 23 cm. ISBN: 1410703452 (paper) 1410703460

Schizophrenia: the cutting edge / Brian O'Shea. Published/Created: Dublin: Eastern Health Board, Dr. Steeven's Hospital, 1997-1998. Description: 2 v.; 21 cm. ISBN: 0948562390

Schizophrenia: the experience and its treatment / Werner M. Mendel; with contributions by Robert E. Allen; foreword by R. Bruce Sloane. Edition Information: 1st ed. Published/Created: San Francisco: Jossey-Bass, 1976. Description: xvi, 174 p.; 24 cm. ISBN: 0875892965

Schizophrenia: the facts / by Ming T. Tsuang, Stephen V. Faraone, with the assistance of Peter D.C. Johnson. Edition Information: 2nd ed. Published/Created: Oxford; New York: Oxford University Press, 1997. Description: xi, 182 p.; 23 cm. ISBN: 0192627600

Schizophrenia: the facts / by Ming T. Tsuang. Published/Created: Oxford [Oxfordshire]; New York: Oxford University Press, 1982. Description: xi, 95 p.; 23 cm. ISBN: 0192613367

Schizophrenia: the major issues / edited by Paul Bebbington and Peter McGuffin. Published/Created: Oxford: Heinemann Professional Pub. in association with the Mental Health Foundation, 1988. Description: viii, 262 p.; 25 cm. ISBN: 0433000457

Schizophrenia: the plight and the promise: hearing before a subcommittee of the Committee on Appropriations, United States Senate, Ninety-ninth Congress, second session: special hearing. Published/Created: Washington: U.S. G.P.O.: For sale by the Supt. of Docs.,

Congressional Sales Office, 1987. Description: iii, 170 p.: ill.; 24 cm.

Schizophrenia: the positive perspective: in search of dignity for schizophrenic people / Peter K. Chadwick. Published/Created: London; New York: Routledge, 1997. Description: xvi, 220 p.: ill.; 24 cm. ISBN: 0415142873 (hbk) 0415142881 (pbk.)

Schizophrenia: the sacred symbol of psychiatry / Thomas Szasz. Edition Information: Syracuse University Press ed. Published/Created: Syracuse, N.Y.: Syracuse University Press, 1988. Description: xvi, 237 p.; 21 cm. ISBN: 0815602243 (pbk.: alk. paper)

Schizophrenia: the sacred symbol of psychiatry / Thomas Szasz. Published/Created: New York: Basic Books, c1976. Description: xiv, 237 p.; 22 cm. ISBN: 0465072224

Schizophrenia: towards a new synthesis / edited by J. K. Wing. Published/Created: London: Academic Press; New York: Grune & Stratton, 1978. Description: xii, 291 p.; 24 cm. ISBN: 0808911406 (Grune & Stratton)

Schizophrenia: treatment of acute psychotic episodes / edited by Steven T. Levy, Philip T. Ninan. Edition Information: 1st ed. Published/Created: Washington, D.C.: American Psychiatric Press, c1990. Description: xv, 223 p.: ill.; 24 cm. ISBN: 0880481641 (alk. paper)

Schizophrenia: treatment process and outcome / Thomas H. McGlashan, Christopher J. Keats. Edition Information: 1st ed. Published/Created: Washington, DC: American Psychiatric Press, c1989. Description: xix, 207 p.: ill.; 24 cm. ISBN: 0880482818 (alk. paper)

Schizophrenia: your questions answered / Trevor Turner. Edition Information: 1st ed. Published/Created: Edinburgh; New York: Churchill Livingstone, 2003. Description: viii, 219 p.: ill.; 20 cm. ISBN: 0443073473

Schizophrenia [sound recording]. Published/Created: Washington, D.C.: National Public Radio, p1986. Description: 1 sound cassette (35 min.): analog.

Schizophrenia <dementia praecox> an investigation of the most recent advances; the proceedings of the Association, Published/Created: Baltimore, The Williams & Wilkins company, 1931. Description: xv, 246 p. illus., diagrs. 24 cm.

Schizophrenia <dementia praecox>; an investigation of the most recent advances, Published/Created: New York, P. B. Hoeber, inc., 1928. Description: xix, 491 p. front., illus. (incl. facsim.) ports., diagrs. 24 cm.

Schizophrenia and affective disorders: biology and drug treatment / edited by Arthur Rifkin. Published/Created: Boston: J. Wright, PSG, 1983. Description: xv, 383 p.; 24 cm. ISBN: 0723670544

Schizophrenia and aging: schizophrenia, paranoia, and schizophreniform disorders in later life / edited by Nancy E. Miller, Gene D. Cohen. Published/Created: New York: Guilford Press, 1987. Description: xxix, 367 p.: ill.; 24 cm. ISBN: 089862228X

Schizophrenia and anti-schizophrenia: the symmetrical theory of mental illness / Harry Wiener. Published/Created: New York: Arrow House Editions, c1978. Description: ix, 266 p.: ill.; 23 cm.

Schizophrenia and bipolar disorders: often misdiagnosed, often mistreated: a family manual / Herbert Wagemaker with Ann Buchholz. Published/Created: Ponte Vedra Beach, FL: H. Wagemaker, [1996?] Description: 155 p.; 22 cm. ISBN: 0965499618

Schizophrenia and civilization / E. Fuller Torrey. Published/Created: New York: J. Aronson, c1980. Description: ix, 230 p.; 24 cm. ISBN: 0087668804

Schizophrenia and comorbid conditions: diagnosis and treatment / edited by Michael Y. Hwang, Paul C. Bermanzohn. Edition Information: 1st ed. Published/Created: Washington, DC: American Psychiatric Press, c2001. Description: xvii, 238 p.; 24 cm. ISBN: 0880487712 (alk. paper)

Schizophrenia and genetics; a twin study vantage point [by] Irving I. Gottesman and James Shields. With a contribution by Paul E. Meehl. Published/Created: New York, Academic Press, 1972. Description: xviii, 433 p. illus. 24 cm. ISBN: 0122934504

Schizophrenia and human value: chronic schizophrenia, science, and society / Peter Barham. Published/Created: Oxford [Oxfordshire]; New York, NY: Blackwell, 1985. Description: viii, 223 p.; 24 cm. ISBN: 0631134743

Schizophrenia and human value: chronic schizophrenia, science, and society: with a new preface / Peter Barham. Edition Information: New ed. Published/Created: London: Free Association Books, c1993. Description: xviii, 223 p.; 24 cm. ISBN: 1853431966

Schizophrenia and madness / Andrew Croyden Smith. Published/Created: London: Boston: George Allen & Unwin, 1982. Description: 174 p.; 23 cm. ISBN: 0041570081 004157009X (pbk.)

Schizophrenia and manic-depressive disorder: the biological roots of mental illness as revealed by the landmark study of identical twins / E. Fuller Torrey in collaboration with Ann E. Bowler, Edward H. Taylor, and Irving I. Gottesman. Published/Created: New York: Basic Books, c1994. Description: xxvi, 274 p.: ill.; 24 cm. ISBN: 0465017460

Schizophrenia and mood disorders: the new drug therapies in clinical practice / edited by Peter F. Buckley and John L. Waddington, with a foreword by Ross J. Baldessarini. Published/Created: Oxford; Woburn, MA: Butterworth-Heinemann, 2000. Description: xiv, 353 p.; 24 cm. ISBN: 0750640960

Schizophrenia and primitive mental states: structural collapse and creativity / Peter L. Giovacchini; with a chapter by Philip Giovacchini. Published/Created: Northvale, N.J.: Jason Aronson, c1997. Description: x, 276 p.; 23 cm. ISBN: 0765700271 (alk. paper)

Schizophrenia and related syndromes / P.J. McKenna. Edition Information: 2nd ed. Published/Created: Hove, East Sussex; New York: Taylor & Francis, 2007. Description: p.; cm. Projected Publication Date: 0705 ISBN: 9781583919286 (hbk) 1583919287 (hbk) 9781583919293 (pbk) 1583919295 (pbk)

Schizophrenia and related syndromes / P.J. McKenna. Edition Information: 1st ed. Published/Created: Oxford: New York; Oxford University Press, 1994. Description: p. cm. Projected Publication Date: 9406 ISBN: 019261780X (hbk)

Schizophrenia and related syndromes / P.J. McKenna. Published/Created: Hove, East Sussex, UK: Psychology Press, c1997. Description: 418 p.; 24 cm. ISBN: 0863777902 (pbk)

Schizophrenia and social care: a comparative follow-up study of 339 schizophrenic patients, by G.W. Brown, Margaret Bone, Bridget Dalison, [and] J.K. Wing. Published/Created: London, New York [etc.] Oxford U.P., 1966. Description: ix, 232 p. tables, diagrs. 26 cm.

Schizophrenia and the family: a practitioner's guide to psychoeducation and management / Carol M. Anderson, Douglas J. Reiss, Gerard E. Hogarty. Published/Created: New York: Guilford Press, c1986. Description: xii, 365 p.; 24 cm. ISBN: 0898620651

Schizophrenia and the family, by Theodore Lidz, Stephen Fleck, and Alice R. Cornelison with the collaboration of Yrjô O. Alanen [and others] Published/Created: New York, International Universities Press [1965] Description: 477 p. 24 cm.

Schizophrenia and the family. Edition Information: 2nd ed. / Theodore Lidz, Stephen Fleck, with the collaboration of Alice R. Cornelison ... [et al.]. Published/Created: New York: International Universities Press, 1985. Description: x, 494 p.: ill.; 24 cm. ISBN: 082366001X

Schizophrenia and the need-fear dilemma, by Donald L. Burnham, Arthur I. Gladstone, and Robert W. Gibson. Published/Created: New York, International Universities Press [1969] Description: xv, 474 p. 24 cm.

Schizophrenia and the poor [by] Paul M. Roman [and] Harrison M. Trice. Published/Created: Ithaca, New York State School of Industrial and Labor Relations, Cornell University, 1967. Description: vi, 78 p. 23 cm.

Schizophrenia and youth: etiology and therapeutic consequences / Christian Eggers (ed.). Published/Created: Berlin; New York: Springer-Verlag, c1991. Description: x, 202 p.: ill.; 24 cm. ISBN: 0387524851 (U.S.: alk. paper)

Schizophrenia as a brain disease / edited by Fritz A. Henn and Henry A. Nasrallah. Published/Created: New York: Oxford University Press, 1982. Description: xii, 298 p.: ill.; 24 cm. ISBN: 0195030885

Schizophrenia as a human process. With introd. and commentaries by Helen Swick Perry. Published/Created: New York, Norton [1974, c1962] Description: xxxv, 363 p. 20 cm. ISBN: 0393007219

Schizophrenia as a human process. With introd. and commentaries by Helen Swick Perry. Edition Information: [1st ed.] Published/Created: New York, W. W. Norton [1962] Description: 363 p. illus. 22 cm.

Schizophrenia as a life style [by] Arthur Burton, Juan J. López Ibor [and] Werner M. Mendel. With a foreword by Otto A. Will, Jr. Published/Created: New York, Springer Pub. Co. [1974] Description: xiv, 160 p. 22 cm. ISBN: 0826115705

Schizophrenia as developmental crisis. [Sound recording] Published/Created: [S.l.]: Big Sur Recordings, [1973] Description: 1 cassette.

Schizophrenia at home / Clare Creer, John Wing. Published/Created: London: Institute of Psychiatry; Surbiton [Eng.]: [sold by] National Schizophrenia

Fellowship, 1974. Description: iii, 78 p.; 30 cm.

Schizophrenia at home: a guide to helping the family / Jacqueline M. Atkinson. Published/Created: New York: New York University Press, 1986. Description: 207 p.; 23 cm. ISBN: 0814705863

Schizophrenia bulletin / National Institute of Mental Health. Published/Created: [Rockville, Md.]: U.S. Dept. of Health, Education and Welfare, Public Health Service, Alcohol, Drug Abuse and Mental Health Administration; Washington, D.C.: [Supt. of Docs., U.S. G.P.O., distributor] Description: v.: ill.; 26 cm. Began with Dec. 1968. ISSN: 0586-7614

Schizophrenia from a neurocognitive perspective: probing the impenetrable darkness / Michael Foster Green. Published/Created: Boston: Allyn and Bacon, c1998. Description: xii, 190 p.: ill.; 24 cm. ISBN: 0205184774

Schizophrenia genesis: the origins of madness / Irving I. Gottesman, with the assistance of Dorothea L. Wolfgram. Published/Created: New York: Freeman, c1991. Description: xiii, 296 p.: ill.; 25 cm. ISBN: 0716721457: 0716721473 (pbk.)

Schizophrenia in a molecular age / edited by Carol A. Tamminga. Published/Created: Washington, D.C.: American Psychiatric Press, c1999. Description: xvii, 181 p.: ill. (some col.); 23 cm. ISBN: 0880489618 (alk. paper)

Schizophrenia in childhood [by] Charles Bradley. Published/Created: New York, Macmillan, 1941. Description: vii, 152 p. 21 cm.

Schizophrenia in children and adolescents / edited by Helmut Remschmidt. Published/Created: Cambridge, UK; New York: Cambridge University Press, 2001. Description: xv, 308 p.: ill.; 25 cm. ISBN: 0521794285 (pbk.)

Schizophrenia in children; collected papers, by J. Louise Despert. Edition Information: [1st ed. Published/Created: New York] R. Brunner [1968] Description: vi, 215 p. 23 cm.

Schizophrenia in focus: guidelines for treatment and rehabilitation / David F.L. Dawson, Heather Munroe Blum, Giampiero Bartolucci. Published/Created: New York, NY: Human Sciences Press, c1983. Description: 190 p.; 23 cm. ISBN: 0898850967

Schizophrenia in late life: aging effects on symptoms and course of illness / Philip D. Harvey. Edition Information: 1st ed. Published/Created: Washington, DC: American Psychological Association, c2005. Description: v, 219 p.; 26 cm. ISBN: 1591471621

Schizophrenia in psychoanalytic office practice: 1956 symposium; thirty contributors. Alfred H. Rifkin, editor. Published/Created: New York, Grune & Stratton, 1957. Description: x, 150 p. 24 cm.

Schizophrenia into later life: treatment, research, and policy / edited by Carl I. Cohen. Edition Information: 1st ed. Published/Created: Washington, DC: American Pyschiatric, c2003. Description: xx, 322 p.: ill.; 23 cm. ISBN: 1585620378 (pbk.: alk. paper)

Schizophrenia research / editors, Carol A. Tamminga, S. Charles Schulz. Published/Created: New York: Raven Press, c1991. Description: xviii, 373 p.:

ill. (some col.); 26 cm. ISBN: 0881676756

Schizophrenia research. Published/Created: Amsterdam: Elsevier Science Publisher B.V., c1988- Description: v.: ill.; 26 cm. Vol. 1, no. 1 (Jan./Feb. 1988)- ISSN: 0920-9964

Schizophrenia revealed: from neurons to social interactions / Michael Foster Green. Published/Created: New York: Norton, c2001. Description: xiv, 207 p.: ill.; 22 cm. ISBN: 0393703347

Schizophrenia simplified: a field guide to schizophrenia for frontline workers, families, and professionals / editors and authors, J.F. Thornton, M.V. Seeman; contributing authors, E.D. Plummer, J.J. Jeffries, S.K. Littman. Published/Created: Toronto; Lewiston, NY: Hogrefe & Huber Publishers, 1991. Description: viii, 136 p.: ill. (some col.); 23 cm. ISBN: 0920887171

Schizophrenia today / edited by D. Kemali, G. Bartholini and D. Richter. Published/Created: Oxford; New York: Pergamon, 1976. Description: xv, 282 p.: ill.; 26 cm. ISBN: 0080209289

Schizophrenia, a bibliography of books in English / by Mark Weiman. Published/Created: Darby, Pa.: Norwood Editions, 1981. Description: iii, 146 p.; 23 cm. ISBN: 0848270649 (lib. bdg.)

Schizophrenia, a biopsychological perspective / Andrew Crider. Published/Created: Hillsdale, N.J.: Lawrence Erlbaum Associates; New York: distributed by Halsted Press, 1979. Description: x, 204 p.: ill.; 24 cm. ISBN: 0470268336

Schizophrenia, a multinational study: a summary of the initial evaluation phase of the international pilot study of schizophrenia. Published/Created: Geneva: World Health Organization; Albany, N.Y.: available from Q Corporation, 1975. Description: 150 p.: ill.; 22 cm. ISBN: 9241300639

Schizophrenia, a psychobiological view: proceedings of the symposium held in L'Aquila, Italy, February 26, 1988 / edited by Massimo Casacchia and Alessandro Rossi. Published/Created: Dordrecht; Boston: Kluwer Academic Publishers, c1989. Description: 136 p.: ill.; 24 cm. ISBN: 074620096X

Schizophrenia, a source of social insight / Brian W. Grant. Published/Created: Philadelphia: Westminster Press, [1975] Description: 252 p.; 21 cm. ISBN: 0664207227

Schizophrenia, by Helge Lundholm. Published/Created: Durham, N.C., Duke University Press, 1932. Description: 117 p. 25 cm.

Schizophrenia, culture, and social work / Jayne Westcott. Published/Created: Norwich: University of East Anglia: Social Work Today, 1984. Description: 39 leaves; 30 cm. ISBN: 0946751056 (pbk.)

Schizophrenia, culture, and subjectivity: the edge of experience / edited by Janis Hunter Jenkins, Robert John Barrett. Published/Created: New York: Cambridge University Press, 2004. Description: xix, 357 p.; 24 cm. ISBN: 0521829550 0521536413 (pb.)

Schizophrenia, edited by Lawrence C. Kolb, Frank J. Kallmann [and] Phillip Polatin. Published/Created: Boston, Little, Brown, 1964 Description: xii, 699-999 p. 24 cm.

Schizophrenia, medical diagnosis or moral verdict? / Theodore R. Sarbin, James C.

Mancuso. Published/Created: New York: Pergamon Press, c1980. Description: xiv, 263 p.: ill.; 24 cm. ISBN: 0080246133 0080246125 (pbk.)

Schizophrenia, the epigenetic puzzle / Irving I. Gottesman, James Shields, with the assistance of Daniel R. Hanson. Published/Created: Cambridge; New York: Cambridge University Press, 1982. Description: xiii, 258 p.: ill.; 24 cm. ISBN: 0521225736 0521295599 (pbk.)

Schizophrenia, theory, diagnosis, and treatment: [proceedings] / edited by Herman C. B. Denber. Published/Created: New York: M. Dekker, c1978. Description: ix, 242 p.; 24 cm. ISBN: 082476711X

Schizophrenia. Published/Created: [Minneapolis, American Schizophrenia Association, etc.] Description: 3 v. ill., ports. 26 cm. v. 1-3, no. 3/4; 1969-71. ISSN: 0036-6129

Schizophrenia. Published/Created: Baltimore, Williams and Wilkins, 1962. Description: 190 p. illus. 23 cm.

Schizophrenia. Published/Created: London, Mental Health Research Fund [1961] Description: 7 p. 21 cm.

Schizophrenia. Published/Created: Morristown, N.J., General Learning Press, [1972] Description: 19 p. 28 cm.

Schizophrenia. Published/Created: New York, Philosophical Library [1958] Description: 335 p. illus. 22 cm.

Schizophrenia. where families fear to tread from despair to hope./ by Donald P. Rothschild. Published/Created: [Wakefield, RI: D.P. Rothschild], 2004. Description: 183 p.: ill.; 23 cm. ISBN: 0974815004

Schizophrenia: behavioral aspects. Published/Created: New York, Wiley [1973] Description: ix, 181 p. illus. 23 cm. ISBN: 0471750913 0471750905 (pbk.)

Schizophrenia: current approaches to a baffling problem. Edition Information: [1st ed. Published/Created: New York, Public Affairs Committee, 1971] Description: 24 p. illus. 19 cm.

Schizophrenia: pharmacotherapy and psychotherapy [by] Lester Grinspoon, Jack R. Ewalt [and] Richard I. Shader. Published/Created: Baltimore, Williams & Wilkins [1972] Description: xxii, 290 p. illus. 24 cm. ISBN: 0683036785

Schizophrenia: the divided mind, by Joyce Emerson and Clare Marc Wallace. Published/Created: London, British Medical Association in conjunction with the National Association for Mental Health [1969] Description: 23 p. 19 cm. ISBN: 090022102X

Schizophrenia: the first ten Dean award lectures, edited by Stanley R. Dean. Published/Created: New York, MSS Information Corp. [1973] Description: 323 p. illus. 24 cm. ISBN: 0842271155

Schizophrenia: the meanings of madness [by] Alexander R. K. Mitchell; with additional sections by Kenneth Myers, H. Y. Robertson and K. D. Armitage; foreword by Christopher Mayhew. Published/Created: London, Priory Press Ltd, 1972. Description: 158 p. 23 cm. ISBN: 0850780500 0850780519 (pbk.)

Schizophrenia: the meanings of madness [by] Alexander R.K. Mitchell. Foreword by Christopher Mayhew. Published/Created: New York, Taplinger Pub. Co. [1974, c1972] Description: 158 p. 23 cm. ISBN: 0800870026

Schizophrenia; a psychopharmacological approach, by Thomas A. Ban. Published/Created: Springfield, Ill., Thomas [1972] Description: ix, 134 p. illus. 24 cm. ISBN: 0398022224

Schizophrenia; a review of the syndrome. With the collaboration of Paul K. Benedict. Published/Created: New York, Logos Press, 1958. Description: xx, 1010 p. illus., diagr., tables. 24 cm.

Schizophrenia; an integrated approach, edited by Alfred Auerback. Published/Created: New York, Ronald Press Co. [1959] Description: viii, 224 p. illus., diagrs. 22 cm.

Schizophrenia; chemistry, metabolism and treatment. Published/Created: Springfield, Ill., Thomas [c1963] Description: xiv, 86 p.

Schizophrenia; conditional reflex studies. Published/Created: Springfield, Ill., Thomas [c1962] Description: xx, 345 p. ill.

Schizophrenia; current concepts and research. Edited by D. V. Siva Sankar. Published/Created: Hicksville, N.Y., PJD Publications [1969] Description: vi, 944 p. illus. 28 cm.

Schizophrenia; research and theory [by] William E. Broen, Jr. Published/Created: New York, Academic Press, 1968. Description: x, 240 p. illus. 24 cm.

Schizophrenia; somatic aspects. Published/Created: London, Pergamon Press, 1957. Description: viii, 181 p. ill.

Schizophrenia--treatment, management, and rehabilitation / edited by Alan S. Bellack. Published/Created: Orlando: Grune & Stratton, c1984. Description: xiii, 417 p.: ill.; 24 cm. ISBN: 0808916408

Schizophrenic disorders: sense and nonsense in conceptualization, assessment, and treatment / Leighton C. Whitaker; with a chapter by Antonio E. Puente. Published/Created: New York: Plenum Press, c1992. Description: xv, 256 p.; 24 cm. ISBN: 030644156X

Schizophrenic disorders: theory and treatment from a psychodynamic point of view / Ping-Nie Pao. Published/Created: New York: International Universities Press, c1979. Description: xv, 456 p.; 24 cm. ISBN: 0823659909

Schizophrenic psychology: new research / Douglas P. French, editor. Published/Created: New York: Nova Science Publishers, c2006. Description: xiii, 387 p.: ill. (some col.); 27 cm. ISBN: 160021035X 9781600210358

Schizophrenic speech: making sense of bathroots and ponds that fall in doorways / Peter J. McKenna, Tomasina M. Oh. Published/Created: Cambridge; New York: Cambridge University Press, 2005. Description: x, 210 p.: ill.; 26 cm. ISBN: 0521810752

Schizophrenic women: studies in marital crisis / Harold Sampson, Sheldon L. Messinger, Robert D. Towne; with a new introduction by Rita J. Simon; with the collaboration of David Ross ... [et al.]. Published/Created: New Brunswick, N.J.: Aldine Transaction, 2005. Description: xv, 174 p.; 23 cm. ISBN: 0202308162 (pbk.: alk. paper)

Schizophrenic women; studies in marital crisis [by] Harold Sampson, Sheldon L. Messinger [and] Robert D. Towne, with the collaboration of David Ross [and] others] Published/Created: New York, Atherton Press, 1964. Description: xiv, 174 p. 22 cm.

Search for the causes of schizophrenia / edited by H. Hafner, W.F. Gattaz, and W. Janzarik. Published/Created: Berlin; New York: Springer Verlag, c1987-<c1995 > Description: v. <1-3 >: ill.; 26 cm. ISBN: 0387173765 (v. 1: U.S.) 3540513663 (v. 2) 0387513663 (v. 2: U.S.)

Searching for the causes of schizophrenia / Eve C. Johnstone. Published/Created: Oxford; New York: Oxford University Press, 1994. Description: 134 p.: ill.; 25 cm. ISBN: 019262296X (cloth)

Season of birth: a study of schizophrenia and other mental disorders / Per Dalén. Published/Created: Amsterdam: North-Holland Pub. Co.; New York: American Elsevier, 1975. Description: 164 p.; 24 cm. ISBN: 0444107959 (American Elsevier)

Serological fractions in schizophrenia; a research symposium sponsored by the Louisiana State Department of Hospitals, Tulane University, and Louisiana State University, New Orleans, June 13-14, 1961. Published/Created: [New York] Harper & Row [c1963] Description: xiv, 239 p. ill.

Serum cortisol in chronic schizophrenia and its relation to psychiatric mental status. Published/Created: Lund, 1971. Description: 40 p. 24 cm.

Social cognition and schizophrenia / edited by Patrick W. Corrigan and David L. Penn. Edition Information: 1st ed. Published/Created: Washington, D.C.: American Psychological Association, 2001. Description: xvii, 353 p.: ill.; 27 cm. ISBN: 1557987742

Social systems and schizophrenia: selected papers/ H. Warren Dunham. Published/Created: New York, N.Y.: Praeger, 1980. Description: xi, 316 p.: maps; 24 cm. ISBN: 0030561345

Some effects of emotion on the use of words by schizophrenics. Published/Created: Washington, Catholic University of America Press, 1957. Description: vi, 39 p. tables 23 cm.

Some mathematical notes on three-mode factor analysis Published/Created: Urbana, Dept. of Psychology, University of Illinois, 1965. Description: 55. 19. 8 l. illus. 28 cm.

Some verbal aspects of primary process thought in schizophrenia. Published/Created: [n.p., n.d.] Description: 29 l.

Soothing the troubled mind: acupuncture and moxibustion in the treatment of schizophrenia / translated by Thomas Dey; edited by Nigel Wiseman; foreword by Richard Warner. Published/Created: Brookline, Mass.: Paradigm Publications, c2000. Description: xxvii, 140 p.; 23 cm. ISBN: 0912111607 (pbk.: alk. paper)

Soteria: through madness to deliverance / Loren R. Mosher, Voyce Hendrix, with Deborah C. Fort. Published/Created: [California?]: L.R. Mosher, c2004. Description: xviii, 340 p.; 22 cm. ISBN: 1413465242 1413465234 (softcover)

Soul murder: persecution in the family. Edition Information: [1st ed.] Published/Created: New York, Random House [1973] Description: xii, 193 p. illus. 23 cm. ISBN: 0394481488

Soul murder: persecution in the family. Published/Created: London, Allen Lane, 1973. Description: xiv, 173 p. illus. 23 cm. ISBN: 071390321X

Special report: schizophrenia 1993 / issue editor David Shore. Published/Created: Rockville, Md.: U.S. Department of Health and Human Services, National Institute of Mental Health, 1993. Description: 273 p.: ill.; 27 cm.

Special report: schizophrenia, 1980 / National Institute of Mental Health; [editors-in-chief, Samuel J. Keith, Loren R. Mosher]. Published/Created: Rockville, Md.: U.S. Dept. of Health and Human Services, Public Health Service, Alcohol, Drug Abuse, and Mental Health Administration; Washington, D.C.: For sale by the Supt. of Docs., U.S. G.P.O., 1981. Description: 160 p.: form; 27 cm.

Special report: schizophrenia, 1987 / guest editor, David Shore; National Institute of Mental Health. Published/Created: Rockville, MD: U.S. Dept. of Health and Human Services, Public Health Service, Alcohol, Drug Abuse, and Mental Health Administration, [1987] Description: 197 p., [12] leaves of plates: ill. (some col.); 27 cm.

Special report: Schizophrenia, 1993 / issue editor, David Shore. Published/Created: Rockville, Md. (5600 Fishers Ln.): U.S. Dept. of Health and Human Services, Public Health Service, National Institutes of Health, National Institute of Mental Health, Division of Clinical and Treatment Research, Schizophrenia Research Branch; Washington, D.C.: [Supt. of Docs., U.S. G.P.O., distributor], 1993. Description: 273 p.; 28 cm.

Special report: schizophrenia, prepared by Loren R. Mosher and David Feinsilver. Published/Created: Rockville, Md., National Institute of Mental Health; [for sale by the Supt. of Docs., U.S. Govt. Print. Off., Washington, 1971] Description: 40 p. 26 cm.

Specific techniques for the psychotherapy of schizophrenic patients / Andrew Lotterman. Published/Created: Madison, Conn.: International Universities Press, c1996. Description: xii, 224 p.; 24 cm. ISBN: 082366130X (hard cover)

Speech and language disorders in psychiatry: proceedings of the Fifth Leeds Psychopathology Symposium / edited by Andrew Sims. Published/Created: London: Gaskell; [Washington, D.C.]: Distributed in North America by American Psychiatric Press, c1995. Description: viii, 206 p.: ill.; 23 cm. ISBN: 0902241796 (Gaskell) 0880486406

Staying well after psychosis: a cognitive interpersonal approach to recovery and relapse prevention / Andrew Gumley and Matthias Schwannauer. Published/Created: Chichester, England; Hoboken, NJ: Wiley, c2006. Description: xi, 287 p.: ill.; 24 cm. ISBN: 0470021845 (hbk.) 0470021853 (pbk.) 9780470021842 (hbk.) 9780470021859 (pbk.)

Strategic intervention in schizophrenia; current developments in treatment. Edited by Robert Cancro, Norma Fox [and] Lester E. Shapiro. Published/Created: New York, Behavioral Publications [1974] Description: xvi, 326 p. 22 cm. ISBN: 087705133X

Stress, fantasy, and schizophrenia: a study of the adaptive processes.

Structural factors related to the substitute value of activities in normal and schizophrenic persons ... by Georgia Bennett ... Published/Created: [Durham, N.C., 1941-42] Description: 2 pt. tables. 23 cm.

Structured learning therapy: toward a psychotherapy for the poor [by] Arnold P. Goldstein. Published/Created: New York, Academic Press, 1973. Description: xviii, 421 p. 24 cm. ISBN: 0122887506

Studies in metaphoric verbal behavior in patients with a psychiatric diagnosis of schizophrenia. Published/Created: Stockholm, Skandinaviskatestfôrlaget, (Stureg. 56), 1968. Description: 125 p. 23 cm.

Studies of schizophrenia: papers read at the World Psychiatric Association symposium Current Concepts of Schizophrenia, London, November 1972 / edited by M. H. Lader. Published/Created: Ashford, Kent: Headley [for] the World Psychiatric Association and the Royal College of Psychiatrists, 1975. Description: x, 160 p., [2] p. of plates: ill.; 25 cm. ISBN: 0900443081

Studies on inpatient care of schizophrenia cases / Julia Chesler-Gampel. Published/Created: Jerusalem: State of Israel, Ministry of Israel, Mental Health Services, 1973- Description: v.: ill.; 27 cm.

Suffering insanity: psychoanalytic essays on psychosis / R. D. Hinshelwood. Published/Created: Hove [England]; New York: Brunner-Routledge, 2004. Description: xi, 187 p.; 23 cm. ISBN: 1583918930 (hardback: alk. paper) 1583918949 (pbk.: alk. paper)

Suicide in schizophrenia / Roberto Tatarelli, Maurizio Pompili, and Paolo Girardi, (editors). Published/Created: Hauppauge, N.Y.: Nova Science, c2006. Description: p.; cm. Projected Publication Date: 0606 ISBN: 1600211992

Suicides in schizophrenia and paranoid psychoses / by Matti Virkkunen; [translated from the Finnish by Jaakko Railo]. Published/Created: Copenhagen: Munksgaard, 1974. Description: 305 p.; 24 cm. ISBN: 8716017579

Surfaces of strangeness: Janet Frame and the rhetoric of madness / Simone Oettli-van Delden. Published/Created: Wellington: Victoria University Press, 2003. Description: 187 p.; 21 cm. ISBN: 0864734565

Surviving schizophrenia: a family manual / E. Fuller Torrey. Edition Information: Rev. ed. Published/Created: New York: Perennial Library, c1988. Description: xviii, 460 p.; 21 cm. ISBN: 0060551194: 0060962496 (pbk.)

Surviving schizophrenia: a family manual / E. Fuller Torrey. Edition Information: 1st ed. Published/Created: New York: Harper & Row, c1983. Description: xiv, 302 p.; 24 cm. ISBN: 0060151129

Surviving schizophrenia: a manual for families, consumers, and providers / E. Fuller Torrey. Edition Information: 4th ed. Published/Created: New York: Quill, 2001. Description: xxiv, 512 p.: ill.; 21 cm. ISBN: 0060959193 (pbk.)

Surviving schizophrenia: a manual for families, consumers, and providers / E. Fuller Torrey. Edition Information: 3rd ed. Published/Created: New York: HarperPerennial, c1995. Description:

xviii, 409 p.: ill.; 21 cm. ISBN: 006055360X 0060950765

Surviving schizophrenia: a manual for families, patients, and providers / E.Fuller Torrey. Edition Information: 5th ed., 1st Collins pbk. ed. Published/Created: New York: Collins, 2006. Description: xxiv, 546 p.: ill.; 21 cm. ISBN: 0060842598 (pbk.)

Symbol and realization: a contribution to the study of magic and healing / by Ronald H. Davidson and Richard Day. Published/Created: Berkeley: Center for South and Southeast Asia Studies, University of California, 1974. Description: ix, 135 p.: ill.; 28 cm.

Symposium on Research in Schizophrenia, Veterans Administration Hospital, Battle Creek, Michigan, March 1, 2, 22 and 23, 1962. Published/Created: [s.l.: s.n., 1962?] Description: 162 p.: ill.; 28 cm.

Symposium on the Biology of Schizophrenia, Veterans Administration Hospital, Battle Creek, Michigan, March 16-17, 1961. Published/Created: [s.l.: s.n., 1961?] Description: 90 p., [63] leaves of plates: ill.; 28 cm.

Symposium: collected papers on schizophrenia. Published/Created: Battle Creek, Mich., Veterans Administration Hospital, 1965. Description: 108 p. 28 cm.

Symptoms of schizophrenia / edited by Charles G. Costello. Published/Created: New York: Wiley, c1993. Description: xi, 322 p.; 25 cm. ISBN: 0471548758 (cloth: alk. paper)

Synopsis of Eugen Bleuler's Dementia praecox, or The group of schizophrenias. [By] Nathan S. Kline. Published/Created: New York, International Universities Press [1952] Description: 57 p. 22 cm.

Technicians of the finite: the rise and decline of the schizophrenic in American thought, 1840-1960 / S.P. Fullinwider. Published/Created: Westport, Conn.: Greenwood Press, 1982. Description: ix, 253 p.; 22 cm. ISBN: 0313230218 (lib. bdg.)

The adaptive behavior of adolescent children whose mothers were hospitalized at Saint Elizabeths Hospital with a diagnosis of schizophrenia. Published/Created: Washington, Catholic University of America Press, 1955. Description: p. cm.

The American Psychiatric Publishing textbook of schizophrenia / edited by Jeffrey A. Lieberman, T. Scott Stroup, Diana O. Perkins. Edition Information: 1st ed. Published/Created: Washington, DC: American Psychiatric Pub., c2006. Description: xvii, 435 p.: ill. (some col.); 29 cm. ISBN: 1585621919 (hardcover: alk. paper) 9781585621910

The behavioral high-risk paradigm in psychopathology / Gregory A. Miller, editor. Published/Created: New York: Springer, c1995. Description: xiv, 303 p.: ill.; 25 cm. ISBN: 0387945040 (New York: acid-free paper)

The biologic basis of schizophrenia, by Jon L. Karlsson. With a foreword by Curt Stern. Published/Created: Springfield, Ill., C.C. Thomas [1966] Description: xi, 87 p. illus. 27 cm.

The Biological basis of schizophrenia / edited by Gwynneth Hemmings and W. A. Hemmings. Published/Created: Baltimore: University Park Press, c1978. Description: xi, 272 p.: ill.; 23 cm. ISBN: 0839113293

The biology of schizophrenia: proceedings of the 7th International Symposium of the Tokyo Institute of Psychiatry, Tokyo, Japan, October 19-20, 1992 / editors, T. Moroji and K. Yamamoto. Published/Created: Amsterdam; New York: Elsevier, 1994. Description: ix, 274 p.: ill. (some col.); 25 cm. ISBN: 0444817727 (alk. paper) 0444801073 (ser.: alk. paper)

The biology of the schizophrenic process / edited by Stewart Wolf and Beatrice Bishop Berle. Published/Created: New York: Plenum Press, c1976. Description: xi, 199 p.: ill.; 26 cm. ISBN: 0306379198

The casebook of a residential care psychiatrist: psychopharmacosocioeconomics and the treatment of schizophrenia in residential care facilities / Martin Fleishman. Published/Created: New York: Haworth Clinical Practice Press, c2005. Description: xxiv, 446 p.; 23 cm. ISBN: 0789023725 (hard: alk. paper) 0789023733 (soft: alk. paper)

The character of the interrelationship of crime and schizophrenia, by H. Warren Dunham. Published/Created: Chicago, 1941. Description: v, 257 l. 32 cm.

The charge of consciousness: energy, chemistry, and the dynamics of the brain / by David Boadella. Published/Created: Abbotsbury: Abbotsbury Publications, 1979. Description: [5], 120 p.: ill.; 28 cm.

The chronic schizophrenias / by Christian Astrup. Published/Created: Oslo: Universitetsforlaget; Irvington-on-Hudson, N.Y.: distributed by Columbia University Press, 1979. Description: xiii, 121 p.; 22 cm. ISBN: 8200018105

The cloud of unknowing / Thomas H. Cook. Edition Information: 1st ed. Published/Created: Orlando, Fla.: Harcourt, c2007. Description: 310 p.; 24 cm. ISBN: 9780151012602 0151012601

The complete family guide to schizophrenia: helping your loved one get the most out of life / Kim T. Mueser and Susan Gingerich; foreword by Harriet P. Lefley. Published/Created: New York: Guilford Press, c2006. Description: xiv, 481 p.: ill.; 26 cm. ISBN: 9781593852733 (hardcover: alk. paper) 1593852738 (hardcover: alk. paper) 1593851804 (pbk.: alk. paper) 9781593851804 (pbk.: alk. paper)

The Concept of schizophrenia: historical perspectives / edited by John G. Howells. Edition Information: 1st ed. Published/Created: Washington, DC: American Psychiatric Press, c1991. Description: xxiv, 211 p.; 24 cm. ISBN: 0880481080 (alk. paper)

The concept of schizophrenia. Published/Created: New York, Philosophical Library [1954] Description: 145 p. 23 cm.

The Construction of madness: emerging conceptions and interventions into the psychotic process / edited by Peter A. Magaro. Edition Information: 1st ed. Published/Created: New York: Pergamon Press, 1976. Description: 221 p.; 23 cm. ISBN: 0080199046. 0080199038

The course and prognosis of schizophrenic psychoses in Helsinki; a comparative study of first admissions in 1950, 1960 and 1965, by Pekka Niskanen [and] Kalle A. Achté. Published/Created: [Helsinki, Helsinki University Central Hospital, Psychiatric Clinic, 1972] Description: 56 p. illus. 25 cm. ISBN: 9517090013

The diagnosis and stigma of schizophrenia / by Charles E. Harman. Published/Created: Brookings, Or: Old Court Press, c2003. Description: xx, 318 p.; 22 cm. ISBN: 0964939134 (alk. paper)

The dialectics of schizophrenia / Philip Thomas. Published/Created: London; New York: Free Association Books, 1997. Description: x, 269 p.; 23 cm. ISBN: 1853433616

The dinosaur man: tales of madness and enchantment from the back ward / Susan Baur. Edition Information: 1st ed. Published/Created: New York, NY: Edward Burlingame Books, c1991. Description: 203 p.: ill.; 25 cm. ISBN: 0060165383

The disordered mind: what we now know about schizophrenia / Patrick O'Brien. Published/Created: Englewood Cliffs, N.J.: Prentice-Hall, c1978. Description: xi, 304 p.; 21 cm. ISBN: 0132164655. 0132164574

The divided self: an existential study in sanity and madness / R.D. Laing. Published/Created: London; New York: Routledge, 1999. Description: 237 p.; 23 cm. ISBN: 0415198186

The early course of schizophrenia / edited by Tonmoy Sharma and Philip D. Harvey. Published/Created: Oxford; New York: Oxford University Press, 2006. Description: vi, 263 p.: ill.; 25 cm. ISBN: 9780198510840 (hbk.) 0198510845 (hbk: alk. paper) 9780198568957 (pbk.) 0198568959 (pbk: alk. paper)

The early stages of schizophrenia / edited by Robert B. Zipursky, S. Charles Schulz. Edition Information: 1st ed. Published/Created: Washington, DC: American Psychiatric Pub. 2001. Description: xx, 259 p.: ill.; 23 cm. ISBN: 0880488409 (alk. paper)

The empty core: an object relations approach to psychotherapy of the schizoid personality / Jeffrey Seinfeld. Published/Created: Northvale, N.J.: J. Aronson, c1991. Description: xiii, 260 p.; 24 cm. ISBN: 0876686110

The encyclopedia of schizophrenia and other psychotic disorders / Richard Noll; foreword by Leonard George. Edition Information: 3rd ed. Published/Created: New York: Facts on File, c2007. Description: xx, 409 p.; 25 cm. ISBN: 0816064059 (alk. paper) 9780816064052 (alk. paper)

The encyclopedia of schizophrenia and other psychotic disorders / Richard Noll; foreword by Susan Naylor. Edition Information: 2nd ed. Published/Created: New York, NY: Facts On File, c2000. Description: xxiv, 344 p.; 24 cm. ISBN: 0816040702 (alk. paper)

The encyclopedia of schizophrenia and the psychotic disorders / Richard Noll; foreword by Leonard George. Published/Created: New York: Facts on File, c1992. Description: xxvi, 374 p.; 26 cm. ISBN: 0816022402 (alk. paper)

The environment of schizophrenia: innovations in practice, policy, and communications / Richard Warner. Published/Created: London; Philadelphia: Brunner-Routledge; Philadelphia, PA: Taylor & Francis, 2000. Description: xii, 136 p.: ill.; 22 cm. ISBN: 0415223067 (hbk) 0415223075 (pbk.)

The epidemiology of schizophrenia / edited by Robin M. Murray ... [et al.]. Published/Created: Cambridge, U.K.; New York: Cambridge University Press,

2003. Description: xvi, 454 p.: ill.; 26 cm. ISBN: 052177540X (hb.)

The etiology of schizophrenia. Published/Created: New York, Basic Books [1960] Description: 456 p. illus. 25 cm.

The European concept of schizophrenia. [Sound recording] Published/Created: Fort Lee, N.J., Sigma Information [1973. 90324] Description: p. 1 cassette. 2 1/2 x 4 in.

The experience of God: portraits in the phenomenological psychopathology of schizophrenia / David Terry Bradford. Published/Created: New York: P. Lang, c1984. Description: x, 331 p.; 23 cm. ISBN: 0820401269

The experience of reality in childhood schizophrenia. Published/Created: New York, International Universities Press [1962] Description: 215 p. 23 cm.

The falling shadow: one patient's mental health care 1978-1993: report of the Committee of Inquiry into the Events Leading up to and Surrounding the Fatal Incident at the Edith Morgan Centre, Torbay, on 1 September 1993 / Louis Blom-Cooper, Helen Hally, Elaine Murphy. Published/Created: London: Duckworth, 1995. Description: xxvi, 230 p.: ill.; 22 cm. ISBN: 0715626620

The family and schizophrenia / John G. Howells and Waguih R. Guirguis. Published/Created: New York, N.Y.: International Universities Press, c1985. Description: v, 346 p.; 24 cm. ISBN: 0823618501

The family shadow: sources of suicide and schizophrenia / David K. Reynolds and Norman L. Farberow. Published/Created: Berkeley: University of California Press, c1981. Description: xi, 177 p.; 24 cm. ISBN: 0520042131

The far side of madness / John Weir Perry; with a new preface by John Beebe. Edition Information: 2nd ed. Published/Created: Putnam, Conn.: Spring Publications, 2005. Description: xii, 209 p.; 23 cm. ISBN: 9780882145570 (pbk.: alk. paper) 0882145576 (pbk.: alk. paper)

The far side of madness / John Weir Perry. Published/Created: Dallas, Tex.: Spring Publications, [1989], c1974. Description: vi, 177 p.; 23 cm. ISBN: 0882145118

The far side of madness. Published/Created: Englewood Cliffs, N.J., Prentice-Hall [1974] Description: viii, 177 p. 21 cm. ISBN: 0133030326 0133030245 (pbk.)

The formal aspects of schizophrenic verbal communication.

The four of us: a family memoir / Elizabeth Swados. Published/Created: New York, N.Y., U.S.A.: Plume, [1993] Description: 243 p.; 21 cm. ISBN: 0452269601

The four of us: the story of a family / Elizabeth Swados. Edition Information: 1st ed. Published/Created: New York: Farrar, Straus, and Giroux, 1991. Description: 243 p.; 24 cm. ISBN: 0374152195

The future of time; man's temporal environment. Edited by Henri Yaker, Humphry Osmond, and Frances Cheek. Edition Information: [1st ed.] Published/Created: Garden City, N.Y., Doubleday, 1971. Description: xvi, 512 p. illus. 22 cm.

The Genain quadruplets; a case study and theoretical analysis of heredity and environment in schizophrenia. David Rosenthal, editor, and colleagues.

Published/Created: New York, Basic Books [1963, i.e. 1964] Description: xiv, 609 p. illus., diagrs., facsims., tables. 25 cm.

The hands of the living God: an account of a psycho-analytic treatment [by] Marion Milner. Published/Created: London, Hogarth P., and the Institute of Psycho-Analysis, 1969. Description: xxxi, 444 p. illus. 23 cm. ISBN: 0701202998

The hands of the living god; an account of a psycho-analytic treatment [by] Marion Milner. Published/Created: New York, International Universities Press [1969] Description: xxxi, 444 p. illus. 23 cm.

The idea of a mental illness. Published/Created: New Haven, Yale University Press, 1971. Description: 140 p. 22 cm. ISBN: 0300014309

The industrial rehabilitation of long-stay schizophrenic patients: a study of 45 patients at an industrial rehabilitation unit / J.K. Wing, D.H. Bennett, and John Denham. Published/Created: London: H.M.S.O., 1964. Description: vi, 42 p.; 25 cm.

The influence of self-disclosure with schizophrenic outpatients / by Richard Francis Formica. Published/Created: Oceanside, N.Y.: Dabor Science Publications, [1977] Description: xv, 123 p.: ill.; 23 cm. ISBN: 0895610604

The madness of Adam and Eve: how schizophrenia shaped humanity / David Horrobin. Published/Created: London; New York: Bantam, 2001. Description: vii, 275 p.; 24 cm. ISBN: 0593046498

The management of the severely disturbed adolescent / William M. Easson. Published/Created: Madison, Conn.: International Universities Press, c1996. Description: viii, 353 p.; 24 cm. ISBN: 0823630919

The meaning of madness; symptomatology, sociology, biology, and therapy of the schizophrenias [by] C. Peter Rosenbaum. Published/Created: New York, Science House, 1970. Description: xix, 411 p. 24 cm. ISBN: 0876680287

The Mesocorticolimbic dopamine system / edited by Peter W. Kalivas and Charles B. Nemeroff. Published/Created: New York, N.Y.: New York Academy of Sciences, 1988. Description: xii, 540 p.: ill.; 24 cm. ISBN: 0897664701 (alk. paper) 089766471X (pbk.: alk. paper)

The mind in chains; the autobiography of a schizophrenic. Edition Information: [1st. ed.] Published/Created: New York, Exposition Press [1955] Description: 315 p. 21 cm.

The natural history of mania, depression, and schizophrenia / George Winokur and Ming T. Tsuang. Edition Information: 1st ed. Published/Created: Washington, DC: American Psychiatric Press, c1996. Description: x, 372 p.: ill.; 24 cm. ISBN: 0880487267 (acidâ‹free paper)

The natural medicine guide to schizophrenia / Stephanie Marohn. Published/Created: Charlottesville, VA: Hampton Roads Pub. Co., c2003. Description: xix, 227 p.; 20 cm. ISBN: 1571742891 (alk. paper)

The nature of schizophrenia: new approaches to research and treatment / Lyman C. Wynne, Rue L. Cromwell, Steven Matthysse, in collaboration with Margaret L. Toohey, Bonnie J. Spring, Jonathan Sugarman. Published/Created: New York: Wiley, c1978. Description: xxi, 726 p.: ill.; 26 cm. ISBN: 0471022098

The Neurochemistry and neuropharmacology of schizophrenia / editors, Fritz A. Henn, Lynn E. DeLisi. Published/Created: Amsterdam; New York: Elsevier; New York, NY: Sole distributors for the USA and Canada, Elsevier Science Pub. Co., 1987. Description: xv, 503 p.: ill.; 25 cm. ISBN: 0444904360 (U.S.)

The neurodevelopmental basis of schizophrenia / [edited by] John L. Waddington, Peter F. Buckley. Published/Created: New York: Chapman & Hall; Austin: R.G. Landes, c1996. Description: 186 p.; 26 cm. ISBN: 0412100819 (alk. paper)

The Neuroleptic-nonresponsive patient: characterization and treatment / edited by Burt Angrist, S. Charles Schulz. Edition Information: 1st ed. Published/Created: Washington, DC: American Psychiatric Press, c1990. Description: xxviii, 164 p.: ill.; 22 cm. ISBN: 0880484616 (alk. paper)

The Neurology of schizophrenia / editors, Henry A. Nasrallah, Daniel R. Weinberger. Published/Created: Amsterdam; New York: Elsevier; New York, NY: Sole distributors for the USA and Canada, Elsevier Science Pub. Co., 1986. Description: xii, 416 p.: ill.; 25 cm. ISBN: 0444904158 (U.S.)

The neuropathology of schizophrenia: progress and interpretation / edited by Paul J. Harrison and Gareth W. Roberts. Published/Created: Oxford; New York: Oxford University Press, 2000. Description: xii, 374 p.: ill.; 25 cm. ISBN: 0192629077 (alk. paper)

The new pharmacotherapy of schizophrenia / edited by Alan Breier. Edition Information: 1st ed. Published/Created: Washington, DC: American Psychiatric Press, c1996. Description: xx, 240 p.: ill.; 22 cm. ISBN: 0880484918

The nonhuman environment, in normal development and in schizophrenia. Published/Created: New York, International Universities Press [1960] Description: xvii, 446 p. 23 cm.

The one / Paul Reed. Published/Created: Edinburgh: Crescent, 2003. Description: 328 p.; 22 cm. ISBN: 1841830550

The origin and treatment of schizophrenic disorders / Theodore Lidz. Published/Created: Madison, Conn.: International Universities Press, [1990], c1973. Description: xii, 144 p.; 22 cm. ISBN: 0823682064

The origin and treatment of schizophrenic disorders. Published/Created: New York, Basic Books [1973] Description: xii, 145 p. 22 cm. ISBN: 0465053378

The origins of schizophrenia; proceedings of the first Rochester International Conference on Schizophrenia, March 29-31, 1967 / Editor: John Romano. Published/Created: Amsterdam, New York, Excerpta Medica Foundation [1967] Description: 288 p. illus. 24 cm.

The out-patient treatment of schizophrenia; a symposium, edited by Sam C. Scher and Howard R. Davis. Published/Created: New York, Grune and Stratton, 1960. Description: x, 246 p. diagrs., tables. 24 cm.

The paradoxes of delusion: Wittgenstein, Schreber, and the schizophrenic mind / Louis A. Sass. Published/Created: Ithaca, N.Y.: Cornell University Press, 1994. Description: xiv, 177 p.; 24 cm. ISBN: 0801422108

The Pathophysiology of schizophrenia / Ray S. Greenberg. Published/Created: Austin: R.G. Landes, 1993. Description: 163 p.; 27 cm. ISBN: 1570590532

The pathways of mind: a neural theory of mental processing: mathematical principles, empirical evidence, and clinical applications / Roland Kalb. Published/Created: Wein; New York: Springer-Verlag, c2001. Description: xx, 355 p.: ill.; 25 cm. ISBN: 3211835652 (alk. paper)

The phenomenological approach to psychiatry; an introduction to recent phenomenological psychopathology. Published/Created: Springfield, Ill., Thomas [1955] Description: 105 p. 22 cm.

The physiology of psychological disorders: schizophrenia, depression, anxiety, and substance abuse / James G. Hollandsworth, Jr. Published/Created: New York: Plenum Press, c1990. Description: xvii, 318 p.: ill.; 24 cm. ISBN: 0306433532

The placenta and neurodisability / edited by Philip Baker and Colin Sibley. Published/Created: London: Mac Keith Press: Distributed by Cambridge University Press, 2006. Description: xi, 153 p.: ill.; 28 cm. ISBN: 1898683441

The politics of schizophrenia: psychiatric oppression in the United States / David Hill. Published/Created: Lanham, MD: University Press of America, c1983. Description: xii, 577 p.; 22 cm. ISBN: 081913614X (alk. paper): 0819136158 (pbk.: alk. paper)

The post-imperative negative variation in schizophrenic patients and healthy subjects / Christoph Klein. Published/Created: Frankfurt am Main; New York: P. Lang, c1997. Description: 386 p.: ill.; 21 cm. ISBN: 3631310781 (Frankfurt am Main) 0820432334 (U.S.)

The prognosis in schizophrenia. Published/Created: Copenhagen, Munskgaard, 1956. Description: 66 p. 25 cm.

The promise / Chaim Potok. Edition Information: 1st Anchor Books ed. Published/Created: New York: Anchor Books, 2005. Description: 368 p.; 21 cm. ISBN: 9781400095414 (pbk.) 1400095417 (pbk.)

The promise / Chaim Potok. Published/Created: Thorndike, ME: G.K. Hall, 1998, c1969. Description: 512 p. (large print); 25 cm. ISBN: 0783802560 (lg. print: hc: alk. paper)

The promise. Edition Information: [1st ed.] Published/Created: New York, Knopf, 1969. Description: 358 p. 22 cm.

The promise. Published/Created: Lancaster, N.Y., Associated Reprinting Co. [c1969] Description: 368 p. 34 cm.

The psyche and schizophrenia: the bond between affect and logic / Luc Ciompi; translated by Deborah Lucas Schneider. Published/Created: Cambridge, Mass.: Harvard University Press, 1988. Description: xii, 327 p.: ill.; 24 cm. ISBN: 0674719905 (alk. paper)

The Psychiatric clinics of North America. Annual of drug therapy. Published/Created: Philadelphia: W.B. Saunders, c1994- Description: v.: ill. Vol. 1 (1994)- Ceased in 2001. ISSN: 1068-3178

The psychiatric team and the social definition of schizophrenia: an anthropological study of person and illness / Robert J. Barrett; foreword by Byron J. Good. Published/Created: Cambridge [England]; New York, NY, USA: Cambridge University Press, 1996. Description: xx, 337 p.: ill.; 24 cm. ISBN: 0521416531 (hardback)

The psychology of dementia praecox / C. G. Jung; translated by R. F. C. Hull. Edition Information: 1st Princeton/Bollingen paperback ed. Published/Created: Princeton, N.J.: Princeton University Press, 1974, c1960. Description: xiv, 222 p.; 22 cm. ISBN: 0691018006

The psychology of schizophrenia / John Cutting. Published/Created: Edinburgh; New York: Churchill Livingstone, 1985. Description: vi, 457 p.: ill.; 24 cm. ISBN: 0443026637

The Psychopharmacology and treatment of schizophrenia / edited by P.B. Bradley, S.R. Hirsch. Published/Created: Oxford, [Oxfordshire]; New York: Oxford University Press, 1986. Description: 457 p.: ill.; 24 cm. ISBN: 0192612603

The Psychopharmacology of schizophrenia / edited by Michael A. Reveley & J. F. William Deakin. Published/Created: London: Arnold, c2000. Description: x, 269 p., [4] p. of plates: ill.; 25 cm.

The Psychotherapy of schizophrenia / edited by John S. Strauss .. [et al.]. Published/Created: New York: Plenum Medical Book Co., c1980. Description: xiii, 305 p.; 24 cm. ISBN: 0306404974

The Psychotherapy of schizophrenia: effective clinical aproaches--controversies, critiques and recommendations / edited by Gaetano Benedetti and Pier Maria Furlan. Published/Created: Seattle: Hogrefe & Huber, c1993. Description: xxii, 407 p.: ill.; 24 cm. ISBN: 088937077X: 3456820313 (Hans Huber Publishers)

The regressed patient / L. Bryce Boyer. Published/Created: New York: J. Aronson, c1983. Description: xvii, 346 p.: ill.; 24 cm. ISBN: 0876686269 (alk. paper)

The relationship of affective complexity to the judged emotional arousal value of the stimulus among process and reactive schizophrenics and normals. Published/Created: [n.p., n.d.] Description: v, 61 l. ill.

The Schizophrenias / edited by Frederic Flach. Edition Information: 1st ed. Published/Created: New York: Norton, c1988. Description: xiv, 233 p.; 24 cm. ISBN: 0393700623

The schizophrenias: a biological approach to the schizophrenia spectrum disorders / Mary Coleman, Christopher Gillberg. Published/Created: New York: Springer Pub. Co., c1996. Description: xiii, 312 p.; 24 cm. ISBN: 0826192904

The Schizophrenias: ours to conquer / by Carl C. Pfeiffer, Richard Mailloux, and Linda Forsythe. Edition Information: Rev. ed. Published/Created: Wichita, Kan.: Bio-Communications Press, 1988, c1970. Description: xi, 365 p.: ill.; 23 cm. ISBN: 0942333020

The schizophrenias--yours and mine / prepared and published by the Professional Committee of the Schizophrenia Foundation of New Jersey. Published/Created: New York: Pyramid Books, c1970, 1976 printing. Description: 158 p.: ill.; 18 cm. ISBN: 0515021784

The schizophrenic disorders: long-term patient and family studies / Manfred Bleuler; translated by Siegfried M. Clemens.

Published/Created: New Haven: Yale University Press, 1978. Description: xxiv, 529 p.: ill.; 26 cm. ISBN: 0300016638

The schizophrenic reactions: a critique of the concept, hospital treatment, and current research; the proceedings. Robert Cancro, editor. Published/Created: New York, Brunner/Mazel, 1970. Description: x, 293 p. 24 cm. ISBN: 0876300220

The schizophrenic syndrome. Leopold Bellak and Laurence Loeb, editors. Published/Created: New York, Grune & Stratton [1969] Description: vii, 879 p. 24 cm.

The Schizophrenic syndrome; an annual review. Published/Created: New York, Brunner/Mazel. Description: 1 v. ill. 24 cm. v. 1; 1971. ISSN: 0080-682X

The self in psychotic process: its symbolization in schizophrenia / John Weir Perry; foreword by C.G. Jung. Published/Created: Dallas, Tex.: Spring Publications, 1987, c1953. Description: xxiii, 184 p., [4] p. of plates: ill. (some col.); 23 cm. ISBN: 0882145096 (pbk.)

The self psychotic process, its symbolization in schizophrenia. Published/Created: Berkeley, University of California Press, 1953. Description: xvii, 184 p. illus. (part col.) 24 cm.

The six schizophrenias; reaction patterns in children and adults. Published/Created: New York, American Orthopsychiatric Association, 1954. Description: 238 p. illus. 26 cm.

The social integration of people with schizophrenia / Lesley Cotterill. Published/Created: Aldershot; Brookfield, Vt.: Avebury, c1994. Description: ix, 144 p.: ill.; cm. ISBN: 1856288412

The spectrum of psychotic disorders: neurobiology, etiology, and pathogenesis / [edited by] Daryl Fujii and Iqbal Ahmed. Published/Created: Cambridge [England]; New York: Cambridge University Press, 2007. Description: p.; cm. Projected Publication Date: 0703 ISBN: 9780521850568 (hardback) 0521850568 (hardback)

The symptom as communication in schizophrenia. Contributors: Bruce L. Bushard [and others] Introd. by David McK. Rioch. Published/Created: New York, Grune & Stratton, 1959. Description: 233 p. illus. 22 cm.

The tangled web: my son, a schizophrenic / by Naomi Smith [i.e. H. Vinter]. Published/Created: London: Johnson, 1975. Description: 48 p.; 22 cm. ISBN: 0853071446

The therapeutic relationship and its impact: a study of psychotherapy with schizophrenics / edited by Carl R. Rogers, with the collaboration of Eugene T. Gendlin ... [et al.]. Published/Created: Westport, Conn.: Greenwood Press, 1976, c1967. Description: xix, 625 p.: ill.; 24 cm. ISBN: 0837183588

The therapeutic relationship and its impact: a study of psychotherapy with schizophrenics. Edited by Carl R. Rogers with the collaboration of Eugene T. Gendlin, Donald J. Kiesler [and] Charles B. Truax. Published/Created: Madison, University of Wisconsin Press, 1967. Description: xix, 625 p. 24 cm.

The three Christs of Ypsilanti: a psychological study / by Milton Rokeach. Published/Created: New York: Columbia University Press, 1981, c1964. Description: xii, 338, iv p.; 21 cm. ISBN: 0231052715

The Transmission of schizophrenia; proceedings of the second research conference of the Foundations' Fund for Research in Psychiatry, Dorado, Puerto Rico, 26 June to 1 July 1967. Editors: David Rosenthal and Seymour S. Kety. Edition Information: [1st ed.] Published/Created: Oxford, New York, Pergamon Press [1968] Description: xi, 433 p. illus. 25 cm.

The treatment of psychoses of the schizophrenic and manic-depressive type: (the treatment of the so-called endogenous psychoses) / 2. Symposion on Psychiatry, Landeck; ed. by H. -J. Haase; with contributions by W. Bister ... [et al.]. Edition Information: Rev. ed. in Engl. Published/Created: Stuttgart; New York: Schattauer, 1978. Description: 116 p.: 4 ill.; 24 cm. ISBN: 3794506243

The treatment of schizophrenia / Leland E. Hinsie. Published/Created: New York: Arno Press, 1980, c1930. Description: xvii, 206 p.; 21 cm. ISBN: 0405119194

The treatment of schizophrenia: a holistic approach based on the Edgar Cayce readings / [David McMillin]. Published/Created: Virginia Beach, Va.: Lifeline Press, c1991. Description: 312 p.: ill.; 28 cm.

The treatment of schizophrenia: a holistic approach based on the readings of Edgar Casey / David McMillin. Published/Created: Virginia Beach, Va.: A.R.E. Press, 1997. Description: xxi, 391 p.: ill.; 22 cm. ISBN: 0876043848 (pbk.)

The treatment of schizophrenia: status and emerging trends / Hans D. Brenner, Wolfgang Bôker, Ruth Genner (editors). Published/Created: Seattle, WA: Hogrefe & Huber Publishers, c2001. Description: xii, 259 p.: ill.; 23 cm. ISBN: 0889371954

The violence of interpretation: from pictogram to statement / Piera Aulagnier; translated by Alan Sheridan. Published/Created: East Sussex; Philadelphia: Brunner-Routledge, 2001. Description: xxxi, 245 p.; 24 cm. ISBN: 0415236754 (hbk) 0415236762 (pbk)

The writer's divided self in Bulgakov's The master and Margarita / Riitta H. Pittman. Published/Created: Houndmills, Basingstoke, Hampshire: Macmillan in association with St. Antony's College, Oxford, 1991. Description: x, 211 p.; 23 cm. ISBN: 0333464338

The writer's divided self in Bulgakov's The master and Margarita / Riitta H. Pittman. Published/Created: New York: St. Martin's Press, 1991. Description: x, 211 p.; 23 cm. ISBN: 031206148X

Theatre discipline and mental health: an acting modality, including the artistic intervention technique / editor, Lyle Kessler. Published/Created: New York City (One Gustave Levy Place, Annenberg 20-210, New York 10029): Imagination Workshop, c1981. Description: 35 p.: ill.; 27 cm.

Theoretical evolutions in person-centered/experiential therapy: applications to schizophrenic and retarded psychoses / Garry Prouty; foreword by Luc Roelens. Published/Created: Westport, Conn.: Praeger, c1994. Description: xxx, 113 p.; 22 cm. ISBN: 027594543X (alk. paper)

Theories of schizophrenia. Edited by Arnold H. Buss and Edith H. Buss. Edition Information: [1st ed.] Published/Created: New York, Atherton Press, 1969. Description: 175 p. 23 cm.

Therapeutic approaches with the schizophrenic patient [sound recording].

Published/Created: New York: Psychotherapy Tape Library, c1979. Description: 1 sound cassette (90 min.)

Therapy, communication, and change, edited by Don D. Jackson. Published/Created: Palo Alto, Calif., Science and Behavior Books [1968] Description: x, 276 p. 22 cm.

This is mental illness: how it feels, and what it means. Pref. by Leston L. Havens. Published/Created: Boston, Beacon Press [1963] Description: 210 p. 22 cm.

This stranger, my son: a mother's story. Published/Created: London, J. Murray, 1969. Description: 247 p. 22 cm. ISBN: 0719518717

Time: experiences, perspectives, and coping-strategies / Gôran Westergren. Published/Created: Uppsala: Uppsala University; Stockholm: Distributor, Almqvist & Wiksell International, 1990. Description: 190 p.: ill.; 22 cm. ISBN: 915542578X

Towards a comprehensive model for schizophrenic disorders: psychoanalytic essays in memory of Ping-Nie Pao, M.D. / edited by David B. Feinsilver. Published/Created: Hillsdale, N.J.: Analytic Press: Distributed solely by L. Erlbaum Associates, 1986. Description: xx, 389 p.: ill.; 24 cm. ISBN: 0881630292

Towards a comprehensive therapy of schizophrenia / Hans Dieter Brenner, Wolfgang Bôker, Ruth Genner, editors. Published/Created: Seattle, WA: Hogrefe & Huber Pub., c1997. Description: xv, 283 p.: ill.; 23 cm. ISBN: 088937175X

Towards a sociology of schizophrenia: humanistic reflections / Keith Doubt. Published/Created: Toronto; Buffalo: University of Toronto Press, c1996. Description: xii, 124 p.; 24 cm. ISBN: 0802008453 (cloth) 0802078303 (pbk.)

Towards mental health; the schizophrenic problem, by Charles Macfie Campbell. Published/Created: Cambridge, Harvard university press, 1933. Description: v, [1] p., 2 l., 3-110 p.

Towards need-specific treatment of schizophrenic psychoses: a study of the development and the results of a global psychotherapeutic approach to psychoses of the schizophrenia group in Turku, Finland / Yrjô O. Alanen ... [et al.]. Published/Created: Berlin; New York: Springer-Verlag, c1986. Description: xi, 295 p.; 25 cm. ISBN: 0387166424 (New York)

Trapped: families and schizophrenia / Lloyd H. Rogler, August B. Hollingshead. Published/Created: New York: R. E. Krieger Pub. Co., 1975, c1965. Description: xiv, 436 p.: ill.; 24 cm. ISBN: 0882753029

Treating mental illness / Robert Byck. Published/Created: New York: Chelsea House Publishers, 1986. Description: 93 p.: ill.; 24 cm. ISBN: 0877547742

Treating schizophrenia / Sophia Vinogradov, editor. Edition Information: 1st ed. Published/Created: San Francisco: Jossey-Bass, c1995. Description: xvii, 372 p.; 24 cm. ISBN: 0787900796 (hc: alk. paper)

Treating schizophrenia / Werner M. Mendel. Edition Information: 1st ed. Published/Created: San Francisco: Jossey-Bass Publishers, 1989. Description: xviii, 244 p.: ill.; 24 cm. ISBN: 1555421512 (alk. paper)

Treating schizophrenic patients: a clinico-analytical approach / Michael H. Stone ... [et al.]. Published/Created: New York:

McGraw-Hill, c1983. Description: vii, 376 p.; 24 cm. ISBN: 0070019177

Treating the treatment failures; the challenge of chronic schizophrenia [by] Arnold M. Ludwig. Published/Created: New York, Grune & Stratton [1971] Description: xvi, 235 p. illus. 24 cm. ISBN: 0808907077

Treatment of schizophrenia: family assessment and intervention / edited by M.J. Goldstein, I. Hand, K. Hahlweg; with contributions by C.M. Anderson ... [et al]. Published/Created: Berlin; New York: Springer-Verlag, c1986. Description: xii, 222 p.: ill.; 25 cm. ISBN: 3540166289 (Berlin) 0387166289 (New York)

Treatment of schizophrenia: progress and prospects / edited by Louis Jolyon West, Don E. Flinn. Published/Created: New York: Grune & Stratton; London: distributed in the United Kingdom by Academic Press, c1976. Description: xv, 291 p.: ill.; 24 cm. ISBN: 0808909703

Treatment of schizophrenia; a comparative study of five treatment methods [by] Philip R. A. May. Published/Created: New York, Science House [1968] Description: 352 p. illus. 23 cm.

Treatment of the chronic schizophrenic patient / Diane Gibson, editor. Published/Created: New York: Haworth Press, c1986. Description: xi, 87 p.; 23 cm. ISBN: 0866565787

Treatment of the severely disturbed adolescent / by Donald B. Rinsley. Published/Created: New York: J. Aronson, c1980. Description: 351 p.; 24 cm. ISBN: 0876684150

Trends in schizophrenia research / Mary V. Lang, editor. Published/Created: New York: Nova Biomedical Books, c2005. Description: viii, 222 p.: ill. 27 cm. ISBN: 159454154X

Twin studies, with especial reference to schizophrenia and certain anthropometric data; a survey of the literature. Published/Created: Bethesda, Md., U. S. Dept. of Health, Education, and Welfare, Public Health Service, National Institutes of Health [1965] Description: 74 l. 27 cm.

Ûber die Psychologie der Dementia praecox: ein Versuch / von C.G. Jung. Published/Created: Halle a S.: Verlagsbuchhandlung Carl Marhold, 1907. Description: iv, 179 p.; 24 cm.

Understanding and helping the schizophrenic: a guide for family and friends / by Silvano Arieti. Published/Created: New York: Basic Books, c1979. Description: xi, 239 p.; 22 cm. ISBN: 0465088554

Understanding and helping the schizophrenic: a guide for family and friends / Silvano Arieti. Edition Information: 1st Touchstone ed. Published/Created: New York: Simon and Schuster, 1980, c1979. Description: xi, 239 p.; 21 cm. ISBN: 0671412523

Understanding and treating schizophrenia: contemporary research, theory, and practice / Glenn D. Shean. Published/Created: New York: Haworth Clinical Practice Press, 2004. Description: xiv, 336 p.; 23 cm. ISBN: 078901887X (alk. paper) 0789018888 (pbk.: alk. paper)

Understanding schizophrenia: a guide to the new research on causes and treatment / Richard S.E. Keefe, Philip D. Harvey. Published/Created: New York: Free Press; Toronto: Maxwell Macmillan Canada; New York: Maxwell Macmillan International, c1994. Description: xv, 283 p., [2] p. of plates: ill. (some col.); 25 cm. ISBN: 0029172470

Understanding understanding [by] Humphry Osmond, with John A. Osmundsen and Jerome Agel. Edition Information: [1st ed.] Published/Created: New York, Harper & Row [1973, c1974] Description: 223 p. 22 cm. ISBN: 0060132396

Vectoriasis praecox; Published/Created: Springfield, Ill., C. C. Thomas [1966] Description: xi, 371 p. 24 cm.

Verlaufsweisen kindlicher und prapuberaler Schizophrenien. Published/Created: Berlin, New York, Springer-Verlag, 1973. Description: ix, 250 p. illus. (1 col.) 26 cm. ISBN: 3540060630

Visual versus tactual receptor preference in normal and schizophrenic children. Published/Created: [n.p., n.d.] Description: viii, 79 l. ill.

Vocabulary knowledge and usage among normal and schizophrenic subjects. Published/Created: [Washington] American Psychological Association [1954] Description: 19 p. 26 cm.

Vulnerability to psychopathology: risk across the lifespan / edited by Rick E. Ingram and Joseph M. Price. Published/Created: New York: Guilford Press, 2001. Description: xv, 476 p.; 24 cm. ISBN: 1572306033 (hardcover)

Water balance in schizophrenia / edited by David B. Schnur and Darrell G. Kirch. Published/Created: Washington, DC: American Psychiatric Press, c1996. Description: xxiv, 278 p.; 22 cm. ISBN: 0880484853

What is schizophrenia and how can we fix it? / Glenn D. Shean. Published/Created: Lanham, MD: University Press of America, 2003. Description: 116 p.; 22 cm. ISBN: 0761826637

What is schizophrenia? / William F. Flack, Jr., Daniel R. Miller, Morton Wiener, editors. Published/Created: New York: Springer-Verlag, c1991. Description: xii, 270 p.; 24 cm. ISBN: 0387976426 (New York: alk. paper) 3540976426 (Berlin: alk. paper)

Why does schizophrenia develop at late adolescence?: a cognitive-developmental approach to psychosis / Chris Harrop and Peter Trower. Published/Created: Hoboken, N.J.: Wiley, c2003. Description: xvii, 222 p.: ill.; 24 cm. ISBN: 0470848774 (hbk: acid-free paper) 0470848782 (pbk: acid-free paper)

Woman within the web / by Cheryl Dolby; illustrated by Turtle Eddins and Brandon Galloway; edited by Karen Henderson. Published/Created: Roanoke, VA: Earthlight Press, c1996. Description: 202 p.: ill.; 22 cm. ISBN: 0965489825

Women and schizophrenia / edited by David J. Castle, John McGrathand Jayashri Kulkarni. Published/Created: Cambridge, U.K.; New York, NY: Cambridge University Press, 2000. Description: xii, 151 p.: ill.; 25 cm. ISBN: 0521786177 (pbk.)

Working with the person with schizophrenia: the treatment alliance / Michael A. Selzer ... [et al.]. Published/Created: New York: New York University Press, c1989. Description: ix, 399 p.; 24 cm. ISBN: 0814778917 (alk. paper)

World issues in the problems of schizophrenic psychoses / edited by Tetsuo Fukuda, Hisatoshi Mitsuda. Edition Information: 1st ed. Published/Created: Tokyo; New York: Igaku-shoin, 1979. Description: xii, 183 p.: ill.; 27 cm. ISBN: 0896400352

Your guide to schizophrenia / Adrianne M. Reveley. Published/Created: London: Hodder Arnold, 2006. Description: xv, 175 p.: ill.; 20 cm. ISBN: 034092747X (pbk.) 9780340927472 (pbk.)

Youth with juvenile schizophrenia: the search for reality / by Kenneth McIntosh and Phyllis Livingston. Published/Created: Philadelphia: Mason Crest Publishers, c2008. Description: p. cm. Projected Publication Date: 0801 ISBN: 1422201481

INDEX

A

B

D

E

H

I

J

K

L

M

N

O

P

Q

R

T

U

V

W

X

Y